Researching Writing

Researching Writing

An Introduction to Research Methods

Joyce Kinkead

UTAH STATE UNIVERSITY PRESS
Logan

© 2016 by the University Press of Colorado

Published by Utah State University Press
An imprint of University Press of Colorado
5589 Arapahoe Avenue, Suite 206C
Boulder, Colorado 80303

 The University Press of Colorado is a proud member of
The Association of American University Presses.

The University Press of Colorado is a cooperative publishing enterprise supported, in part, by Adams State University, Colorado State University, Fort Lewis College, Metropolitan State University of Denver, Regis University, University of Colorado, University of Northern Colorado, Utah State University, and Western State Colorado University.

The paper used in this publication meets the minimum requirements of the American National Standard for Information Sciences—Permanence of Paper for Printed Library Materials. ANSI Z39.48-1992

ISBN: 978-1-60732-478-2 (paperback)
ISBN: 978-1-60732-479-9 (e-book)
DOI: 10.7330/9781607324799

Library of Congress Cataloging-in-Publication Data

Names: Kinkead, Joyce A., 1954– author.
Title: Researching writing : an introduction to research methods / written by Joyce Kinkead.
Description: Logan : Utah State University Press, [2016] | Includes bibliographical references.
Identifiers: LCCN 2015042393 | ISBN 9781607324782 (pbk.) | ISBN 9781607324799 (ebook)
Subjects: LCSH: English language—Rhetoric—Textbooks.
Classification: LCC PE1408 .K6624 2016 | DDC 808/.0420711—dc23
LC record available at http://lccn.loc.gov/2015042393

Cover photograph © Mark Poprocki/Shutterstock.

For David F. Lancy

Contents

Acknowledgments

A book is a lonely project, but it is not done alone. I have been fortunate to have encouragement at all levels. I thank Utah State University for sabbatical-leave funding (2011–2012) to work on this manuscript, in particular Department Head Jeannie Banks Thomas and Dean John Allen.

USU's IRB office—True Fox Rubal, Nancy Sassano, and Janet Roberts—provided their expertise on research ethics and support of my students' IRB-approved projects. In fact, the Office of Research and Graduate Studies, during my tenure there as associate vice president and even since my departure to return to a faculty role, has been a stellar support system. I miss that office family.

Colleagues are invaluable resources. Rebecca Walton, especially, offered advice on usability studies and on the role of technical communication in third-world countries. Wendy Holliday, formerly a librarian at Utah State University and currently at Northern Arizona University, generously gave advice and guidance regarding databases and the research process. Mary-Ann Muffoletto contributed counsel on student researchers and media relations.

We don't always know our colleagues who offer support. Anonymous reviewers provided invaluable feedback and advice on an early draft of this manuscript. I am particularly indebted to one, who said the proposal was "whip smart" but chapter 1, well, not so much. That was inspiration for an overhaul.

By happenstance, I met Laurie Grobman, founding editor of *Young Scholars in Writing*, at a Research and Writing Conference hosted by the University of California, Santa Barbara. That meeting led to a lasting friendship and academic partnership. Next to Laurie, I feel undercaffeinated. Jane Greer, editor of *Young Scholars in Writing* (volumes 7–12), has also been very helpful. The same is true of Doug Downs, who succeeded Jane as editor of *YSW*, beginning with volume 13.

In 2014, I surveyed writing studies degree programs around the country about research-methods courses. I drew on the very helpful work of the CCCC Committee on the Writing Major, which compiled a database of such programs; they number well over one hundred. People were generous in answering my queries. I single out Dominic DelliCarpini of York College of Pennsylvania and Richard Enos of Texas Christian University, but also worthy of mention are the following: Barry Maid, Arizona State University; Beth Godbee, Marquette University; Dànielle Nicole DeVoss, Michigan State University; Joddy Murray, Texas Christian University; Libby Miles, University of Rhode Island; Rebecca Pope-Ruark and Jessie Moore, Elon University; Steven Price, Mississippi College; Greg Giberson, Oakland University; Michael Pemberton, Georgia Southern University; Jaqueline McLeod Rogers, University of Winnipeg; Shevaun E. Watson, University of Wisconsin–Eau Claire; Gary Sue Goodman, University of California, Davis; Lois Agnew and Kate Navickas, Syracuse University; I. Moriah McCracken, St. Edward's University; Elizabeth Robertson, Drake University; Sid Dobrin, University of Florida; Linda Gray, Oral Roberts University; Cameron Bushnell, Clemson University; Patricia Sullivan, Purdue University; Teresa Henning, Southwest Minnesota State University; Andrea Greenbaum, Barry University; Sanford Tweedie, Rowan University; Traci Zimmerman, James Madison University; Janice Neuleib, Illinois State University; Chris Anson, North Carolina State University; Rodney F. Dick, University of Mount Union; Carl Glover, Mount St. Mary's University; Peggy O'Neill, Loyola University; Suzanne Lane, Massachusetts Institute of Technology; Jonathan Hunt, University of San Francisco; Anthony Baker, Tennessee Tech University; Kate Kiefer, Colorado State University; and, Peter Vandenberg, DePaul University.

Naturally, students matter greatly in the creation of this book. I've been fortunate to have stellar undergraduate research assistants: Marissa Shirley (2013–2014) and Sarah Barton (2011). Students in English 3040 Honors (Spring 2013) and students from English 6810 (Spring 2014) used this textbook in manuscript form and gave valuable feedback. Students profiled in this book include Lenaye Howard, Carlos Junior Guadarrama, Brianne Palmer, Sara Calicchia, Eric Stephens, Samantha Latham, Kristin Lillywhite; and writing fellows Chad Adams, Keri Anderson, Sunni Brown, Cody Clark, Marchet Clark, Natalie Hadfield, Angela Hill, Brooke Jones, Aimee Kawakami, Jared Madsen, Leah Madsen, Betsy O. Moore, Julia Moris, Denise Natoli, Jeffrey Nilson, Debbie Raymond, Jessica Staheli, Bryan Tilt, Craig Wise, and Teri Brown.

Michael Spooner was a stellar director of NCTE Publications when I first met him. He has made Utah State University Press a leader in composition studies. As do my colleagues in composition and writing studies, I think highly of his contributions to the field. The staff members at USU Press and the University Press of Colorado are truly incredible.

In the 1980s, when I was working on a research grant and needed advice, I was told to seek out colleagues recognized as research experts on campus, one being David F. Lancy. Reader, I married him. I thank him for the conversations over the last twenty years as the idea for this book percolated.

Preface

This book is designed for those who wish to conduct research on writing and who consider themselves novices in the field. It prepares students for undergraduate research in writing studies by introducing a range of methodological approaches—both humanistic and social scientific. It also showcases published undergraduate research and coaches students in conducting research as well as writing and presenting it. My objective in authoring this textbook is to makes research an achievable goal and an integral part of all students' undergraduate educations.

Researching Writing is designed to be appropriate particularly to undergraduates, including those majoring in writing, studying to become teachers, or writing creatively. In addition, it is highly appropriate to those interested in investigating writing in the disciplines, which includes a wealth of majors. Students who are practitioners of writing—tutors, especially—will find in this volume ways to interrogate practice. Finally, it is appropriate for those undertaking capstone or thesis projects that focus on writing. The skills and critical thinking that result from undertaking research in writing studies will transfer to other settings, too. Being an authentic researcher has lifelong implications.

It is likely that graduate students may also use this book, particularly if they are embarking on research in writing studies for the first time. An added benefit to the graduate-student user is that writing programs increasingly are embracing *writing about writing* content and pedagogy. This textbook will help graduate students who envision a career teaching in writing programs and writing studies to become more familiar with undergraduate research in writing. And, in fact, I have used early versions of the manuscript both in a graduate seminar and an undergraduate course.

The book is divided into two parts. Part 1 overviews the research process while part 2 introduces methodological approaches. Conducting research is a complex and messy process that cannot truly be represented in a linear book, yet a book is very helpful in overviewing research and getting started. Student activities, embedded in the chapters, are designed for a range of students. A sufficient number to choose among is deliberate to accommodate that possible range.

The end goal of this volume, though, is to conduct ethical, authentic research during a term, beginning a project and seeing it through to dissemination. That is a tall order, but it is possible. And, it can be very rewarding. I have taught such a course, both to graduate students and students in majors across the curriculum. In each case I was delighted with the final products but even more with how engaging in authentic research can be an important learning process—for both its successes and failures.

REFERENCES

Hadfield, Leslie, Joyce Kinkead, Tom Peterson, Stephanie H. Ray, and Sarah S. Preston. 2003. "An Ideal Writing Center: Re-Imagining Space and Design." In *The Center Will Hold: Critical Perspectives on Writing Center Scholarship*, edited by Michael Pemberton and Joyce Kinkead, 166–76. Logan: Utah State University Press.

Kinkead, Joyce. 1997a. "Documenting Excellence in Teaching and Learning in Writing-Across-the-Curriculum Programs." In *Assessing Writing across the Curriculum*, edited by Kathleen Blake Yancey and Brian Huot, 37–50. Greenwich, CT: Ablex.

Kinkead, Joyce. 1997b. *A Schoolmarm All My Life: Personal Narratives from Early Utah*. Salt Lake City: Signature Press.

Kinkead, Joyce, and David F. Lancy. 1990. "Looking for Yourself: The Classroom Teacher as Researcher." *Utah English Journal* 18: 2–13.

Kinkead, Joyce, and Jeanne Simpson. 2000. "The Administrative Audience: A Rhetorical Problem." *WPA Journal* 23 (3): 71–84. (Reprinted in *The Allyn & Bacon Sourcebook for Writing Program Administrators*, edited by Irene Ward and William J. Carpenter [Boston: Allyn and Bacon, 2002]).

PART I
The Research Process

Research is formalized curiosity. It is poking and prying with a purpose.
—Zora Neale Hurston

Part 1 lays out the primary aspects of doing research and explains the parameters and contexts for research in writing.

1

The Research Process

WHY DO RESEARCH?

Researchers are curious. They wish to know the *why* or *how* of an issue, and they hope the findings of their research result in additional knowledge and, perhaps, even make a difference. Being a researcher means seeing more intensely. Research also has the power to change people. It can be, in fact, a transformative experience, as the investigator is empowered to pose questions, design studies, investigate, report on results, and recommend alterations in policy or practice. Thus, research adds to the knowledge base of the field of study and has the potential for significant impact.

Hardly anyone worries about polio now, as the vaccination Dr. Jonas Salk developed in 1955 meant people could avoid the devastating disease. But prior to 1955, polio literally terrorized the nation, reaching epidemic proportions with almost sixty thousand cases in 1952. Many people died or were crippled for life. Some were placed in machines called iron lungs that helped them breathe, as they could not breathe on their own. As a child, I watched a television show that featured an adult in an iron lung. Talk about claustrophobia. The disease affected children primarily, but adults, like Franklin D. Roosevelt, were also victims. The subject of Andrew Wyeth's painting *Christina's World* was a polio victim. The well-known violinist Itzhak Perlman performs sitting due to the debilitating effects of the disease. Dr. Salk began working on a vaccine in 1948. When it proved successful, he was hailed as a hero, yet he refused to profit by taking out a patent on the drug.

While Dr. Salk's research was scientific, the current research that seeks to eradicate polio worldwide is sociocultural. It seemed at one time that polio could be completely eliminated; however, lore about the vaccine permeated some rural areas around the globe, particularly those populated by people with Muslim beliefs, that the vaccine would hurt children. As a result, hundreds of cases still appear. But with researchers working through community and religious organizations to educate leaders about the devastating effects of the disease and the value of the vaccine, the number of cases is decreasing in some areas of the world, a hopeful sign.

Humanistic research plays a role in the fight against polio, too. Technical communicators design appropriate technical documentation to educate and inform community members. Researchers such as Rebecca Walton note that standard technical documentation that puts the facts forward to users may not be effective. Instead, technical communicators do a needs assessment of the issue and then design appropriate documentation for the specific purpose. This may include showing people in familiar garb and surroundings. Such an approach brings the situation closer to being recognizable by users. The power of narrative and storytelling may also be evoked in effective documentation. Walton (2013; Walton, Zraly, and Mugengana 2015) works in user-centered design, and her particular interest is enhancing technical communication in third-world countries.

Researchers are working at this very minute trying to find cures for Alzheimer's disease, cancer, and even the common cold. Research in health-related issues is a high priority for any nation, as it contributes to economic, social, and personal well-being. The United States is known particularly for its research in health, defense, technology, energy, and space exploration. And, over half the nation's basic research is undertaken at its colleges and universities.

Students who engage in research are helping to ask questions and solve problems in a wide range of fields. This is important work. In addition, students benefit in multiple ways. Undergraduate research has been identified as a "high impact" practice by researcher George Kuh (2008, 20) and his team, who, through the National Survey of Student Engagement (NSSE), found that many colleges and universities provide research experiences for students in all disciplines. Students' early and active involvement in systematic investigation and research offers a "sense of excitement that comes from working to answer important questions." Students grapple with "actively contested questions, empirical observation, and cutting-edge technologies."

Personally, students gain tremendously when engaging in research. The following attributes have been substantiated by researchers such as David Lopatto (2009) and Laursen et al. (2010). Student researchers benefit by

- experiencing the rewards of designing a project, making discoveries, and sharing findings;
- understanding some of the ways in which research differs across disciplines;
- increasing ability to think, learn, and work independently;
- strengthening oral and written communication skills;
- sharpening critical thinking skills;
- developing close relationships with faculty mentors;
- preparing for graduate school;
- getting work published;
- traveling to conferences and working with people who share their interests;
- enhancing a resume;
- participating in and contributing to the life of their chosen field.

Participation in research has the capability of increasing students' sense of responsibility and independence, yet it provides experience in learning to work as members of a team when a project is done collaboratively with other students or with faculty mentors. It can also help clarify career goals. Is this what I wish to do with my life? And even if the subject matter differs from the postgraduation job, research skills are transferable to other settings. Employers consistently cite good communication skills, problem solving, facility with technology, and the ability to work with others as highly valued attributes.

WHY DO RESEARCH IN WRITING?

Charles Bazerman (2007) argues that the study of writing is the study of "how people come to take on the thought, practice, perspective, and orientation of various ways of life; how they integrate or keep distinct those perspectives in which they are practiced; and how we organize our modern way of life economically, intellectually, socially, interpersonally, managerially, and politically through the medium of texts" (35). Throughout history, to be literate has been key to a person's success. Writing is not only about personal success but also about a person's well-being. It can be used to discover oneself, to write one's way through problems, and to communicate feelings.

Writing is what makes us human.

Important studies in writing have changed the way writing is taught from an emphasis on *product* to an emphasis on *process*. They have also helped teachers understand how students become literate or why they make errors. These studies have argued for valuing alternative voices. They have explored digital environments and the intersections of technology and rhetoric. They have gone outside academe to explore writing in business settings. They have analyzed how writers collaborate.

Writing studies is a capacious field. Researchers do not necessarily need to be studying or majoring in English. Writing belongs to everyone. A psychology major can study the differences in writing done by clinical and research psychologists, a premed student can study how physicians use information technology to improve communication with patients, a business major can study how a hotel chain uses comments on customer feedback forms in its reports or in the employee newsletter, a student in ethnic studies can research newspaper representations of local civil-rights activists.

So many topics call to the researcher for investigation: authorship, collaboration, intertextuality, visual rhetoric, digital and multimedia platforms, narrative, storytelling, gender and writing, race and writing, social class and writing, writing and power. The possibilities are really limitless.

THE RESEARCH PROCESS

The goal of this textbook is for students to engage in *authentic* or real research. You may have experience in writing research papers that draw exclusively on others' previous research. Much of "school" research looks at what is termed *secondary* research sources. This is material written about others' research. *Primary* research resources are the original studies or documents. For instance, if you were to study tribal-school diaries housed in a special collections or archives, you would be looking at primary documents. Your writing about these diaries then becomes primary research. When another scholar incorporates your work into an analysis, that is *secondary research.*

Writing academic research papers, whether in secondary school or college, has the benefit of introducing the research process to the writer and providing practice in the skills of finding information and citing sources. In some cases it can be seen as regurgitating information found in common sources such as *Wikipedia* or popular media. These can be valuable foundational experiences. Please understand that the research you will do as a result of reading this book differs. The goal is to produce research that contributes to our understanding of writing studies.

Research is considered to add new knowledge and as such is termed a *discovery activity*. This means information is collected systematically and then analyzed for *findings*. These findings can influence practice and policy. For some researchers a study is not so much about discovering new knowledge as about adding to the conversation; it may take compiling several studies before new knowledge is discovered.

The overarching goal is for research to meet *RAD* criteria: *replicable, aggregable,* and *data supported.* Let's look at each of those terms. *Replicable* means another researcher can repeat the study and get the same results. This lends to the study's *validity. Aggregable* means the study can be associated with others or compiled to arrive at even richer interpretations. In other words, it fits in with a group of studies. *Data supported* refers to the fact that the study draws on evidence, usually quantitative evidence, that supports the conclusions made by the research.

The hope is that research offers the opportunity to generalize from specific instances. Most research contributes to *generalizable knowledge.* How can the results have an effect on, let's say, another college not in the same state? Federal regulations define research as a "systematic investigation, including research development, testing, and evaluation designed to develop or contribute to generalizable knowledge." Some qualitative studies that may not directly "contribute to generalizable knowledge" are still research. In addition, course research assignments conducted by students may be research even if they are limited in scope. Generalizable knowledge is knowledge "expressed in theories, principles, and statements of relationships" that can be widely applied to our experiences (Code of Federal Regulations 2009). Generalizable knowledge is usually shared with others through presentations and publications. Audience members or readers of the research may experience a flash of recognition and say, "Oh, that has implications for my own work."

The research process is a series of stages. But as Flower and Hayes (1981) found with the writing process, it's not just prewriting, writing, and rewriting. It's a *recursive* process in which the writer loops back to earlier stages. While the research process is more complex than writing an essay, it has that same characteristic of recursiveness. The project may be reviewed and revised numerous times before it reaches its conclusion. Think about it as a looping process, constantly winding back on itself. A misperception among novice researchers is that experienced researchers never make a misstep. That is simply not true. Expert researchers have become skilled through practice and feedback from mentors.

Ranjit Kumar (2014, 34) offers an "eight-step model" for the research process. As he remarks, "The eight steps cover the complete spectrum of a research endeavour, from problem formulation through to writing a research report." The figure below summarizes the eight steps with the use of arrows.

While a step-by-step guaranteed process would be ideal, and Kumar's model is helpful, fortunately or unfortunately, that's not the way it works in real research. Researchers experience failures, they change their minds about design based on information gained in the process, they decide the study is operationally flawed. *Recursiveness* is common, and the student researcher should not feel discouraged if a project does not truly follow step by step to success. As teachers, we sometimes simplify such processes for novices, as we don't want research to seem overwhelming, but the nature of authentic research in which the researcher reassesses throughout can strengthen the final results.

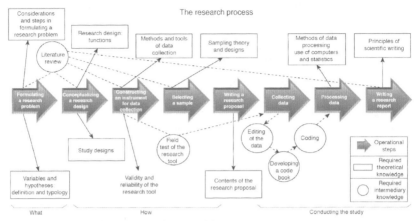

FIGURE 1.1. Kumar's process of researching.

Profile of a Student Researcher: Sara Calicchia

To illustrate how a researcher uses recursiveness to advantage, let's look at Sara, a student who was enrolled in an honors seminar on researching writing with special attention to writing in the disciplines. Sara was majoring in equine science, and she had represented the university in the National Equestrian Challenge. She also worked in the ruminant nutrition laboratory. She was able to study the digestive system of a cow that has been surgically fitted with a cannula, which is similar to a porthole that allows access to the rumen. She was focusing on epigenetics for her undergraduate honors thesis. With that background, I assumed Sara would be interested in doing a project focused on scientific writing. I was rather surprised that, instead, she was curious about how music affects writers. She knew music was important to her own composing process and wanted to investigate whether that were true for others.

Sara conducted a case study through interviews with twelve subjects—nine professors and three students at her university in the fields of English, biology, and history. Through her research she determined that experienced writers tend to prefer silence or white noise to lyrical music to produce their work. These results show that some of the problems students may find with writing may stem from an overwhelming number of distractions hindering their writing abilities. Sara's progress did not necessarily flow in a step-by-step progression. Although she carefully crafted her interview questions, she found that she needed to return to her participants for a follow-up question about their own ability to play a musical instrument. And, she made a late-stage breakthrough in understanding her project when she returned to review further literature, finding an important article on "environmental self-regulation" that she said was enlightening and changed the way her final report was conceived and structured.

Sara disseminated her research in three venues: the state conference on undergraduate research, the National Conference on Undergraduate Research (NCUR), and *Young Scholars in Writing: Undergraduate Research in Writing and Rhetoric* (*YSW*). The process for publishing her research report reveals that even when an essay is accepted, revisions can continue. "To 'Play That Funky Music' or Not: How Music Affects the Environmental Self-Regulation of High-Ability Academic Writers" was revised dramatically for publication. *YSW* has a system whereby an editorial board member is assigned to authors whose work is accepted by the journal. Sara received a detailed message about her submission; it read in part,

> The reasons we liked your piece so much have to do with its subject of study, your intriguing methodological approach to that study, the quality of your literature review, and the well-structured organization of the piece, which was therefore highly readable and interesting. Personally, I have a long-running fascination with the relationship of music and writing and the role of music for various writers in the writing process—it's an important area of study, definitely under-developed, and your article will truly be able to contribute to the field's knowledge on this subject. Your idea for comparing, through careful surveying/interviewing, faculty writing habits and undergraduate writing habits, and the way that you lay out the results in your piece, is really smart and works well for the kind of knowledge you're trying to develop. And you did an unusually good job of locating your study within existing conversation in the field, including beautifully setting up the open question of why some studies show music as an impediment while others show music as enhancing the thinking that underlies the writing process. In short, many excellent qualities come together to make this piece attractive to us at *YSW*, and suggest that with development in some other areas, it will be a terrific addition to this volume.

Working with this mentor, Sara spent some time in revising her essay, and it was published in volume 11 of *YSW*, much to her delight. It has become an important part of her portfolio as she looks to graduate study in biomedical science.

Student Activity

READING

"Anatomy of an Article: How an Undergraduate Researcher Turned a Passionate Project into a Published Essay" (Source: http://kairos. technorhetoric.net/16.1/topoi/zabielski-janangelo/Anatomy_of_an_ Article/Part_1.html)

Sara's story of how she embarked on a research project in writing studies that eventually appeared in a peer-reviewed journal is necessarily brief. For a more detailed case study of a similar student, read Joseph Janangelo's case study, which appears in the online journal *Kairos* (Janangelo 2010–2011). The article demonstrates beautifully how the researcher's own intellectual development was enhanced through his work and the give and take with mentors. Janangelo's interview methods also come to the fore. This essay also serves as an example of a case study, which is one of the approaches addressed in this textbook.

Finding and Defining Questions

Researchers are curious and ask questions. Here are some questions that have been asked—and answered—through research.

- What makes writers anxious, creating writer's block, and how might this anxiety be measured (Daly and Miller 1975)?
- What kinds of writing are students in secondary schools asked to do (Langer and Applebee 2007)?
- What is the history of writing across the curriculum, and how does contemporary practice reflect historical origins (Russell 2002)?
- Can the architecture of a writing center have an effect on the efficacy of tutoring (Hadfield et al. 2003)?
- How do nontraditional students differ from traditional students, and what effect does that difference have on teachers or tutors (Hirschi 1996)?
- What are trends in website design (Kator 2000)?
- What do beginning graduate teaching assistants believe about their students' writing (Dryer 2012)?
- What do *rhetorical heirlooms*, such as grocery lists and menu planners, say about women's roles (White-Farnham 2014)?

While some of these questions have been posed by professionals in the field (Daly and Miller 1975; Dryer 2012; Langer and Applebee 2007; Russell 1990, 2002; White-Farnham 2014), others have been posed by students. Charlene Hirschi (1996) asked how she, as a reentry student and tutor, brought special understanding to working with nontraditional students. Leslie Hadfield et al. (2003) and two students in interior design used their combined expertise to design an ideal writing center. And Corinne Kator (2000) wrote her honors thesis on trends in website design circa 2000. While trends in website design is a topic that is addressed frequently, the results also change regularly. On the other hand, before the Hadfield project on writing center architecture, no other researchers had undertaken this question. It is entirely possible for a student to be first in addressing a question.

Student researchers are no doubt already aware of *problems* or *questions* to be addressed through their own experiences. The problem, which may involve a specific situation, phenomenon, or a classroom, for instance, can then be explored, described, and analyzed. Recall that Sara was curious about the role of music in purposeful writing, which led her to a question outside herself.

Student Activity

THE WRITING AUTOBIOGRAPHY

To begin to study writing, it's helpful to analyze one's own writing and writing processes. This is also called *autoethnography* and draws upon participant-observation tools for gathering information. Ethnography is a social sciences approach to studying peoples and cultures. In contrast, *autoethnography* focuses on the researcher's personal experiences and includes self-reflection and analysis. The *auto* in *autoethnography* is just like *auto* in autobiography, referring to the self. That analysis can then be examined to look for connections to larger culture. Following are guidelines to help you begin to do just that.

Part 1

Write an autobiography in which you think about the story of you as a writer. This project may be an opportunity to query your family about your early writing habits. Such opportunities to reminisce are almost always welcome.

Here are some questions to help you think of possible directions to take in your essay.

- What are your earliest memories of writing?
- Did you have toy writing implements? Real writing implements? Were you a pencil collector?
- Did you write poetry?
- Did you put out your own newspaper?
- Did someone guide you in writing?
- What was school writing like for you?
- When did you transition from learning to write to writing to learn?
- What are good memories about writing? Not-so-good memories?
- Did you have readers of your writing who provided feedback?
- Do you like to write for particular audiences?

Bring the autobiography to the present and consider

- how you feel about writing;
- anything that's difficult for you about writing;
- things about the writing you have done in the past year(s) that were successful for you or that you liked;
- things about the writing you did in the past year(s) that you didn't like or that were not successful for you;
- any goals you have for yourself in writing this year.

Part 2

Using the following list, write about how you write. You may use any or all of the questions to stimulate your thinking about your writing processes. Do include other topics not listed here. You do not have to address these in any particular order.

- Where do you write?
- Do you have a certain body position?
- Do you need background noise (e.g., music, television)?
- Do you need a certain kind of paper?
- Do you have a favorite writing instrument?
- What kind of technology do you use?
- Do you ask others for help?
- What time of day do you like to write?
- What must happen before you are able to begin writing?
- How do you handle interruptions or breaks?
- Must you be alone or with others?
- Does correctness—spelling or punctuation—affect how you write?
- Are you concerned about neatness?

- How do you begin? Do you have trouble beginning to write?
- How do you go about planning what you will write?
- Does your mind wander while you are writing?
- How frequently do you reread what you are writing?
- Do you evaluate as you write? Rewrite?
- If others were to read your writing, what characteristics of your person would they perceive? In other words, what does your writing say about you?

Part 3—The Writing Log

Tally the types and kinds of writing you do for one week. Make a note of the date (perhaps even the time). Include what may seem insignificant, such as signing a debit form at the grocery store checkout. For academic writing, note the class number/name. (If the academic writing task is part of a larger assignment, note that, too. For instance, an annotated bibliography might be leading up to a longer research paper.) For non-academic writing, include grocery lists, e-mail messages, texts. For the analysis, try to uncover themes, quantify, and compare. A tracking sheet in a notebook might be organized as follows.

TABLE 1.1. Writing log template

Date	Academic Writing	Nonacademic Writing

TABLE 1.2. Sample—Samantha's writing log

Date	Academic Writing	Nonacademic Writing
Feb. 3	Note-taking over reading (NTR) Engl 6350	Texting (3 texts sent)
	NTR Engl 6810	Filled out schedule for week
	Annotated bibliography Engl 6810 (included NTR, library searches, and e-mail instructor)	Google search for events
	Discussion response	Filled out timecard
	Typing PowerPoint	List for counseling
	Writing lesson plans	
	Writing notes on dry erase board	

continued

TABLE 1.2. Sample—Samantha's writing log—*continued*

Date	Academic Writing	Nonacademic Writing
Feb. 4	NTR Engl 6610	Google Translate
	Note-taking in class (NTC) Engl 6610	Texting (7 sent)
	NTC Engl 6810	E-mail (3 sent)
	Practice quiz Engl 6350	To-do list
	Notes for discussion Engl 6350	
	Notes in writing center	
	Form completion in writing center	
Feb. 5	NTR Engl 6610	Google Translate
	Writing lesson plans	E-mail (5 sent)
	Writing notes on dry erase board	Text (5 sent)
	Grading, writing feedback	Grocery list
	NTR Engl 6350	
	NTC Engl 6350	
	Quiz Engl 6350	
	Paperwork for counseling	
Feb. 6	Note-taking in class (NTC) Engl 6610	Google Translate
	NTR Engl 6610	Texting (21 sent)
	Grading and feedback	Search for flights
	Notes in writing center	Search for hotels
	Form completion in writing center	E-mail (3 sent)
		Journal
Feb. 7	Grading and feedback	Texting (35 sent)
	Writing notes on board	E-mail (5 sent)
	NTR Engl 1010	Search flight and hotel
		Book flight and hotel
Feb. 8	NTR Engl 6810	E-mail (2 sent)
	Grading and feedback	
	Discussion paper Engl 6350	
	Discussion paper Engl 6610	
	Text (68 sent)	
Feb. 9	NTR Engl 6350	Timecard
	Discussions Engl 6810	Note to husband
	Revise conference paper (including library searches for additional sources and some note-taking)	
	E-mail students (4 sent)	
	Paperwork (Chrysalis)	

Part 4

What questions about writing interest you? Rereading your autoethnography may reveal topics that can be explored through research. Begin to catalog a list of research questions you would like to explore.

In the sample above, the student, a graduate teaching assistant, was curious about the amount of time spent in writing for her own classes as opposed to the classes she was teaching. She also pondered her personal writing and whether she devoted sufficient time to writing in her journal. For her, *time* became a key word and a consideration for follow-up research.

Finding Your Own Research Question

How do you find a research question that interests you and is viable in terms of adding to the knowledge base of the scholarly literature? Authentic research generally helps fill a gap in what we know about writing studies. From your writing autobiography, you probably have already discovered areas of interest. Making a list of *topics* that interest you is a good start. Recall that writing studies is a capacious field. Writing touches every person and reaches into all corners of our daily lives. In the writing log tally, entries may include writing that seems almost invisible: putting search terms in a browser; writing a check; signing a greeting card; completing a time card.

Another possibility may focus on a question about writing that you've pondered. For instance, how does a field other than English view writing, or more particularly, how does a particular department set its writing standards—not only in contemporary terms but also historically. What does a field say about the importance of writing in its recruitment literature, and is that carried through in reality? The focus of the question will influence the method of investigation.

Or, consider questions outside academe and school. How does writing manifest itself at work? At play? In interpersonal communication? What is the nature of any applied writing that you do? *Applied* writing generally refers to real-world writing applications. Again, the field is practically limitless, but here are a few: contracts, grants, correspondence, usability studies, websites, personnel reviews, performance reports, advertisements, and programs.

Develop a working draft of your question. What is it you want to explore or know? What questions will help you find the answers? What will you study in order to get answers—people, texts, artifacts, practices? Why is this question important or significant? How will it make a contribution to the field, and, finally, is it doable in the amount of time allotted?

Here are some sample topics:

- Has the blue book (used for writing essay exams) seen its day? What is its history?

- The classic advice for designing a research poster is this: 40 percent white space, 40 percent pictures/illustrations, 20 percent text. These proportions are based on good communication principles for this medium. At a particular event (e.g., NCUR), are the posters designed with these proportions? If they are not, what do follow-up interviews with the researchers reveal about poster design?

- The National Council of Teachers of English (NCTE) has a policy on gender-neutral language. Is such as policy common in other fields? How knowledgeable are college-aged writers about gender-neutral language?

- Atul Gawande and Jerome Groopman are both physicians who also write for the *New Yorker*. How do these two physicians' essays differ and how are they alike? What personas do their essays project?

- Writer's block doesn't just strike young writers; it can also affect mature, professional writers. Consider a case study of one to three mature scholars who are experiencing or who have experienced writer's block. The *New Yorker* article, "Draft No. 4," by John McPhee, which begins with his own description of writer's block—even though he's a Pulitzer Prize-winning writer—might be an inspiration. http://www.newyorker.com/magazine/2013/04/29/draft-no-4)

- What is the standard for writing in a particular field of study (e.g., a major); how is it defined, and how did it get to be that way?

- What written documents about responsible conduct of research (RCR)—research ethics—exist in any particular field on campus? How are these concepts transmitted from mentor to student novice?

- Writing exams for entry into particular fields (e.g., teacher education) exist on campuses. What are their histories? Why were they instituted? How do students feel about these writing exams? What is their pass rate? Is there room for improvement?

- What are the lore and myths about grammar among college-aged writers in a particular class or field?

- What mnemonic devices do students use to write—strategies about how to succeed in writing that may or may not be valid?

- Why don't students take advantage of the writing center or writing-fellows program?

- The writing-fellows program suggests that its participants/graduates acquire skills that help them with graduate studies and professional schools. What do WF alumni say about their experience as WFs looking back?

- "Writing is a skill that develops slowly over time but atrophies quickly," according to Erika Lindemann (1989). What is the prevalence of frequent writing in classes? Or is it a case of the Big Paper at the end of the term?

- What are faculty beliefs (in a field other than English) about how students learn to write?

- Does your family have any historical journals/diaries that would be of interest for understanding the times in which they were written?

- What rhetorical devices are common in ecclesiastical documents? How are audience, organization, and style reflected in these documents?

- What documents (and arguments) are written to convince a university campus to make a significant change (e.g., Aggie Blue Bikes, the arts fee, the GLBTQ Center)? How are these documents perceived from a historical perspective, say, ten years later?

- The honors program requires application essays for entrance. How might these essays be mined to understand the profile of the entering class? What are red flags for readers/evaluators that might torpedo a student's entrance?

- How is the IMRAD structure of scientific reports communicated by mentors to their student researchers?

- Analyze the texts of university admissions documents from (1) research universities, (2) land-grant institutions, or (3) state institutions. What messages are being communicated to prospective students and parents?

- The poster is an unusual—almost unknown—medium for communicating research results in the humanities, yet humanities students must learn how to prepare posters for many venues, such as CUR's annual Posters on the Hill in Washington, DC. How are students and their mentors coping with this new medium?

- How does academic writing differ from real-world writing, using the lens of your own experiences?

- Why is an app like Hankz Writer, which adds retro manual typewriter sounds to an iPad, attractive to users?

Student Activity

DEVELOP A RESEARCH QUESTION

You are looking for a topic that (1) interests you, (2) is worthwhile, (3) has not yet been addressed in the literature, and (4) is doable in the time constraints of this class. Once this question is developed, the review of literature can begin, which then leads to the methodology development and study.

Refining Research Questions

Once a question is decided upon, it must be refined and defined. Consider the *scope, timing, setting,* and *size of the participant population* of the research study that will be used to answer the question or solve the problem posed. The *scope* of the study refers to both the amount of *time* involved and the *size* of the participant population, often referred to as *n* or *number* of participants. Note that *participants* is the preferred alternative to the term *subjects*, which is viewed as being more hierarchical. The amount of time from start to finish of the study is often a common-sense question and answer: a workshop or short-course period, a semester, an academic year.

The *method* or *approach* taken is yet another important question. *Methods* are techniques used to gather information while *methodology* is a theory of how research should be done. Methodology also indicates a philosophical basis for the research. A researcher may *approach* a study using various theoretical lenses. I recall an important book from my own undergraduate career, Wilford L. Guerin's (1966) *A Handbook of Critical Approaches to Literature.* My professor used the first edition, which employs approaches such as Freudian and Jungian analyses. In the sixth edition it is easy to see how literary criticism has changed with the addition of eco-criticism, feminist and cultural studies, and postcolonial studies. These schools of thought really did not exist in the 1970s, although in the case of feminism, there were beginning signs of feminist criticism. *Researching Writing* will explore various approaches to writing studies research; Part 2 develops some of these in detail.

The following chart outlines how the question for the study may be defined by site, method, and scope. These problems were defined by teacher-practitioners pursuing graduate studies. They had real questions, encountered from their work in K–12 classrooms, that they wished to pursue. These are *teachers-as-researchers* engaging in research and reflection in order to improve practice. As such, they join a distinguished group of teachers-as-researchers who have experienced discovery and change— sometimes borne out of frustration. Nancie Atwell (1987), for instance, had an epiphany as a middle-school teacher: "I didn't know how to share responsibility with my students, and I wasn't sure I wanted to. I liked the vantage of my big desk" (179). Lucinda Ray (1987) similarly felt frustrated "with the lack of success . . . in talking to students about their writing." As a result, she studied the distribution of talk in teacher-student writing conferences, finding that teacher talk dominated about 75 percent of the time. Clearly, the inspiration to do research can come from within.

TABLE 1.3. Chart outlining research question, site, method, and scope of sample research projects

| | | | Scope | |
Problem	Site	Method	Time	Size
How does a writing specialist influence writing tasks in the cross-curricular classroom?	High school, grades 10–12	Case Study: • Interviews • Surveys • Counting	1 academic year	63 teachers over-all but then a selected few for in-depth study
What happens to students when introduced to a writing-workshop approach in the classroom?	Elementary school	Case Study: • Interviews • Observations • Video recording • Audio recording • Logs • Interest surveys	18 weeks	27 sixth-grade writing-workshop students

A Heuristic for Defining Research Questions

The chart that appears above in Table 1.3 offers a fairly simple way of defining a study. The classifications of a study can become increasingly narrowed by definition as the project is refined. A *heuristic* offers questions that help a writer determine the scope of a study. It can serve as an *invention* or *prewriting* stage that spurs the researcher to craft the research question. *Invention* is the classical term used by Aristotle and is more generally termed *prewriting* in contemporary times.

As you develop your research question, consider the questions that follow. How do these help you define your study? These questions do not represent inclusive categories, as other items could be added to any of the fields.

- What are the ages of the participants?
- Are they children? Elderly? Writers who have already passed and whose work is in archives?

- Who are the participants?
- Are they members of a group such as a service club or a profession?
- Where are the participants located?
- Is the location in the home or in a professional setting or even outdoors? Consider, too, the importance and pervasiveness of the digital environment.
- What genres will be considered? Genres number in the dozens, if not more.
- What time period will the study cover?
- Is the time period a day in the life of a writer? Perhaps a longitudinal study will cover a writer's undergraduate career.
- What is the sample size? A case study may include only a few participants while a large study may have as many as three thousand participants—or even texts.
- What research approach will be used and what instruments from a researcher's toolkit will be employed?

Student Activity

CHARTING A RESEARCH STUDY

In the following chart (Table 1.4), columns are defined for some of the typical aspects of a study. These are sample topics as well as scope and setting for the study. The toolkit of methods to be used begins to come into play. And the notion that some studies will need approval from review boards (e.g., those using human participants or animals) is also introduced.

Do any of the topics give you ideas for developing your research question? Perhaps it is difficult to see connections among some of these items. Think, though, of Charlotte Hogg's (2006) interesting work, *From the Garden Club: Rural Women Writing Community*, which might have evolved from thinking about *farms* as a literacy setting. At the bottom of the chart, begin filling in items that apply to your particular study: information about participants; the setting; what genres of writing might be studies; the time required to complete the study; the size of the sample (e.g., of people or artifacts); and possible methods. This is a draft to begin to develop the research question into a study. You may return to this chart as your thinking about the research question develops. Use the items listed to explore possibilities.

TABLE 1.4.

Participants: Age	Participants: Details	Setting	Genres	Scope: Time	Sample Size	Research Method	Toolkit	RCR: Ethics
preschool	ABC blocks	home	letters	1 day	N of 1	history/archival	survey	IRB
kindergarten		school	essays	1 week		case study	interview	data management
grades 1–3		church	blogs	1 term		feminist	data mining	IACUC
grades 4–6	4-H Club	club	manuscripts	month		text/rhetorical analysis	counting	authorship
grades 7–10	sports teams	outdoors	PostSecret	year		ethnography	participant-observation	
grades 11–12	debate team	retreat	social media	longitudinal		mixed method		
college undergrad	First Year Composition	sports setting	books			empirical/quantitative		
college graduate		international	autobiography			qualitative		
20s		business	memoir			Marxist		
30s		library	recipes			queer studies		
40s	service club (Rotary)	prison	minutes			critical discourse analysis		
50s	physicians	program	poems					
60s		Internet	fiction		N of 1000			
70s	Red Hat Society	writing center	reports					
80s		hospital	lab reports					
90s		farm	scientific reports					

continued

Table 1.4.—continued

Participants: Age	Participants: Details	Setting	Genres	Scope: Time	Sample Size	Research Method	Toolkit	RCR: Ethics
100s			white papers					
deceased			executive memos					
			technical reports					
			powerpoint					
			journals					
			diaries					
			blogs					
			lists					
			advertising					
			comics/graphics					
			flyers/brochures					
			children's books					
			medical docs					
			confessions					
			textbook					
			yearbook					

YOUR STUDY

FINDING INFORMATION AND RESOURCES

A crucial step in the research process is determining whether the research question you are investigating has already been answered. If it has, it is no longer a viable question, and it's back to the drawing board to see how the question may be tweaked or a new line of research developed. The goal in authentic research is to add to the knowledge base in the field. Certainly, finding information about the topic can be done through Internet sources, but libraries continue to be repositories that are most helpful to the student researcher.

Truly, librarians are the unsung heroes of any college campus. The resources of a library and its librarians are immeasurable. For the researcher who is just entering the conversation on a particular topic, books provide the best synthesized approach and don't overwhelm, as a wealth of articles tend to do. A rather old-fashioned, but still a reliable, idea is to find one helpful book and then browse the shelves adjacent to it. This may reveal other valuable resources. Likewise, dissertations are excellent resources, as their writers must defend their ideas through an extended review of the literature, building on the work already done by others. Another resource is the *review essay*, which provides an overview of several articles or books on the topic. Finally, although more rare, a meta-analysis essay or book provides an overview of the topic by looking at as many studies as possible on the topic, drawing them together, and then generalizing.

Citation chaining is a pre-Internet search strategy in which the list of references in an essay or chapter is mined for further valuable sources. This mining helps build context in which the researcher finds an idea and then chains it backward. At any and every stage of the research process, librarians can provide assistance. But this same strategy can be used in digital environments.

In addition to books and journals, electronic databases provide a wealth of information. Writing is a topic that has universal appeal, and as a result, it may be addressed in what seem like disparate databases: ERIC, Education Abstracts, MLA Bibliography, Arts and Humanities Search, Dissertation Abstracts, Social Sciences Abstracts—to name but a few. The interdisciplinary nature of writing means that some sources may be found in educational psychology. To demonstrate the interdisciplinary nature of writing, consider the following titles from a National Conference on Undergraduate Research (NCUR) program and where they are categorized in the program.

- "Writing Apprehension and the Impact on Learning in Undergraduate Nursing Students" (nursing)
- "Rhetoric and Reality in Mainline Protestant Decline: Doctrine or Demographics?" (religious studies)

- "Looking into Song: Rhetoric versus Reality in the Crafting of Protest Lyrics" (American studies)
- "Adapting Campaign Rhetoric to New Media: A Linguistic Analysis of Senate Candidate Web Messages" (political science)
- "Contrastive Rhetoric: Cultural Differences between Chinese and American Business Letters" (English as a second language)
- "Putting Student Research into Context: Lessons from Over 25 Years of Integrating Student Initiated Research with Interdisciplinary Writing and Departmental Assessment" (biology)
- "Wen I Rite Gud It Cuz I Dun Did It Lots: The Effects of Repeated Practice on the Improvement of Writing Skills of General Psychology Students" (psychology)
- "Assessing the Validity and Reliability of Curriculum-Based Measurement in Writing for Elementary-Aged English Language Learners" (education)
- "'Matters of the Soul': Rhetoric of the Black Intellectual" (communications)

Databases may have different names depending on the vendor; each academic library will have a different package. One library may purchase Education Abstracts while another acquires Education FullText. Entering a database search through the library portal of a campus website generally ensures that the researcher will have access to these databases, as libraries pay a subscription fee. Each discipline has tools, and each library has some—but perhaps not all—of the tools. Accessing works electronically also ensures that bibliographic information and perhaps even the work itself can be downloaded, which makes writing the report much easier. Librarians can also point to useful software that allows bibliographic information to be transformed from one citation style to another.

Sometimes, searches lead to dead ends. Take Data Database (below), which initially looks like a gold mine of information for conducting empirical research in writing. As it turns out, it was a semester-only project for a graduate course.

RESOURCE FOR DATABASES IN WRITING STUDIES RESEARCH

Welcome to Data Database, where you can explore and find tools for conducting empirical research in writing. Search by tool name, related tags, or the stage of your current research in Rhetoric and Composition. This resource was created by a seminar held at Purdue University (2011). http://datadatabase.wordpress.com/

A truly terrific resource is CompPile (http://comppile.org/site/history .htm.), which offers a database on scholarly work published in composition studies since World War II. It presents "an inventory of publications in post-secondary composition, rhetoric, technical writing, ESL, and discourse studies." Its search engine is effective at locating relevant sources. It catalogs postsecondary writing scholarship published in journal articles, review essays, notes and comments, books, dissertations, ERIC items, and edited collections. CompPile is a collaborative project, and a group of volunteers add to this resource. Another resource is REx (the Research Exchange Index, http://researchexchange.colostate.edu), a searchable database of researcher-authored, peer-reviewed reports on contemporary research.

Other resources include video and audio. It's not only print-based materials that can be drawn on for a research question, particularly when there are excellent online journals that allow multimedia submissions.

Web resources are yet another good venue for finding information. Although *Wikipedia* is enormously helpful as a resource, it may not always be considered a good source. Why? *Wikipedia* features user-created content, which may or may not be credible. *Wikipedia* even affixes notes to entries that are suspect. A primary purpose of citations and references is for the reader to check the original source. That's yet another reason why *Wikipedia* may not be the best source: its content is not static. How do we judge web resources? Consider the accuracy of any documents, their authority, their objectivity, their currency (how recent are they?), and the breadth of coverage.

The increasing interest in digital humanities projects is also a boon to the writing studies researcher. Digital humanities, which encompasses both research and pedagogy, focuses on the intersection of humanities disciplines and computing. There is a long-standing history—certainly from the early 1980s—of a relationship between composition and computing. As director of a university writing program at this time, I headed the transition to a computer-based writing program, which featured a computer lab in our writing center. Students were not happy. They asked, "Is this a computer class or a writing class?" The notion of composing in longhand seems archaic now. A professional journal, *Computers and Composition*, arose as a result of technology integration in writing programs. Digital humanities is much more broad based but is still a worthy venue for finding sources and resources. The National Endowment for the Humanities (NEH) correctly states the impact of technology on the humanities:

> In a short period of time, digital technology has changed our world. The ways we read, write, learn, communicate, and play have fundamentally changed due to the advent of networked digital technologies. These changes are being addressed in fascinating ways by scholars from across the humanities, often working in collaboration with scientists, librarians, museum staff, and members of the public. (Source: http://www.neh.gov/divisions/odh/about.)

Special Collections and Archives

Libraries have specialized collections featuring items that generally do not circulate as materials in the general collection do. What is housed in these areas? Archives and special collections encompass rare and unique materials in various formats. Materials may range from papyrus to digital records. Illuminated manuscripts and early printed books may be included but also business records, personal and family papers, maps, artifacts, images, motion-picture films, and audio recordings. And these items are not derived from historical artifacts only. More recent areas of collecting include websites, blogs, and other digital content.

Visitor and user policies should be reviewed prior to any visit, although special collections librarians often give tours to groups of students as part of a class. In general, given the rarity of the materials, users are requested to have in hand note-taking materials that cannot harm the artifacts. This includes, generally, pencils, laptops, and even digital cameras. Users are asked to register in special collections. Some items may require white-glove treatment—literally. For instance, a student researcher working on a translation of the flyleaf of an illuminated book not only wore white gloves, but the book rested on a special platform to ensure it was supported.

Profile of a Student Researcher: CJ Guadarrama

Carlos Junior ("CJ") Guadarrama is an English education major, and as part of one of his courses, he visited the Special Collections and Archives area of the university library. The librarian reviewed various areas of emphasis for its collection: Western history; local poet May Swenson; Jack London papers; forest-service records; and agricultural papers. CJ perked up noticeably when the Intermountain Indian School was mentioned. His mother had worked at Head Start in the building that had housed the tribal boarding school, and he knew the buildings were to be razed in the near future. As he began to look at the papers in the files, he found newspapers from the 1970s that included articles about a "riot" at the school. He latched onto this topic, and by interviewing school alumni, he came to a final project about the appearance and reality of rhetoric about the conflict among students of the various tribes housed at the school. "The lightbulb illuminated for me," CJ said. "I finished that research project and prepared a poster for the undergraduate research day at the state capitol." CJ was so "on fire" about the possibilities of research arising out of this special collection that he proceeded to complete three projects, each one disseminated in poster format.

Reviewing the Literature

For students, it may seem contradictory to think about *literature* as scholarly works when it so often means Shakespeare, *To Kill a Mockingbird*, or *Catch-22*. But in the context of research, *literature* means that which has been published on the topic. Reviewing the scholarly literature gives the researcher insight into what has been done already by other scholars. It sets up the opportunity for the researcher to know if the project will truly fill a gap in the literature. Researchers review the scholarly literature on the topic, but they may also review appropriate scholarly references on the setting and even the research design. Skimming sources quickly is a first stage, followed by more careful review once the researcher determines that there is truly something *there*. In short, is the topic of significance, and can the researcher add to what's known? These questions are sometimes abbreviated as the *so what* test.

A *review of literature* demonstrates whether or not research questions have already been addressed sufficiently. It's also possible to take a problem that has been explored in one setting and transplant it to a different setting; in other words, vary the *site* for the research or the *population* studied. For instance, Piaget's theories on child development were developed in a Western culture. Would those still hold true in a tribal setting? For instance, how is information technology used in a third-world country? Does a computer-for-every-child initiative have an impact on literacy rates? It's also possible to replicate a study to see if the findings are consistent. A replication may also vary the context of the setting.

How is this part of the research process recorded? The best way to proceed is to begin building an *annotated bibliography*. This list of references includes the citation—using the style appropriate to the topic. Students in English may be most familiar with the citation format of the Modern Language Association (MLA), which is used for writing scholarly essays on literature. On the other hand, for professional journals that include research on writing, the more common citation form is the current edition of the *Publication Manual of the American Psychological Association* (APA 2001). Some publications in writing may opt for Chicago style. This brings to the forefront the fact that research on writing is often considered a social science as opposed to the humanistic scholarship in literature. Why do citation styles differ? In terms of APA format, note that two differences are immediately apparent: (1) the author's initials are used rather than the full first name, and (2) the date of publication comes early in the citation. In terms of the preference for initials, gender-neutral identification is guaranteed. How current the work is becomes very important in the social sciences, which is why the date is given primacy.

Following is a sample from the Annual Annotated Bibliography published in the journal *Research in the Teaching of English*, which uses APA style:

Wolfe, C. R. 2011. "Argumentation across the curriculum." *Written Communication* 28 (2): 193–219.

Analyzes 265 undergraduate writing assignments from 71 university courses as explicitly thesis-driven assignments, text analysis, empirical arguments, decision-based arguments, proposals, short answer arguments, and compound arguments. Most assignments (59%) involved argumentation with the highest percentages occurring in engineering, fine arts, interdisciplinary studies, social science, education, and natural science, with less focus in the humanities (47%) and business (46%). While argumentative writing in general is valued at the university level, the types of arguments required also varied across different disciplines.

Yang, Y. F. 2010. "Students' reflection on online self-correction and peer review to improve writing." *Computers & Education* 55 (3): 1202–10.

Investigates an online system to arouse students' reflection on both self-correction (one's own problem-solving process in writing) and peer review (peers' problem-solving process in writing) to improve their texts. Students were encouraged to reflect on their actions during and after text construction. A sample of 95 undergraduate students wrote a reflective journal, which was analyzed by content analysis to compare their reflection on self-correction with peer review in writing. Finds that reflecting on the differences between self-correction and peer review enabled students to monitor, evaluate, and adjust their writing processes in the pursuit of text improvement. Furthermore, students claimed that self-correction helped them detect grammatical errors (local revision) while peer review allowed them to view their own texts from others' perspectives. (*RTE*, Volume 46, November 2011; http://www.ncte.org/journals/rte/biblios)

A good annotation includes the bibliographic information as well as a summary. In addition, it's important to note the date of the study, where it was conducted, the size of the sample, demographic information, and choice of methodology. Finally, reflection on how this publication has relevance to the study helps frame the context. This detailed work is invaluable when the actual report on the project is being written and saves much stress for the researcher. (For work found on a website, the date the website was accessed should also be recorded.)

WRITING THE PROPOSAL

Before the research is undertaken, a proposal for the research is written. This is especially true when the researcher seeks IRB approval or grant funding. Many institutions have grant programs that support students' research projects. No matter other considerations, it is always wise to write a proposal, as it lays out what is to be done, and it's the first check on the credibility of the project. It's a place where the need for revisions in the topic may come to light. Once the proposal is done, it's a plan for the work, but that plan may be revised as the project develops.

The following is a general outline for writing a proposal:

- project title
- project abstract (briefly describes the project)
- project description (describes the basic idea or question you will explore and illustrates your planned approach)
- review of literature (describes the significance of your proposed work and the contribution it will make to the field by offering a review of the literature on the chosen topic and an explanation of how your project fills a gap in scholarly knowledge)
- budget (describes funds needed to complete the project, perhaps in an Excel form like the one below)

TABLE 1.5. Project budget form

	Brief Explanation	Request	In-Kind Match
Travel			$0
Supplies and Materials			$0
Other (Please Specify)			$0
Other (Please Specify)			$0
Total Expenses			$0

- Here's an example of a budget submitted to conduct archival research.

Research Budget: Archival Research to Study Papers of 19th-Century Woman Physician

Photocopies:	$120
Printer Cartridge:	$75
Blank CDs for Microfilm Copying:	$5
Pens and Paper:	$8
Research Software, Endnotes:	$110
Travel:	
• Airfare to Salt Lake City:	$325
• Car rental, 4 days:	$125
Total Cost:	$768

COLLECTING AND ANALYZING DATA

In part 2 of this textbook, specific strategies for collecting data will be addressed in tandem with the research approach addressed. This section provides a broad overview of the toolkit available to researchers for gathering information. Please note that *data* is the plural form while *datum* is singular. This sometimes trips up researchers in terms of subject-verb agreement. Thus, to be grammatically correct, *data are* reported.

Strategies for collecting information or data are many and should be selected in accordance with the research question, site, and methodology. Inherent in any data collection is the responsible conduct of research (RCR) that is discussed more fully in chapter 3. Permissions may need to be obtained in order to conduct the study, and if people are involved, the researcher must be certified in studying human subjects. While information obtained through digital sources may seem fair territory, people are behind content, and their work must be treated fairly and ethically. But first, a look at the ways in which information may be obtained.

Content Analysis

Most likely, you are already familiar with *content analysis*, having interpreted texts in previous assignments: understanding a historical document, analyzing a novel, arguing a political point. In fact, the writing autobiography of an earlier assignment in this text called for analysis. The systematic examination of data gathered is *content analysis*. This analysis may be quantitative—literally *counting*—or qualitative.

Content analysis is sometimes called *textual analysis*. Students who have worked with literary criticism will find similarities in understanding factual occurrences and interpreting fictional characters and events. While the people in fiction are *characters*, the key elements of *motivation, plot,* and *conflict* can apply in research as well. For instance, why does a tutor use a particular approach in working with a basic writing student? What is the motivation behind the writer who revises a piece multiple times? How do collaborative authors work together successfully and resolve conflict?

A word here about an approach to criticism and analysis that appeared in the last part of the twentieth century is appropriate. *Critical discourse analysis* is yet another form of analysis. *Discourse,* most commonly applied to spoken word, can also refer to written text. Critical discourse analysis studies the relationship between discourse and ideology. By *ideology,* we mean a set of beliefs and attitudes that form a certain perspective on the world. Critical discourse analysis is particularly keen on how language and power are interrelated. Most critical discourse analysts approach a text with a political goal or agenda of some kind and are often advocates for social justice and social change, seeking to show how a text could be biased toward a particular ideology. While critical discourse analysis relies on the content-analysis tool, in itself it is not a method but a lens through which to look at the research topic. Scholars who engage in critical discourse analysis are looking to raise the downtrodden, support equal rights, and uncover unfairness.

In content analysis, what text is being analyzed? It may be an existing text, or it may be one that is created, as in *transcriptions,* when scripts are written based on interviews or other means of capturing conversations or monologues. Transcriptions may reveal kinds of statements and quantitative information. Through such analysis, patterns or themes may be established.

Transcriptions of interviews can be an arduous process, so it is important for the researcher to take into account the time and effort needed when choosing this research tool. Something like an interview but more like a monologue, *protocol analysis* allows the researcher to get inside the thoughts of writers in order to look at process, not just product. This method arises from cognitive studies. Three kinds of protocol analysis were popular in research on writing, largely in the 1980s: the *think-aloud protocol, talk-aloud protocol,* and *read-aloud protocol.* Think-aloud protocols operate like this: a writer begins a task and thinks aloud while writing, the voice captured on a recording device. The data produced from this approach include the writing as well as the transcription of the think-aloud protocol. Flower and Hayes (1981; Flower et al. 1986) used this approach to good effect to uncover the cognitive processes of writers and to strategize on how novice and expert writers differ in their approaches. The think-aloud protocol is sometimes applied in usability studies so observers can understand a user's experience when working with a piece of equipment, an object, or, say, an app.

The talk-aloud protocol asks participants to describe their behaviors but not comment on or interpret them. In the read-aloud protocol, students read aloud a text; they may also interrogate the text as they read. This process is not to be confused with simply reading aloud in class.

David Bartholomae (1980) found that having students do read-aloud protocols of their own work offered insight into their thinking and writing processes. When basic writers read their own texts aloud, they actually corrected many of the errors; however, when they were asked to locate those errors in the writing itself, they could not! This kind of protocol has lost some popularity as a method because it is viewed as less objective than once believed.

Transcriptions carry with them possible drawbacks. Equipment does fail. If that is the case, the researcher should transcribe as much of the conversation as possible and note the omissions in the record. The transcription may be a word-for-word record (including pauses, notes about laughter, etc.), or it may be a summary of the conversation, which can be done more quickly. The approach depends on the question and methodology of the overarching project.

Coding labels may be determined in advance of the coding, or the codes may be teased out as the researcher reviews the data. Some examples follow below. For one example codes were determined, at least in part, in advance of the transcription analysis, and for the other, the terms emerged through careful review of the transcripts. In terms of coding systems, it is highly recommended to use codes recognizable in the field, which will be helpful when the study is presented or published. Using familiar coding systems helps make the research *replicable* and *aggregable.*

Rebecca R. Block's (2010) dissertation focuses on tutoring sessions and the belief that addressing higher-order concerns is more important than addressing lower-order concerns. There are commonly accepted notions of which concerns in writing are higher and which are lower. Higher concerns generally include thesis, organization, development, purpose, and audience while lower concerns include sentence structure, word choice, punctuation, and spelling. The abstract for her dissertation explains the approach Block employed to get at a question on efficacious approaches for read-aloud tutorial sessions.

> Reading aloud in writing center sessions is a common practice, one that is both under-studied and under-theorized. In an attempt to begin to address this gap, this dissertation conducts an empirical analysis of three different methods of reading aloud in the writing center: client-read, tutor-read, and point-predict. Client-read and tutor-read are traditional approaches to reading in writing centers; point-predict was adapted into a tutoring method from a peer-review method by Barbara Sitko. In order to examine these methods, a study of 24 writing center sessions—eight of each method—was conducted. Sessions were recorded, transcribed, and coded for initiator and writing issues discussed.

> This dissertation is divided into four chapters. Chapter One provides a literature review, Chapter Two addresses the transcript and survey analysis, Chapter Three uses tutor interviews to question common assumptions within writing center lore, and Chapter Four offers ideas for future research and implications for practice. The most striking finding of this study is the strong suggestion that reading methods have a significant impact on the outcome of tutoring sessions—especially on the amount of attention given to global and local issues—and that current beliefs that having clients read aloud is the best way to ensure a global focus, client control, and client engagement may be incorrect. Specifically, this study found that traditional tutor-read sessions focused three-fourths of their conversation on local issues, whereas point-predict sessions focused only a fourth of their discussion on these issues and gave far more attention to organization, signposting, and content. Clients were also about twice as likely to initiate globally focused discussions in point-predict sessions as in other session types. Consequently, this dissertation concludes that writing center practitioners need to more closely analyze the current reading methods they employ and seek out new reading methods

that might be better suited at catalyzing global, engaged, client-focused sessions.

David Bartholomae's (1980) Braddock Award[1]–winning essay, "The Study of Error," describes how he used error analysis to understand basic writers' intentions with the goal of uncovering internal strategies that could be mined to improve their writing.

> The mode of analysis that seems most promising for the research we need on the writer's sequence of learning is error analysis. Error analysis provides the basic writing teacher with both a technique for analyzing errors in the production of discourse, a technique developed by linguists to study second language learning, and a theory of error, or, perhaps more properly, a perspective on error, where errors are seen as (1) necessary stages of individual development and (2) data that provide insight into the idiosyncratic strategies of a particular language user at a particular point in his acquisition of a target language. (256)

> Error analysis begins with a theory of writing, a theory of language production and language development that allows us to see errors as evidence of choice or strategy among a range of possible choices or strategies. They provide evidence of an individual style of using the language and making it work; they are not a simple record of what a writer failed to do because of incompetence or indifference. Errors, then, are stylistic features, information about this writer and this language; they are not necessarily "noise" in the system, accidents of composing, or malfunctions in the language process. Consequently, we cannot identify errors without identifying them in context, and the context is not the text, but the activity of composing that presented the erroneous form as a possible solution to the problem of making a meaningful statement. (257)

Bartholomae found that having students read aloud their work can be helpful to improving their writing, but he also found that there was not just one response but several, which he then classified by type. In essence, he set up a coding system for his findings. In other words, the themes emerged from the review of the data.

In general, when writers read, and read in order to spot and correct errors, their responses will fall among the following categories:

1. overt corrections
2. spoken corrections
3. no recognition
4. overcorrection

5. acknowledged error

6. reader miscue

7. nonsense in which the writer reads the sentence as though it were correct. (266)

It should be clear that analyzing data can be time intensive. Software specially designed for qualitative research data analysis, such as Nud*ist or Atlas TI, is powerful, but it is expensive and not necessarily easy to learn quickly. Computer assisted/aided qualitative data analysis software (CAQDAS) provides tools for transcription analysis, content analysis, discourse analysis, coding, and textual interpretation. The Saturate application (http://www.saturateapp.com/) is simple and free. Technological innovations for qualitative research will be continually evolving. As a result, listings here will be quickly dated.

With the rise of digital humanities projects, the number of text-analysis tools has also grown. One of these is TAPoR 2.0, the revised edition of TAPoR (Text Analysis Portal for Research), which was developed by faculty at the University of Alberta in Canada. As the creators note, "It is a both a resource for discovery and a community. The TAPoR team has created a place for Humanities scholars, students and others interested in applying digital tools to their textual research to find the tools they need, contribute their experience and share new tools they have developed or used with others." (Source: http://www.tapor.ca/.) When I was an undergraduate, I focused one of my essays on the use of the word *honor* in Henry Fielding's 1725 book *The True and Genuine Account of the Life and Actions of the Late Jonathan Wild*. My research method was to count each and every occurrence of the term by turning page by page. The trials of an undergraduate in the precomputer age!

Observations and Notes

Recording information stems from the *field-notes* concept used by anthropologists. By this time it may be obvious that research in writing derives many of its methods from anthropology. Bronislaw Malinowski, considered the founder of anthropology, established the practice in which the researcher lives for an extended time among the people being researched and conducts research in the native language. This ethnographic approach to fieldwork influenced his many students, including, famously, Margaret Mead, who studied maturation rites in the South Pacific. For an example of research on literacy away from the United States, Kulick and Stroud (1993) looked at the acquisition of literacy in a village in Papua New Guinea. The found that "children learn very little during their first two or three years . . . due . . . to their inability to cope with instruction in English. . . . Outside of school . . . literacy skills are almost never used. . . . After they leave school at ages fourteen to fifteen, many of these young people may never read and will almost certainly never write again" (32).

The practice of *participant observation*, in which the researcher is placed within the culture of the study to gather information, is the basis of ethnographic practice. Clifford Geertz (1973), another anthropologist influential for writing studies, suggested that "thick description," detailed notes from observation, is the best approach for understanding the situation and context. For the purposes of studying writing, the culture is often the classroom.

Note taking is an essential skill for the researcher as it involves careful observation, analysis, and critical thinking in order that meaning can be derived. Hardly anyone can be like Truman Capote, who practiced memorizing conversations so he could recall later in the day the details and record them; this approach stood him in good stead during his research for the groundbreaking "nonfiction novel" *In Cold Blood* (Capote 1965).

The researcher may be in the role of observer as an outsider, or the researcher may be in the role of observer as an insider—someone invested in the culture. The setting may be so familiar to the insider that it's more difficult to see aspects of the culture. A researcher is responsible for making the familiar unfamiliar so it is more readily assessed; conversely, the researcher may also make the unfamiliar familiar, offering explanations for the phenomenon. Alice Goffman was a sophomore at the University of Pennsylvania when she began tutoring an African American high-school student from a low-income neighborhood. Through this student she met crack dealers, whom she followed after asking their permission, tracking their lives. For the next six years, Goffman lived in the neighborhood and observed and took the notes that became *On the Run: Fugitive Life in an American City* (Goffman 2014). That is a dramatic example of true immersion in a culture.

Returning to writing studies research, how is it best to take notes during an observation? Admittedly, capturing the details of a setting can be overwhelming, as there are the physical description of the place, the interactions that go on among the people who inhabit the space, and even what is *not* happening. Does the researcher enter notes electronically or in longhand? The setting may determine whether an electronic method is intrusive or not. Certainly it is much easier to begin with notes typed so they are more accessible; however, transcribing notes from longhand may also reveal much to the researcher. Keeping notes carefully is one of the standard principles of responsible conduct of research although the principle typically assumes lab notebooks. Note keeping is discussed in more depth in the section on the ethics of data acquisition and management, but in brief, the researcher is responsible for taking

Table 1.6. "T" Journal or dialogic notebook sample.

Observations	Comments
8 March 2012, 10:25 a.m.	1:30 p.m.
The students enter classroom 201B noisily. Counting. 29 students (16 female; 13 male).	
The desks are arranged in front of the teacher's desk.	
One student approaches the teacher to discuss a paper.	I asked H about this after class, and she said this was a late assignment.
10:30: Ms H calls the class to order and asks them to do a task "correct the sentence."	H said in interview following class that she likes "bell-ringer" assignments to get the class into learning mode right away.
Students share their answers to sentence exercise.	Students seem to get this right. I'm wondering about a grammar lesson out of context? Effectiveness? What does this signal about importance of grammar when it's first thing on agenda?
10:35: H asks student to read Poem of the Day. . .	H told me she uses Poetry 180 website to find poem of day. This seems a different priority from the sentence error task. . . .

accurate notes and not selecting only data that conform to the hypothesis or question. The participant-observer takes in all details and then draws meaning from them.

The format may vary from a simple notebook in which observations are dated and recorded to a "T" journal or dialogic notebook in which two columns are used, the first for observation and the second for reflection and comment. Even if the researcher is not an artist, it's helpful to have a sketch of the physical setting or photographs.

Student Activity

OBSERVATIONS: SPEND SOME TIME
PRACTICING TAKING FIELD NOTES

I have adapted these guidelines for making observations from *Field-Working: Reading and Writing Research* by Bonnie Sunstein and Elizabeth Chiseri-Strater.

Option 1: In a direct observation (about thirty to fifty minutes on average), take notes as much as possible on what you observe, hear, perhaps even smell. The left-hand column includes notes from the observation (e.g., physical characteristics of the setting, conversations between and among those in the setting, nonverbal behavior); the right-hand column includes the researcher's reactions, feelings, thoughts, and speculations. Also note what is not happening if appropriate as the absence of activity may be illuminating.

Option 2: Participate in an activity of about an hour's length—as an actual participant, which means notes cannot be taken at the time. It requires good memory and using mnemonic devices so that when notes are written, they are as accurate as possible. Record in as much detail as possible in the field notes as soon as you can. This is participant observation in its true sense.

In general, any good record of participant-observation includes the following items:

- date, time, and place of observation
- specific facts, numbers, details
- sensory impressions
- personal responses to the act of recording (Are others watching you as you watch them?)
- specific words, phrases, summaries of conversations, and insider language
- questions about people or behaviors at the site for future investigation
- continuous page-numbering system for future reference
  (Sunstein and Chiseri-Strater 2011)

Interviews

Observations may lead naturally to interviews. Talking to informants can provide important information if the groundwork is prepared carefully. For novice interviewers, in fact, it is best to use the interview as a methodological tool only after considerable effort has been put into the development of questions and also after practice conducting an interview. This is not to say that the casual interview is not valuable; spur-of-the-moment conversations may reveal information that serves as instigation for a project. The researcher may be struck by a student's or teacher's comment in such a way that it serves as the basis for further investigation. For more formal information gathering, the researcher must always be aware that the participants' time is valuable, which means being as organized as possible. An interview is not a fishing expedition but a series of questions designed to gather information that will help illuminate the topic. Because interviews are time and energy intensive, it's important to use this tool wisely.

How to begin? Consider this set of steps. Drafting a set of questions for review by a mentor is a good initial move. In general, it's wise to begin with a few warm-up questions to put the interviewee at ease. These may be easy-to-answer factual or demographic questions. Subject questions should be open ended and neutral, as the researcher's agenda should not influence the interviewee. Questions that elicit only a yes or no answer should be avoided unless a clarifying follow-up question is added. Any terms that may be unfamiliar to the interviewee should be defined. The interviewee should feel comfortable, not threatened, in answering the questions. Trying out a series of questions in a dry run with a friend or mentor is a good idea. The questions can be revised, then, based on the feedback. The interviewer should feel comfortable in asking follow-up questions not originally on the list if a comment seems worth further investigation.

Comfort is a key part of any interview. In addition to the interviewee's feeling at ease about the content of questions, it is also helpful for the interview to take place in a comfortable setting with no distractions. The time of day and even the day itself should be set carefully so as to avoid any Monday-morning blues or TGIF haste. Interviews may take place in person or through Skype or other technology. The researcher should explain (most likely reinforce) what the interview is about, as it is assumed that the project was explained earlier in order for the participant to agree to be interviewed. It's crucial that issues of confidentiality are once again noted and that necessary permissions have been obtained. For some interviews results are shared with participants, including the researcher's analysis and interpretation.

The nuts and bolts of an interview can make the process flow smoothly or provide disastrous distractions. Assuming that the interview is being recorded, it's important to check the equipment, not just at the beginning but also during the session. If a second person is available, it's advantageous for the researcher to have another recorder and listener in the room—assuming the participants agree. Frankly, it can be difficult for one person to both ask and record comments. And, memory is fallible. Explaining the mechanics of the interview—length, format, recording devices, what will happen next—helps the participant understand the process and feel relaxed. The body language of the interviewer should also express neutrality. Likewise, the interviewer should not engage in a debate with the participant but have an open attitude to all answers. That said, some interviewees may try to take control of the session, and it's important that the interviewer keeps the session on track and on time. A good interviewer might offer an affirming comment such as "that's a fascinating story" but then steer the conversation back to the set of questions with "let's continue with the next point." A mock interview set up to practice might introduce these potential hurdles so the interviewer can be alert and prepared.

At the beginning and end of any interview, the interviewee should be asked, "Do you have any questions?" Another good question to ask is, "Is there anything you wish to share with me that you did not?" This question can uncover hidden information that may be useful, and the interviewees also depart the session believing their opinions mattered. Once the participant has departed the session, the interviewer should take additional notes on observations and reflections. Be alert to surprises from the interview. Consider whether further follow up will be needed. Assuming the session was recorded, transcribe it as soon as possible.

Profile of a Student Researcher: Kristin Lillywhite

To illustrate a sample interview (and some other aspects of conducting research as well), a research project undertaken by Kristin Lillywhite will be used. Kristin, a secondary-education major with subject specialization in English, was interested in these questions for her honors thesis: How does linguistic research inform teaching practices to address the learning needs of ELL (English language learners) in today's classrooms? How can teachers help students achieve higher-level proficiency, called cognitive academic language proficiency (CALP)? Interviews were the primary tool to collect information in this study. Kristin described her purpose and methods as follows:

> In order to determine how teachers conceptualize second language acquisition and literacy instruction, eight secondary language arts teachers were interviewed. The interview component of this project was a qualitative case study relying heavily on thick descriptions. Participants were selected from five different sites: two middle schools and three high schools from mostly rural and suburban communities. The average class size for most teachers ranged from 20–35 students. Teaching experience of the individuals varied from 5 to 33 years. . . . The teachers interviewed in this study worked mostly

with Hispanic students in transitional bilingual programs. (Lillywhite 2011, 8–9)

Kristin's research study was approved by the university's Institutional Review Board (IRB), as human-subject research was integral to her study. Five guiding research questions structured the study and thus influenced the interview questions.

1. How do the learning needs of ELL students differ in terms of number or degree from the needs of mainstream students?
2. How do teachers think CALP is relevant to their teaching practices?
3. How do teachers negotiate possible differences between home literacies and CALP?
4. What significant trends or changes in literacy instruction and students' learning needs have occurred?
5. What should novice teachers know regarding students' learning needs, literacy or language instruction? (10)

The list of questions Kristin developed for her research project was revised based on consultation with her mentors following a practice session. It should be noted that she began communication with her teacher-participants through a preinterview survey. These questions are included in the survey section; they set the stage for the following interview questions.

Student Activity

INTERVIEWS

Your classmates have developed writing autobiographies in an earlier assignment in this text. Working with a partner, share these texts. Prepare a set of three to five questions you would like to address to the author based on the autobiography. Questions may focus on attitudes, processes, goals, or other issues. Ensure that the questions are worded in such a way as to elicit meaningful responses. When beginning the interview, introduce yourself to your interviewee. Note the purpose of the interview and how the responses will be used. At the conclusion of the interview, note themes or patterns you discovered as a result of the conversation. When one interview has been concluded, switch roles. At the conclusion of the conversation, both partners should reflect on the interview process. Which questions worked particularly well? Which questions didn't work or needed refinement?

Elicited Oral Histories

Also called *life histories* or *personal accounts,* oral history is a special kind of interview focusing on an individual. Noted ethnographer Harry Wolcott's (2003) justly famous study *The Man in the Principal's Office* focused on the life of a school administrator. Sally Crisp (1995) focused her dissertation on four women in rhetoric and composition for her dissertation *Women Scholar-Leaders.*

The Journal of Narrative and Life History was created in 1990 to capitalize on this emerging tradition of looking at narrative to better understand life experiences. Morphing into *Narrative Inquiry* in 1998, the journal provides a "forum for the theoretical, empirical, and methodological work on narrative" (website: http://www.clarku.edu/~mbamberg/nar rativeINQ/ Access: February 16, 2012). This scholarly work builds on the belief that understanding the human experience may be best done through life-history narratives. Jerome Bruner (1986a, 1986b, 1990) feels that narrative is an effective way to communicate research. (For a discussion of narrative as a research method, see Journet 2012.)

Oral histories may illuminate the lives of first-year students in writing or, conversely, the lives of the graduate students who so often teach first-year writing. What happens during their first year of being a student or teacher? Certainly, the first year, generally considered an important rite of initiation, is a common theme. Glen Walter (1981) described that pivotal first year of teaching in *So Where's My Apple? Diary of a First-Year Teacher.* Nancie Atwell (1987), who has already been mentioned, found inspiration for conducting research during her first days of sitting behind the "big desk." Robert Bullough (1989) wrote *First-Year Teacher,* drawing on the personal account of "Kerrie," a novice teacher.

Laurie Grobman (2009, 2013) has been particularly active in establishing projects within her community of Berks County, Pennsylvania, where students in her classes work on African American history, Latino/Latina history, and Jewish history. The students examine artifacts of the community and also interview its members with the goal of developing products (e.g., videos, books, museum exhibits) that will be useful and valued. Oral histories form the core of this *community-based research*—the intersection of service learning and undergraduate research—collecting information in the service of the participants.

While these examples focus on personal accounts in the here and now, it is also feasible to study historical personal accounts. Such life histories can illuminate a particular historical period, address women's roles, be used to establish a timeline of events and historical change, or provide a contrast to contemporary practice. Working with archival life histories will be explored in more detail in the chapter on historical research methodology.

Biography

In contrast to autobiographical personal accounts, biography is generally developed from the researcher's reviewing all available primary and secondary materials and then constructing the life of a person (or persons) from those sources. It is an interesting mix of fact (based on evidence) and fiction (supposition and conclusions drawn from interpretation of evidence). In terms of research on figures in writing studies, biography looks at the *intellectual* history of an individual.

Most likely, a biography will be written about a historical person. Aspasia from classical Greece is one of the subjects of *Reclaiming Rhetorica* (Glenn 1994; Lunsford 1995), a collection of essays that seeks to recover the voices of women in rhetoric over the ages. James Moffett (1929–1996), another leading rhetorician, coined the term "universe of discourse," which has influenced teachers and students K–16 (Moffett 1987). John Warnock (2000) portrays Moffett's significant reach in an essay in *Twentieth-Century Rhetoric and Rhetoricians*. The impact of Louise Rosenblatt (1904–2005), a worthy subject for biography given her influential introduction of reader-response theory in *Literature as Exploration* (Rosenblatt [1938] 1995), is addressed by Roen and Karolides (2005) in *The ALAN Review*. Still, there are many, many more scholars in writing worthy of biographical treatment.

While the intellectual history and biography may seem an enormous undertaking, it is possible for a team of researchers to divide the work into sectional assignments so the task is not so daunting. This kind of research is most closely related to historical scholarship but also brings to bear analysis of intellectual contributions to the field.

Surveys

Surveys can be an informal or formal way to gather information about behaviors. But even with an informal survey, researchers tend to structure surveys carefully so the data obtained have validity. An informal survey might be used in the planning phase of the research to get a better sense of the issue. The researcher may try out questions and, in doing so, revise procedures or even the focus of the study.

The ease of access to electronic survey instruments has made these attractive vehicles for conducting research. SurveyMonkey and Qualtrics are just two of the most popular. (The latter may be licensed on your campus.) These companies provide templates for various types of surveys: academic research, market research, demographic data collection, job satisfaction, usability polls, and so on. Online responses can even be measured by the amount of time a participant takes to decide on an answer. But such sophisticated feedback is only appropriate if response time is part of the study. In any tool used to collect data, the emphasis lies with the goal of the research study.

Kristin's Preinterview Survey

1. What is your name?
2. How long have you been teaching language arts?
3. Briefly (3–4 sentences) describe your teaching assignments.
4. Briefly list the top three learning needs of English Language Learner (ELL) students in your classroom that you are most concerned about.
5. Briefly list the top three teaching strategies you use to address those needs.
6. Circle below to indicate how often you think about the language needs of students when planning lessons.

Let's return to Kristin, our honors student, who engaged in research to ascertain how practicing teachers felt about instruction for ESL students. The questions Kristin developed for her interviews were discussed, but she also used a written survey or questionnaire to elicit information prior to the interviews. Her survey used old-fashioned pen and paper. Those questions appear below. The goal was to be a more informed researcher and to ask the teachers to begin to think about the questions at hand so they were entering the interview knowledgeable about the topic. This design meant the teachers considered the topic in more depth and were not answering spontaneously.

Experts on survey construction generally exist on campuses and can provide helpful feedback on the development and administration of the survey. Survey participants will not look kindly on a slipshod survey and may not finish answering the questions. Designing effective questions is key to a reliable survey. Drafts of questions should be tested with potential respondents to ensure they are easily understood.

Questions may elicit simple yes or no answers. These are easily tabulated. Other types of questions, which are known as open-ended questions, include the possibility for additional comment. Or, questions may request a response on a Likert-type scale, normally offering five possible answers: 1. Strongly disagree, 2. Disagree, 3. Neither agree nor disagree, 4. Agree, 5. Strongly agree. Notice that the middle area indicates a neutral response.

A survey done by a national task force on undergraduate research in writing studies used several types of questions to get at the state of student research in the field. In the following questions, responders provided factual information, but the door is also open for variant answers the researchers did not anticipate.

Where are you located within your institution?
Department of English
Department of Writing & Rhetoric (or similar name)
Stand-alone Writing Program
Other (please describe)

Does your department have a degree program in writing?
It has a writing major or track or concentration
It has a writing major/track/concentration *and* minor
It has a writing minor
It has a certificate in writing studies
Other (please describe):

Does your department provide opportunities for undergraduate research to engage in original research and scholarship? (E.g., do students engage in authentic research through classroom assignments—as opposed to "term papers.")
Yes
No
Not sure
Please describe:

The following questions are structured with a list of answers. In the first example it is a check-all-that-apply multiple-choice structure, while in the second participants are asked to rank the items.

What type(s) of research methodologies do the students that you mentor employ? (Check all that apply, please.)
Historical/archival research
Community-based research
Practitioner inquiry
Discourse/textual analysis
Case Study
Ethnography
Experimental
Other (please describe)

What are the most effective ways to increase support for undergraduate research (rank them in order of importance with 1 being most important):
Develop undergraduate curricula
Develop graduate curricula
Develop undergraduate research textbooks and other pedagogical materials

Develop policy statements and best practices

Create new conferences for undergraduate research

Create new presentation opportunities at existing conferences

Create new publications

Create new publication opportunities within existing publications

Create a clearinghouse for information about undergraduate research in/relevant to writing studies

Additional strategies

Demographic information helps the researcher understand who the participants are. These questions may vary widely; they typically include sex and age of the participant but may also include educational level, salary, and other information pertinent to the study. For the survey on undergraduate research given to the membership of the Conference on Composition and Communication (CCCC), the committee was interested in these demographics:

DEMOGRAPHICS

I currently belong to the following type of institution:

Two-year

Bachelor

Masters

Doctoral

None of the above

Other (insert description)

My role/rank at my institution is

Adjunct/part-time

Instructor

Assistant Professor

Associate Professor

Professor

Other (insert description)

I have been a member of CCCC for

1–5 years

6–10 years

10–19 years

20–29 years

30+ years

The answers to these demographic questions helped the researchers understand where undergraduate research is occurring and in what institutional types. Demographic questions tend to come at the end of any survey as they are inherently not as interesting as content-focused questions, which are designed to hook participants and keep them answering questions.

A letter of information must preface surveys. This letter to potential participants lays out the goals of the research, benefits to the field, procedures, and any risks. It also informs participants about how the results will be used and how their confidentiality will be protected. Because surveys involve human participants, conducting a survey may require approval by the Institutional Review Board (IRB). A sample letter of information follows.

Student Activity

TAKE A SURVEY: WRITING APPREHENSION

John Daly and Michael Miller developed a survey on writing apprehension featuring multiple questions to uncover the participant's level of comfort with writing. Is the writer fearful? Nervous? Uncomfortable? Daly and Miller used this survey to understand better why students may be fearful of writing—and as a goal, to help students overcome that fear. The test has been used widely since its creation in 1975; an updated version allows students to self-assess their apprehension with the idea that awareness is a first step in improving. The rubric on scores then offers advice to the writer. (See http://www.csus.edu/indiv/s/stonerm /The%20Daly-Miller%20Test.htm.)

Take the survey. Then analyze the results with the scoring rubric provided. How well has this 1975 survey stood the test of time? Are there questions you found particularly effective? Are there questions you would revise? Are there differences in the way students write now and the way they did in 1975?

Source: From John Daly and Michael Miller's "The Empirical Development of an Instrument to Measure Writing Apprehension." *Research in the Teaching of English* 12 (1975): 242–49. Adapted by Michael W. Smith in *Reducing Writing Apprehension* (Urbana: NCTE, 1984).

WHAT TO DO WITH SURVEY DATA

When the surveys are submitted, it is time to begin analysis. One simple data point to assess is the *response rate*. This is the number of surveys submitted in relationship to the number sent. If one hundred surveys were sent, and thirty were returned, then the response rate is 30 percent. Is that a good rate? For an online survey, that is about average. Response rate may be increased through incentive or pay. The National Novel Writing Month (NaNoWriMo) program conducted a survey; its incentive was to offer gifts from the program, such as logo items—"There's a novel inside this pencil." For the survey on undergraduate research in writing studies noted above, no response rate was given as CCCC has thousands of members, and it was understood that not all would be interested, but it was convenient to send to the membership. The report indicated that 365 members had responded. Instead of indicating a response rate, the authors of the report described the demographics, noting, for instance, that over 50 percent work at research universities.

Collecting data is only a first step. Analyzing the information means looking for themes or patterns in the answers. Being able to quantify the results is helpful. Take, for instance, this statement:

> 83% of respondents noted that opportunities exist on their campuses for undergraduates to conduct research. These are largely curricular experiences with almost 80% checking "advanced or upper-level courses in which students have opportunities to learn about and conduct research." (CCCC Committee on Undergraduate Research 2014)

An analysis of results is part of the research study. This analysis may include discussion and implications or findings. In the undergraduate-research survey, the researchers teased out implications, particularly with perceived hurdles.

CHALLENGES
- The continued gold standard of sole authorship reduces the chance that faculty will seek undergraduates as coauthors or even as research assistants.
- The major barrier for faculty to work with students is time and the willingness to take on students to mentor. A second barrier is lack of experience in working with undergraduates.
- In terms of faculty roles and rewards, faculty and their department leaders should advocate for tenure and promotion decisions as well as merit decisions to include mentorship of students, whether those are undergraduate or graduate students.

In sum, when using survey as a research tool, do a dry run to test the questions, draw on expertise for the design, use an appropriate format (e.g., online, print), consider incentives for the participants, seek IRB approval as needed, and don't go overboard on the time needed to complete the survey.

AVOIDING PITFALLS AND
ESTABLISHING A TIMELINE

Setting a reasonable schedule may be the single most important attribute of bringing a good research project to a successful conclusion. Just as in carpentry, the adage "measure twice, cut once" applies. For projects that require detailed consideration and coordination, the advice might be "plan the work and work the plan." When a complex project must be undertaken, it's much easier if it's broken into doable segments. This is especially true for any project that must be completed within the framework of a quarter or semester. A capstone project such as a thesis may be undertaken over a longer period, perhaps a year.

An experienced mentor can provide advice on what's reasonable in terms of time frames. For instance, IRB approval may take only a couple of weeks for an expedited review, or it may be a longer period of two months, particularly if the review requires full board approval and the board meets on a monthly basis. Anticipating delays and building in flexibility can be very helpful in avoiding frustration and disappointment— and even abandonment of a worthy project.

WRITING THE REPORT

Reports on research vary from a few pages, as in a microstudy, to many more pages for a thesis. Particularly long reports may be fronted by an abstract or executive summary. Scientific papers often rely on the IMRAD format, an acronym for introduction, methods, results and discussion. That's actually a good starting point for research in writing, too, but there are no rigid rules. The point is to communicate the research in a clear and accessible manner. Basically, the research describes what was done and what it means, usually ending with a note that future research might take the project in a particular direction. The researcher is also frank about any limitations of the study. It's important to place the study in the context of what other researchers have done, and it's also essential to explain why the study has significance or meaning.

There is no one right way to structure the report on the research project, but the sections below are typical, building on the IMRAD format.

- Introduction with problem statement
  - Explanation of the research question and the overarching purpose of the study
- Theoretical overview and review of literature
  - Explanation of how this study is situated in the literature of what has come before, the theory or philosophy that informs the research, and what methodology is being used. (*Methodology* is the overarching theory of investigation while *methods* are the tools used in the research process.)

- Context of the investigation
  - Information about the researcher, the purpose of the research, or the origin of the research question
- Method
  - Explanation of the approach of the research: classroom observation, surveys, interviews, discourse analysis. (In short, how were data collected and analyzed? If multiple methods were used, these may be addressed in subheadings.)
- Results
  - Explanation of what was discovered or uncovered during the investigation
- Discussion
  - Explanation of what it all means, what is significant about the findings
- Implications for policy change and/or further research
  - Suggestions for where to go from here (Are there implications for changes in practice or policy? Or is this study just a brick in the wall and the researcher recommends further research?)
- References
  - The bibliography developed at the proposal stage and augmented through the research process
- Appendices
  - Location of lengthy documents (e.g., transcripts, examples) that would detract from the flow or argument of the report, providing the evidence for readers
- Acknowledgments
  - List of funding sources as well as acknowledgment of mentors and any participants (not including personal information of protected informants)

ABSTRACTS

Once the report is written, an *abstract* or, perhaps, an executive summary is added. In general, abstracts are one hundred to two hundred words in length. The abstract offers readers an immediate road map of the research. Following is a fairly standard organization.

1. A sentence that summarizes the research problem
2. A sentence that notes why it is significant
3. A sentence that describes the methods used
4. A sentence that summarizes results obtained
5. A sentence that says why these results are significant
6. A return to the first of the abstract with a sentence added that "hooks" the reader (e.g., a rhetorical question). To determine

whether the abstract meets its objectives, subject it to the following Abstract Evaluation Rubric.

TABLE 1.7. Abstract rubric

Components	Poor	Fair	Good	Excellent
Subject and Purpose	The topic and purpose are not clear.	The author describes main idea and purpose of the research/project.	The main idea and purpose are described as well as the significance of the project.	The project is explained within its larger context.
Method	The method of inquiry is inadequately described.	The method is described.	The methodology, sources, and methods of research are described.	The researcher not only describes the methods but also understands why this method is the best approach.
Results	It is not clear what was found.	What was learned is described.	Outcomes are described in either qualitative or quantitative terms or both.	The results are contextualized within the larger context, and recommendations for further study may be made.

Following is a sample abstract developed by Sara Calicchia (2014) for a presentation at the National Conference on Undergraduate Research.

To "Play That Funky Music" or Not:
How Music Affects the Environmental Self-Regulation of High-Ability Academic Writers

Successful writing, achieved by *self-regulated* writers, depends not only upon focus and content, but also the writing environment, including the physical and social setting, which varies greatly among writers. Just as musical tastes differ among individuals, there are strong preferences regarding the role of music in a writing setting. To better understand the *environmental self-regulation* of writers, I selected a group of twelve high-achieving writers with a range of musical interests, including nine professors and three undergraduate students across three academic fields. The results suggest that musical background impacts a writer's preferred setting, and academic writers should strongly consider this impact when establishing a successful writing environment.

BIG-DATA RESEARCH

Sherlock Holmes believed that "it is a capital mistake to theorise before one has data. Insensibly one begins to twist facts to suit theories instead of theories to suit facts" (Doyle 1895). The importance of data in evaluating and thus improving writing programs is crucial. In general, writing program research is undertaken to assess current practices and policies and to determine whether improvements can be made. In this way it is much like teacher research, but writing program research is done on a much larger scale. As such it may employ—as tutor and teacher research does—a mixed-methods approach.

Lauer and Asher (1988) suggest that writing program research may take two forms, either formative evaluation or summative evaluation. In the former, curricula, faculty qualifications and attitudes, student progress, administrative support, environmental factors, teaching methods, kinds of assignments, and grading may be examined. On the other hand, summative evaluation focuses on the results of a program and may be used to seek additional funding, to make administrative decisions about continuance, or to test faculty effectiveness (221). Writing programs tend to be complex entities, whether they are lower-division writing requirements for an entire campus—and the freshman composition course, historically, is the one course all students take; writing-across-the-curriculum or writing-in-the-disciplines programs; writing centers; writing-fellows programs; technical writing; or upper-division or advanced writing programs. They involve not only classroom information but also institutional data on student credit hours produced, salaries and wages of teachers, policy statements on adjuncts, professional-development activities, and graduate-student training.

The Council of Writing Program Administration (CWPA) offers several excellent documents for anyone looking at programs on a big-picture scale. One is an outcomes statement for first-year composition. (See http://wpacouncil.org/positions/outcomes.html.) A second is a consultant-evaluator service in which two experts in writing program administration visit a campus as an external review team. This occurs after the writing program itself has done a thorough self-study. (For this document, see the appendix on page 313.) An external review is a formal study of a program with results communicated generally to central administration. It may be considered a specialized form of accreditation, although organizations such as CWPA are not accreditors. The organization functions in the role of peers helping peers.

Research on and evaluation of writing programs can take place on a smaller and less formal basis. Writing fellow Jennifer Corroy (2003) investigated institutional change as a result of the tutoring program in which she worked at the University of Wisconsin–Madison. To do so, she interviewed faculty members who had been involved in using fellows in their classrooms. Corroy's thesis is that institutional change begins with individuals. In her conclusion she makes recommendations to program directors about how to encourage change. Corroy demonstrates that it is possible to conduct research on writing programs on quite a small scale.

To improve the practices of writing programs, large-scale assessment and design are often required. Big-data research has come to the fore as writing program administrators increasingly are faced with issues of accountability and assessment (e.g., Moxley 2013). Literally thousands of documents may be examined. In order to do research on this scale, an army of researchers may be necessary—or sophisticated technological tools. That army may arise from those involved in the program already: staff members, graduate assistants, undergraduate tutors. To demonstrate how such large-scale evaluation may take place using limited funds, an extended example of how one university analyzed all of its campus syllabi to investigate the use of writing in courses across the curriculum is presented below. The approach relies heavily on gathering data. The impetus for the research arose from two factors: (1) a writing-fellows program interested in enhancing the teaching of writing on campus and (2) a general-education-reform task force assessing important skills for undergraduates.

Extended Example of a Research Study: Writing Programs

The research questions were, what courses integrate writing into the syllabi and what kinds and types of writing assignments are there? Writing fellows[2] enrolled in a training seminar took on the task of analyzing syllabi and developing a report for the general education committee. Their task was to review *every syllabus* at the undergraduate level and determine the amount and kinds of writing. The final report offered information and recommendations for curricular change.

Such an undertaking requires the precision of a military operation. The students were tasked with reviewing more than seven hundred syllabi from forty departments. They needed both a theoretical background on writing across the curriculum as well as the nuts and bolts process of getting their hands dirty, so to speak, in physically getting access to the syllabi and reviewing them. These students became, in essence, the army required in order to undertake large-scale assessment. How was the problem of the ubiquitous lack of funding solved? Done on a shoestring, the project was aided by the fact that the students received credit for the course in which the project was done.

To begin, the twenty students[3] involved in analyzing and assessing the syllabi of courses undertook a theoretical overview—a review of literature—to learn about the history of writing across the curriculum (WAC). They read such studies as Walvoord and McCarthy (1990), which looks at how students think and write in college, focusing on four classrooms with one hundred students at three different institutions. As Barbara

Walvoord and Lucille McCarthy found, "Twelve of the fifteen major assignments in the four classes asked students for evaluation and/or problem solving in the form of what we call good/better/best questions" (7). The student researchers noted Peter Elbow's (1986, 33) admonition that "real learning is the ability to apply discipline-based concepts to a wide range of situations and to relate those concepts to the students' own knowledge and experience." An earlier WAC study by Bridgeman and Carlson (1984, 271) surveyed academic writing tasks at thirty-four institutions involving 190 academic departments. They found that instructors at that time favored comparison/contrast essays in addition to "argumentation with audience designation."

The student researchers also reviewed literature about assignment design, particularly Harris's (2010) wonderful "Assignments from Hell," Lindemann's (1995) advice on using heuristics, and Walvoord, Hunt, Dowling, and McMahon's (1997) study on faculty-development workshops. An assignment from hell, for instance, has no stipulated purpose or audience, asks for too much, and assumes knowledge the student does not have (Harris 2010). The student researchers also looked at institutional WAC newsletters such as Boise State University's *Word Works*. The investigators were charmed by the candor of a piece on writing assignments as one faculty member reflected on her own assignments: "The papers were dogs. And the mama dog was the assignment" (Leahy 1996). These readings gave the students sufficient background to understand what they would be looking for when reviewing syllabi across the campus.

Institutional policies about general education, writing requirements, and the mission statement formed a second corpus of documents reviewed. For instance, the philosophy statement for general education includes a competency for students "communicating effectively for various purposes and audiences" (Utah State University 1998a). The Institutional Review Board (IRB) was consulted to see whether the research project needed to go through human-subjects approval. The answer at the time was given that the project met the exempt classification for "research conducted in established or commonly accepted educational settings, involving normal educational practices, such as research on regular instructional strategies or research on the effectiveness of or the comparison among instructional techniques, curricula, or classroom management methods" (Utah State University 1998b).

A number of approaches can be used in this kind of project. The students reviewed possible strategies in our toolkit, deciding which to use and which to discard: interviews, observations, video or audiotaping, log or field notes, interest surveys, pre- and posttests. A range of artifacts could be gathered for analysis: journals, essays, protocol analyses, metacognitive reflections, tests, correspondence, personal accounts, syllabi, curriculum statements, institutional catalogs. In this section of the project, it was important to look at a global picture of the research methodology available.

Supported by the background readings and approaches to methodology, the actual process of collecting and analyzing syllabi began. Before soliciting permission to review syllabi campus wide, the students looked at one department's offerings in order to develop a coding technique for reviewing all syllabi. This analysis was done during class time and provided a dry run or pilot so the students could tinker with the proposed research process. This dry run helped crystallize our definitions so information would be categorized in the same way. For instance, keeping a journal counted as one assignment rather than multiple assignments for each entry. Student researchers noted that *writing-to-learn* tasks may not be graded as opposed to writing used to assess a student's knowledge. Classes associated with internships, independent studies, and student teaching were deleted as were syllabi of courses taught at the institution's regional campuses.

The result was a two-page form the student researchers could use when reading syllabi. The first page captured information on the college, department, course number and title, instructor, enrollment, and number of pages in the syllabus. The number of sections of the course as well as any cross-listing information was recorded. (*Cross-listing* occurs when multiple departments have ownership over a single course, resulting in rather unusual numbering such as Anthro/English/History 450). A second section asked yes/no questions about writing assignments. If the answer was "no writing assignments," the syllabus review for that course was completed. Syllabi that included writing assignments in some way were differentiated by "yes; it has a complete description" or "yes; mentioned in evaluation but with little, if any, directions or description." For the former, the assignment and any references to it in the syllabus were photocopied. For the latter, a follow-up phone call or e-mail to the faculty member asked for a written description or a retelling of oral instructions given in class. The writing assignments collected were described using a table adapted from Walvoord et al.'s *In the Long Run* (1997) (see Table 1.8). This table in its final format was then used to analyze all other campus syllabi.

Prior to the collection of syllabi, a formal process of asking permission took place. Fortunately, this project coincided with a regional accreditation visit, and each department was required to house all syllabi in the department office, making them accessible. Having informed central administration and the deans and secured their approval, the researchers sent the following message to the department heads.

Each year the Writing Fellows undertake a major writing assignment, typically on some aspect of writing across the curriculum. One of the

TABLE 1.8. Table for gathering data on types and kinds of writing assignments (adapted from Walvoord et al. 1997)

	Writing assignment type/genre	*# of writing assignments*	*Page requirement*	*Purpose specified*	*Audience specified*	*Documentation format (e.g., APA, MLA)*	*Model papers provided?*	*Evaluation Criteria specified?*	*Peer Response Group*	*Faculty/Student Conferences*	*Referrals to Writing Center*
In-class											
Formal essay											
Lab report											
Journal											
Book review											
Essay exam											
Other?											

Note. Please consider number and types of peer revision (e.g., in-class; virtual; take home). Are multiple drafts encouraged? If faculty/student conferences are employed, how many are there? Also record anything that is unusual, notable, or not addressed in these questions.

goals of this assignment is to introduce the students to the scholarly literature in this area and a second is to teach them research methods. For this fall's project, the Fellows are investigating "the nature of writing assignments in the disciplines." Given that the recent accreditation visit has created a situation in which every department on campus has its fall quarter syllabi available, this seems the perfect opportunity to see what kinds of assignments occur in classes. We are asking your permission for the Writing Fellows to visit the department at a convenient time and review syllabi. This will be a descriptive report. When we find exemplary writing assignments, we may ask permission of the faculty member to use them in our campus newsletter, *Writing and Speaking @ USU.* Please do not hesitate to share comments with us. We will assume that your administrative assistant is the contact person with whom to set up the appointment for the review. Thank you!

Each of the heads of the forty-five departments on campus was contacted individually by a student to ascertain that permission was truly given and to get an introduction to the administrative assistant. For the most part, each student took on two departments; for instance, one might review Accounting and Business Information Systems while another fellow asked for three departments in the College of Engineering.

Once permission was granted, the student contacted the designated administrative assistant. Leaving nothing to chance, the students created a guide sheet titled "The Nature of Writing Assignments-across-the-Curriculum Research Process for Data Collection." The script for introducing themselves to the department contact follows:

> Hello, I'm Julia, a Writing Fellow, and we're doing a research project on "the nature of writing assignments across the curriculum." The department head, Dr. X, has given us permission to review syllabi. Am I in the right place to do that? [Assuming yes.] Is this a convenient time to do that? [Assuming yes.] Is there a place where I can sit out of your way? [Assuming yes.] After I finish the review, we may need photocopies of the actual assignments. Is it possible to do that here, or is it better to take them to the college office and photocopy there. I would return them quickly if you prefer that method. [After the review, return the syllabi in the same order and condition as you received them and thank the secretary.]

The student then read each syllabus, cross-referencing the *Schedule Bulletin*'s list of courses to ensure all classes listed as being offered during the term actually had representative syllabi on file. As each syllabus was read, the form was completed to capture the details about any writing assignments. If the office staff was reluctant in any way to have assignments photocopied, the student contacted the program director.

Once the department office visit was concluded, the students followed up with faculty members from whom they needed additional information but only after the program administrator had alerted the faculty that they might be contacted. In a memo to university faculty sent a month into the data-collection process, the director explained the writing-fellows program, noting it employed "outstanding undergraduates who are nominated by faculty to serve as tutors for communication across the curriculum." The information that had been shared with their department heads about the project was included. The names of the students were listed so they would be known should a contact be made. Here is the faculty request:

> In many cases, the instructions for writing assignments are included in the syllabus, but when they are not, the student researcher assigned to the department will seek out a copy of the assignment by contacting you. If you feel comfortable in sharing, please do help them. If you prefer not to share, then please let the student know. If you give oral instructions for writing assignments, then the student will interview you and transcribe those. Thank you for your

assistance.

NEXT STEPS: ANALYZING THE DATA

The enormity of the task of analyzing seven hundred syllabi was greatly reduced by the numbers on the team—the "army." Some syllabi took only a few minutes to review. Once all syllabi were reviewed and writing assignments noted and copied, each student began the process of looking for patterns. They counted assignments and looked at aspects such as genre, methodology, and documentation. The group created a tally guide.

Department _____ offers _____ (number) of classes during this term.
Of these, _____ (number) of classes have multiple sections.
Of the total number of classes, _____ (number) included writing assignments.

The writing assignments offered in classes in this department may be characterized in this way:

HOW OFTEN WRITING OCCURS

Typically, students had to write _____ (average) number of papers/tasks.
The number of writing assignments in classes that were included ranged from a low of _____ to a high of _____.

LENGTH OF PAPERS

The required length of papers ranged from a low of ____ to a high of _____.
The average length of papers was _____.

PURPOSE

Purpose for the writing task is specified in _____ (number) of classes.
Purpose of writing includes _____.

AUDIENCE

Audience for the writing is specified in _____ (number) of classes.
Typical audiences include the following: _____.

DOCUMENTATION FORMAT

The documentation format specified is APA/MLA/Turabian/other.
___ (number) of classes specified a format for documenting references while ___ (number) required documentation but did not specify a format.

STUDENT/FACULTY CONFERENCES

Conferences to help student writers were found in ____ (number) of courses.

These conferences typically occurred _____ times during the term.

I would characterize these conferences as _____.

MULTIPLE DRAFTS

In _____(number) of classes, students were required to submit or work on multiple drafts.

In classes where multiple drafts are required or encouraged, when did evaluation occur? Before or after the final version? In other words, did students revise before receiving a grade or after?

PEER RESPONSE/EDITING

In _____(number) of classes, peer response groups are required.

In these classes, the group work occurred during class? Outside of class? Online?

WRITING CENTER

In _____(number) of classes, students are referred to the Writing Center as a place where they may receive assistance.

MODEL PAPERS

Model or exemplary papers were offered in _____(number) of classes.

These model papers could be found in the syllabus? On reserve in the Library? Other?

EVALUATION

Evaluation criteria are specified in _____(number) of classes.

These criteria might be characterized in the following way:_____.

A concern for correctness or grammar, usage, and mechanics in evaluation criteria in _____(number) of classes. [*Concern* is defined as prominent listing or mention in the syllabus.]

From these quantitative and qualitative comments, student researchers began to formulate thesis statements about what writing assignments mean to a particular department. They decided to differentiate courses taught to meet general education requirements as opposed to those taught for majors. The students also pointed out that the academic fall term may be an atypical one for a department and not represent its values on writing accurately; in other words, limitations to the study were noted. They also found that the enrollment of a particular course affects the number and kinds of writing assignments. In preparing the final compiled report, the students agreed on these commonalities: that *programs, departments,* and *colleges* must be differentiated; that a logical organization moves from lowest course number to highest course number;

that course-catalog descriptions may provide additional background; that course names as well as numbers must be included for clarity; and that any assertion must be backed up by data. The students also agreed on stylistic issues of point of view and ethnographic present tense.

COMING TO AND DISSEMINATING CONCLUSIONS

Each department's writing assignments were described in an overview written by the student who had reviewed the syllabus. A portion of the description for a department in the College of Agriculture appears below.

> In the Department of Plants, Soils, and Climate, the majority of classes include writing assignments, mostly lab reports but also short answer essay exams. The emphasis for all classes is on understanding the science of the discipline and participating in fieldwork, which results in the many reports that students write. Two classes—Soil and Water Conservation as well as Seed Physiology and Production, require in-depth research papers. For the latter class, the research paper counts for 20% of the final grade. Evaluation criteria and instructions on how to structure the paper are delivered orally in class. The syllabus contains a list of possible topics (e.g., seed production and energy expenditure). For the Soil and Water Conservation course, students work collaboratively on a written conservation plan for the ten-week period of the course. The results are presented orally to the other class members, who offer critiques of the plan. This assignment stands as unique in the department.

Students drew on their data counts to develop the picture of writing in a particular department, such as the following from accounting:

> Of the 12 courses offered this term, 11 require at least one writing assignment, but the high number of tasks is indicated in the fact that students average 8 assignments per class, the most common task being written answers to homework questions. Almost one-half of the classes include evaluation criteria, and these criteria emphasize the importance of correct grammar. "All written assignments are to be in a form worthy of professional presentation to the CEO or Board of Directors of a large corporation." In an Introduction to Financial Accounting course, students analyze a company's annual financial report, an assignment that reinforces concepts learned in class and applied to real-life situations. In Income Tax Accounting, a senior-level course, students are given a case study in which they are to prepare information for a situation that is headed to court. They are instructed to "prepare the strongest case possible for both the taxpayer and the

IRS." The purpose of this assignment is to prepare accountants who can "see both sides of an issue and communicate the information in written form."

Classes within accounting set high standards for written communication. Sample papers are available for review in faculty offices, and students are encouraged to make use of the writing center. In addition, multiple drafts of papers may be required, and teamwork is encouraged. The Department of Accounting, while focusing on numbers, does not overlook the importance of written and oral communication in the workplace.

The student researchers shared their results in draft versions of their reports with each other. By looking across departments in each college, the students began to detect patterns. This was particularly true of colleges such as the College of Natural Resources, where students, upon completion of their degrees, work in professional careers, usually in state and federal agencies. An orientation course to the fisheries major, for instance, requires resumes and personal-interest statements. Problem-solving assignments for Natural Resource Management are common, particularly in understanding and resolving conflicts among users of public lands. On the other hand, the College of Engineering features very few writing assignments. Writing instruction was found to be relegated primarily to a specific course in technical writing taught within the college by a member of the English department. The capstone project for engineers, however, is a senior design project completed by teams, which typically requires a one-page letter of intent, a thirty-page proposal, and a formal report.

Each of the student's reports was destined to become part of a much larger report to be delivered to the institution's general education committee and also shared more widely with departments and colleges. The following organization for the final report included these sections: problem statement, review of literature, definition of the methodology, results, discussion, implications and recommendations.

MAKING RECOMMENDATIONS

Once all the reports on departmental writing assignments were compiled and edited into one document, the students drew on their theoretical knowledge and practical experience of writing across the curriculum to develop a set of recommendations. The students suggested particular writing assignments that should be featured in the *Writing & Speaking @ USU*, a monthly newsletter sent to the more than eight hundred faculty members on campus. The students recommended workshops for faculty interested in exploring, integrating, or improving writing assignments, drawing on expertise within the English faculty but also including faculty whose assignments had been found exemplary. The student research-ers found when interviewing faculty members that they were particularly concerned about "paper-load" issues and suggested that at least one workshop offer suggestions on evaluating writing.

The research team also believed that courses with intensive writing in the major should be designated as such (e.g., *WI* for *writing inten-sive*). Such a designation reflects well on a student's transcript, and it also honors the faculty member who invested the extra time and energy to integrate writing into the course. They knew from their reading in the scholarly literature that this designation is common in institutions that promote writing across the curriculum.

The final report characterized writing in the institution and used tables and graphs to illustrate. Although the students wanted to com-pare the university's commitment to writing with other land-grant or research universities, that information was not accessible. The research question—what is the nature of writing assignments at this institution?—was not one developed by the students, but from that point on, they engaged in the research process and decision making. As writing tutors, they immediately understood why this question was important to the institution, and they felt the methodology could be transferable to other institutions to undertake similar assessments. Their theoretical overview helped them situate the research question in relevant theory and justi-fied an empirically grounded inquiry.

The students decided what methodology to use for data collection and analysis. As they collected information, they also noted confound-ing factors. For instance, although courses such as internships and independent studies were not included, the students had not taken into account the large number of courses in which writing would be imprac-tical. Introductory courses in foreign languages offer limited writing opportunities, if worksheets can be thus termed. In theatre arts, thirty-two of its forty-three classes focus on technical aspects of production such as makeup, stage lighting, and design. Likewise, in music, thirty-two of the sixty-two classes are devoted to performance, rehearsal, and skills. Thus, when we tallied the total number of classes ($n = 725$) with syllabi analyzed and found that 41 percent of them included writing tasks of some sort or another, it was not a true picture of the amount of writing at the institution. Eliminating classes in which writing was not practical would have created a much higher percentage. In formulat-ing results and conclusions, the students learned there may be outliers or anomalous data that can distort the picture, and these should be discussed in the research report. A final aspect of the data collection they felt should have been noted was the difference between general education courses taught by departmental faculty and courses designed for majors and minors.

Conducting research responsibly requires clearly defined processes. One of the issues that appeared in first drafts of the reports was that the researchers sometimes felt it necessary to be cheerleaders for a department. Students practiced writing objective descriptive statements that are not necessarily positive or negative. The students who developed the data-driven report "The Nature of Writing Assignments at Utah State University" made an impact on curriculum and innovation,[4] and they acquired methodological skills for developing their own inquiry-based projects.

LESSONS LEARNED

For large-scale assessment projects, there are guidelines to keep in mind.

- Objectivity must be maintained: A good piece of advice is "avoid validating your own opinion or hope"; the goal of research is not necessarily to prove something works.
- The scope of the question must be narrowed to a workable study; can something useful or new be learned within the timeframe allocated?
- Terms should be operationalized to be concrete and specific to the extent possible.
- Whether the question is of real interest to the profession must be addressed.
- Questions about what has been done on this topic before, what the researchers have learned from a review of literature, and the foundation for the study must be answered.
- Researchers must ask themselves whether the research question interests them sufficiently that they will invest in the long haul.
- Generalizing from the research sample to the world is a pitfall and must be avoided.
- Problems should be identified; forthrightness is appreciated.
- The interpretation of the data must be credible.

These guidelines can lead to defining a research project by the problem or question, to zeroing in on a site, to picking subjects and method, and to defining the scope of the project by time and size. The results of the project described above included a descriptive report, which was of value to the institution at a time it was making sweeping changes in curriculum and the academic calendar. As Gerald Graff (2008) notes, "Once we start asking whether our students are learning what we want them to learn, we realize pretty quickly that making this happen is necessarily a team effort, requiring us to think about our teaching not in isolation but in relation to that of our colleagues." Thus, the research report was of value not only to the institution but also to the students who engaged in the data collection and analysis.

Reports such as the one generated by the writing fellows on an institution's commitment to writing need not be one-time studies; in fact, it makes sense to replicate such a detailed study on a regular schedule. In this instance, the outcome of the report resulted in a revamped general education program that featured upper-division writing-intensive (WI) courses. To achieve that designation, syllabi were submitted to a writing subcommittee of the general education committee. A few years after the inclusion of WI courses, the project was replicated, focusing on these specific courses and asking the question, do they meet the original criteria for approval? The results were that only 55 percent did so, which led to communication with the teacher of a course to (1) enhance the teaching of writing in the course or (2) to have the WI designation removed. This process is part of a regularly scheduled feedback loop to ensure that principles for general education are followed. The same research process could be used to investigate any aspect of the curriculum: quantitative skills, research skills, honors instruction.

Writing program research can address any one of a number of topics: training composition staff, testing and evaluating students and programs, collaborating with other institutions, outreach to secondary schools, electronic portfolios, admission standards. Likewise, a range of methods can be employed: historical study, textual analysis, case study, ethnography, teacher or tutor research. Writing programs offer some of the most vibrant spaces on a campus for learning and can be exciting sites for practitioner inquiry.

In the two chapters that follow, writing studies is explained in more detail and conducting research ethically is addressed. Both of these chapters further illuminate the research process. By the end of part 1, you should have a good idea about a viable research question, an appropriate method by which to address it, and the tools that can be used to uncover information.

NOTES

1. Richard Braddock, a noteworthy researcher in writing whose work includes such articles as "The Frequency and Placement of Topic Sentences in Expository Prose" (Braddock 1974), is the namesake of the Braddock Award, given to the outstanding essay of the year in *College Composition and Communication*. It was first awarded in 1975, and the corpus of winning essays provides excellent background in writing studies.

2. The writing-fellows program (formerly called *Rhetoric Associates*) is described in Kinkead 1997.

3.   The following students conducted the research study "The Nature of Writing Assignments at Utah State University": Chad Adams, Keri Anderson, Sunni Brown, Cody Clark, Marchet Clark, Natalie Hadfield, Angela Hill, Brooke Jones, Aimee Kawakami, Jared Madsen, Leah Madsen, Betsy O. Moore, Julia Moris, Denise Natoli, Jeffrey Nilson, Debbie Raymond, Jessica Staheli, Bryan Tilt, and Craig Wise. Teri Brown assisted in the final compilation of the report.

4.   The General Education Reform Task Force recommended that courses that include intensive writing and speaking assignments be designated as *communications intensive* (*CI*). The committee preferred to integrate both writing and speaking into these courses.

RESOURCES: BOOKS ABOUT RESEARCH METHODS

Babcock, Rebecca Day, and Terese Thonus. 2012. *Researching the Writing Center: Toward an Evidence-Based Practice.* New York: Peter Lang. http://dx.doi.org /10.3726/978-1-4539-0869-3.

Bazerman, Charles, and Paul Prior. 2004. *What Writing Does and How It Does It: An Introduction to Analyzing Texts and Textual Practices.* Mahwah, NJ: Erlbaum.

Bishop, Wendy. 1999. *Ethnographic Writing Research: Writing It Down, Writing It Up, and Reading It.* Portsmouth, NH: Heinemann.

Blakeslee, Ann, and Cathy Fleisher. 2007. *Becoming a Writing Researcher.* Mahwah, NJ: Erlbaum.

Connors, Robert J., and Andrea A. Lunsford. 1988. "Frequency of Formal Errors in Current College Writing, or Ma and Pa Kettle Do Research." *College Composition and Communication* 39 (4): 395–409. http://dx.doi.org/10.2307 /357695.

Cresswell, John W. 2013. *Research Design: Qualitative, Quantitative, and Mixed Methods Approaches.* 4th ed. Thousand Oaks, CA: SAGE.

DeVoss, Danielle, and Heidi A. McKee. 2007. *Digital Writing Research: Technologies, Methodologies, and Ethical Issues.* Cresskill, NJ: Hampton.

Fitzgerald, Lauren, and Melissa Ianetta. 2015. *The Oxford Guide for Writing Tutors: Practice and Research.* New York: Oxford University Press.

Grobman, Laurie, and Joyce Kinkead. 2010. *Undergraduate Research in English Studies.* Urbana, IL: NCTE.

Hughes, Michael A., and George F. Hayhoe. 2007. *A Research Primer for Technical Communication: Methods, Exemplars, and Analyses.* 2nd ed. New York: Routledge.

Kirsch, Gesa E., and Liz Rohan, eds. 2008. *Beyond the Archives: Research as a Lived Process.* Carbondale: Southern Illinois University Press.

Kirsch, Gesa E., and Patricia A. Sullivan, eds. 1992. *Methods and Methodology in Composition Research.* Carbondale: Southern Illinois University Press.

Lancy, David F. 1993. *Qualitative Research in Education: An Introduction to the Major Traditions.* New York: Longman.

Lauer, Janice, and J. William Asher, eds. 1988. *Composition Research: Empirical Designs.* New York: Oxford University Press.

MacArthur, Charles A., Steve Graham, and Jill Fitzgerald, eds. 2008. *Handbook of Writing Research.* New York: Guilford.

McKee, Heidi A., and James E. Porter. 2009. *The Ethics of Internet Research: A Rhetorical, Case-Based Process.* New York: Lang.

Nickoson, Lee, and Mary P. Sheridan. 2012. *Writing Studies Research in Practice: Methods and Methodologies.* Carbondale: Southern Illinois University Press.

Ramsey, Alexis, Wendy Sharer, Barbara L'Eplattenier, and Lisa Mastrangelo, eds. 2010. *Working in the Archives: Practical Research Methods for Rhetoric and Composition.* Carbondale: Southern Illinois University Press.

Schell, Eileen, and K.J. Rowson, eds. 2010. *Rhetorica in Motion: Feminist Rhetorical Methods and Methodologies.* Pittsburgh: University of Pittsburgh Press.

Shaughnessy, Mina. 1979. *Errors and Expectations: A Guide for the Teacher of Basic Writing.* New York: Oxford University Press.

Smagorinsky, Peter, ed. 2006. *Research on Composition: Multiple Perspectives on Two Decades of Change.* New York: Teachers College Press.

REFERENCES

American Psychological Association (APA). 2001. *Publication Manual of the American Psychological Association.* 5th ed. Washington, DC: American Psychological Association.

Atwell, Nancie. 1987. "Everyone Sits at a Big Desk: Discovering Topics for Writing." In *Reclaiming the Classroom: Teacher Research as an Agency for Change,* edited by Dixie Goswami and Peter R. Stillman, 178–87. Portsmouth, NH: Heinemann.

Bartholomae, David. 1980. "The Study of Error." *College Composition and Communication* 31 (3): 253–69. http://dx.doi.org/10.2307/356486.

Bazerman, Charles. 2002. "The Case for Writing Studies as a Major Discipline." In *The Intellectual Work of Composition,* edited by Gary Olson, 32–38. Carbondale: Southern Illinois University Press.

Bazerman, Charles. 2007. *The Handbook of Research on Writing: History, Society, School, Individual, Text.* Mahwah, NJ: Erlbaum.

Block, Rebecca R. 2010. "Reading Aloud in the Writing Center: A Comparative Analysis of Three Tutoring Methods." PhD diss., University of Louisville.

Braddock, Richard. 1974. "The Frequency and Placement of Topic Sentences in Expository Prose." *Researching in the Teaching of English* 8 (3): 287–302.

Bridgeman, Brent, and Sybil B. Carlson. 1984. "Survey of Academic Writing Tasks." *Written Communication* 1 (2): 247–80. http://dx.doi.org/10.1177/0741088384001002004.

Bruner, Jerome. 1986a. *Actual Minds, Possible Worlds.* Cambridge, MA: Harvard University Press.

Bruner, Jerome. 1986b. "Life as Narrative." *Language Arts* 65 (6): 574–83.

Bruner, Jerome. 1990. *Acts of Meaning.* Cambridge, MA: Harvard University Press.

Bullough, Robert V. Jr. 1989. *First-Year Teacher: A Case Study.* New York: Teachers College Press.

Calicchia, Sara. 2014. "To 'Play That Funky Music' or Not: How Music Affects the Environmental Self-Regulation of High-Ability Academic Writers." National Conference on Undergraduate Research, Lexington, KY.

Capote, Truman. 1965. *In Cold Blood.* New York: Random House.

CCCC Committee on Undergraduate Research. 2014. Report on Survey to CCCC Members on Undergraduate Research. Urbana, IL: NCTE.

Code of Federal Regulations. 2009. 45 CFR § 46. Revised January 15, 2009. Effective July 14, 2009. http://www.hhs.gov/ohrp/regulations-and-policy/regulations/45-cfr-46/index.html.

Corroy, Jennifer. 2003. "Institutional Change and the University of Wisconsin–Madison Writing Fellows Program." *Young Scholars in Writing* 1:25–44.

Crisp, Sally Chandler. 1995. "Women Scholar-Leaders." PhD diss., University of Arkansas.

Daly, John A., and Michael D. Miller. 1975. "The Empirical Development of an Instrument to Measure Writing Apprehension." *Research in the Teaching of English* 12: 242–49. Adapted by Michael W. Smith in *Reducing Writing Apprehension* (Urbana: NCTE, 1984).

Doyle, Sir Arthur Conan. 1895. A Scandal in Bohemia. New York: G. Munro's Sons.

Dryer, Dylan B. 2012. "At a Mirror, Darkly: The Imagined Undergraduate Writers of Ten Novice Composition Instructors." *College Composition and Communication* 63 (3):420–52.

Elbow, Peter. 1986. *Embracing Contraries: Explorations in Learning and Teaching.* New York: Oxford University Press.

Fielding, Henery. 1725. *The True and Genuine Account of the Life and Actions of the Late Jonathan Wild.* London: John Applebee.

Flower, Linda, and John R. Hayes. 1981. "A Cognitive Process Theory of Writing." *College Composition and Communication* 32 (4): 365–87. http://dx.doi.org/10.2307/356600.

Flower, Linda, John R. Hayes, Linda Carey, Karen Schriver, and James Stratman. 1986. "Detection, Diagnosis, and the Strategies of Revision." *College Composition and Communication* 37 (1): 16–55. http://dx.doi.org/10.2307/357381.

Geertz, Clifford. 1973. "Thick Description: Toward an Interpretive Theory of Culture." In *The Interpretation of Cultures: Selected Essays*, 3–30. New York: Basic Books.

Glenn, Cheryl. 1994. "Sex, Lies, and Manuscript: Refiguring Aspasia in the History of Rhetoric." *College Composition and Communication* 45 (2): 180–99. http://dx.doi.org/10.2307/359005.

Goffman, Alice. 2014. *On the Run: Fugitive Life in an American City.* Chicago: University of Chicago Press. http://dx.doi.org/10.7208/chicago/9780226136851.001.0001.

Graff, Gerald. 2008. "Assessment Changes Everything." *Inside Higher Ed*, February 21. Accessed May 30, 2008. https://www.insidehighered.com/views/2008/02/21/assessment-changes-everything.

Grobman, Laurie. 2009. "Speaking with One Another": Writing African American History in Berks County, Pennsylvania." *Reflections: Writing, Service-Learning, and Community Literacy* 9 (1): 129–61.

Grobman, Laurie. 2013. "'I'm on a Stage': Rhetorical History, Performance, and the Development of the Central Pennsylvania African American Museum." *College Composition and Communication* 65 (2): 299–323.

Guerin, Wilford L. 1966. *A Handbook of Critical Approaches to Literature.* 1st ed. New York: Harper and Row.

Hadfield, Leslie, Joyce Kinkead, Tom C. Peterson, Stephanie H. Ray, and

Sarah S. Preston. 2003. "An Ideal Writing Center: Re-Imagining Space and Design." In *The Center Will Hold*, edited by Michael A. Pemberton and Joyce Kinkead, 166–76. Logan: Utah State University Press.

Harris, Muriel. 2010. "Assignments from Hell: The View from the Writing Center." *What Is College-Level Writing?* Vol. 2: *Assignments, Readings, and Student Writing Samples*, edited by Patrick Sullivan, Howard Tinberg, and Sheridan Blau, 183–206. Urbana, IL: NCTE.

Hirschi, Charlene A. 1996. "The Re-Entry Student: On Both Sides of the Table." *Writing Lab Newsletter* 21 (2): 9–10.

Hogg, Charlotte. 2006. *From the Garden Club: Rural Women Writing Community*. Lincoln: University of Nebraska Press.

Janangelo, Joseph. 2010-2011. "Anatomy of an Article." *Kairos* 16 (1).

Journet, Debra. 2012. "Narrative Turns in Writing Studies Research." In *Writing Studies Research in Practice: Methods and Methodologies*, edited by Lee Nickoson and Mary P. Sheridan, 13–24. Carbondale: Southern Illinois University Press.

Kator, Corinne. 2000. "Trends in Web Site Design." Honors thesis, Utah State University.

Kinkead, Joyce. 1997. "Documenting Excellence in Teaching and Learning in Writing-Across-the-Curriculum Programs." In *Assessing Writing Across the Curriculum*, edited by Kathleen Blake Yancey and Brian Huot, 37–50. New York: Ablex.

Kuh, George D. 2008. *High-Impact Educational Practices: What They Are, Who Has Access to Them, and Why They Matter*. Washington, DC: American Association of Colleges and Universities.

Kulick, Don, and Christopher Stroud. 1993. "Conceptions and Uses of Literacy in a Papua New Guinean Village." In *Cross-Cultural Approaches to Literacy*, edited by Brian Street, 30–61. Cambridge: Cambridge University Press.

Kumar, Ranjit. 2014. *Research Methodology: A Step-by-Step Guide for Beginners*. 4th ed. London: SAGE.

Langer, Judith A., and Arthur N. Applebee. 2007. "How Writing Shapes Thinking: A Study of Teaching and Learning." WAC Clearinghouse Landmark Publications in Writing Studies. http://wac.colostate.edu/books/langer _applebee/. (Originally published in print, 1987, by National Council of Teachers of English, Urbana, Illinois.)

Lauer, Janice M., and J. William Asher. 1988. *Composition Research: Empirical Designs*. New York: Oxford University Press.

Laursen, Sandra, Anne-Barrie Hunter, Elaine Seymour, Heather Thiry, and Ginger Melton. 2010. *Undergraduate Research in the Sciences: Engaging Students in Real Science*. San Francisco: Jossey-Bass.

Leahy, Richard. 1996. "Designing Assignments." *Word Works* 80 (April). Accessed May 30, 2008. http://www.boisestate.edu/wcenter/ww80.htm.

Lillywhite, Kristin M. 2011. "Developing Cognitive Academic Language Proficiency (CALP) in Diverse Classrooms." Honors thesis, Utah State University.

Lindemann, Erika. 1989. "Writing to Learn." For Your Consideration series. The University of North Carolina at Chapel Hill's Center for Teaching and Learning website. Accessed May 1, 2004. http://ctl.unc.edu/fyc4.htm.

Lindemann, Erika. 1995. *A Rhetoric for Writing Teachers*. New York: Oxford

University Press.

Lopatto, David. 2009. *Science in Solution: The Impact of Undergraduate Research on Student Learning.* Tucson: The Research Corporation.

Lunsford, Andrea A., ed. 1995. *Reclaiming Rhetorica: Women in the Rhetorical Tradition.* Pittsburgh, PA: University of Pittsburgh Press.

Moffett, James. 1987. *Teaching the University of Discourse.* Portsmouth, NH: Heinemann.

Moxley, Joseph M. 2013. "Big Data, Learning Analytics, and Social Assessment Methods." *Journal of Writing Assessment* 6 (1). http://www.journalofwritingassessment.org/article.php?article=68.

Ray, Lucinda C. 1987. "Reflections on Classroom Research." In *Reclaiming the Classroom: Teacher Research as an Agency for Change*, edited by Dixie Goswami and Peter R. Stillman, 219–41. Portsmouth, NH: Heinemann.

Roen, Duane, and Nicholas Karolides. 2005. "Louise Rosenblatt: A Life in Literacy." *The ALAN Review* 32 (3): 59–61.

Rosenblatt, Louise. (1938) 1995. *Literature as Exploration.* New York: MLA.

Russell, David R. 1990. "Writing across the Curriculum in Historical Perspective: Toward a Social Interpretation." *College English* 52 (1): 52–73. http://dx.doi.org/10.2307/377412.

Russell, David R. 2002. *Writing in the Academic Disciplines: A Curricular History.* 2nd ed. Carbondale: Southern Illinois University Press.

Sunstein, Bonnie Stone, and Elizabeth Chiseri-Strater. 2011. *FieldWorking: Reading and Writing Research.* 4th ed. Boston: Bedford/St. Martin's.

Utah State University. 1998a. General Education Citizen Scholar Philosophy Statement. Logan, UT. http://www.usu.edu/provost/academic_programs/geduc_univstud/.

Utah State University 1998b. Institutional Review Board. http://rgs.usu.edu/irb/.

Walter, Glen. 1981. *So Where's My Apple? Diary of a First-Year Teacher.* Long Grove, IL: Waveland Press.

Walton, Rebecca. 2013. "How Trust and Credibility Affect Technology-Based Development Projects." *Technical Communication Quarterly* 22 (1): 85–102. http://dx.doi.org/10.1080/10572252.2013.726484.

Walton, Rebecca, Margaret Zraly, and J. P. Mugengana. 2015. "Values and Validity: Navigating Messiness in a Community-Based Research Project in Rwanda." *Technical Communication Quarterly* 24(1): 45–69.

Walvoord, Barbara E., Linda Lawrence Hunt, H. Fil Dowling Jr., and Joan D. McMahon. 1997. *In the Long Run: A Study of Faculty in Three Writing-Across-the-Curriculum Programs.* Urbana, IL: National Council of Teachers of English.

Walvoord, Barbara E., and Lucille P. McCarthy. 1990. *Thinking and Writing in College: A Naturalistic Study in Four Disciplines.* Urbana, IL: National Council of Teachers of English.

Warnock, John. 2000. "James Moffett." In *Twentieth Century Rhetoric and Rhetoricians*, edited by Michelle Ballif and Michael G. Moran, 258–65. Westport, CT: Greenwood.

White-Farnham, Jamie. 2014. "'Revising the Menu to Fit the Budget': Grocery Lists and Other Rhetorical Heirlooms." *College English* 76 (3): 208–26.

Wolcott, Harry. 2003. *The Man in the Principal's Office.* Lanham, MD: Altamira.

2

Writing Studies

WHAT IS WRITING STUDIES?

The study of writing is a big tent. To rephrase Walt Whitman, writing studies is large; it contains multitudes. Because writing is ubiquitous in our lives, from birth to death—literally, with certificates of birth, diplomas, degrees, marriage licenses, and wills—we tend to take it for granted. We should not. Because writing is such a large area, it also means research topics in writing are equally expansive. In the next few pages, we'll look at just how encompassing writing as topic can be.

School Writing

Writing about writing. Now there's an interesting thought. For some time, college and university writing courses turned to thematic readers for content, asking students to focus on the environment, death, monsters, food—almost any topic. More recently, the subject of writing courses is writing itself: the process of writing, how texts are constructed and how they affect readers, what counts as writing. How and what writing is taught in higher education, though, is just the tip of the iceberg in terms of writing subjects.

School writing is one very important part of writing studies, as learning to write and writing to learn are essential parts of what makes people literate. Academic writing can be investigated by looking at how writing is taught in higher education but also in primary and secondary schools. How do individuals learn to write? What happens when literacy studies are delayed? How do adults learn to write? Is it easier or more difficult to learn to write in a second language? How do communication disorders affect a person's ability to write?

What are the methods used to teach writing? Have these remained consistent or changed over the ages? If they have changed, what are the reasons for the changes? Can the instruction of writing be charted over the centuries? How has writing been used as punishment or as therapy?

In ancient Rome, composition exercises included these tasks in ascending order of difficulty:

1. Retelling a fable
2. Retelling an episode from a poet or a historian
3. Amplification of a moral theme
4. Amplification of a proverb
5. Refutation or confirmation of an allegation
6. Confirmation of a thing admitted
7. Eulogy of a person or thing
8. Comparison of things or persons
9. Impersonation—in the character of the given person
10. Description, or vivid presentation of details
11. Thesis, or argument for/against an answer to a general question
12. Laws, or arguments for or against a law. (Murphy 2012, 74)

School continued to have set exercises for teaching writing for centuries. The three primary areas of study in antiquity were grammar, rhetoric, and logic. These were known as the *trivium*. Later, as knowledge developed, they were joined by arithmetic, geometry, astronomy, and music, called the *quadrivium*. Together, these seven areas formed the *liberal arts*—known as liberal because these are the areas a free person must know in order to function well as a citizen.

Likewise, a history of schools and writing is a meaty topic. And some writing teachers have achieved fame over the ages. How is writing evaluated, and who assesses it? Are there ways of handling the paper load that teachers face who subscribe to the notion that fluency in writing is achieved through frequent practice?

A History of Writing

The subject of writing is more expansive than just school writing. Consider the role of writing and law and how important it was to put laws into writing as Hammurabi did in eighteenth-century BCE. These nearly three hundred laws codified behaviors ranging from work to family relationships and laid the basis for future rules, such as the Napoleonic Code (1804), that outlined civil law.

Writing also played and continues to play a major role in religions. Writing and copying sacred texts was the province of religious houses and resulted in such products as stunningly beautiful illuminated books. The printing press helped to make reading, and thus writing, more democratic when in the fifteenth century Gutenberg perfected movable type. Notably, the Bible was the most important book to be produced during the Middle Ages. Of course, this is a Western viewpoint. Advances in writing and printing were being made in other cultures too. In contemporary times the printing press has gained some prominence in the artistic production of books. Some people eschew the digital production of text in preference for a book that looks and feels like a "real" book.

The history of typography and technologies used in writing extends from the printing press to digital representations. Book design and even the concept of authorship are part of research on writing. The earliest tools for writing were embedded in people's desire to express themselves, not just make tally marks for trade and business. The origins of writing is a fascinating research area exploring how peoples developed systems of writing in order to communicate. Generally, the first successful peoples to code language are considered to be the Sumerians and Mayans, both establishing alphabets around 3400 BCE. Cuneiform and glyphs serve as these representations. Cuneiform was produced by using a stylus in wet clay. Imagine that pencils were not widely available until the early part of the twentieth century, with ink pens coming decades later and manual typewriters being viable in the 1920s. It was the invention of the personal computer that eventually transformed writing.

Egyptian scribes developed hieroglyphics to help an empire keep track of its people and lands. And the Egyptians are credited with developing a type of paper using papyrus. I am particularly fond of one Egyptian goddess: Seshat, "She who is foremost in the house of books" (see Figure 2.1). Not surprising for a professor of English. She is depicted with a stylized papyrus above her head, signifying the importance of paper, along with a stylus. A house of books—the library—in an Egyptian temple is a notably small room, like the one at the temple of Edfu, where papyrus scrolls and clay tablets could be kept.

Early writing materials included clay tablets but also wax tablets, papyrus, vellum, and, thankfully, paper, which was developed in China. Even so, in the nineteenth century schoolchildren might have practiced their "pothook" *s*'s on slates or, on the frontier, using cedar bark. I found when researching teacher diaries from the frontier that students used whatever was at hand.

Alphabets take various forms; English-language speakers rely on a version that harkens back to Greco-Roman origins. Although it would seem that alphabets have long been enshrined, it is possible for new alphabets to be created, as Sequoyah did in the early 1800s for the Cherokee

FIGURE 2.1. Seshat, Egyptian Goddess of writing.

language, and as Brigham Young did later in that same century with the Deseret Alphabet, trying to create a more sensible system for converts to learn English.

Secular and Spiritual Writing

Religion and state have not always been separate and continue to be joined in some countries. *Secular* writing refers to writing that is not theological in content but is about worldly topics. Governments rely heavily on writing. And journalists report on news through discourse—spoken and written. In the arts, writing is present on stage, in exhibition catalogs, and in performance. Imagine how writing plays a part in almost any profession.

In both secular and spiritual writing, women have been practitioners although invisible much of the time. Volumes such as *Reclaiming Rhetorica* have brought to the fore important writers such as Aspasia and Hortensia from antiquity and Christine de Pizan and Margery Kemp from the Middle Ages. Women's rights have been the subject of Mary Wollstonecraft, Sojourner Truth, and Susan B. Anthony, among others. Thus, another theme in writing studies can be the role of gender. But women do not have the market cornered on civil rights. It takes only a reading of "Letter from Birmingham Jail" by Martin Luther King Jr. to understand the power of writing to make a case and effect change.

Finally, although not the end of the possible angles from which to view writing, text can be analyzed for its linguistic and grammatical aspects. Words, sentences, paragraphs, essays—these can be areas for exploration. Genres, forms, or types of writing provide rich areas for investigation. And, returning to Aristotle's classic definitions of rhetoric, writing can be analyzed for its purposes, such as persuasion or argument, and its various audiences.

This laundry list of topics within writing studies only begins to scratch the surface of possibilities for investigation. They are necessarily telegraphic. Entire volumes have been written on any one of these subjects (see Bazerman 2002, 2007; Lunsford 1995; Murphy 2012 for examples). Charles Bazerman notes, "In short, the study of writing is a major subset of the history of human consciousness, institutions, practice, and development over the last five millennia" (Bazerman 2002, 36). A tall order to be sure, but one that is vast in its possibilities and opportunities. Similarly, Douglas Downs and Elizabeth Wardle have suggested that writing should be studied as a subject in first-year writing courses (Downs and Wardle 2007).

In sum, topics in writing studies that may be explored—although some will require years of study—include the following:

- history of writing, its tools, and technologies
- writing in society, particularly in and as power

- school and academic writing
- writing and the writer
- writing as text
- writing and professions
- writing, gender, ethnicity, class, and culture

LANDMARK WRITING RESEARCH

Zeroing in on just one period of research on writing when so many valuable studies exist is difficult but not impossible. Research done in the 1960s through the 1980s brought about a paradigm shift in the teaching of writing at all school levels, including higher education. This dramatic shift focused on *process writing*. *Invention*, or *prewriting*, moved to the forefront of process writing, followed by drafting, peer reviewing, revising, and publishing. In this section we will review some of the landmark studies that brought about this change from writing as product to writing as process.

Janet Emig's (1971) case study of high school writers, *The Composing Processes of Twelfth Graders*, helped pioneer the *writing process movement*, which focuses much more on how a student writes as opposed to looking only at the end product. Emig's study launched composition research. By focusing on a few students in depth, Emig offered insight into how they actually composed. The case-study method, paired with composing-aloud protocols, revealed that the writing process was really multiple processes and subprocesses. She also noted teaching approaches that did not square with the writing processes students employed. This single volume mobilized the profession to change the way writing was taught, not only at the high-school level but also in college classes.

Emig began a trend of looking at writers cognitively. Sondra Perl, drawing on Emig's approach, studied basic writers and wrote about her findings in the essay "The Composing Processes of Unskilled College Writers." Perl's dissertation focused on five "basic writers" in college, and the essay focused on one. She used the students' written texts, their composing-aloud protocols, and answers to interview questions. Perl was an innovator in finding a way to describe what happens when a student writes; she developed a sophisticated coding system that replaced more cumbersome narrative styles. For instance, over multiple sessions, "Tony," the student profiled in the essay, made 234 changes in revising his work; however, only 24 of those were significant revisions. The other 210 revisions included surface-level changes such as correcting spelling (n = 95). Even so, misspelled words remained.

Emig's students ranged in ability level, but Perl was tapping into the consternation and concern created as more underprepared students entered college. Faculty members wanted these students to succeed.

TABLE 2.1. Perl's system of coding for revising

1. Elaborations of ideas through the use of specification and detail;

2. Additions of modals that shift the mood of a sentence;

3. Deletions that narrow the focus of a paper;

4. Clause reductions or embeddings that tighten the structure of a paper;

5. Vocabulary choices that reflect a sensitivity to language;

6. Reordering of elements in a narrative;

7. Strengthening transitions between paragraphs;

8. Pronoun changes that signal an increased sensitivity to audience.

The 210 changes in form included the following:

Additions	19	Verb Changes	4
Deletions	44	Spelling	95
Word choice	13	Punctuation	35
Unresolved problems	89		

Source: Perl (1979)

What were the students thinking as they composed? Where might they be getting off track, and how could teachers learn more so they could help them succeed? The implications of Perl's research led teachers to focus much more on prewriting activities to help students construct content before beginning to write. They also worked with students to help them avoid error hunting and focus on more useful revision strategies.

Mina Shaughnessy's (1979) landmark study *Errors and Expectations* showed that basic writers, thought to make multiple errors, essentially produced patterns of errors, which was a more manageable problem. To arrive at this result, Shaughnessy analyzed four thousand placement exams. Not only did she help modify the way basic writers are taught, her legacy as a caring teacher and thoughtful researcher is memorialized in a prize awarded by the Modern Language Association (MLA) in her name.

Linda Flower and John Hayes from Carnegie Mellon University continued to tease out how writers think in their study "A Cognitive Process Theory of Writing" (Flower and Hayes 1981). What guides the decisions writers make? They used protocol analysis, too, but over a five-year period. For Flower and Hayes the composing process was much more complex than previously envisioned. They found that processes looped back upon one another in a *recursive* way. "This process of setting and developing sub-goals and—at times—regenerating those past goals is a powerful creative process. . . . By placing emphasis on the inventive power of the writer, who is able to explore ideas, to develop, act on, test, and regenerate his or her own goals, we are putting an important part

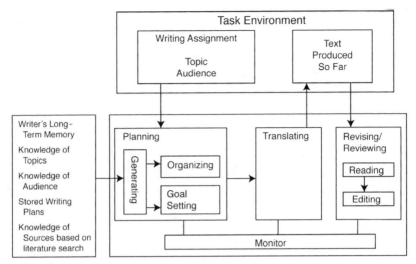

FIGURE 2.2. Flower and Hayes's diagram of the cognitive processes in composing.

of creativity where it belongs—in the hands of the working, thinking writer" (366).

Thus, the implications for teachers are that students do not begin at one point in the writing process and proceed to a logical end; instead, revision and reenvisioning can happen efficaciously at several points. To map what they observed in writers, Flower and Hayes created the following diagram.

These are just a few researchers in writing who have had a significant influence on the way writing is taught. Donald Graves (1994), Lucy Calkins (1986), and Nancie Atwell (1987) had similar influences on teaching writing in the primary grades. The excitement of this period of teaching and investigating effective practices is embodied in the development of the National Writing Project, which arose from the Bay Area Writing Project, started in 1974. Summer workshops for teachers, using a teachers-teaching-teachers model, energized and provided faculty development. It's important to note that teachers of writing, kindergarten through college, came together to share best practices. In addition, the National Writing Project (NWP) and its research partners conduct research. "How Teens Do Research in the Digital World" (Purcell et al. 2012) is just one example.

Student Activity

READING RESEARCH

Choose a landmark study or a research article that won CCCC's Braddock Award, given for outstanding scholarship in composition. (For a list of essays, see this site: http://www.ncte.org/cccc/awards/braddock.)

The goal of this assignment is to read research critically, to interrogate the procedures, methods, and findings that were used. Prepare a written reaction in the following format:

- bibliographic information, including title, author, date of publication, journal. (Chicago Style preferred)
- two to three sentences that summarize the research study, particularly noting the "gap" in the scholarly base that was to be addressed or filled
- review of literature (What sources did the researcher use that informed the study?
- methods used in the research
- results and discussion (What was found?)
- implications for practice, policy, or future study
- critique of the study (What might the researcher have done differently? Were there limitations?)
- added information on the author(s) of importance, particularly about credibility and life history

COMPOSITION STUDIES AND WRITING STUDIES

We are using the term *writing studies* as the more inclusive term throughout this book. The term *composition studies* is derived from required lower-division writing courses and programs on college campuses and has been used in the profession consistently. Since 1885, beginning at Harvard, composition courses have been the one universal requirement at any campus. Some people in the profession use *composition studies* and *writing studies* interchangeably. And there is some disagreement about the origins of each term. For our purposes we will use *writing studies*, but it's helpful to review the source of the term *composition studies*, which arises from the required composition courses omnipresent on campuses.

No doubt, you are familiar with the required lower-division writing courses on your own campus, as a student or as a graduate teaching assistant. Writing programs, though, may structure their curriculum in various ways. At some institutions required writing is completed in year one. This requirement may involve one, two, or even three courses, depending on the calendaring system of the institution: quarters versus semesters. A year-one approach may be considered as getting it "out of the way," as some students speak of their general education requirement.

Writing is a developmental process. As Erika Lindemann (2001) pointed out, "Writing is a skill that develops slowly over time but atrophies quickly." Writing programs constructed with this philosophy in mind may include a required first-year course as well as a second-year course. The former is generally in expressive and academic writing while the second in the series focuses on the researched paper.

The Council of Writing Program Administration (CWPA) is a professional organization for those who direct writing programs. CWPA has several position statements about writing, including one about expected outcomes for first-year composition. This outcomes statement offers research-based advice on what students should know at the conclusion of required writing courses, including rhetorical knowledge; critical thinking, reading, and composing; processes; and knowledge of conventions, the formal rules writers use.

Let's continue to explore a vertical approach to writing on a college campus. Advanced composition, typically taught as an upper-division course, may focus on writing in the subject area (e.g., medical writing, technical writing in engineering, writing as a social scientist), or it may continue to develop the essay in increasingly complex and sophisticated ways. Yet another approach is for a campus to institute writing-intensive (WI) or communications-intensive (CI) courses in which curricula in the majors ensure that writing is taught within the discourse conventions of the discipline. Does the field use present tense or past tense in its reports or essays? Is voice active or passive? What is the style sheet for crediting sources?

Capstone experiences in the baccalaureate may include a culminating portfolio, honors thesis, research grant, conference proposal, design project, or exhibition. The goal is for the student writer to move from general academic writing to career-driven tasks.

How might writing programs be graphically depicted? Here is a summary of how composition might be found throughout a curriculum, not just in a lone first-year course.

Obviously, a campus is a fertile field for investigating writing, and much is still to be learned about writing and the teaching of writing. Kathleen Blake Yancey (2009) has posited, "Seen historically, this 21st century writing marks the beginning of a new era in literacy, a period we might call the Age of Composition, a period where composers become composers not through direct and formal instruction alone (if at all),

TABLE 2.2

First Year	Sophomore Year	Junior Year	Senior Year
1–3 courses (FY comp; research; writing about literature)	1 course, if any, generally focusing on research	Advanced composition (English); subject-specific writing; "rising-junior" assessment	Capstone, portfolio, honors thesis
Writing across the curriculum (WAC)	Writing across the curriculum (WAC)	Writing in the disciplines (WID)	Writing in the disciplines (WID)

but rather through what we might call an extracurricular social co-apprenticeship" (5). We see new models of composing all around us. David Russell (1995) suggests that writing can and should be an object of study. This emphasis on the study of writing offers you the opportunity to add your voice to the work being done in important new research on writing. The sites of study are numerous.

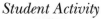

Student Activity

READING, RESEARCH, AND REACTION

Describe the writing program you experienced as an undergraduate, beginning with first-year composition. What courses did you take? Map the sequence of writing courses required for all students. What was the underlying philosophy of the writing program? How can you find out? In class, compare your findings. Are there differences? If so, what are they? What can you learn from comparing approaches to college and university writing courses?

Read the Statement on Outcomes for First-Year Composition at the CWPA website: http://wpacouncil.org/files/WPA%20Outcomes%20Statement%20Adopted%20Revisions%5B1%5D_0.pdf. Thinking about your own experience in first-year writing courses, how well did these criteria map onto your courses?

Student Activity

RESEARCH AND WRITING: WRITING STUDIES PROGRAM ANALYSIS

The purpose of this assignment is to become familiar with a wide range of writing studies programs. Adopt one writing studies program at a university or college other than your own. Writing studies programs generally offer a degree (major, minor, graduate degree) in writing. These may be housed in departments of English, or they may be in what are termed *stand-alone writing departments*. The CCCC Committee on the Major in Writing and Rhetoric (2016) created a list of these programs: http://www.ncte.org/library/NCTEFiles/Groups/CCCC/Committees/Writing_Majors_Final.pdf. Other resources include *What We Are Becoming: Developments in Undergraduate Writing Majors*, edited by Gregory A. Giberson and Thomas A. Moriarty, plus a second volume extending this work, *Writing Majors: Eighteen Program Profiles* (Giberson and Moriarty 2010; Giberson et al. 2015).

Write a summary of no more than one page explaining the structure and philosophy of the program and be prepared to share it with other class members.

Student Activity

RESEARCH AND WRITING: KEYWORDS ESSAY

Keywords in Composition Studies (*KCS*) by Heilker and Vandenberg (1996) defines terms that focus on academic text, the writing student, and the classroom: *academic discourse, argument, basic writing/writers, coherence, collaboration, critical thinking, discourse community, error, essay, evaluation, form/structure, grammar, invention, logic, marginalization, peer evaluation, portfolio, process, revision, students, teacher, voice, writing center.*

Vocabulary in a discipline evolves. The authors of *Keywords*, almost twenty years later, produced a new edition, notably changing its title to *Keywords in Writing Studies* (*KWS*) (Heilker and Vandenberg 2015). Their goal "is not to provide fixed, unitary meanings of a term or even to privilege some meanings above others, but rather to illuminate how many divergent and contesting significations reside within our field's central terms" (9).

The authors of *KCS* and *KWS* offer a systematic inquiry into the vocabulary of writing theorists and teachers through brief yet well-researched entries, noting the term's historical definition and how it has evolved. Terms interconnect within the volume, providing a window into the principal ideas in the field.

Write an essay of no more than one thousand words in which you define a term in the same fashion as *Keywords in Composition Studies* (and the more recent *Keywords in Writing Studies*) does through a lens of writing studies. Provide a glossary-type definition at the beginning of your essay. Possible keywords to define: *authority, citizen scholar, community, community-based research, computer, discourse, ecology, genre, identity, invention, multimodal, literacy, location, performance, queer, reflection, research, service, sustainability, technical communication, transfer, usability, voice, WAC-WID,* and *CWPA.*

Note that Linda Adler-Kassner and Elizabeth Wardle focus on "threshold concepts" in writing studies, yet another approach that could be analyzed as are keywords (Adler-Kassner and Wardle 2015).

REFERENCES

Adler-Kassner, Linda, and Elizabeth Wardle. 2015. *Naming What We Know: Threshold Concepts and Writing Studies.* Logan: Utah State University Press.

Atwell, Nancie. 1987. *In the Middle: Writing, Reading, and Learning with Adolescents.* Portsmouth, NH: Heinemann.

Bazerman, Charles. 2002. "The Case for Writing Studies as a Major Discipline." In *The Intellectual Work of Composition,* edited by Gary Olson, 32–38. Carbondale: Southern Illinois University Press.

Bazerman, Charles, ed. 2007. *The Handbook of Research on Writing: History, Society, School, Individual, Text.* New York: Routledge.

Calkins, Lucy. 1986. *The Art of Teaching Writing.* Portsmouth, NH: Heinemann.

CCCC Committee on the Major in Writing and Rhetoric. 2016. "Listing of Writing Majors." Conference on College Composition and Communication. http://www.ncte.org/cccc/committees/majorrhetcomp.

Downs, Douglas, and Elizabeth Wardle. 2007. "Teaching about Writing, Righting Misconceptions: (Re)Envisioning 'First-Year Composition' as 'Introduction to Writing Studies.'" *College Composition and Communication* 58 (4): 552–84.

Emig, Janet. 1971. *The Composing Processes of Twelfth Graders.* Urbana, IL: NCTE.

Flower, Linda, and John R. Hayes. 1981. "A Cognitive Process Theory of Writing." *College Composition and Communication* 32 (4): 365–87. http://dx.doi.org/10.2307/356600.

Giberson, Gregory A., and Thomas A. Moriarty, eds. 2010. *What We Are Becoming: Developments in Undergraduate Writing Majors.* Logan: Utah State University Press.

Giberson, Greg, Jim Nugent, and Lori A. Ostergard, eds. 2015. *Writing Majors: Eighteen Program Profiles.* Logan: Utah State University Press.

Graves, Donald. 1994. *A Fresh Look at Writing.* Portsmouth, NH: Heinemann.

Heilker, Paul, and Peter Vandenberg. 1996. *Keywords in Composition Studies.* Portsmouth, NH: Heinemann.

Heilker, Paul, and Peter Vandenberg, eds. 2015. *Keywords in Writing Studies.* Logan: Utah State University Press. http://dx.doi.org/10.7330/9780874 219746.

Lindemann, Erika. 2001. *A Rhetoric for Writing Teachers.* 4th ed. New York: Oxford University Press.

Lunsford, Andrea, ed. 1995. *Reclaiming Rhetorica: Women in the Rhetorical Tradition.* Pittsburgh, PA: University of Pittsburgh Press.

Murphy, James J. 2012. "Roman Writing Instruction as Described by Quintilian." In *A Short History of Writing Instruction: From Ancient Greece to Contemporary America,* 3rd ed. Edited by James J. Murphy, 36–76. New York: Routledge.

Perl, Sondra. 1979. "The Composing Processes of Unskilled College Writers." *Research in the Teaching of English* 13 (4): 317–36.

Purcell, Kristen, Lee Rainie, Alan Heaps, Judy Buchanan, Linda Friedrich, Amanda Jacklin, Clara Chen, and Kathryn Zickuhr. 2012. "How Teens Do Research in the Digital World." *Pew Internet.* http://www.pewinternet.org /2012/11/01/how-teens-do-research-in-the-digital-world/.

Russell, David. 1995. "Activity Theory and Its Implications for Writing Instruction." In *Reconceiving Writing, Rethinking Writing Instruction,* edited by Joseph Patraglia, 51–78. Hillsdale, NJ: Erlbaum.

Shaughnessy, Mina. 1979. *Errors and Expectations: A Guide for the Teacher of Basic Writing.* New York: Oxford University Press.

Yancey, Kathleen Blake. 2009. "Writing in the 21st Century." A Report from NCTE. http://www.ncte.org/library/NCTEFiles/Press/Yancey_final.pdf.

3

Considering Ethics and Responsible Conduct of Research

WHY ETHICS MATTER

Too often in writing, only one principle of ethical research comes into play: avoiding academic dishonesty, more commonly known as *plagiarism*, the willful copying of others' ideas and writing. Responsible conduct of research (RCR) is much more than avoiding plagiarism. A code of ethics for research grew out of the horrifying human experiments conducted during World War II, and while this code may not seem applicable to research in writing, the general principles can be applied. This history of research ethics, beginning with the Nuremberg Code of 1949 and extending to the Belmont Report of 1979, is fascinating. Several resources (e.g., National Academy of Sciences, National Academy of Engineering, and Institute of Medicine 2009; Steneck 2007) cover these important principles in more depth. Yes, these ethical codes were designed with scientific research in mind, but it behooves all researchers to be familiar with the principles of RCR.[1] While it's unlikely that writing researchers will be working with animal subjects, for instance, it's helpful to be knowledgeable about the overarching principles of ethical inquiry. It is much more likely that writing researchers will work with human subjects.

CCCC ETHICAL CONDUCT OF RESEARCH IN COMPOSITION STUDIES

Paul V. Anderson (1998) raised the question of ethical issues in conducting composition research involving students in an article in CCC.

It triggered action by the organization. The Conference on College Composition and Communication (CCCC) developed "Guidelines for the Ethical Treatment of Students and Student Writing in Composition Studies" (2000). It was updated in 2003 and again in 2015, and the result is "CCCC Guidelines for the Ethical Conduct of Research in Composition Studies" (CCCC 2003). Note that writing researchers are termed *composition specialists* in these guidelines. What to call writing researchers has been problematic, as there's no easily recognizable term like *scientists, humanists,* or *artists.* Some use the term *compositionists,* but it does not have universal acceptance. It's a mark of the youth of the profession that no one satisfactory term has been established. The professional organization for composition specialists, CCCC, was not organized until 1949.

Preamble

Composition specialists share a commitment to protecting the rights, privacy, dignity, and well-being of the persons involved in their studies. These guidelines are intended to assist them in fulfilling this commitment.

The guidelines apply to all efforts by scholars, teachers, administrators, students, and others directed toward the publication of a book or journal article, a presentation at a conference, preparation of a thesis or dissertation, a display on a website, or other general dissemination of the results of research and scholarship. The guidelines apply to formally planned investigations and to studies that discuss writers and unpublished writing composition specialists encounter in other ways, such as when teaching classes, holding student conferences, directing academic programs, conducting research in nonacademic settings, or going about their professional and personal lives.

The guidelines do not apply to studies composition specialists conduct solely for the purpose of improving their own practices or solely for discussion within their own schools, school districts, colleges, or universities. However, even in the latter types of studies, composition specialists carefully protect the rights, privacy, dignity, and well-being of the persons they study. These guidelines suggest ways to accomplish this goal.

Composition specialists are encouraged to seek additional ways beyond those identified in these guidelines to assure they treat other people ethically in their research.

Compliance with Policies, Regulations, and Laws

Composition specialists learn about and comply with all policies, regulations, and laws that apply to their studies. If their work is subject to review by an Institutional Review Board (IRB),[2] they submit their plans for advance review and approval, and they conduct their studies in accordance with the approved research plans. If their studies are subject to an alternative review process at an institution that does not have an IRB, they comply with this process. Composition specialists who believe their studies are exempt from any regulation or review process contact the appropriate committee or authority for confirmation. If they do not work or study at an institution with an IRB or other review process, they contact colleagues at other institutions so they can learn about and follow the procedures IRBs require. Composition specialists uncertain about whether their institutions have an IRB or alternative review process initiate the inquiries necessary to find out for certain.

When conducting studies their IRBs determine to be exempt from IRB review, composition specialists follow the applicable provisions of these guidelines.

While complying with the final decision of their IRBs, composition specialists may negotiate concerning IRB requirements or restrictions that hamper research without increasing protection of the rights, privacy, dignity, and well-being of the persons studied.

Maintaining Competence

Composition specialists assure that they and their assistants are appropriately trained and prepared to conduct the studies they undertake. Training and preparation may include enrollment in courses, study of relevant published research and methodological discussions, and consultation or collaboration with experienced researchers. Composition specialists strive to refine their competence and to keep apprised of the ongoing discussion of best practices in research.

Obtaining Informed Consent

When asking people to volunteer to participate in a study, composition specialists explain the study in a way that enables the potential participants to understand the following points:

- the purpose of the research and its possible benefits
- what participants will be asked to do and how long the process will take
- what the composition specialists plan to do with the information or data they obtain from participants
- any potential discomforts or harms participants might incur as a result of participating

Whether or not composition specialists intend to include information in research reports that would render participants identifiable, composition specialists always honor participants' requests that reports contain no personally identifiable information, including information that would make them identifiable to persons familiar with the research site.

In addition, composition specialists emphasize the following points:

Participation is completely voluntary.

Participants may withdraw at any time without penalty or loss of
benefits to which they are otherwise entitled.

For studies involving minors or adults who have legal guardians, composition specialists obtain written permission from the parents or legal
guardians and also the assent of the minors or adults. If required, composition specialists also gain the permission of sponsoring institutions, such
as public schools or private workplaces. They are careful to observe that
whatever terms of access they agree to are consistent with the stipulations
of applicable IRB regulations and the provisions of these guidelines.

These guidelines concerning informed consent are intended to com-
plement (not replace) any additional requirements of applicable policies,
regulations, and laws.

Conducting Studies Involving Classes

When conducting studies involving classes, composition specialists give
primary consideration to the goals of the course and fair treatment of all
students. Toward that end, they take the following measures, whether the
students are members of their own classes or are from classes taught by
other people:

1. They design their studies so participation is completely voluntary.
2. They assure that volunteering, declining to volunteer, or deciding
    to withdraw after volunteering will not affect a student's grade.
3. They assure that pursuit of their research goals will not hinder
    achievement of the course's educational goals.
4. They assure that all students will receive the same attention,
    instruction, support, and encouragement in the course, whether
    or not they have volunteered to participate in the composition
    specialists' study.
5. They assure that reports on the research do not include informa-
    tion about students who did not volunteer.
6. If there is a possibility that one or more of the volunteering
    students have changed their minds since the study began, com-
    position specialists obtain confirming consent at the end of the
    course.

Recruiting

When conducting studies with individuals, such as subordinates or others whose well-being depends on the composition specialist's opinions,

decisions, or actions, the composition specialist takes special care to protect prospective participants from adverse consequences of declining or withdrawing from participation.

To avoid situations in which students feel their decision to participate (or not) in a study might affect their instructors' treatment of them, composition specialists recruit participants from other classes or other sources unless the topic of the research or other special circumstances require that the study involve the composition specialists' own students.

Responding to Questions

Composition specialists provide those invited to participate an opportunity to ask questions about the study. When asked questions by participants during or after a study, composition specialists reply in as timely a manner as possible without jeopardizing the integrity of the project.

Quoting, Paraphrasing, and Reporting Statements

In their publications, presentations, and other research reports, composition specialists quote, paraphrase, or otherwise report unpublished written statements only with the author's written permission. They quote, paraphrase, or otherwise report spoken statements only with written permission or when the speaker uttered the words in a public forum. Composition specialists always obtain written permission to use a spoken statement they believe was made in confidence with the expectation that it would remain private.

When quoting, paraphrasing, or reporting unpublished writing and when reporting (with permission) oral statements made in private, composition specialists respect the writer's or speaker's wishes about whether or not to include the writer's or speaker's name or identifying information. When the writers or speakers are minors, composition specialists obtain written permission from the parents or legal guardians and also the assent of the minors. When composition specialists have used a consent process approved by an IRB or similar committee, they have obtained the necessary permission.

Composition specialists report written and spoken statements accurately. They interpret the statements in ways faithful to the writer's or speaker's intentions, and they provide contextual information that will enable others to understand the statements the way the writer intended. When in doubt, composition specialists check the accuracy of their reports and interpretations with the writer or speaker. They are especially sensitive to the need to check their interpretations when the writer or speaker is from a cultural, ethnic, or other group different than their own.

When discussing the statements they quote, paraphrase, or otherwise report, composition specialists do so in ways that are fair and serious and cause no harm.

Using Videotapes, Audiotapes, and Photographs

Because videotapes, audiotapes, and photographs allow individuals to be identified, composition specialists include them in conference presentations, publications, or other public displays only with written permission from all persons whose voices and/or images were recorded or shown unless these persons were taped or photographed while speaking in or attending a public forum. When the persons taped or photographed are minors or adults with legal guardians, composition specialists obtain written permission from the parents or legal guardians and also the assent of the minors or adults. When composition specialists have used a consent process approved by an IRB or similar committee, they have obtained the necessary permission.

Describing Individuals and Groups

Composition specialists describe individuals and groups fairly and accurately, in ways accountable to the data, observation, or other evidence on which the descriptions are based. They describe other people in ways that are fair and serious, cause no harm, and protect privacy.

Using Unpublished Writing Collected Outside of an IRB-Approved Study

When studying unpublished writing samples (e.g., job-application essays) that have been collected outside of a study approved by an IRB or other process, composition specialists determine whether their planned use of these samples is consistent with the policies governing research at their institutions or at the institution at which the samples were collected.

SELECTED BIBLIOGRAPHY

CCCC has compiled a selected bibliography of sources on the ethical conduct of research involving human participants. It is available at http://www.ncte.org/cccc/resources/positions/ethicalconductbiblio.

NOTES

1.   An institutional review board is a committee established under the federal regulation for the protection of research participants (45 CFR 46). Each IRB is legally responsible for assuring that all research involving human participants conducted under the aegis of

its institution complies with this regulation. For more information, visit the website of the federal Office for Human Research Protections: http://www.hhs.gov/ohrp/.

2. This sentence is adapted from the American Psychological Association Ethics Code, 6.10.c.

The CCCC Guidelines reflect many of the national standards on RCR, generally categorized as nine areas:

- data acquisition, management, sharing, and ownership
- conflict of interest and commitment
- human subjects
- animal welfare
- research misconduct
- publication practices and responsible authorship
- mentor/trainee responsibilities
- peer review
- collaborative science

Within the humanities, some disciplines believe themselves exempt from Institutional Review Board (IRB) oversight; these include anthropology, history, and folklore. The *Common Rule* of federal regulations defines *research* as "a systematic investigation, including research development, testing and evaluation, designed to develop or contribute to generalizable knowledge" and *human subject* as "a living individual about whom an investigator (whether professional or student) conducting research obtains (1) data through intervention or interaction with the individual, or (2) identifiable private information" (46.102[d] and [f]).

Humanistic research is often framed as documentation, interpretation, or conversation not needing IRB approval. The ethics of research in folklore or anthropology takes into account that the researcher is entering a community, and the researcher learns and follows the community's rules of conduct and follows the community's lead in the direction of the research. To qualify as exempt, the research meets all of the following conditions: (1) subjects are exposed to no more than minimal risk; (2) the waiver or alteration does not adversely affect subject rights and welfare; (3) the research would not be feasible without the waiver or alteration; and (4) subjects will be provided with additional pertinent information after participation, when appropriate. Participants may sign an informed consent form although some researchers balk even at that amount of intrusion in the field.

Laurie Grobman (2015) reminds researchers that balance and power are always important issues to negotiate in research, particularly community-based research and service learning that draw on participants who may not be in positions of power. She notes, "But these partnerships also raise complex issues of unequal, fluid, and shifting discourses among community partners, students, and faculty, and, consequently, inform ways to enact publicly shared meaning in community literacy partnerships" (237). The outcome of students engaging as "rhetorical citizen historians" (239) can result in extremely important community publications.

In disseminating research, whether in presentation or print, a statement such as the following should be included, leaving no doubt that the researcher conducted the project with integrity: this project was approved by the institutional review board and follows CCCC Guidelines for the Ethical Conduct of Research in Composition Studies; informed consent was obtained to conduct and cite all interviews and to quote all student work in this report.

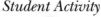

Student Activity

COMPLETE HUMAN SUBJECTS CERTIFICATION

Complete CITI (Collaborative Institutional Training Initiative) certification. First, *create an account* by registering. A drop-down menu allows you to pick your home institution. Select Social & Behavioral Research Modules, Basic Course (80 percent is a passing grade). This includes an introduction, History and Ethical Principles, Research with Human Subjects, Regulations for Social and Behavioral Research, Assessing Risk, Informed Consent, Privacy and Confidentiality, and Conflicts of Interest. Once you have passed these modules, then you will be certified through your home institution to conduct human subjects/participants research. Allow two to three hours for completion. The certificate is valid for three years. CITI is online at this URL: https://www.citiprogram.org/.

Profile of a Student Researcher: An IRB-Approved Honors Thesis

Kristin Lillywhite, an honors student in English at Utah State University, felt it was her responsibility as a preservice educator to understand second-language acquisition in order to better meet the needs of her future students. As a result, she focused her honors thesis (Lillywhite 2011)—the culminating project of her undergraduate education—on how teachers of English language learners (ELL) help students develop cognitive academic language proficiency (CALP). What practices help students become proficient? Kristin was particularly interested in two model approaches: sheltered instruction that integrates content and language goals and whole language that considers multiple contexts. (While whole language is typically viewed as an approach in elementary school settings, Kristin was interested in secondary literacy instruction.) In order to investigate her project, she planned to observe teaching behaviors and interview teachers to explore attitudes in a local high-school setting.

Because Kristin chose to use human subjects—high-school teach-ers—for her research, permission and approval from the Institutional Review Board (IRB) were required. Generally, IRBs have a minimum of five members with at least one scientist, one nonscientist, and one com-munity member. According to federal regulations, IRBs must also have gender balance. The overarching purpose of the IRB is to focus on limit-ing harm to human subjects and insuring informed consent; IRBs have legitimate concerns about how subjects will be protected and how data collected will remain confidential. On the other hand, these boards also use common sense in insuring that researchers are not overburdened with unnecessary paperwork. As a result, projects may receive *expedited* review, which does not require review by the full board.

The IRB at Kristin's home institution required that both she and the faculty mentor—designated as the principal investigators (PIs)—were certified for human-subjects research via the CITI (Collaborative Insti-tutional Training Initiative) Program, which provides research-ethics education to all members of the research community. To be certified at this university, a set of nine modules in the curriculum choice Social & Behavioral Research Investigators and Key Personnel, Basic Course must be completed via the CITI website with an overall score of 80 percent. Once the training is completed, CITI issues a completion certificate valid for a three-year period and notifies the local IRB.

To apply for approval, Kristin submitted five documents to the IRB:

1. A general application
2. Honors Thesis Proposal (with the committee signature page)
3. Interview questions
4. Classroom observation sheet
5. Informed consent (formatted to the template provided by the IRB)

The process of writing, reviewing, and compiling these documents helped Kristin plan her project. She received comments from her men-tor and committee members throughout the writing and research pro-cess, revising as she refined her investigation.

The fifteen-page general application is contained in appendix 3.1. While such an application may seem overwhelming, its purpose is to ensure protection of the human participants, particularly any groups that may be considered *vulnerable*: children, the aged, the infirm, or prison populations. Likewise, the IRB wants to ensure that students in classes taught by the researcher do not feel *coerced* to participate. Such forms must cover a broad range of research types. For much writing research, questions can be answered as "not applicable": NA. The forms vary depending on the type of institution. For instance, Kristin's university is a land-grant institution with an agricultural experiment station; thus, the form queries researchers about funding from the AES.

In addition to avoiding risk to the participants, confidentiality of their information is another important aspect of the research. For Kristin's project she chose to use pseudonyms for her participants in the thesis, to keep the interview documents secure, and to destroy the materials a year from the approval of her thesis.

Staff members of the IRB office, the IRB chair, or the board itself may engage in a dialogue with the researcher, asking for revisions before approving. Then a formal approval is given to the researcher; a sample follows. In the final report of the research, these assurance and protocol numbers are included.

USU Assurance: FWA#00003308
    Protocol # 2649
        MEMORANDUM
        TO: Joyce Kinkead
                    Kristin Lillywhite
        FROM: Kim Corbin-Lewis, IRB Chair
                    True M. Fox, IRB Administrator
        SUBJECT: Developing Cognitive Academic Language Proficiency in Diverse Classrooms

Your proposal has been reviewed by the Institutional Review Board and is approved under expedite procedure #7 (see below).

X There is no more than minimal risk to the subjects.
    There is greater than minimal risk to the subjects.

This approval applies only to the proposal currently on file for the period of one year. If your study extends beyond this approval period, you must contact this office to request an annual review of this research. Any change affecting human subjects must be approved by the Board prior to implementation. Injuries or any unanticipated problems involving risk to subjects or to others must be reported immediately to the Chair of the Institutional Review Board.

Prior to involving human subjects, properly executed informed consent must be obtained from each subject or from an authorized representative, and documentation of informed consent must be kept on file for at least three years after the project ends. Each subject must be furnished with a copy of the informed consent document for their personal records.

The research activities listed below are expedited from IRB review based on the Department of Health and Human Services (DHHS) regulations for the protection of human research subjects, 45 CFR Part 46, as amended to include provisions of the Federal Policy for the Protection of Human Subjects, November 9, 1998.

7. Research on individual or group characteristics or behavior (including, but not limited to, research on perception, cognition, motivation, identity, language, communication, cultural beliefs or practices, and social behavior) or research employing survey, interview, oral history, focus group, program evaluation, human factors evaluation, or quality assurance methodologies.

INFORMED CONSENT

Once a project is approved, the researcher can proceed with obtaining consent from the participants. The following informed-consent document is printed on letterhead and includes the appropriate information about IRB approval. Participants are thus informed about the research project before they sign and agree to participate. (If participants are children, informed consent must be cosigned by parents, and the language of the informed consent is written so as to be understandable by the child. IRB offices often have samples of such age-appropriate documents.)

The preinterview survey and the interview questions developed by Kristin have been included in an earlier section. She also submitted to IRB her classroom observation sheet (see Figure 3.2).

At the end of the research, Kristin defended her honors thesis and submitted the IRB Protocol Status Report so the project could be formally closed out. In her summary statement, she explained the results.

The process of second language acquisition was studied by examining the distinction between basic interpersonal conversation skills (BICS) and cognitive academic language proficiency (CALP). This distinction, originally proposed by linguist Jim Cummins, relates to current trends in the U.S. public education system. A review of the literature was conducted and integrated with information obtained by interviewing local language arts teachers. The primary goal of the study was to learn how public school teachers conceptualize second language acquisition and literacy instruction. The thesis also addresses how the BICS/CALP distinction can be applied in real classroom settings. Teachers reported that low student motivation and various cultural factors affect second language acquisition. Further study is needed to determine the extent to which these factors affect the development of CALP. While developing CALP is especially critical for English Language Learner (ELL) student populations, teachers felt that intervention strategies will benefit all students.

What did Kristin learn from this experience? Most important, she became expert in an area of literacy that will be important in her career as a teacher. In addition, she developed deeper relationships with a group of faculty mentors who guided the research process. She also learned much more about research methodology and methods, including the time-consuming task of transcribing oral interviews for transcripts. As she notes in the acknowledgments section of the thesis, one of the most valuable aspects of the project was getting to work one-on-one with a group of practicing teachers, whom she found inspirational. While research in writing can involve a significant investment, the rewards for the student can be considerable. Kristin also found that her individual project and her initiative paid dividends when entering the job market. It also has the potential to influence graduate-school admission.

FIGURE 3.1. Informed consent.

USU IRB Approved: July 1, 2010; Page 79 of 265
Approval Terminates: 06/30/2011
Protocol #2649
IRB Password Protected per IRB Administrator

Department of English
1450 Old Main Hill
Logan UT 84322-1450
Telephone: (435) 797-1706

INFORMED CONSENT
Developing Cognitive Academic Language Proficiency (CALP) in Diverse Classrooms

Introduction/Purpose: Professor Joyce Kinkead, Professor Jennifer Sinor, and Kristin Lillywhite, an undergraduate honors student researcher, in the Department of English at Utah State University (USU) are conducting a research study to find out more about the role of secondary teachers in second language acquisition. The goal of the project is to analyze the ways in which linguistic models can inform the practice of secondary language arts teachers. Experience with teaching ELL or CLD students is preferred, but not required for this study. There will be 9-10 total public high school teachers participating in the research study.

Procedures: If you agree to be in this research study, the following events will occur:

Interviews: You will be asked to participate in an informal interview in which you will be asked a series of questions related to your professional opinions and teaching practices. The interview is expected to take about 30 minute and will be audio recorded on cassette tapes and transcribed.

Observation: The researcher will observe one full-length class period. The student researcher will take notes on classroom activities and interactions between teachers and students. The types of data that will be collected include specific learning activities (Whole class discussion, Large/Small group work, Individual work time, etc.), types of questions posed, use of manipulatives, etc. The researcher will describe the students' general behavior and perceived level of engagement without including identifiable information. Student work will not be collected by the researchers.

Document analysis: You may be asked to provide copies of relevant curriculum materials such as lesson plans, homework assignment descriptions, assessment materials, grading rubrics, supplemental handouts etc. for analysis by the researchers.

Risks: There is minimal risk in participating in this study. You may experience discomfort with some questions when queried about your teaching practices. To minimize discomfort, you may choose to not answer certain questions and still proceed with the interview. There is a possibility of a loss of personal privacy and confidentiality; however, measures have been put into place to minimize this risk and it is explained below, under "Confidentiality."

Benefits: There may or may not be any direct benefit to you from these procedures. The investigator, however, may learn more about significant literacy trends found in local mainstream classrooms. The investigator may also learn about effective approaches to developing cognitive academic language proficiency. Relevant curriculum materials may be collected and analyzed if teachers have them available. The research will demonstrate specific ways in which linguistic models can inform the practice of secondary teachers

New Findings: During the course of this research study, you will be informed of any significant new findings (either good or bad), such as changes in the risks or benefits resulting from participation in the research, or new alternatives to participation that might cause you to change your mind about continuing in the study. If new information is obtained that is relevant or useful to you, or if the procedures and/or

methods change at any time throughout this study, your consent to continue participating in this study will be obtained again.

Explanation & offer to answer questions: Kristin Lillywhite has explained this research study to you and answered your questions. If you have other questions or research-related problems, you may reach Kristin at 801-458-4582 or Professor Kinkead at (435) 797-1706.

Extra Cost(s): There are no additional costs for participating in this study.

Payment/Compensation: While your participation is appreciated, there is no compensation available for participating in this study.

Voluntary nature of participation and right to withdraw without consequence: Participation in research is entirely voluntary. You may refuse to participate or withdraw at any time without consequence. The researchers will not use any data from the study if you withdraw.

Confidentiality: Research records will be kept confidential, consistent with federal and state regulations. Only Professor Joyce Kinkead, Professor Jennifer Sinor, and Kristin Lillywhite will have access to the data, which will be kept in a locked file cabinet in a locked room to maintain confidentiality. To protect your privacy, a pseudonym will replace your name on all notes and transcripts from classroom observations and interviews. This code will also be used in the final research texts/reports. No personal identifiable information will be included in the final report. The code will be stored separately from the data collected in a locked cabinet. You will be given the opportunity to review the interview transcripts, observation notes, and reports prior to any publications that may result from this study. Personal, identifiable information will be kept for the duration of the study from August 2010 until May 2011. All personally identifiable information, including audiotapes and notes, will be destroyed after data collection is completed.

IRB Approval Statement: The Institutional Review Board for the protection of human participants at USU has approved this research study. If you have any pertinent questions or concerns about your rights or a research-related injury, you may contact the IRB Administrator at (435) 797-0567 or email irb@usu.edu. If you have a concern or complaint about the research and you would like to contact someone other than the research team, you may contact the IRB Administrator to obtain information or to offer input.

Copy of consent: You have been given two copies of this Informed Consent. Please sign both copies and retain one copy for your files.

Investigator Statement: "I certify that the research study has been explained to the individual, by me or my research staff, and that the individual understands the nature and purpose, the possible risks and benefits associated with taking part in this research study. Any questions that have been raised have been answered."

Joyce Kinkead, Principal Investigator   Kristin Lillywhite, Student Researcher
(435) 797-1706; joyce.kinkead@usu.edu   (801) 458-4582; kristin.l@aggimail.usu.edu

Jennifer Sinor, Honors Thesis Advisor
(435) 797-3440; jennifer.sinor@usu.edu

Signature of Participant: By signing below I agree to participate.

_____   _____
Participant's Signature   Date

FIGURE 3.2. Classroom Observation Sheet

Classroom Observation Data Sheet

Sketch of Classroom:

Observed Teacher Behavior   Comments

Student Activity

RESPONSIBLE CONDUCT OF RESEARCH (RCR)/ RESEARCH ETHICS SLIDE PRESENTATION

Each student will develop PowerPoint slides, having been assigned one topic to present to the class as a whole. The title slide will be *Conducting Research Responsibly with Particular Attention to Research in Writing*. Each slide will present information on the topic briefly, which its author will present orally. A second part for most topics will be the answers to the question, what would happen if this standard were not followed? In other words, look at the pitfalls of not adhering to RCR.

Topics include the following:

PART 1: IMPORTANT DOCUMENTS AND STATEMENTS ABOUT RCR

- Nuremberg Code (1949)
- American Psychological Association (APA) Ethical Standards of Psychologists (1953)
- American Anthropological Association Code of Ethics (1973)
- National Research Act (passed 1974)

- Belmont Report (1979)
- American Historical Association Statement on Standards of Professional Conduct (1987)
- Modern Language Association (MLA) Statement of Professional Ethics (1992)
- Guidelines for the Ethical Treatment of Students and Student Writing in Composition Studies (CCCC 2003)

PART 2: NINE AREAS OF RCR INSTRUCTION

- data acquisition, management, sharing, and ownership
- conflict of interest and commitment
- human subjects
  - institutional review boards (IRB)—seven criteria for review of research proposals
- animal welfare
- research misconduct
- publication practices and responsible authorship
- mentor/trainee responsibilities and relationships
- peer review; and
- collaborative science

PART 3: WHEN RESEARCH GOES WRONG

- What routes may students involved in research take when witnessing research misconduct?

The template for the slide presentation will be shared. Slides will be compiled before the scheduled presentation so they are ready for the class session. Each speaker has two to three minutes to present the information on the slide. For the areas of RCR instruction, an additional minute may be taken to present the pitfalls of ignoring the standard.

ETHICS IN DIGITAL ENVIRONMENTS

We have already discussed how the Internet provides a rich tool for researchers. Another use of the Internet is as a venue for research. The Association of Internet Researchers (AoIR) has issued guidelines for conducting research (AoIR 2012). Authors McKee and DeVoss (2007) weave ethical issues throughout the chapters in their volume. In general, the same ethical principles we have already discussed apply to the Internet, but there are special issues in what may seem a public and anonymous space. Following are practical guidelines to consider.

Data privacy and confidentiality, integrity of data, and protection of participants are key to conducting research in digital environments. It may seem contradictory that protection should be given to those who willingly and freely post in public spaces. What harm or risk is involved after all? Nonetheless, researchers have ethical obligations to protect the privacy of subjects even when they are engaged in public digital environments. Entering a socially mediated space in a deceptive manner or lurking and then using information gathered from the experience are not acceptable.

Privacy and confidentiality in traditional research are generally assured through "scrubbing" data of any identifying attributes. This cleanup is nearly impossible in a digital environment, as people can be tracked in numerous ways: IP addresses, cookies, data sets, and online data trails. The researcher, when seeking informed consent, should acknowledge these limitations. Similarly, information stored in the "cloud" is also vulnerable. Participants may be asked to recognize this heightened vulnerability by agreeing to a statement such as this: I understand that online communications may be at greater risk for hacking, intrusions, and other violations. Despite these possibilities, I consent to participate.

Recruitment of participants in digital environments can be difficult—to say the least. Consider whether or not participants are using their real names or an avatar. How can people be solicited to participate in a study? Plans for recruitment must be detailed in the IRB application. Remarkably, a tweet may be used or even YouTube videos. E-mail solicitations may or may not be effective recruitment tools. When recruiting from a moderated site, it is important that the moderators are in the communication loop and have agreed to the study. Then the recruitment invitation should note this agreement.

Informed consent will, no doubt, occur electronically, which requires that traditional information be delivered nontraditionally. Participants must be informed that their activity is entirely voluntary and offered the opportunity to check "I do not agree" rather than "I agree." Other important information includes risks, benefits of the research, an ending date, proposed dissemination of the research, and an invitation to submit feedback. Note that no identifying information will be used. Explain how the data gathered will be protected and kept secure. It will likely be in a password-protected file. In some cases encryption may be necessary—the electronic equivalent of a locked filing cabinet.

"On the Internet, no one knows you're a dog." This famous caption from the *New Yorker* cartoon is prescient for research ethics (find the cartoon in chapter 7). On the Internet, is it possible to tell the age of users? Federal regulations for protections of human subjects note that minors—those under eighteen—are vulnerable audiences. Age-verification procedures must be enacted to protect both participant and researcher.

Undertaking research in digital environments increases the complexity of the process for the researcher. Textual analysis that does not

involve human participants may not be subject to the ethical considerations discussed here. But always consider whether there are people who
are invisible behind any text. The Internet provides a rich environment
for researchers, not only as a tool but also as a venue. In both instances,
research integrity is critical.

AUTHORSHIP

A key tenet of RCR is authorship. The student may be sole author or
may collaborate with others, including mentors. One of the first issues
to clarify in any student-mentor relationship is the question of *authorship*. In general, the person who conceptualizes and analyzes the data is
termed *first author*. In writing studies, authorship may be single authorship (following a humanistic model) or coauthorship by two or more
(following a more collaborative social sciences model). Simply being
a mentor does not qualify for joint-author status. Authors must make
a significant intellectual contribution to the project. The APA (2001)
notes that authorship includes those who have made substantial contributions to a study, such as "formulating the problem or hypothesis,
structuring the experimental design, organizing and conducting the
statistical analysis, interpreting the results, or writing a major portion of
the paper" (350–51).

THE IMPORTANCE OF A MENTOR

Standards of conduct apply not just to authorship but also to the overall
student-mentor relationship. Typically, the novice researcher is guided
through the research process by a mentor. In classical Greek mythology,
Mentor was a friend of Odysseus, who placed Mentor in charge of his
palace and asked him to look after his son Telemachus. During the difficult period when suitors for Penelope were besieging Odysseus's family, Athena—goddess of wisdom—inhabited Mentor's body and provided
advice. From this historical meaning comes the current use of the term
mentor: a trusted and experienced guide and counselor.

A research mentor has an important role in introducing the student
to practices and policies of research in the particular field (see Temple,
Sibley, and Orr 2010). Conceptualizing and designing research studies
can be difficult, and having a mentor to guide the student through the
process is essential. A good mentor teaches by example and can model
how to read scholarly literature, critique it, and write and revise it.

The mentor should provide direct instruction and advice about the
responsible conduct of research (RCR) in the field. The essential nature
of the role of the mentor cannot be underestimated. Because of this, it
is important for the student to choose wisely. It's helpful to resee faculty

who teach classes as possible mentors, as these are special relationships that can result in lifelong friendships and be important to career networking. In choosing a mentor, students should look for a good fit but not necessarily the most popular teacher, who may be overwhelmed with independent study and advising. Doing a search of faculty members' interests through webpages is a good way to become informed about their expertise and research interests. Likewise, setting up appointments with possible mentors to get a sense of their character and work is also a good way to proceed. One of the most important facets of the mentor-apprentice relationship is communication; consequently, understanding communication styles and expectations is crucial. Likewise, make sure the faculty mentor is interested in *you* and asks about aspirations and career plans.

Working with Your Mentor

Set regular meetings with the mentor and arrive prepared with an agenda, or send written documents for comment and response in sufficient time for the mentor to review and be ready to respond. Some mentors may prefer electronic communication for review and response, but face-to-face meetings (even if those are electronic) are helpful for relationship building.

If there are problems with the project or personal stumbling blocks, communicate openly and in a timely manner with the mentor. An adage says "be the first to relate any bad news," which is often a wise policy. Mentors appreciate honesty as well as responsibility. They are well aware that there will be difficulties along the way for any novice, and that's one of the reasons they sign on as mentors—to provide guidance.

While it's difficult to change horses midstream, if the relationship between the mentor and mentee is not working, perhaps a different mentor may be selected, or a third party may be invited to mediate and help solve any issues. But the student researcher should first ask "Have I met all of my responsibilities?" before abandoning the relationship or the project. If there are inappropriate behaviors (e.g., sexual harassment) on the part of the mentor, this qualifies as violating ethical principles. The student researcher should make contact with the mentor's supervisor and lodge a report.

The development of a researcher is on a continuum from novice to expert. A good mentor helps the student mature as a researcher, and in the process, the student's critical thinking and skills are enhanced. In the final analysis, the relationship between mentor and mentee should be beneficial to both.

Student Activity

FINDING A MENTOR

Begin by making a list of possible mentors for a research project. The teacher of a research methods in writing studies course is an obvious choice. What do you know of that person's research and scholarly agenda? How can you find out? Consider interpersonal communication styles. How would you like to be viewed as a possible researcher? What do you value in a mentor's behavior?

APPENDIX 3.1: AN IRB-APPROVED HONORS THESIS

KRISTIN LILLYWHITE'S GENERAL APPLICATION TO THE IRB AT USU

Research projects that involve human participants must be reviewed and approved by the USU Institutional Review Board prior to beginning research.

IMPORTANT NOTICE: IRB review and approval of research using the General Application usually takes 3–4 weeks and research cannot be initiated until IRB approval is granted.

Note: USU policy requires that all researchers successfully (80% +) complete training in the protection of human subjects in research. Click the following link to check current IRB certification status: http://rgs.usu.edu/irb/htm/facultystaff-completed-certifications. To complete CITI Certification click the following link for login procedures and instructions: https://www.citiprogram.org/default.asp.

Basic Project Information Date:
Project Title:

Principal Investigator(s) (USU researchers only):
   Email:
   Phone:
   College:
   Department:
   UMC: *(University Mail Code)*

Date IRB certification expires: Click Here to access the IRB certification database to check expiration date

Co-Principal Investigator(s) *(who are not students)*:
    Email:
    Phone:
    College:
    Department:
    UMC: *(University Mail Code)*

Date IRB certification expires: Click Here to access the IRB certification database to check expiration date

Student researcher(s):
    Email:
    Phone:
    College:
    Department:
    UMC: *(University Mail Code)*

Date IRB certification expires: Click Here to access the IRB certification database to check expiration date

Graduate Students:
Is this research for:

Plan A (thesis or dissertation)? **Yes** ☐   **No** ☐
Date of committee approval

Plan B (creative project)? **Yes** ☐   **No** ☐
Date of committee approval

Plan C (extra class—no project)? **Yes** ☐   **No** ☐

If Plan A or B, committee must approve prior to IRB submission (send copy of signed committee approval page to IRB

Anticipated Start Date of Research:

Anticipated End Date of Research:

Will this project / protocol be supported by an external funding agency? **Yes** ☐   **No** ☐
If yes, name of funding agency or source:

Is there a grant award number for this project/protocol?
Yes ☐   **No** ☐   **List:**

Is this project funded with Agricultural Experiment Station/ Extension funds? **Yes** ☐   **No** ☐   **UTA00**

Scientific Validity

The Common Rule (45 CFR 46) requires that for all non-exempt research, "In order to approve research . . . the IRB shall determine that . . . risks to subjects are minimized: (i) by using procedures which are consistent with sound research design and which do not unnecessarily expose subjects to risk . . . " The requirement to ensure sound research design can be fulfilled through several means at USU. The Investigator is encouraged to obtain a review using the Scientific Validity Review Checklist and provide the results of the review to the IRB.

A review of the proposed study has been performed through one of the following mechanisms:

❑ The proposal has been reviewed by a peer group through a funding agency. Identify agency (e.g., NIH, NSF, DOE):   (NOTE: Attach any documentation stemming from the agency review; however, the Scientific Validity Review Checklist is not required)

❑ The proposal has been reviewed through an internal review process (e.g. CURI grant, Ag Experiment Station) and any documentation stemming from this review (including the Scientific Validity Review Checklist) is attached to this application.

❑ The proposal is for thesis or dissertation research (Plan A). It has been reviewed and has received approval from the student's committee. Documentation of this approval (cover sheet signed by committee) and any documentation stemming from this review (including the Scientific Validity Review Checklist) are attached to this application.

❑ The proposal is a Plan B or Plan C project. It has been reviewed and has received approval from the student's committee (minimum of 3 faculty members). Documentation of this approval (cover sheet signed by committee) and any documentation stemming from this review (including the Scientific Validity Review Checklist) are attached to this application. **(Note:** Not all Plan B or Plan C projects go through a committee approval process—please note that documentation of committee approval MUST be included for this box to be checked).

❑ The proposal has not yet been reviewed

If none of the reviews outlined above has been performed, the IRB will appoint one of its members or a qualified consultant to conduct a review, using the Scientific Validity Review Checklist.

STUDY BACKGROUND

What is the purpose of this research (provide a concise statement of 2–3 sentences):

Provide a description of procedures already being performed on the participants for non-research purposes, that may be related to this study: *(Type N/A if not applicable)*

List the research question(s) for this study (do not include your rationale for why you have chosen your research questions):

Is this a multi-center study (e.g. research being conducted at two or more separate universities or research being conducted in partnership with community agencies)? **Yes** ❐   **No** ❐

- If yes, list other participating institutions/agencies and explain the responsibilities and obligations of each center and/or each investigator:
- If yes, has this study been, or will it be reviewed by another IRB? **Yes** ❐   **No** ❐

Was the research approved by the participating IRB? **Yes** ❐   **No** ❐

- If yes, give contact information (name, address and telephone) for the participating IRB:
- If compensation (e.g., money, gift cards) or incentives (e.g., extra class credit) are offered to participants, provide a description of the amount of money and schedule of payments or type of incentive.   *(Type N/A if not applicable)*

PARTICIPANT INFORMATION

Explain who the human participants will be (if only males or only females are to be used, include the rationale):

Estimated number of participants involved: Male__Female__Total__

Provide justification for your sample size:

Number of participants must be sufficient to appropriately answer the research question(s). Small scale designs are acceptable if such designs adequately answer the research question(s).

Age range of participants:

Explain how participants will be recruited:

Will recruitment materials be used? **Yes** ❐   **No** ❐

(Click Here to access IRB Advertising Guidelines)

Explain what participants will be asked to do as part of your research (survey, interview, treadmill test, blood test, assessments, etc.). Provide a step by step explanation of the study procedures:

How long will participants be involved in this research (e.g., one session, multiple sessions, minutes, hours, days, etc.):

What is the proposed duration of this study:

Provide a description of the setting in which the research will be conducted:

Provide a description of provisions to protect the privacy interests of participants. (Privacy interests refer to how much a participant has control over the extent, timing, and circumstances of sharing oneself (physically, behaviorally, or intellectually) with others).

INCLUSION/EXCLUSION CRITERIA

Note: Federal guidelines indicate that participants cannot be excluded from research on the basis of race, gender, age, language, or disability status.

List the inclusion criteria for participants:

List the exclusion criteria for participants:

Does this study involve participants (or parents, guardians, or wards) who are not fluent in English? **Yes** ❐ **No** ❐ *If yes, please submit both the English consent form and translation in the appropriate language(s). Participants (or parents, guardians, or wards) who do not read and/or speak English must have the consent form written and/or read to them in their native language. They must sign a form indicating that the informed consent has been explained to them in their native language, and all questions have been answered. Participants may not be excluded from research based solely on language ability.*

Will the researcher be asking about individuals *other than those from whom informed consent has been received?* **Yes** ❐ **No** ❐

If yes, explain:

If yes, can these people be identified? **Yes** ❐ **No** ❐

VULNERABILITY OF PARTICIPANTS

Participants who are vulnerable are often included in research even though they are in protected categories. If you answer yes to any of the items below, explain your rationale for selecting vulnerable participants. If you check yes, indicate if the use of such participants is a necessary *part of the research or if such participants are included* incidentally *as members of a more general population.*

Are participants younger than 18 years of age? **Yes** ❐ **No** ❐
If yes, is this necessary ❐ or incidental ❐ ?
If necessary, explain:

Are participants older than 65 years of age? **Yes** ❐ **No** ❐
If yes, is this necessary ❐ or incidental ❐ ?
If necessary, explain:

Are participants cognitively impaired? **Yes** ❐ **No** ❐
If yes, is this necessary ❐ or incidental ❐ ?
If necessary, explain:

Do participants have a known physical or mental illness or condition that impairs their ability to consent? **Yes** ❐ **No** ❐

If yes, is this necessary ❐ or incidental ❐ ?
If necessary, explain:

Are participants potentially pregnant *(most females over age 10 and under age 55 are potentially pregnant)?* **Yes** ❐   **No** ❐
If yes, is this necessary ❐ or incidental ❐ ?
If necessary, explain:

Are participants prisoners? **Yes** ❐   **No** ❐
If yes, is this necessary ❐ or incidental ❐ ?
If necessary, explain:

Are participants institutionalized or adjudicated *(in prison, hospital, or other residential setting)?* **Yes** ❐   **No** ❐
If yes, is this necessary ❐ or incidental ❐ ?
If necessary, explain:

Are participants at risk for coercion *(e.g. students in your class, employees, etc.)?* **Yes** ❐   **No** ❐
If yes, is this necessary ❐ or incidental ❐ ?
If yes, explain how you will minimize the perception of coercion:

COERCION GUIDELINES

If you answered 'yes' to any of the above questions, describe additional safeguards for vulnerable population(s), (e.g., children, prisoners, pregnant women, mentally disabled, economically or educationally disadvantaged) and demonstrate to the IRB that risks have been minimized to protect the rights and welfare of participants, (e.g., a process for obtaining informed consent and a monitoring process, a data safety monitoring plan). This description will become an attachment to the application. If your research is found to pose greater than minimal risk to participants, then you may be asked to provide a data safety monitoring plan that explains how you will monitor and facilitate the reduction of risk. See SOP, Chapter 10, page 67 (b.15)

Risks and Benefits (Both risks and benefits must be addressed)

The IRB takes the position that research involving participants is unethical if the research has no educational or scientific value. All research has some risk, even if it is minimal. Risks may include loss of confidentiality, anonymity, economic, social, or psychological or physical harm. Address all risks and benefits below:

What are the potential benefits to be gained from this study:

What are the risks or discomforts to the participant(s) (e.g., loss of confidentiality, anonymity, economic, social, psychological or physical harm):

What measures will be taken to minimize the risks:

What decision rules (e.g., stopping rules) will be considered;

How will unexpected harms be detected promptly?

If the research involves more than minimal risk to participants, provide a description of the provisions for monitoring the data collected to ensure the safety of participants (Data and safety monitoring plan, e.g., propose a plan that will provide ongoing review of data as it is collected and of participant profiles as they are enrolled to identify unexpected outcomes and to ensure participant safety. See IRB Handbook, Chapter 6, page 25).

Informed Consent (Informed Consent Checklist)

Informed Consent Template

How will the informed consent be obtained (e.g., verbally for phone interview, via use of video tape, in person or via letter sent to home, etc.):

Who will obtain the informed consent (e.g., PI, research assistant, teacher, counselor, parent):

Who will provide consent or permission (e.g., participant, parent(s), or legally authorized representative):

What is the waiting time, if any, between informing the prospective participant about the study and obtaining consent:

What steps will be taken to minimize the possibility of coercion or undue influence regardless of whether participants have been identified as being vulnerable to coercion or undue influence:

What procedures are in place other than the translation of the consent document to allow research staff to communicate with non-English speaking participants in a language the participants can understand:

Are you requesting a waiver or alteration to the informed consent process or to the documentation of the informed consent? Refer to the IRB Investigator's Guide: 'Waiver of Informed Consent' or 'Waiver of Documentation.' **Yes** ☐ **No** ☐

Confidentiality

Participants are identifiable when:

- *The researcher or colleague maintains a coded list that could be used to match names and codes.*
- *Addresses or social security numbers or birth dates or other relatively specific information is collected.*
- *Please realize that in a state, unit, or area with a small population it is often very easy to identify participants from data sets with relatively small sample sizes.*

Will the research participants be identifiable to the researchers?
Yes ❐   **No** ❐
If yes, how long will identifying information be kept:
What measures will be taken to protect participants' confidentiality:
How will data be stored (e.g., locked file cabinet in locked room, secured computer, etc.)
Who will have access to the data:
Will electronic records be made (e.g. audiotapes, video tapes / DVDs, photographs, etc.) **Yes** ❐   **No** ❐   *(If yes, this information must be included in the informed consent)*
 • If yes, specify:
 • If yes, what measures will be taken to ensure confidentiality of these records:
 • If yes, when will these records be destroyed *(If yes, destruction of information must be included in the informed consent)*:

Reporting
Is it possible you will discover a participant's previous unknown condition (e.g., disease, suicidal thoughts, etc.) as a result of the study procedures? **Yes** ❐   **No** ❐
If yes, explain how you will deal with this:
Is it possible you will discover a participant engaging in illegal activities (e.g., child abuse, use of illegal drugs)? **Yes** ❐   **No** ❐
If yes, explain how you will deal with this:

Deception (Deception Research Checklist)
Does this project involve giving false or misleading information to participants or withholding information from them such that their "informed" consent is in question? **Yes** ❐   **No** ❐
If deception is being used, attach a copy of the debriefing/disclosure statement (to be read to the participant(s)) to this application

Health Records—(HIPAA Checklist) (Additional Reading)
Will any of the data you collect/record consist of existing health records (e.g., medical case notes, evaluations, etc.): **Yes** ❐   **No** ❐
 If yes:
 • Are there any personal identifiers on the data (e.g., names, birth dates, social security numbers, medical chart numbers, etc.)
   Yes ❐   **No** ❐
 • Will participants authorize use of data as part of the informed consent process for this study to authorize use of these data?
   Yes ❐   **No** ❐

Biological Specimens (Tissue Banking)

Will the research involve the collection of biological specimens (e.g., blood, saliva, urine, skin cells, etc.)? **Yes** ❐   **No** ❐

If yes, will these specimens be stored in some manner? **Yes** ❐   **No** ❐

If stored, explain where they will be stored and how long they will be kept:

Conflict of Interest (Definition)

The following conflict of interest section pertains to the Principal Investigator and all other key personnel involved with this project. The term 'you' in these questions refers to the respondent or any member of the respondent's first degree relatives (spouse, children, parents, siblings, or in-laws).

Do you have a significant financial interest in or serve as a director or officer in a commercial organization:

- that could be involved in this study? **Yes** ❐   **No** ❐   If Yes, explain:
- whose business is substantially related to subject matter of this study? **Yes** ❐   **No** ❐   If Yes, explain:
- which has requested rights to USU/USURF intellectual property? **Yes** ❐   **No** ❐   If Yes, explain:

Do you plan to use University facilities or personnel in the conduct of work for your outside interest that will be related to this study? **Yes** ❐   **No** ❐   If Yes, explain:

Have you or do you expect to receive gifts of $100 or more from a commercial entity that is connected to this study? **Yes** ❐   **No** ❐ If Yes, explain:

Do you supervise any students or other personnel who will be working on this study and who also work for your outside interest? **Yes** ❐   **No** ❐ If Yes, explain:

Is this study related to subject matter in which you are aware that another sponsor or entity has a claim to ownership or any rights granted by USU/USURF? **Yes** ❐   **No** ❐   If Yes, explain:

"Significant Financial Interest" (SFI) means anything of monetary value, including but not limited to, salary or other payments for services (e.g., consulting fees or honoraria); equity interests (e.g., stocks, stock options or other ownership interests); and intellectual property rights (e.g., patents, copyrights and royalties from such rights).

THE TERM SFI DOES NOT INCLUDE:

- salary, royalties, or other remuneration **from the institution** (Note: royalties paid to an investigator on behalf of Utah State University are not considered reportable SFIs);
- income from seminars, lectures, or teaching engagements sponsored by public or nonprofit entities;
- income from service on advisory committees or review panels for public or nonprofit entities; or
- an equity interest that when aggregated for you meets both the following tests: is less than $10,000 in value as determined through reference to public prices or other reasonable measures of fair market value, and is less than a five percent ownership interest in any single entity; or
- salary, royalties or other payments that when aggregated for you over the next 12 months are not expected to exceed $10,000.

If any answer to the above questions is 'yes' or if you have existing conflicts of interest in relation to previously awarded projects that have not been resolved through the Office of Compliance Assistance, you should contact the Federal Compliance Manager at (435) 797–8305.

Investigator's Assurance

As Principal Investigator, I have ultimate responsibility for the performance of this study, the protection of the rights and welfare of the human subjects, and strict adherence by all co-investigators and research personnel to all Institutional Review Board (IRB) requirements, federal regulations, and state statutes for human subjects research. I hereby assure the following:

- The information provided in this application is accurate to the best of my knowledge.
- All named individuals on this project have read and understand the procedures outlined in the application.
- All experiments and procedures involving human subjects will be performed under my supervision or that of another qualified professional listed on this protocol.

I understand that, should I use the project described in this application as a basis for a proposal for research funding (either intramural or extramural), it is my responsibility to ensure that the description of human research used in the funding proposal(s) is identical in principle to that contained in this application. I will submit modifications and/or changes to the IRB as necessary.

- I and all the co-investigators and research personnel agree to comply with all applicable requirements for the protection of human subjects in research including but not limited to, the following:
  - ◆ Making no changes to the approved protocol without first having submitted those changes for review and approval by the Institutional Review Board; and
  - ◆ Promptly providing the IRB with any information requested relative to the project; and;
  - ◆ Promptly reporting the premature completion of a study;
  - ◆ Promptly and completely complying with an IRB decision to suspend or withdraw its approval for the project; and
  - ◆ Obtaining continuing review prior approval to the expiration of approval.

I understand if I fail to apply for continuing review, approval for the study will automatically expire, and study activity must cease until current IRB approval is obtained.

I understand that the report of an unanticipated problem may require me to inform participants.

I assume responsibility for ensuring the competence, integrity and ethical conduct of the student researcher(s). I certify that any student researcher(s) is/are fully competent to accomplish the goals and techniques stated in the attached proposal, and that all researchers (faculty and student) have a current IRB certification.

As PI, I have read and accept the Investigator's Assurance   *(Type initials in box)*

Are you Ready to Submit Your Application?

Your application MUST be accompanied by the supporting documents (listed below) at the time of submission or the application will be returned to you as "not reviewable":

- Proposal, if available (e.g., thesis, dissertation, grant) OR a summary of the methods and objectives (Your proposal and IRB application must be congruent. Do not cut/paste information from your proposal into the IRB application form.)

- Data collection forms / instruments / measures (see Section C, #5, Participant Information)

- Draft Informed Consent / Letter of Information (see Section G, Informed Consent) (see Section D, Inclusion/Exclusion Criteria). Format the informed consent using our template

- Recruitment materials (fliers, advertisements)—applicable?
  Yes ❒ **No** ❒   If yes, attach recruitment materials to your application (see Section C, #4, Participant Information)

- Description of the additional safeguards to protect vulnerable participants' rights and welfare—applicable?
  Yes ❒ **No** ❒   If yes, attach description to your application (see Section E, Vulnerability of Participants)

- Data and safety monitoring plan—applicable?
  Yes ❒ **No** ❒   (see Section F, #4, Risks and Benefits)

- Signed committee approval page—applicable?
  Yes ❒ **No** ❒   If yes, mailed or delivered to the IRB?
  Yes ❒ **No** ❒

- Approval letter(s) from participating IRB(s)—applicable?
  Yes ❒ **No** ❒   (see Section B, #4, Study Background) If yes, letters mailed or delivered to USU IRB?
  Yes ❒ **No** ❒

- Debriefing/disclosure statement (deception research)—applicable?
  Yes ❒ **No** ❒   If yes, mailed or delivered to the IRB?
  Yes ❒ **No** ❒   (see Section J, #1, Deception)

- Scientific Validity Review Checklist—applicable?
  Yes ❒ **No** ❒   (see Section A, Scientific Validity)

Once the application is complete, email all components (this application and the above supporting documents) to the IRB by clicking here

Institutional Review Board
9530 Old Main Hill
Logan, UT 84322

NOTE

1.   While readers may feel that issues of research integrity are in the past, we are not that distant from instances of scientific misconduct, as was exemplified in the Tuskegee case in which participants in an experiment were uninformed, to their own detriment, of the failure of the National Cancer Institute to link tobacco smoking to cancer in the 1950s; or the scenario described in Rebecca Skloot's 2010 *The Immortal Life of Henrietta Lacks*. Being an educated citizen—not just a researcher—means being informed about responsible conduct of research.

REFERENCES AND FOR FURTHER READING

Anderson, Paul V. 1998. "Simple Gifts: Ethical Issues in the Conduct of Person-Based Composition Research." *College Composition and Communication* 49 (1): 63–89. http://dx.doi.org/10.2307/358560.

American Psychological Association. 2001. *Publication Manual of the American Psychological Association.* 5th ed. Washington, DC: American Psychological Association.

Association of Internet Researchers (AoIR). 2012. *Ethical Decision-Making and Internet Research.* Version 2.0. http://aoir.org/reports/ethics2.pdf.

CCCC. 2003. "Guidelines for the Ethical Conduct of Research in Composition Studies." Conference on College Composition and Communication. Revised March 2015. http://www.ncte.org/cccc/resources/positions/ethicalconduct.

Eynon, Rebecca, Jenny Fry, and Ralph Schroeder. 2008. "The Ethics of Internet Research." In *The SAGE Handbook of Online Research Methods,* edited by Nigel G. Fielding and Raymond M. Lee, 23–41. San Francisco: SAGE. http://dx.doi.org/10.4135/9780857020055.n2.

Grobman, Laurie. 2015. "(Re)Writing Local Racial, Ethnic, and Cultural Histories: Negotiating Shared Meaning in Public Rhetoric Partnerships." *College English* 77 (3): 236–58.

Lillywhite, Kristin M. 2011. "Developing Cognitive Academic Language Proficiency (CALP) in Diverse Classrooms." Honors thesis, Utah State University.

McKee, Heidi A., and Danielle Nicole DeVoss. 2007. *Digital Writing Research: Technologies, Methodologies, and Ethical Issues.* Cresskill, NJ: Hampton.

McKee, Heidi A., and James E. Porter. 2008. "The Ethics of Digital Writing Research." *College Composition and Communication* 59 (4): 711–49.

McKee, Heidi A., and James E. Porter. 2009. *The Ethics of Internet Research: A Rhetorical, Case-Based Process.* New York: Peter Lang.

National Academy of Sciences, National Academy of Engineering, and Institute of Medicine. 2009. *On Being a Scientist: A Guide to Responsible Conduct of Research.* 3rd ed. Washington, DC: National Academies Press.

Office of Research Integrity. n.d. "Responsible Conduct of Research." US Department of Health and Human Services. http://ori.hhs.gov/education/.

Skloot, Rebecca. 2010. *The Immortal Life of Henrietta Lacks.* New York: Crown.

Steneck, Nicholas. 2007. "Introduction to the Responsible Conduct of Research." Office of Research Integrity. US Department of Health and Human Services. http://ori.hhs.gov/education/products/RCRintro/.

Temple, Louise, Thomas Q. Sibley, and Amy J. Orr. 2010. *How to Mentor Undergraduate Researchers.* Washington, DC: Council on Undergraduate Research.

Traywick, Deaver. 2010. "Preaching What We Practice: RCR Instruction for Undergraduate Researchers in Writing Studies." In *Undergraduate Research in English Studies,* edited by Laurie Grobman and Joyce Kinkead, 51–73. Urbana, IL: NCTE.

4

Sharing Research through Oral Presentation, Poster Presentation, and Publication

Research is not completed until it is shared. The most common forms of sharing are oral presentation, poster, and publication. For the humanities, oral presentations usually mean a paper is read, while the social sciences tend to prefer a PowerPoint-style presentation or a poster. Those traditions are changing though, and professional conferences in writing are seeing the introduction of poster sessions. What is important—no matter the medium of dissemination—is that the research is communicated clearly to the audience. A handout for audience members helps a "read" paper, particularly if there are sections of the paper that are complex or dense. Likewise, if some concepts or aspects of the subject are unfamiliar to a large part of the audience, it's helpful to explain. For instance, a student presenting a paper on Francophone Africa would be well advised to include a map that delineates those countries.

WebGURU[1]—a website that offers a Guide to Undergraduate Research—includes extremely helpful advice for disseminating research. The following is an adaptation of that advice, modified to suit the context of writing studies.

ORAL PRESENTATIONS

Delivering an effective talk requires preparation and practice to ensure that the research is communicated well to the audience. The advice that follows assumes an illustrated talk, using PowerPoint or another product. Be aware that "death by PowerPoint" is an issue for audiences who have been saturated with dull presentations populated with clip art or text-heavy slides.

Visual Aids

Use a landscape (horizontal) rather than a portrait (vertical) layout when preparing visual aids. Portrait-formatted slides when projected have a greater likelihood of being obscured either at the top or the bottom of the slide than do landscape-formatted slides. In addition, the comparatively larger width of the landscape-formatted slide allows for better use and display of information.

When creating your presentation aids, use light text on a dark background, as this is easy to read and also easy on the eyes. Avoid using colorful backgrounds with words or complicated patterns or pictures on them. Plain single-color backgrounds are the most effective.

Use an appropriate font size on your slides for the room in which you will present. Note that this means you will need to do some homework in advance. The minimum type size you should use for any text on a slide is eighteen-point font, although larger may be advisable.

A mixture of upper- and lowercase text is easier to read than text printed in all uppercase.

Make good use of graphics when preparing slides. Audience retention is about 20 percent when a speaker uses words alone but rises to 70 percent when text is supplemented with graphics. If you do use graphics, avoid the use of tired clip art. Graphics should not distract the audience from your content. Use medium-quality graphics whenever possible. If you must use animation, use it sparingly and only if it will help the audience understand and appreciate your work better.

When preparing and using graphs and/or tables for a presentation

- always label your axes and include the units;
- use standard graph and/or table formats; the purpose of graphic aids should be to uncover the data, not to obscure it;
- avoid the use of insets if at all possible;
- construct and use tables only when you are displaying ten or fewer numbers.

Organize your information. Arrange your information in bite-size chunks. A good guideline for slide content is the 6x6 rule. Use no more than six words per line and six lines per slide.

Pace your slide presentation. On average, plan to show a new slide every thirty to forty-five seconds.

KISS. "Keep it simple, stupid." Plan to introduce a maximum of one new idea per slide. Provide only enough detail to convey your message.

Title your slides. Title your slides succinctly, specifically, and clearly with the slide's purpose. For example, a poor title might be "Results." A more effective title serving both you and your audience's need for information might be "Classroom Evidence for Effective Peer-Response Groups." The title reminds you of what it is that you want to say, and it conveys to the audience the significance of the information shown on the slide.

Proofread visual aids. Typos, misspellings, and the like rob you of your authority as a speaker. This is especially true for presentations that focus on writing. If the author doesn't seem to know the difference between *its/it's*, credibility may go in the trash bin.

Prepare a final slide. End with a slide that says "Questions? Comments?" or something that offers a visual. Never end the presentation with a blank slide, as it hurts the audience's eyes. There should be something on the screen while you are fielding questions.

Brand visual aids. Most institutions have wordmarks used in presentations. Some colleges and universities may even supply researchers with templates for visual aids. Your institution will wish to be associated with a good presentation, so do use the appropriate wordmark. Likewise, if the project received funding—intramural or extramural—be sure to credit that support with the appropriate icons or wordmarks. The introductory slide may also be branded with the logo of the conference at which the presentation is being made—along with the date of the presentation.

Public Speaking

Identify your audience and speaking environment. What is their education? Interests? Are they generalists or specialists—what does your audience likely already know about your topic? Is this a formal presentation? Is a one-way or interactive style of presentation expected?

KISS. "Keep it simple, stupid." Prioritize your presentation—what message is it that you want to convey to your audience? Make sure this message is the focus of your presentation. Avoid the use of acronyms and technical jargon whenever possible. Acronyms can be very divisive. When your audience isn't familiar with the terminology, and too many acronyms are introduced, the audience may become lost and even hostile.

Follow the T3 rule. Tell the audience what you are going to tell them. Tell them. Tell them what you told them. This means you should provide an outline of your talk to your audience, deliver the actual content, and then summarize the key points.

Don't read your slides. If you find that you are, this means your slides aren't correctly designed. The text on the slide should act as a visual prompt for the speaker in terms of the information they intend to convey orally.

Practice your talk in advance several times. Practice makes perfect. Make sure you stay within your allotted time.

Dress appropriately and comfortably. Find out in advance if formal clothing (business attire) is expected, and dress appropriately. Why does how you dress matter? Networking is important in anyone's career, and there can be in the audience people who can be helpful.

Arrive early. Make sure that you are comfortable with room layout and the A/V equipment before your presentation. If you are using technology, be sure to bring backup visual aids, such as a set of transparencies, with you. If you are using a laptop for your presentation, make sure it is compatible with the projector. An important consideration is the display resolution of the laptop and of the projector. If you are using a PC computer, don't attempt to switch at the last minute to a Mac or vice versa. Have multiple ways to access your presentation: on a memory stick, from an Internet site, or emailed as an attachment. These backup procedures will be helpful if disaster strikes. If handouts are to be shared, estimate the number of copies needed as closely as possible, as those without handouts will feel neglected.

Be enthusiastic. Deliver your speech with animation in your voice. Face the audience. Make eye contact with them. Speak loudly, clearly, and slowly so everyone in the audience can hear and understand what you are saying. "Punch" important words or concepts to ensure you are communicating well.

Take charge. If you feel uncomfortable fielding questions during your presentation, be sure to make your feelings known to the audience up front, and if you are interrupted, don't be afraid to defer the question until the end of your presentation. You might do this by saying at the beginning "I'll answer questions at the end of the talk" or "If you have a question while I'm speaking, please do ask." Make sure the audience members can hear you and even query them, "Can everyone hear?"

Don't attempt to use humor in your presentation if you aren't funny. While a funny hook—like a cartoon—can engage an audience, use humor with care, which is particularly important for novices who are trying to establish that they are serious about their research.

Make judicious use of the laser pointer. If you use one, turn it on and point to the specific text or graphic element you wish to highlight, then turn it off. Try not to swing the laser pointer all over each and every slide, and be careful not to point it into the audience.

End your presentation on time. This is particularly important to the other speakers on a panel, as it exemplifies professional courtesy. Some conferences schedule each speaker for a specific time so audience members may attend for a particular topic and then move to another session. (On the other hand, panel members should never enter their session late or depart their session early.)

Anticipate questions. Believe it or not, you really can anticipate the questions most folks will ask, and if you take the time to do this and to prepare, then fielding questions becomes a piece of cake! To anticipate questions, think about who your audience is and what their interests are likely to be related to the subject of your talk. Once you have done this, write down every question that comes to mind. These are likely to be the questions your audience will ask. Consult your advisor, other members of your research group, or friends. When you do a dry-run practice session with your advisor or others, ask them to pose questions. Once you have created this list, prepare an answer for every question and practice delivering the answers until you are confident. Keep in mind that you have expertise about this content.

Listen to every question. This is perhaps the most frequent mistake speakers make. They don't listen to the question being asked, so it makes sense that they have a tough time answering the question. A good technique to adopt that will help you to listen is to plan to restate the questioner's question out loud before you answer. This technique is also useful in that it provides the speaker with time to frame an answer, and it ensures that the speaker is truly answering the question actually asked.

- **What do you do as a speaker if you didn't hear the question?** Simply ask the questioner to repeat the question. Frequently, the speaker isn't the only person who couldn't hear it.
- **What do you do as a speaker if you didn't understand the question being asked?** State that you aren't sure you understood the question and ask the questioner to rephrase the question.
- **What do you do as a speaker if you don't know the answer?** Simply state that you don't know it. No one knows everything. One option is to turn to the audience and ask for their input. Another option is to thank the questioner and note that you intend to follow up postconference.

Treat every questioner respectfully. Compliment a good question. Think about how you answer every question before you answer it. Be careful not to embarrass your questioner if they ask a question that might seem stupid to you. Always treat them with dignity and respect even if they speak disrespectfully to you. Don't attack hostile questioners. Do challenge inappropriate questions, but don't get personal.

Remain in the session until all presenters have concluded. The presenter is responsible not only for making a presentation but also for being a participant through the entire session. Help other presenters by asking them questions.

Tips on How to Use a Laser Pointer

Test the pointer in advance to ensure its batteries are good. A laser pointer is most effective when it is used intermittently in a presentation as a visual aid to highlight key points or to assist the audience in visually identifying specific content on a table, graph, or figure on a slide. The laser pointer loses its value when speakers use it constantly. Depress the button and simply point the beam at the text or visual element you wish to highlight. Do not wave the laser pointer around in circles, and make sure the pointer is never directed at the audience. Also, constant activation of the laser pointer will betray a nervous speaker. Holding the laser pointer with both hands when you activate it can help. Finally, intermittent activation will also conserve the batteries so the laser pointer will work when you need it.

Evaluating an Oral Presentation

Judging takes place at many events in which research is shared. Knowing the rubric judges use can be helpful in preparing (see Figs. 4.1a and b)

POSTER PRESENTATIONS

The poster is an extremely powerful form of communication. It has been a mainstay at professional conferences in the sciences and often in the social sciences but is more rare at writing conferences.

Poster presentations have several advantages over oral presentations. Poster sessions often allow for one to two hours of discussion with interested visitors. In addition, at most meetings multiple oral sessions are scheduled to run simultaneously in small rooms, allowing for a limited audience.

Poster sessions often take place in large rooms and accommodate hundreds of presenters. Posters are mounted on display boards in the room, sometimes on triangular displays so three posters share space; at other times the display boards may be back to back. Consequently, there is potentially greater exposure of your work, but visitors must be attracted to the poster in order for that to occur. As a result, the preparation of the poster is important and involves communicating the results of the work both in content and appearance. (At professional conferences, poster sessions may be coupled with a social reception at the end of the day, and these sessions may take on heightened conviviality.)

Preparation

Sometimes people have the mistaken impression that creating a poster involves less work than developing an oral presentation. Both involve a lot of advance planning, and neither can be done well when the effort is initiated at the last minute. This is especially true for poster presentations, which must include time for printing.

2011 Undergraduate Research Festival Presentation Rubric

RESEARCH DESIGN

Introduction of Research				
No introduction given.	Introduction present, but not clear or informative.	Introduction provided basic information about research design.	Introduction was informative and insightful.	Introduction provided unique insight and exceptional clarity.

Statement of Hypothesis/Research Question				
No hypothesis/RQ given or hypothesis/RQ exceptionally weak.	Hypothesis/RQ given, but not clear or well constructed.	Hypothesis/RQ clearly presented and well constructed.	Hypothesis/RQ offered insight into the rationale for the project.	Student argued that hypothesis/RQ addresses a pressing question in his/her field.

Goals and Objectives				
Goals and objectives not presented or of poor quality.	Goals and objectives presented, but not clearly explained.	Goals and objectives clearly and thoughtfully presented.	Goals and objectives provided an excellent overview of the project.	Student presented goals and objectives as a way to fill a unique gap in his/her field.

Explanation of Methodology				
Methodology not or poorly explained.	Methodology explained, but seem inadequate for study goals/purpose.	Methodology adequate and clearly explained.	Methodology clearly connected to hypothesis/RQ and study's goals.	Methodology shows evidence of exceptional insight and meticulous investigation.

Presentation of Results and Conclusions				
Results and conclusions not presented.	Results and conclusions presented, but unclear.	Results and conclusions clearly presented.	Results and conclusions illustrated insight and achievement.	Student emphasized the impact of results and conclusions on his/her field.

Understanding of The Problem or Challenged Addressed				
Student's presentation did not illustrate student understanding.	Student's presentation illustrated minimal understanding.	Student's presentation illustrated clear understanding.	Student's presentation illustrated unique understanding.	Student's presentation illustrated exceptional understanding.

Use of Literature in The Field				
Student relied on little or no literature.	Student's references to literature did not illustrate understanding.	Student referenced literature that illustrated knowledge of the field.	Student's references to literature illustrated insight into the field.	Student referenced an exceptional depth and breath of literature.

FIGURE 4.1A. Rubric for posters from Abilene Christian University.

Content

A poster is a visual presentation of research. The significance of the research must be clear. Consequently, your focus should be on making sure the information presented on the board reflects the quality of your work.

PRESENTATION AND PERSUASIVENESS

Organization and Preparation				
Student's presentation was obviously unorganized and unprepared.	Student's presentation lacked sufficient organization and preparation.	Student's presentation was prepared and well organized.	Student's presentation showed evidence of practice and flowed well.	Student's presentation was poised, confident, and exceptionally organized.

Use of Visual Aids				
No visual aid.	Visual aid was unclear, cluttered, distracting, and/or grammatically incorrect.	Visual aid was free of errors and informative.	Visual aid added clarity to presentation and illustrated insight of topic.	Visual aid enhanced audience understanding and was smoothly integrated into the presentation.

Use of Voice for Maximum Effect				
Student's voice distracted from his/her presentation.	Student's voice was not distracting, but did not add to his/her presentation.	Student's voice added clarity and interest to his/her presentation.	Student's voice helped capture the audience's attention.	Student's voice conveyed poise and communicated appropriate enthusiasm.

Use of Gestures, Movement, and Facial Expression for Emphasis				
Student's movement and expressions distracted from his/her presentation.	Student's movement and expressions were not distracting, but did not add to his/her presentation.	Student's movement and expressions added clarity to his/her presentation.	Student's movement and expressions emphasized key ideas in his/her presentation.	Student's movement and expressions conveyed poise and appropriate enthusiasm.

Use of Eye Contact				
Student did not maintain eye contact with the audience for a majority of his/her presentation.	Student maintained eye contact with the audience for a portion of his/her presentation.	Student maintained eye contact with the audience throughout his/her presentation.	Student's eye contact enhanced his/her presentation.	Student's eye contact established a meaningful connection with the audience.

Answers to Audience's Questions				
Speaker was not able to address any of the audience's questions.	Speaker was able to address some of the audience's questions.	Speaker was able to address most of the audience's questions.	Speaker's answers added to and extended topics discussed in his/her presentation.	Speaker's answers showed exceptional insight into his/her field.

Explanation of the Project's Significance				
Speaker did not explain his/her project's significance.	Speaker persuaded the audience his/her project was important, but not significantly so.	Speaker argued that his/her project was significant.	Speaker effectively persuaded the audience that his/her project fulfilled a need.	Speaker effectively persuaded the audience of the crucial significance of his/her project.

FIGURE 4.1B. Rubric for posters from Abilene Christian University.

Although the size of a poster may vary somewhat, in general, poster boards tend to be four feet high by six feet long. Some are three feet high and four feet long. Be sure to check with the conference organizers (website), as the size may be specified. Since there is variation in poster dimensions, be sure to find out in advance what the dimensions of your poster board will be, as this will determine what/how much information you can put on your poster. Also find out whether the poster is to be in landscape or portrait format.

The title of your presentation and the names of all the authors and their institutional affiliations should appear at the top center of your

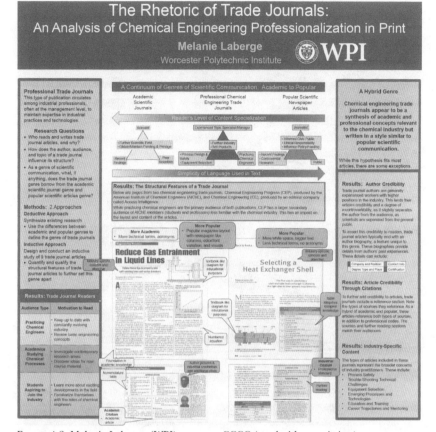

FIGURE 4.2. Melanie Laberge (WPI) poster at CCCC (used with permission).

poster. Use a font size that produces lettering at least one and one-half inches high so interested attendees can quickly identify the subject of your poster.

Guidelines

Most posters use the same general format: title, authors and institutional affiliations, abstract, introduction, methods, results, conclusions, acknowledgments, and references. We will discuss the needed content for each of these sections briefly below:

- The title should effectively highlight the subject of your research in ten words or less.
- The list of authors and institutional affiliations includes the names of all those who have contributed to the project in a significant

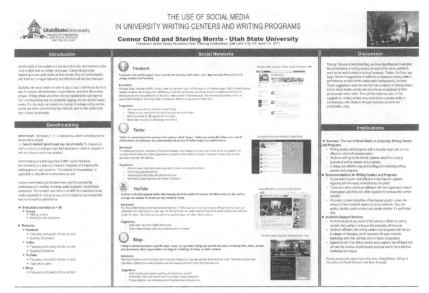

FIGURE 4.3. Poster on the use of social media in writing centers.

way. Be sure to consult your advisor to assure your list is complete. Authorship has serious implications with regard to intellectual property issues and research integrity. For multiple authors, identify the department and institution for each.

- The abstract is a succinct summary, usually 150 words or less, that identifies the research problem studied, the methods used, the results obtained, and the significance of those results.

- The introduction should provide a brief overview of the reasons the research was initiated and provide a background on the materials and methods used in the study.

- In the methods section, the experimental methods used to accomplish the research should be succinctly outlined.

- The results section should outline the results of your work. Since posters are a visual method of presentation, the bulk of this section should be graphic rather than textual.

- The conclusion should provide a succinct summary of the conclusions you have derived from your work as well as a statement of the direction of any future work, if relevant and appropriate.

- The acknowledgments should credit all of those individuals who have provided assistance to you in accomplishing your work. First and foremost, be sure to credit any funding sources that may have underwritten your research. This is particularly important if a federal agency or foundation provided funding for your project. As

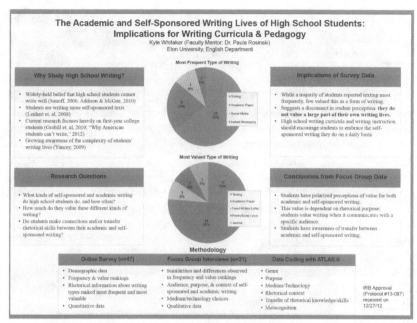

FIGURE 4.4. "The Academic and Self-Sponsored Writing Lives of High School Students," a CCCC 2013 poster.

always, it is best to check with your advisor in order to identify all of the appropriate individuals and/or agencies.

- Since research isn't accomplished in a vacuum, you will need to credit the relevant work of others in one or more sections of your poster. Include a citation for each and every source. Since the format for references differs from discipline to discipline, be sure to consult your advisor concerning the preferred format for citations. This format may also vary depending on the professional organization hosting the conference.

Layout

Historically, posters were composed of a series of 8½" × 11" panels— regular paper in a landscape format—that used sufficiently large font for visitors to read. Hardly anyone uses this approach now, preferring a single large poster printout from a special printer. Posters of this type can be printed at the institution or at local copy shops. They are more expensive to prepare, but their professional appearance cannot be underestimated. Because they are printed, it is doubly important that they are proofread in advance. Mistakes are costly. Protective plastic tubes are used to store and transport posters. (If you are flying to a conference, definitely carry the poster onto the plane rather than checking it to ensure that it arrives with you.)

Lay out your information in a logical pattern on your poster so visitors can readily follow your presentation. Note that there is a normal viewing pattern for posters. Arrange your poster in columns intended to be read from left to right. The poster must be visually attractive. To get the attention of viewers, include one large illustration or photograph that draws them in—from a distance of six feet. A second illustration that is visually arresting helps reel viewers in as they move closer. Graphics, rather than text, should constitute the bulk of the poster, and the text used should contain easy-to-read sentences. Avoid acronyms, excessive text, or complicated figures.

Make sure the poster is readable from a distance of three feet away—this includes lettering and captions on any figures and/or tables. Select a font size that produces lettering at least one-half inch high.

Delivery: Presenting Your Poster

In advance of the meeting prepare a brief (two-to-three-minute) talk about your research, and practice that talk in front of your poster several times. Think of it as the "elevator talk" in which there's only a short amount of time to communicate your message. Ask your advisor, your research group, and/or friends and family to act as audiences for your poster presentation. Make changes to your poster and/or presentation as needed based on the feedback you receive from them.

Identify in advance the location of your poster session and be sure to arrive early (at least thirty minutes) to put up your poster. (If you are relying on conference shuttle buses to get to the venue, be aware that these may not always be on time.)

Although pushpins or Velcro are frequently provided, it is wise to bring your own supply.

Don't be a wallflower. Ask people if they would like to hear about your work and then begin speaking.

Plan to stay by your poster throughout the scheduled poster session. You can check out the other posters presented during your session before the official start of the session—assuming others are like you and prepared in advance. During the session, talk to the presenters of posters close at hand.

Some poster presenters hand out copies of their poster in an 8½" × 11" format. You may do this if any coauthors have agreed and given permission. If visitors express an interest in obtaining a copy of your work, ask for their business cards and/or take down their names, addresses, and/or e-mail addresses so you (and your advisor) can follow up on this contact after the meeting. At the end of the poster session, be sure to remove all of your poster materials, as anything left behind will be thrown out.

Poster Rubric

Rubrics designed to evaluate posters are widespread and vary in design, but for the most part, they follow the organization of this sample that follows.

Posters

Student Name(s):

Please place an X over the description you think most accurately describes the student's performance of each category. (Each row is a new category.)

Research Design

	Poor/Not Addressed	Fair	Good	Great (Rare Rating)	Exceptional (Very Rare Rating)
Introduction of Research	No Introduction	Present but not clear or informative	Provided basic information about research design	Informative and insightful	Provided unique insight and exceptional clarity
Statement of Hypothesis/ Research Question	No Hypothesis/ RQ Given, Or was exceptionally weak	Hypothesis/RQ was not clear or well constructed	Hypothesis/ RQ was clearly presented and well constructed	Hypothesis/ RQ provided insight into the rationale for the project.	Student argued that the hypothesis/ RQ addresses a pressing question in the field
Goals and Objectives	Not presented or of poor quality.	Presented but not clearly explained.	Clearly and thoughtfully presented.	Provided an excellent overview of the project.	Presented in a way to fill a unique gap in the field.
Explanation of Methodology	Not or poorly explained	Explained, but seemed inadequate for the study goals/ purpose	Adequate and clearly explained	Clearly connected to the hypothesis/ research question and study's goals	Showed evidence of exceptional insight and meticulous investigation.
Presentation of Results and Conclusions	Not presented	Presented, but unclear	Clearly Presented	Illustrated insight and achievement	Emphasized the impact of the results on the field.
Understanding of The Problem or Challenge Addressed	Presentation did not illustrate student understanding	Presentation illustrated minimal understanding.	Presentation illustrated clear understanding	Presentation illustrated unique understanding	Presentation illustrated exceptional understanding
Use of Literature in The Field	Relied on little or no literature	References to literature did not illustrate understanding	References to literature that illustrated knowledge of the field	References to literature that illustrated insight into the field	Referenced an exceptional breadth and depth of the field.

Presentation and Persuasiveness

	Poor/Not Addressed	Fair	Good	Great (Rare Rating)	Exceptional (Very Rare Rating)
Overall Poster Design	Disorganized and hard to follow	Adequate organization, but somewhat hard to follow	Well organized	Attractive and the organization added in the understanding of the topic	Poster had a professional appearance
Use of images and text	Images detracted from the message of the poster. Text is unreadable.	Images did not add or detract from the effectiveness. Text is readable but not easily so.	Images added to the understanding of topic. Text is easily readable	Images added clarity and insight to the topic. Text is easily readable and well organized.	Images and the arrangement of text greatly enhanced the understanding of the topic.
Grammar, spelling and style	Gross spelling and grammatical errors, inappropriate writing style for the medium	Some spelling and grammatical errors	Well written with few or no spelling or grammatical errors	Well written, no spelling or grammatical errors. Style increases the understanding of the topic	Exceptionally well written.
Verbal presentation	Did not interact with listener, movements, expression detracted from the presentation.	Movements and expression did not add or take away from the presentation. Interacted poorly with the listener.	Movement and expression added to presentation. Interacted with the listener. Made good eye contact.	Movement and expressions emphasized key points. Interacted well with the listener	Movement and expressions conveyed poise and enthusiasm while explaining the project.
Explanation of the significance of the project	Did not explain significance of the topic	Persuaded the listener that the topic was important, but not significantly so.	Argued that the topic was important significant.	Persuaded the listener that the topic filled a need in the field.	Persuaded the listener of the critical significance of the project.
Answers to Questions	Unable to address questions	Able to partially address some of the questions	Able to address most of the questions	Answers added to and extended the topics discussed	Answers showed exceptional insight into the field.

FIGURE 4.5. Poster rubric.

Student Activity

PRESENTATION: PREPARE A LIGHTNING TALK

Once you have a research project on which to report, consider various forms of presentations. Most research presentations are fifteen to twenty minutes in length. Lightning talks are much shorter, perhaps three to five minutes. Lightning talks are informal (or seem that way) but engaging. Much preparation goes into a good lightning talk. Presenters often line up before the event to move quickly and seamlessly between presentations. The event is fast paced: presenters jump up to the microphone to deliver timed five-minute presentations. Following the series of presentations, all presenters engage in a panel Q&A. Presenters may also ask questions of each other.

The format of the talk is a maximum of twenty slides delivered in no longer than five minutes. Either a PowerPoint or Prezi can be used for presentation. It's important to make the presentation highly visual, using simple graphics and key concepts. In other words, avoid text as much as possible. Practice the lightning talk so it is polished before delivery.

For examples of undergraduate research lightning talks, see this site: http://www.youtube.com/watch?v=G20QjGgZRII.

An alternative to lightning talks is the Ignite initiative. Ignite is called a "fast-paced geek event" (http://www.ignitetalks.io/) in which speakers have five minutes to talk using twenty slides, each slide advancing automatically every fifteen seconds. The first Ignite took place in Seattle in 2006, and since then the event has become an international phenomenon, with gatherings in Helsinki, Finland; Paris, France; New York; and one hundred other locations. More information can be found at Ignite's website: http://www.ignitetalks.io/.

Yet one further option exists for research talks—using the TED format, which is short, powerful talks of eighteen or fewer minutes. TED began in 1984 as a conference where technology, entertainment, and design converged, and today it covers almost all topics—from science to business to global issues—in more than one hundred languages. Some campuses host independently run TEDx events to help share ideas. In such venues, lightning or Ignite talks may be seen as tryouts for TEDx presentations.

Practice sessions for talks benefit from having feedback from a coach. The following form provides criteria to evaluate.

First author, Last Name: _____   Notes

Poster

Content

Introduction/Literature	1	2	3	4	5
Hypotheses/Questions	1	2	3	4	5
Methodology	1	2	3	4	5
Results/Conclusions	1	2	3	4	5

Expression

Organization	1	2	3	4	5
Images & Text	1	2	3	4	5

Presenter(s)

Content

Project knowledge	1	2	3	4	5
Content knowledge	1	2	3	4	5

Expression

Professional presentation	1	2	3	4	5

FIGURE 4.6. Research presentation feedback form source: http://srs.usu.edu/awards-and-judging.

Student Activity

DISSEMINATION: IDENTIFYING CONFERENCE VENUES

Create a list of possible places to present your research. Begin by looking for possibilities at your home institution. Many colleges and universities host events to showcase student research. Some provide mentoring and advice on what makes a good presentation and may even provide feedback on dry runs. This is a great way to try out a presentation. Once the presentation is polished, it may be taken on the road to state or regional student-research conferences or to discipline-specific conferences. Graduate students will lean to the latter. A list of venues for undergraduates follows.

National Undergraduate Conferences for Students in English

- The Conference on College Composition and Communication Undergraduate Research Poster Session
- The National Undergraduate Literature Conference (NULC), established in 1985, hosted each April at Weber State University (Utah)

- An annual convention hosted by Sigma Tau Delta, the International English Honor Society, where all members are invited to submit critical essays, creative nonfiction, original poetry, fiction, drama/ screenplays, panel proposals, and/or works focusing on the common reader for the conference
- The Undergraduate Conference in Medieval and Early Modern Studies, hosted at Moravian College, started in 2006
- The National Conference on Peer Tutoring in Writing (NCPTW), started in 1984, which has included undergraduates as participants since its first days; regional affiliates also feature undergraduate presenters
- The National Conferences on Undergraduate Research (NCUR), which annually includes about three thousand participants, a sizeable group of those coming from English studies
- A national "Posters on the Hill," hosted by CUR for a limited number of students to present in Washington, DC; this event has been mirrored in several state venues, again including posters, an unusual medium for humanistic inquiry but growing in acceptance

PUBLICATIONS

Delivering an oral or poster presentation is often the step that precedes publication. Conference presentations usually include comments from audience members that help the researcher rethink and revise. Preparing a publication requires care and thought. It's important to submit the best work possible, as this process begins to contribute to the researcher's professional standing in the field and has long-range implications. The members of the editorial staff at a journal (and reviewers, too) spend a great deal of time reviewing each manuscript, so it's important that their investment is taken seriously.

In considering journals for submission, researchers may look at student-focused publications, that is, journals that focus specifically on an undergraduate or graduate audience. Conversely, the researchers may look at the professional journals in the field. Whichever the course, the researchers should become familiar with the journal and the types of articles published. Read the submission guidelines carefully and prepare the manuscript accordingly. Below is a sample of submission guidelines from *Young Scholars in Writing*.

Guidelines for Submissions for Articles:

Young Scholars in Writing: Undergraduate Research in Writing and Rhetoric seeks theory-driven and/or research-based submissions from undergraduates on the following topics: writing, rhetoric, composition, professional writing, technical writing, business writing, discourse analysis, writing technologies, peer tutoring in writing, writing process, writing in the disciplines, and related topics.

An electronic copy of manuscript in Microsoft Word is submitted to the editor.

Author's name must not appear on the manuscript.

Submissions should be 10–25 double-spaced pages in MLA format. Essays exceeding 25 pages will not be considered.

Send a separate file, which includes author's name, address, institutional affiliation, email address, and phone number.

All submissions must be accompanied by a professor's note that the essay was written by the student. The professor should email this note to the editor.

Typically, the journal's editor(s) reads the manuscript first to ensure that the essay is a good fit. If the response is affirmative, the essay is sent to reviewers for comment and response in what is termed a *blind review.* That is, the author's name and institutional affiliation are not included. The editor collects those responses and communicates with the author. The decision is generally one of these: accept, accept with minor revisions, revise and resubmit, or reject. Rarely is a manuscript accepted outright. In all cases, the author thanks the editors for their work. If revisions are encouraged, they should be made as quickly as feasible and the manuscript resubmitted. It's wise to include a faculty mentor in the process to have a second pair of eyes looking over the essay.

Good communication skills in this editorial process are essential. Just as in working with a faculty mentor or advisor, the researcher, as standard practice, checks e-mail daily and responds promptly. That does not mean responding in haste but responding thoughtfully and thoroughly using formal language appropriate to the context. Understanding the etiquette and professionalism of the field is part of advancing on the novice-expert continuum.

Students have opportunities to disseminate their work in many places, both at conferences and in print. Discipline-specific professional journals, also appropriate for graduate students, include *Composition Studies, CCC, College English, WLN: A Journal of Writing Center Scholarship,* and *The Writing Center Journal*—among others. The following list is undergraduate oriented.

National Undergraduate Research Journals for
Students in English

- *The Dangling Modifier* is an international newsletter for peer tutors in writing. http://sites.psu.edu/thedanglingmodifier/

- *The JUMP: Journal of Undergraduate Media Projects* is an electronic journal dedicated to providing an outlet for the excellent and exceedingly rhetorical digital/multimedia projects occurring in undergraduate courses around the globe as well as providing a pedagogical resource for teachers working with (or wanting to work with) new media. http://jump.dwrl.utexas.edu/
- *The Oswald Review: Undergraduate Research and Criticism in the Discipline of English* is a refereed undergraduate journal of criticism and research in the discipline of English and includes articles primarily in literary studies. www.usca.edu/english/pubs/oswald/oswald.html
- The *Pittsburgh Undergraduate Review* (*PUR*) publishes research articles written by students, the majority in the humanities, arts, and social sciences. www.pur.honorscollege.pitt.edu/
- The *Stanford Undergraduate Research Journal* is an annual peer-reviewed publication of research articles in all academic fields. Since 2007, the journal has published articles written by undergraduates across the nation. http://surj.stanford.edu/
- The *Undergraduate Journal of Service Learning and Community-Based Research* is a refereed, multidisciplinary, international online undergraduate journal. http://www.bk.psu.edu/academics/33679.htm
- The *Valley Humanities Review* is an online undergraduate research journal in the humanities and is housed in the Department of English at Lebanon Valley College. http://lvc.edu/vhr
- *WLN: A Journal of Writing Center Scholarship* publishes a Tutors Column. https://wlnjournal.org
- *Xchanges* is an interdisciplinary technical communication, writing/rhetoric, and writing-across-the-curriculum journal. The fall issue each year features undergraduate research. http://www.xchanges.org/
- *Young Scholars in Writing: Undergraduate Research in Writing and Rhetoric* is a refereed journal dedicated to publishing research articles written by undergraduates in a wide variety of disciplines associated with rhetoric and writing. http://arc.lib.montana.edu/ojs/index.php/Young-Scholars-In-Writing/index

On occasion, some professional journals have featured undergraduate research special issues for students doing research in writing studies:

- *Kairos.* "(Re)mediating the Conversation: Undergraduate Scholars in Writing and Rhetoric" (a special issue dedicated to undergraduate research in new media) 16, no. 1 (2011).
- *Writing Center Journal.* "Special Issue: Undergraduate Research" 32, no. 1 (2012).

PARTICIPATING IN PUBLIC RELATIONS

It may be surprising to student researchers that their institutions wish to brag about their accomplishments, but it is often true that institutions highlight the accomplishments of undergraduate and graduate students. Publicity about student successes may take the form of news releases, radio interviews, or videos. Some institutions prepare hometown-news stories—or may even ask the student to write the first draft of the story. How to prepare for these encounters? First of all, know that institutional public-relations teams wish to put their students in the most positive light possible. They are interested in the content of the work as well as the educational context. How did a faculty member assist the student researcher? Did an institutional grant support the research? Did an office provide travel support for presenting the research? Following is some advice about preparing for an interview with media relations.

- Be professional in manner and dress, as the interview may also include a photograph.
- Prepare an "elevator speech" of two to three minutes that succinctly describes the research and its significance.
- Know how the research has influenced your own professional development.
- Be prepared to answer questions about what's next, including further research or study.
- Give credit to any faculty mentors, advisors, and institutional support.
- Be positive and avoid criticism or negative comments.

Student researchers who work well with public-relations units may find themselves called on to present to other audiences, including alumni and foundations. They may become ambassadors for the institution, sterling examples of the educational enterprise.

PROFESSIONAL ORGANIZATIONS IN COMPOSITION AND WRITING FOR STUDENTS

One way to begin to become a member of the club of professionals in the field is to join a local student chapter of a professional organization. These might include the English honor society, Sigma Tau Delta; the student chapter of the National Council of Teachers of English (NCTE); the Society for Technical Communication (STC); or another professional organization in the field. Faculty members generally serve as sponsors and are good contacts. Being an informed member of a department or program—even as a student—means attending special lectures and events, signing up for newsletters and electronic alerts, and paying attention to postings in the buildings. Faculty members who are approached about serving as a mentor wish to know that the student has done the legwork and is well informed. The mentor-apprentice relationship is an enormous investment on the part of each. Increasingly, mentors are sharing coauthorship on collaborative projects. This kind of collaboration may very likely lead to students participating in the professional organizations associated with composition and writing studies.

COMPOSITION'S PROFESSIONAL ORGANIZATIONS

The Conference on College Composition and Communication (CCCC) was organized in 1949 as a subgroup of the National Council of Teachers of English (NCTE). The journal *CCC* appeared in 1950. The *professionalization* of composition took off in the late 1960s/early 1970s. Academics began to gravitate to composition and rhetoric as a career path. The emphasis on writing also coincided with social changes: the GI Bill, open admissions, an increase in two-year colleges, and the democratization of college.

In the 1970s/1980s, local and national conversations about how to teach writing effectively brought together a growing number of teachers and administrators. The Council of Writing Program Administration (CWPA) and its journal began in 1977. While CWPA includes any writing program, including writing centers, the latter group felt the necessity for a separate organization. Why? Writing centers/laboratories increased in number and were viewed first as fix-it shops to assist in remedial (basic) writing. Muriel "Mickey" Harris, director of the Purdue Writing Lab, cut and pasted together the first issue of the *Writing Lab Newsletter* in 1976. *The Writing Center Journal* was created in 1980 by editors Lil Brannon and Stephen North. The National Writing Centers Association was formed in 1982, putting together already-existing regional writing centers associations, such as the one for the east central part of the United States.

Other subgroups formed as outgrowths of the emphasis on writing. One of these was computers and composition (circa mid 1980s), with Cynthia Selfe and Gail Hawisher at the helm. Yet another theme in the profession was writing across the curriculum (WAC). The WAC Clearinghouse is a treasure trove of scholarly resources about communication across the disciplines: http://wac.colostate.edu/index.cfm. A group dedicated to the mission of advanced composition also formed. The Rhetoric Society of America draws on the classic definition of rhetoric and appeals to those interested in the art of effective communication. Technical writing is yet another vibrant community; on the other hand, business communications never really aligned with CCCC.

CCCC, the professional organization for writing teachers, has developed a number of position statements that address policy and practice in teaching writing, including Students' Right to Their Own Language and a research ethics statement. Its journal, *CCC*, also has a mission statement.

Current CCCC Mission Statement

The Conference on College Composition and Communication (CCCC) supports and promotes the teaching and study of college composition and communication by (1) sponsoring meetings and publishing scholarly materials for the exchange of knowledge about composition, composition pedagogy, and rhetoric; (2) supporting a wide range of research on composition, communication, and rhetoric; (3) working to enhance the conditions for learning and teaching college composition and to promote professional development; and (4) acting as an advocate for language and literacy education nationally and internationally.

CCC Mission Statement

College Composition and Communication publishes research and scholarship in rhetoric and composition studies that supports college teachers in reflecting on and improving their practices in teaching writing and that reflects the most current scholarship and theory in the field. The field of composition studies draws on research and theories from a broad range of humanistic disciplines—English studies, rhetoric, cultural studies, LGBT studies, gender studies, critical theory, education, technology studies, race studies, communication, philosophy of language, anthropology, sociology, and others—and from within composition and rhetoric studies, where a number of subfields have also developed, such as technical communication, computers and composition, writing across the curriculum, research practices, and the history of these fields.

Student Activity

INVESTIGATE: INSTITUTIONAL SUPPORT FOR STUDENT RESEARCHERS

What support does your institution offer for student researchers? Is grant funding available? Is there financial support to travel to conferences to present research results? Where can institutional support be found: department, college, university, student government? Sometimes multiple units fund an individual student, providing *matching* funds. Do a search of your institution's webpages to find information about central or unit-specific offices that support student inquiry. Learn about application processes and forms.

NOTE

1.   WebGURU was originally funded by the National Science Foundation Division of Undergraduate Education's Educational Materials Development Program (Award DUE-0341080); further support is from the Camille & Henry Dreyfus Foundation, Inc.

REFERENCE

WebGURU. http://www.webguru.neu.edu/.

PART II

Approaches to Research

Following are chapters that focus on a particular method for research:

- "Textual and Discourse Analysis"
- "The Case Study"
- "Ethnographic Research"
- "Mixed Methods"

This is not an exhaustive list of methods but a list of approaches chosen for their accessibility to students and to the length of an academic term. Quantitative strategies are approached inductively and integrated appropriately in chapters. Each chapter ends with an exemplary published essay employing the research methodology.

5

Analyzing Text and Discourse

Discourse in its strictest sense refers to spoken language; however, more recently it has been applied to oral, written, and even sign language. We will be using it in its broadest sense. This type of analysis is not the sole province of writing studies. Take for example political pundits who analyze speeches by candidates, presidents, and other government leaders. These analysts may have very different reactions to the same texts. Disciplines within social sciences—social work, anthropology, psychology, education, for instance—make use of this method.

Discourse analysis is sometimes also termed *textual analysis* and *content analysis*. They are the marriage of rhetoric and writing studies in which text is analyzed, sometimes along the lines of sociocultural, political, and historical themes. A linguist may analyze at the sentence level while more rhetorical analysis occurs at the essay or speech level. The context of writing may also be studied, particularly the social constructs in which the writing is produced or are inherent in the text. This latter emphasis is based on the understanding of the social nature of language. As with historical research, discourse analysis tends to be a humanistic approach to research, grounded in reading and interpretation.

Writing may also be analyzed through any number of theoretical lenses: Marxism, feminism, queer studies—among others. *Critical discourse analysis* is a more recent approach in which text is examined in its context with the specific aim to address issues of inequality, ethics, and institutions and with particular interest in abuses of power (Huckin et al. 2012). While this is an important method of analysis, it is not discussed in detail here.

Mike Rose gained prominence in composition and rhetoric as an impassioned teacher and the author of several books, including *Lives on the Boundary: The Struggles and Achievements of America's Educationally Underprepared* (Rose 1989), which recounts in part his own struggles as a student deemed a problem student. Because of his own experience, he believes public education is important to a democracy and provides educational opportunity for its citizens. He takes up the cause of teacher education in opinion pieces, knowing that such programs are under attack. Rose resists simple explanations. He uses textual and rhetorical analysis to good effect in a series of three articles in Valerie Strauss's *Washington Post* blog, The Answer Sheet. The third article in the series, posted on January 13, 2014, asks "Is Teacher Education a Disaster?" and by analyzing the language and rhetorical frames of two national reports on teacher education, Rose gets at the problem of painting all teacher-education programs as disastrous. One report, *Educating School Teachers* (Levine 2006), includes institutional, demographic, and survey data that would support the language of failure about 30 to 50 percent of the time. As Rose points out, "The other 50 to 70 percent of the data get much less attention and analysis." The result is a report slanted negatively and not true to these data. As evidence, Rose cites the enormous variability in teacher-education programs. But as he notes, "The language of the current criticism of teacher ed, at least the most public language, doesn't allow for this variability. Nor does the dismissive rhetorical stance of the most vocal critics, the tone and attitude running through their language."

A BRIEF HISTORY OF RHETORIC

Rhetoric dates back to ancient times and has been a crucial part of the Western tradition. The ability to speak well—elocution—and persuasively was highly valued in ancient Egypt and Greece. Even in these times, rhetoric sometimes took on pejorative meaning, particularly with the Sophists, who were infamous for proposing that a weaker stance or argument might gain the upper hand if the audience could be persuaded of its value through an excellent speaker. This approach ran counter to those who believed argument should be true and ethical. The Sophists were also itinerant teachers, ironically, sometimes considered the first humanists. From this classical viewpoint, public speaking "makes the man," which can only be brought about through education. Likewise, public speaking was an important facet of civic engagement and thus a path for good (read: high-born, patrician) citizens to be successful in government.

Aristotle (384–322 BCE) wrote *The Art of Rhetoric*, and he is still credited with being the leading authority on rhetoric. He called rhetoric "the faculty of observing in any given case the available means of persuasion" (Aristotle 350 BCE). But rhetoric was also dialectic, an approach that suggested that the best way to argue was for two or more people to engage in reasoned discussion, which would eventually lead to a resolution, and a true resolution at that. Aristotle felt that excellent persuasive techniques stemmed from one of three appeals: the appeal to logic (*logos*), the appeal to emotion (*pathos*), and the appeal to ethics (*ethos*). The latter focuses on the credibility of the speaker: is the person an ethical, honorable person with expertise in the subject matter? An appeal to emotion might draw in examples, such as animal or child abuse, that brings the audience to empathize. On the other hand, logic invokes quantitative evidence (e.g., 24 percent of 1,214 respondents felt that X is the case). Inductive and deductive reasoning are also brought to bear in argument.

In addition to these three primal bases for argument, Aristotle also laid out five major aspects of rhetoric, tasks that are part of creating a persuasive speech (or text): *invention, arrangement, style, memory,* and *delivery.* Obviously, for nonspeech discourse, memory takes a back seat. But invention, the creation of something to say, has been labeled in composition studies as *prewriting.* And another Greek term comes into play to help rhetoricians develop what is to be said, *heuristics,* which is in essence a set of questions to assist in creating content. Jacqueline Berke's popular textbook, *Twenty Questions for the Writer,* provides a standard set of heuristics to help writers think about the topic. This is a discovery technique, as other techniques have been, such as freewriting, looping, clustering, and tagmemic invention. Delivery is another of the five parts that lost favor when public speaking declined at the end of the nineteenth century. Arrangement (read: organization) and style remained and were equally appropriate for written discourse. These two were carried out for the purpose of presenting the best argument and thus winning the case. Not surprisingly, rhetoric was not only the province of government officials—the Roman senator, for instance—but also of the legal profession. As John Quincy Adams famously said of his part in the Amistad case in which an African slave was being tried, "I realized after much trial and error, that in the courtroom, whoever tells the best story wins" (Nowlan 2012, 247).

Perhaps surprisingly, the field of rhetoric was not solely the province of men. Well-born women in classical Rome could be educated according to the principles of the rhetorical tradition. In fact, Andrea Lunsford's (1995) edited volume *Reclaiming Rhetorica* rescues several women from the historical fog, one of them being Hortensia, who delivered a powerful speech in 42 BCE that resulted in a partial waiver of taxes on wealthy Roman women. Historical inquiry to address the question of whether there were female rhetoricians has uncovered several such women, one of them being Christine de Pizan (1364–1430), a medieval writer who argued against male writers who took stereotypical stances that devalued women. She is considered perhaps the first feminist writer. In *The Treasure of the City of Ladies*, de Pizan argues that "skill in discourse should be a part of every woman's moral repertoire" (Redfern 1995, 74) and that women have special powers as peacemakers and mediators. The US National Women's History Museum has adopted de Pizan as the namesake of its honors program to celebrate women in history and in contemporary times whose work may have otherwise gone unnoticed.

Rhetoric was one of the big three of classical-discourse education, known as the *trivium*, which included grammar and logic. It was joined by four other important fields of study—arithmetic, geography, music, and astronomy (but the latter was more likely astrology in the Middle Ages)—which were known as the *quadrivium*. The threesome and four-some became the seven liberal arts. Note that *liberal* is a reference to *liberated* or *free*; thus, the *quadrivium* is the basis of an education for a free person. All study was labeled *philosophy*, which is the origin of the title *doctor of philosophy* or *PhD*, appropriate no matter the field.

From ancient to contemporary times, numerous people have written about rhetoric: Cicero, Quintilian, Thomas Aquinas, Erasmus, Thomas Hobbes, Hugh Blair, Kenneth Burke. Classical rhetoric was for centuries an important part of the curriculum. In US institutions, departments of rhetoric became popular at the turn of the twentieth century in something of a revival. In contemporary higher education, the required writing course remains the one constant of any institution. Thus English 101 (by any of its various names) is imbued with epochs of value-laden philosophy and bears the heavy weight of providing the means by which students can describe, argue, persuade, or explain. Notably, speaking skills were relegated to communication studies or similar departments when rhetoric split in two in the mid-twentieth century.

Edward Corbett's (1965) *Classical Rhetoric for the Modern Student* began a process of recovering and discovering the classical tradition in modern writing studies. An interest in the historical antecedents of contemporary approaches to writing led Patricia Bizzell and Bruce Herzberg to compile an anthology of primary texts, *The Rhetorical Tradition: Readings from Classical Times to the Present* (Bizzell and Herzberg 1990). The edited volume begins with an overview of classical rhetoric to the twentieth century, bringing not only Aristotle to the fore but also an international cast of modern rhetoricians such as Michel Foucault and Mikhail Bakhtin. The former focuses on power and relationships while the latter introduces Marxist analysis.

For a fine concise history of rhetoric as well as an overview of composition studies, see Nedra Reynolds et al. (2012); an earlier edition is available online: http://www.macmillanhighered.com/Catalog/static/bsm/bb/history.html.

RHETORICAL ANALYSIS

In general, rhetorical analysis grows out of the same principles Aristotle posited eons ago. What is the thesis? What is the subject of the text? What are the arguments the writer advances? On what claims are these based? What evidence is provided? What strategies are used to win the audience? How is the argument arranged or organized to be effective? Are there stylistic devices the writer uses to make the argument more powerful? Is the writer's motivation discernible? Is the writer trustworthy? What clues exist to reveal the writer's biases? Is the style of the writing highbrow or plain-spoken language?

As Corbett notes in his seminal text, the terminology of classical rhetoric may be foreign to contemporary students. For instance, *rhetoric* is sometimes thought of only in the context of *empty rhetoric*. In truth, it is so much more. Its roots are in the Greek use of *rhetoric* as *words* or *rhetor* as *speaker* or *orator*. But the vocabulary of rhetorical analysis is important as it provides a common language with which to discuss texts. This section of the chapter seeks to introduce and define some of the most important terms.

The *aim* of the text may be persuasive or argumentative, but it may also simply seek to describe or to explain. It may also use narration, telling a story or anecdote, to drive home a point. Any one text may use a number of modes to drive its thesis. For instance, definition provides essential information about what something is. But defining what that something is *not* may be used to further explain. Likewise, the subject can be compared or contrasted to something else. An extended definition may enumerate its parts or describe how something is done with the subject—what is the process associated with this topic? Where does this something fit in a larger classification system? And how might it have changed over time? What is its history? Knowing the etymology, or word origin, may also prove enlightening to understand the topic. Providing examples is yet another way a topic is illuminated. What have those with authority or expertise said on this topic? Does the text hang on an apt quotation? Are there helpful statistics, precedents, or even legal cases that contribute to the understanding of this topic?

A text may employ deductive or inductive reasoning. For the latter, several examples are presented, and from these a conclusion is drawn. For deductive reasoning, the *syllogism* provides a test. A syllogism reasons from premises, statements, or propositions. Corbett (1965) calls the following syllogism "Exhibit A in almost every elementary book of logic":

> All men are mortal beings.
> Socrates is a man.
> Therefore, Socrates is a mortal being. (61)

The *enthymeme* is a syllogism in which one of the premises is implied. For instance, take this statement: Jesse Hawkes would not make a good president of the United States, as she/he is an atheist. The implied statement is that atheists would not make good presidents (which also is not necessarily a true statement).

Being able to unlock the logic behind assertions becomes important in rhetorical analysis. That is also one reason most writing courses include instruction in fallacies and how to recognize them. An *either/or fallacy* occurs when it is stated that there are only two choices available. For instance, in a gun-control debate, someone might argue that all guns will be scooped up by authorities when there may be multiple options that do not involve *all* guns but are differentiated among gun registration, user training, gun types, ammunition types, and background checks.

Begging the question is a form of circular argument in which there is not true support for the premise. *Argument ad hominem* occurs when the focus of the argument switches from issues to personalities. On the other hand, *argument ad populum* appeals to prejudices—as in flag characterizing waving, apple pie, and baseball as "all-American" activities while socialism may be used to incite fear. A *red herring* is a false detour from the topic, yet another dodge.

These are only a few of the instances of logic that may be used in analyzing a text rhetorically.

Yet another approach in rhetorical analysis is to focus on the *structure* of the text. Simplified, this is an introduction, a body, and a conclusion. The introduction provides the *exposition* or explanation of what is to come. In public speaking, the introduction has the crucial role of getting the audience's attention (and keeping it). The same is true of written discourse. Writing and delivering celebratory or memorial speeches involves hooking the readers/listeners quickly. Does the introduction offer a startling statistic or data point? Does it tell a story that grabs the reader's heart? Does it lay out a future scenario? Does it begin with a quotation and then build from it? Does it rely on a metaphor that will serve as the structure of the entire text?

The body of any text is the meat in the sandwich, so to speak, a metaphor that has been used at times to help novice writers understand essay structure. The substance may be the evidence to support a thesis, or it may be a series of examples or refutations. The conclusion is not simply the end of "here's what I'm going to say, this is what I have to say, and this is what I just said." Rather, a worthy conclusion curries favor with the audience, perhaps inspiring readers. Or it may be a call to action. It may introduce a "what if" scenario or a prediction. It may add further facts as a final thrust.

Style may seem an elusive target for the analyst. It is *how* something is written. Style refers to a range of writer's tools: word choice, sentence structure, and figures of speech. Abraham Lincoln was known for his *plain style* in his writing and speeches, a style common people could understand. But a speaker may opt for a more formal or high style. Depending on the purpose of the text, the writer might opt for jargon or slang. For professional writing, the vocabulary of the field—called *cant*—may be used. What is true of these latter approaches is that all readers may not understand the meaning. Words can carry tremendous significance, and the repetition of certain words may signal themes in the writing. For instance, Henry Fielding's *Jonathan Wild*, which is an eighteenth-century novel about a disreputable but handsome character, uses the word *honor* to good effect.

In general, a variety of sentence patterns is desirable in a text although that may vary depending on the purpose of the piece. Sentence variety contributes to the rhythm of the text. Likewise, paragraph structure carries with it a certain style. Each paragraph may be a mini essay, complete with a thesis—usually termed a *topic sentence*. The patterns of paragraphing help readers, in part, track the subject. That indentation (or additional spacing) at the beginning of a paragraph gives the reader pause. Signposting in the form of headings and subheadings, particularly appropriate to technical or business writing, signals for readers topics or changes in the narrative thread.

Most word processors have a statistical tool to count aspects of style. This tool can quantify the number of words, lines, paragraphs, and pages.

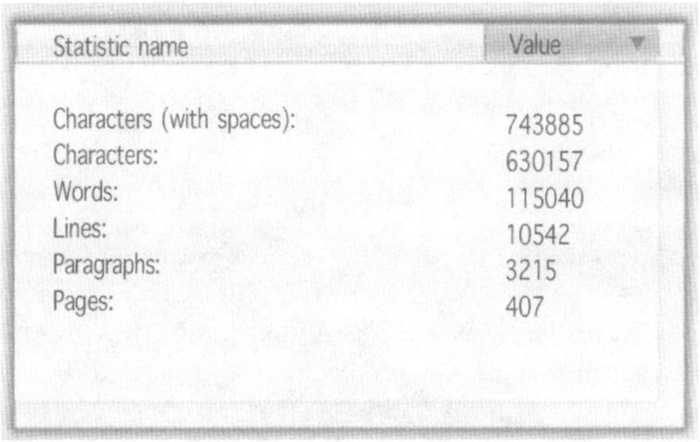

Statistic name	Value
Characters (with spaces):	743885
Characters:	630157
Words:	115040
Lines:	10542
Paragraphs:	3215
Pages:	407

FIGURE 5.1. Statistics about a document file.

Other counts that may be useful include the number of sentences and their lengths (shortest, longest, average); number of paragraphs and their lengths (shortest, longest, average); types and variety of sentence beginnings; use of specific punctuation marks (e.g., semicolon, colon); use of conjugations of "to be" verbs.

Figures of speech number well over one hundred; as a result, only a few will be addressed here. Some, like *metaphor*—a comparison between two

Table 5.1. A sample of figures of speech

Denotation

The direct or dictionary meaning of a word, in contrast to its figurative or associated meanings.

Diacope

A rhetorical term for repetition broken up by one or more intervening words.

Diatyposis

A rhetorical term for recommending useful precepts or advice to someone else; it is also a compact expression of enargia.

Distinctio

Explicit references to various meanings of a word—usually for the purpose of removing ambiguities.

Dysphemism

Substitution of a more offensive or disparaging word or phrase for one considered less offensive.

Effectio

Personal description; a head-to-toe inventory of a person's physical attributes or charms.

Ellipsis

The omission of one or more words, which must be supplied by the listener or reader.

Encomium

A tribute or eulogy in prose or verse glorifying people, objects, ideas, or events.

Enthymeme

An informally stated syllogism with an implied premise.

Epanalepsis

A rhetorical term for repetition at the end of a clause or sentence of the word or phrase with which it began.

things—are well known, as is *simile*, a type of metaphor but one that uses *like* or *as*. (These figures of speech are also known as *tropes*.)

Parallelism refers to similarity in a series of words or phrases. A classical example of parallel structure is Caesar's "*Veni, Vidi, Vici*"—I came; I saw; I conquered.

For a contemporary example, look at these lines from President Barack Obama's second inaugural address:

> We, the people, declare today that the most evident of truths—that all of us are created equal—is the star that guides us still, just as it guided our forebears through Seneca Falls and Selma and Stonewall.

Note the parallel structure of Seneca Falls, Selma, and Stonewall—as well as the *alliteration* of the initial *s* in each word. The *s* is also a sibilant sound. But Seneca Falls, Selma, and Stonewall are more than three places; they embody women's rights, African Americans' civil rights, and queer (or LGBTQ) rights. This short series of words is a very strong statement for civil rights for groups that historically have been disenfranchised.

Other common figures of speech readily recognizable include *hyperbole*, outlandish exaggeration; *irony*, using a word to convey its opposite meaning; or *oxymoron*, two terms together that ordinarily contradict one another, as in *peacemaker bomb*.

THE ROLE OF AUDIENCE

Without a doubt, audience is one of the most crucial choices a writer makes in the prewriting or invention stages. Who are the designated readers or listeners? Is there a venue or event for which the text is being written? Obviously, a eulogy, memorializing someone who has died carries with it a much more formal, weighty tone than, say, an e-mail to a college friend. In short, the audience has tremendous power in shaping the writing. A heuristic can help define the audience.

- Who is the reader?
- What is the age of the reader?
- What is the educational level of the reader?
- Does the reader have prior knowledge or expertise of the subject, or conversely, is the reader naïve about the topic?
- Does the reader carry any prejudices or biases about the topic?
- What is the reader's interest level in the topic? (Will the reader read the text no matter what, or does the text need to hook the reader to maintain interest?)

A real audience rather than one imagined or implied is typically much easier for the writer to address. But an audience may also be the self. A writer may be writing in order to understand a concept or delineate a philosophy.

The form of the text is often an outcome of considering the audience. A report to a supervisor, for instance, or an analysis that will affect policy change will determine in large part how the writing is organized. A deliberative essay probably is not the right format for a report, which, more typically, would begin with the point or recommendation, probably in an executive summary. And the document itself may be a series of bullet points so the message is delivered efficiently. The same may be true of a PowerPoint slide presentation. On the other hand, several research approaches in this book—the case study, the ethnography, the history—carry with them particular formats.

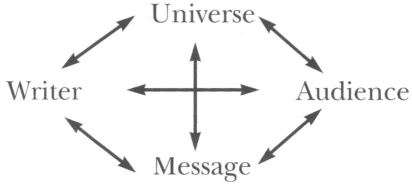

FIGURE 5.2. Corbett's model of "The Rhetorical Interrelationships" (Corbett 1981).

Profile of a Student Researcher: Eric Stephens

Eric works as a tutor in his university's writing center and is also a graduate instructor of first-year writing. In the latter role he emphasizes the concept of *audience* in teaching. As a tutor, he had an epiphany that he wasn't serving as an audience for the students he worked with but as a *reader*. He undertook a study to explore the relationship tutors have with their tutees. How do tutors see themselves rhetorically in a writing session? Do they enter the session in the role of reader but act as the audience? How often do tutors discuss audience awareness? Do tutors see audience awareness as a rhetorical tool? Is there a difference in what tutors believe and how they actually behave?

Eric conducted a review of literature and tutor guidebooks to see how the terms *audience* and *reader* are used. He drew on graphic representations of the rhetorical situation.

In addition to textual analysis, Eric, in an IRB-approved study, surveyed and observed tutorial sessions to analyze further the use of *audience* and *reader* as terms. He concluded that tutor training would be enhanced by more precise attention to audience and readers.

GENRE

In analyzing text rhetorically, identifying the form or *genre* is a key aspect. *Genre* is closely associated with literature; fiction, creative nonfiction, poetry, and drama are the forms of literature. However, the application of the term *genre* has broadened considerably to include a wide variety of types of writing such as the personal statement for medical school or a graduate-school application; it also includes grant applications and proposals. Traci Gardner (2009) has suggested a comprehensive list of types of writing forms. This list can aid in categorizing or classifying various genres and forms of writing.

List of Genre Types

acrostic

advertising giveaway—buttons, pens, calendars

almanac article

anagram

anthology or submission to a class anthology

application (e.g., job, college, grant)

bad-news letter or memo

banner ad

billboard

blank verse

blog—personal, corporate

book cover or dust jacket

bulletin board (on the wall)

business card

campaign speech

cartoon

CD or DVD collection (e.g., the items in the collection)

CD or DVD cover

census report

chart, diagram, or graph

cinquain

claims letter

classified ad (e.g., personal, want ad)

coffee-table book

collage—word, visual, aural

collections letter

comic book or strip

commercial (radio, television, or online)

congratulatory letter

contract

cookbook or recipe collection

cover story or front-page news

crossword puzzle

declaration

dialogue

diamante

diary entry

dictionary or dictionary entry

direct mail—letter, pamphlet, postcard

directory (e.g., staff, telephone, member)

dramatic monologue

dramatic scene or skit

eBay listing

editorial column

e-mail message—personal, customer service, interoffice, etc.

eulogy

expository essay

eyewitness account

fake news—comedic or corporate government produced

feature article

flyer, pamphlet, or brochure

found poem

free verse

friendly/personal letter

fund-raising letter

game instructions

good-news letter or memo

government report

grave marker/tombstone

greeting card—birthday, holiday, condolence, thank you, etc.

grocery list

haiku

homepage on a website

hospital chart

illustration

IM or chat-room transcript

infomercial

interview or interview transcript

item description for a mail-order catalog

item description for an online store

letter of recommendation

letter or memo of introduction

letter poem

limerick

list, or catalog, poem

log entry

lyrics and/or music—pop, country western, ballad, heavy metal, rap

magazine or journal ad

map with legend

math problem

meeting transcript

memo—departmental or interoffice

memoir

List of Genre Types (*continued*)

memo of understanding
menu
monologue
monument or statue
MP3 player playlist
newsgroup posting or thread
newspaper ad (e.g., full to partial-page ad for businesses, etc.)
newspaper or magazine insert
news teaser
notebook
obituary
ode
online bulletin-board posting or thread
online forum posting
online profile (such as on Facebook)
PA announcement
pantoum
performance appraisal
personal commentary
personal-interest article (as in newspapers, magazines, etc.)
photo gallery/album
photograph with caption, keywords/tags, and/or descriptions
picture book
play
police report—CSI-style, coroner's, moving-violation ticket, etc.
political advertisement
pop-up ad
postcard
poster
press release
product or service website
product-placement recommendation (e.g., placement in movie or television show)
proposal
public-service announcement
quiz
ransom note
recipe
recipe poem
recommendation report

reference book or entry/article in a reference book
report card
resignation letter or memo
resume
sales letter
sandwich board
scrapbook
script—television, radio, podcast, etc.
short story
social worker's report
sonnet
special news report or update
sports score and story
survival kit
tanka
telegram
telemarketer's script
telephone-book ad
testimonial ad/endorsement
text message
thank-you letter, memo, or note
timeline
trading card
transcript of phone call, conversation, etc.
transit ad (i.e., ad on bus, plane, or train)
treaty
trip report
t-shirt message
video- or computer-game vignette
villanelle
voicemail message
wanted poster
warning sign
web page—personal, corporate, organization, educational, etc.
wiki or wiki entry
will
word-seek puzzle
yearbook—spread on student life, class section, feature on academics, special profile, sports section, ad, or special event
zine

DISCOURSE COMMUNITY

Over the past few decades, the realization that language is a social construct has come to the fore. A discourse community is a group of people who share values and assumptions and ways of communicating. For instance, the medical-school application will be read by a discourse community of physicians and medical staff who understand its values and will evaluate applicants based on those values. A group of computer-software developers share vocabulary and language common to the field. John Swales (1990), a leading figure in discourse community theory, notes that a discourse community shares six characteristics:

1. Has a broadly agreed set of common public goals
2. Has mechanisms of intercommunication among its members
3. Uses its participatory mechanisms primarily to provide information and feedback
4. Utilizes and hence possesses one or more genres in the communicative furtherance of its aims
5. In addition to owning genres, has acquired some specific lexis (word usage or vocabulary)
6. Has a threshold level of members with a suitable degree of relevant content and discoursal expertise

As a result of association among its members, a discourse community shares common language characteristics and patterns. The ethnographic study in a later chapter focuses on those engaged in a Waco, Texas, punk community in the mid-1980s.

THEORETICAL LENSES FOR RHETORICAL ANALYSIS

A text may be viewed not only rhetorically but also from a theoretical stance. For instance, analysis based in Karl Marx's theories might identify any markers that indicate capitalism or focus on labor and the status of the working person. Thus class and socioeconomic status play key roles in any **Marxist** analysis. Material wealth and possessions are suspect in a preferred society where everyone owns everything; wealth is shared.

A **cultural studies** lens focuses more on the context of the events and the people involved. Because people are products of their time, place, and culture, writing is influenced by those aspects. Likewise, those who are analyzing or interpreting writing bring their own time, place, and culture to the analysis. That is a simplified definition, but the key is on cultural context.

Postcolonial criticism or analysis acts on the assumption that Western powers who colonized have been the authoritative authors of history, but those oppressed by colonization have not had voices to share their side of the story. Thus, the story presented is lopsided. History textbooks have been accused of telling only the story of the victors. James Loewen's (1995) *Lies My Teacher Told Me* famously set about debunking the jingoism and blind patriotism of US-history textbooks in high schools. Acknowledging oppression is a significant part of postcolonial criticism.

Although no longer in favor, **Freudian** and **Jungian** critiques focus on the psychological motivation in texts. A psychoanalytical analysis looks for instances of the unconscious at work and even for repression. It takes into account childhood events that may have affected adults, events generally of a sexual nature.

Sexuality or gender is also a hallmark of two other lenses: **feminism** and **queer studies**. In each, oppression and suppression can be themes. For women, how is patriarchy responsible for keeping them marginalized and out of power circles and positions of authority? What are the effects of a male-dominated culture on women's psychology, socioeconomic class, political authority, and social stature? For gender studies and queer studies, the notion of binaries—male/female, masculine/feminine, heterosexual/homosexual—may not be appropriate. What is gender? In textual analysis this may translate into looking at texts for markers of sexual identity or status. What markers indicate power and authority (masculinity) or passivity and marginalization (femininity)? Robin Lakoff (1975) explored texts linguistically in her *Language and Woman's Place*, which later influenced Deborah Tannen's (1990) seminal work deconstructing language in *You Just Don't Understand: Women and Men in Conversation*.

CLOSE READING

Analysis at the text or discourse level requires close reading, a careful, sustained analysis or explication. Almost any text can be studied rhetorically, looking at its organization, style, form, genre, audience, and purpose. Here is a sample of essay titles from *Young Scholars in Writing* that suggest the diversity of topics for rhetorical analysis:

- "Seeing Is Believing: Using the Rhetoric of Virtual Reality to Persuade";
- "Speaking without Words: Silence and Epistolary Rhetoric of Catholic Women Educators on the Antebellum Frontier, 1828–1834";
- "Reframing the Victim: Rhetoric for Segregation in the *Greenville News*";

- "Redefining Interfaith Discourse: Applying Invitational Rhetoric to Religion";
- "Modifying Masculinity, Forging Femininity: Male Feminist Discourse and the Manifestation of an Independent Female Identity";
- "When Writing Cuts Deep: The Rhetoric of Surgical Short Stories";
- "The Rhetoric of Teacher Comments on Student Writing."

Corbett (1965) defined rhetoric as "the art or the discipline that deals with the use of discourse, either spoken or written, to inform or persuade or move an audience, whether that audience is made up of a single person or a group of persons. Broadly defined in that way, rhetoric would seem to comprehend every kind of . . . expression" (3). Eighteenth-century rhetorician George Campbell said of rhetoric that it is "to enlighten the understanding, to please the imagination, to move the passions, or to influence the will" (Campbell [1776] 2013, 26). For those who engage in rhetorical analysis, the same may be true.

At the end of this chapter is a student research essay for reading, analysis, and reflection. Heather Bastian and Lindsey Harkness's essay, "When Peer Tutors Write about Writing: Literacy Narratives and Self Reflection," appeared in the very first issue of *Young Scholars in Writing* in 2003. As with other chapters in part 2 of *Researching Writing*, this essay is designed to exemplify the research approach addressed. Bastian and Harkness (2003) draw upon literacy narratives—tutors' histories as writers—to come to a better understanding of how good or proficient writers see themselves. How do tutors' perceptions of their own development as writers influence their work as tutors?

REFERENCES AND FOR FURTHER READING

N.B. Rhetorical and textual analysis is a favorite approach for essays in *Young Scholars in Writing.* A sampling is included in this list.

Anton, Karen. 2009. "'My Country! 'Tis of Thee, Stronghold of Slavery': The Musical Rhetoric of the American Antislavery Movement." *Young Scholars in Writing* 7:30–40.

Aristotle. 350 BCE. *Rhetoric.* Translated by W. Rhys Roberts, 1954. http:// rhetoric.eserver.org/aristotle/.

Bastian, Heather, and Lindsey Harkness. 2003. "When Peer Tutors Write about Writing: Literacy Narratives and Self Reflection." *Young Scholars in Writing* 1:101–24.

Berke, Jacqueline. 1994. *Twenty Questions for the Writer: A Rhetoric with Readings.* 6th ed. Belmont, CA: Wadsworth.

Bizzell, Patricia, and Bruce Herzberg. 1990. *The Rhetorical Tradition: Readings from Classical Times to the Present.* Boston: Bedford/St. Martin's.

Campbell, George. (1776) 2013. *The Philosophy of Rhetoric.* Cambridge: Cambridge University Press.

Corbett, Edward P.J. 1965. *Classical Rhetoric for the Modern Student.* New York: Oxford University Press.

Corbett, Edward P.J. 1981. *The Little Rhetoric and Handbook.* 2nd ed. Glenview, IL: Scott, Foresman.

Elder, David. 2005. "Chris Rock: Epideictic Rhetor." *Young Scholars in Writing* 3:55–60.

Fielding, Henry. 1725. *The True and Genuine Account of the Life and Actions of the Late Jonathan Wild.* London: John Applebee.

Gardner, Traci. 2009. *Designing Writing Assignments.* Urbana, IL: NCTE.

Heimburger, Susan West. 2004. "Of Faith and Fact: Haywood N. Hill's 'This I Believe.'" *Young Scholars in Writing* 2:29–38.

Hockersmith, Lindy. 2003. "A New Deal for the American People: A Marxist Analysis of FDR's First Inaugural Address." *Young Scholars in Writing* 1:45–59.

Huckin, Thomas, Jennifer Andrus, and Jennifer Clary Lemon. 2012. "Critical Discourse Analysis and Rhetoric and Composition." *College Composition and Communication* 64 (1): 107–28.

Lakoff, Robin Tolmach. 1975. *Language and Woman's Place.* New York: Oxford University Press.

Levine, Arthur. 2006. *Educating School Teachers.* The Education Schools Project. http://www.edschools.org/teacher_report.htm.

Loewen, James. 1995. *Lies My Teacher Told Me: Everything Your American History Textbooks Got Wrong.* New York: New Press.

Lundgren, Jessica. 2009. "Eating Fresh in America: Subway Restaurant's Nutritional Rhetoric." *Young Scholars in Writing* 6:110–17.

Lunsford, Andrea A., ed. 1995. *Reclaiming Rhetorica: Women in the Rhetorical Tradition.* Pittsburgh, PA: University Press of Pittsburg.

Magee, Sarah-Kate. 2009. "College Admissions Essays: A Genre of Masculinity." *Young Scholars in Writing* 7:116–21.

Nowlan, Robert A. 2012. *The American Presidents, Washington to Tyler: What They Did, What They Said. What Was Said about Them.* Jefferson, NC: McFarland & Company.

Pearson, Jonathan. 2009. "From Wellesley to Yale, 1969–1979: A Textual Analysis of Hillary Rodham's Early Written Rhetoric." *Young Scholars in Writing* 7:53–62.

Redfern, Jenny. 1995. "Christine de Pisan and *The Treasure of the City of Ladies*: A Medieval Rhetorician and Her Rhetoric." In *Reclaiming Rhetorica: Women in the Rhetorical Tradition,* edited by Andrea A. Lunsford, 73–91. Pittsburgh, PA: University of Pittsburgh Press.

Reynolds, Nedra, Jay Dolmage, Patricia Bizzell, and Bruce Herzberg. 2012. *The Bedford Bibliography for Teachers of Writing.* 7th ed. Boston: Bedford/St. Martin's.

Rose, Mike. 1989. *Lives on the Boundary: The Struggles and Achievements of America's Educationally Underprepared.* New York: Penguin.

Skonieki, Stefanie. 2004. "Tear Apart This Speech: A Burkean Analysis of Ronald Reagan's 'Tear Down This Wall' Speech." *Young Scholars in Writing* 2:18–28.

Swales, John M. 1990. *Genre Analysis: English in Academic and Research Settings.* Cambridge: Cambridge University Press.

Tannen, Deborah. 1990. *You Just Don't Understand: Women and Men in Conversation.* New York: Ballentine.

"When Peer Tutors Write about Writing: Literacy Narratives and Self Reflection"

Heather Bastian and Lindsey Harkness,
Lafayette College

For many years in the discipline of composition studies, students have been referred to in certain and common ways. Most of the professional literature seems to represent student writers as remedial—deficient in grammatical and creative skills and political awareness. While this attention to the basic student is important for many reasons (much can be learned about writing from students who are struggling to learn), it is also limited in its focus. We want to argue in this paper that the story of the proficient student also needs to be told, because there is much to be learned from it. In this paper we will discuss the research we conducted on the proficient writer, using a training tool referred to by the College Writing Program at Lafayette College as the "literacy narrative" (see Appendix 1 and 2). As we hope to demonstrate, the proficient writer can provide composition studies with an invaluable resource.

This essay is organized into three sections. First, we provide background information about our college writing program. Second, we discuss how students have traditionally been represented in composition studies. And third, we consider the literacy narratives as a reflection of the attitudinal changes and the identities of our peer tutors. The literacy narrative assignment is undertaken every year by peer tutors in the College Writing Program at Lafayette College.[1] Later in our discussion we will explain the importance of the literacy narrative materials for gaining

Heather Bastian and Lindsey Harkness, "When Peer Tutors Write about Writing: Literacy Narratives and Self Reflection," *Young Scholars in Writing* 1 (2003):77–94.

an understanding of how students who provide support in writing to other students regard their own work as writers and as tutors of writing. We believe that our findings have significance for how the discipline of composition understands and represents the work of a "good writer."

BACKGROUND

We attend Lafayette College, a highly selective, small (roughly 2000 students), liberal arts college located in Easton, Pennsylvania. For many years, Lafayette College has had a strong commitment to writing instruction. In fact, writing courses have been offered since the mid-nineteenth century, instituted by the famed philologist Francis A. March. In the 1950s, 60s, and 70s, the head of the English Department, William W. Watt, was also the author of one of the most widely used composition textbooks in the country: *An American Rhetoric.* Also, since 1986, Lafayette College has had in place The College Writing Program, which provides support to various writing intensive courses across the curriculum. This support comes primarily in the form of the hiring, training, and supervising of undergraduate "Writing Associates." Writing Associates are sophomores, juniors, and seniors from all disciplines who are assigned to a single course for an entire semester and who meet with every student in the course at least three times in one-on-one conferences. Writing Associates also meet regularly with the faculty member teaching the course to discuss writing assignments and methods of evaluation.

THEORETICAL BACKGROUND AND CONTEXTS

Our research involved examining the writing of other Writing Associates. While examining the writing of our student colleagues, we became aware of the problems, issues, and difficulties that arise when talking for and representing others. When one talks for others, instead of letting others talk for themselves, one can easily misrepresent the group's concerns, attitudes, behaviors, etc. This has often happened in the field of composition. Composition scholars are often in a position of power where they discuss and reflect upon students—student writing, student attitudes, and even student behavior. Even though composition scholars often interact with students, they are not students. Therefore, they may unintentionally misrepresent students, because they do not allow the students to speak for themselves.

To determine how students have been traditionally represented in composition studies over the years, we reviewed academic essays from the 1930's to the present in *College Composition and Communication (CCC)* and *College English.*[2] We will briefly summarize our findings, which support the claims made by Marguerite H. Helmers in her important book,

Writing Students: Composition Testimonials and Representations of Students, published in 1994. Furthermore, we are providing this background to establish how students have traditionally been understood in composition studies before we argue for a new representation of the student. Students have often been represented as "others" who are lacking various skills; however, this representation is problematic and even dangerous.

Helmers' main argument is that testimonials about student writing provided by teachers and professors—like those found in *College Composition and Communication* and *College English*—do not reflect reality but are actually a genre with conventions that must be observed. However, these conventions are often not recognized as such because the composition discourse community accepts them as second nature; they have become invisible to those who use them. Additionally, Helmers explains that these testimonials can be analyzed and divided into four parts: 1) an argument in favor of a teaching method is provided; 2) students are presented as characters who lack; 3) students are presented as having been transformed by the teacher; 4) the teacher is exalted as a hero. This format has several effects. First, it constructs students as faceless and transhistorical. Second, it creates a binary opposition between the teachers and the students. And third, it creates students as "others;" within this category of "otherness," students are additionally said to be deviant, mystical, orientalized, or bestialized (Helmers 81). In light of her investigation, Helmers concludes that representations of students in testimonials should be understood as rhetorical rather than grounded in fact.

Through the course of our reviewing academic essays in *College Composition* and *Communication and College English,* we found certain trends that support the claims made by Helmers. As we discovered, during the 1930s–1950s teachers discuss students as deficient in writing skills, especially in grammar and mechanics. The following passage from Ruth Davies' "A Defense of Freshmen" points to the common perception that students are lacking in these skills: "Are you a reader of freshmen themes? Do you find yourself nervous, run-down, and tired? Do you see red-pencil marks before your eyes, and are you haunted at night by dangling participles, split infinitives, disagreement between subject and verb, and comma splices? Do freshmen and their papers cause you palpitations and give you pain?" (*College English 441*). During this period students are also described as lazy, cynical, and poorly prepared. None of the essays we reviewed from this time period offered any examples of student writing. As a result, the student voice is never heard; instead, teachers speak for and about their students.

In the 1960s–70s, students are still being labeled as deficient by compositionists, but the nature of that deficiency changes; instead of lacking grammatical and mechanical skills, they are now said to lack creative and inventive skills. For example, in her essay "Transforming the 'Same Paper' Syndrome," Gayle Whittier discusses students' *lack* of creativity, which leads to the "same paper syndrome":

> Most teachers of literature encounter students whose work in a given semester stagnates in quality and range. The depressing phenomenon of the "arrested" student occurs at every level of accomplishment: one may be just as arrested with a uniform sequence of A grades as with an unbroken series of D's. Indeed, the "success" of the high grade essay tends towards a special kind of conservatism. (*College English 151*)

Student writing is first cited in the mid 1960s; however, in these years student writing is typically inserted into an essay to support research claims or the argument. Very few examples of writing are examined in depth. And even then, examples that are provided tend to be written by women and minority students.

Finally, from the 1980s to the present student representation has not really changed much from its earlier years. One difference, however, is that a wide range of students are represented. While students continue to be described as deficient, they are now said to lack political awareness. For example, in her essay "Professing Multiculturalism: The Politics of Style in the Contact Zone," Min Zahn Lu addresses this issue of political awareness in the context of style. In this, she connects perceived errors to cultural differences. She writes: "In arguing for a multicultural approach to styles traditionally displaced to the realm of 'error,' I align my teaching with a tradition in 'error' analysis which views even 'error-ridden' student writing as texts relevant to critical approaches available in English Studies" (*CCC* 447). Unlike the other examples we have used, Lu does not directly criticize students; instead, her explanation of the "errors" in student writing alludes to the common perception of educators that students lack political awareness.

In her essay, Lu discusses how the composition community has traditionally viewed "student" writers as being separate from "real" writers. According to Lu, when students write in a style that does not follow the conventions of academic discourse, they are thought to be making "errors" due to their lack of political awareness. She claims that this is due to the standard that educators often hold students to (but do not always abide by): the criteria that stipulates "until one can prove one's ability to produce 'error-free' prose, one has not earned the right to innovative 'style'" (*CCC* 446). Lu finds this standard as problematic, for educators, and thus their students, often fail to acknowledge the social and political forces that act on students' writing styles. Ultimately, Lu believes that students will come to have a new understanding of style and a less negative view of the "errors" in their writing if they are given the opportunity to gain political awareness through a multicultural approach.

The trends we have discussed up to this point involve how students are represented, but another interesting trend concerns the type of student represented. That is, in *College English*, the articles mainly focused on first-year student writers. Beginning in the 1930s and through 1990s, many articles focused on how first-year composition courses should be structured to accommodate for the poor writing skills of first-year students. In addition to the focus on first-year writers, other articles focused on basic writers and the techniques needed to aid these writers. In only a few instances were "competent" or "experienced" writers the focus of study. While *College Composition and Communication* essays expanded the types of students discussed, the competent writer still remained nearly invisible. *CCC* articles mostly focused on basic or remedial writers, although English as a Second Language (ESL) students, women students, minority students, non-traditional students, and first-year students were also discussed. Once again, only a few articles in *CCC* discussed the proficient college writers. In both *CCC* and *College English*, the type of students, regardless of their labeling, attended large state universities.

These findings suggest to us that the discourse community of composition has mainly constructed students as "others" who lack various skills and are in need of help from enlightened and heroic teachers and professors. More importantly, within this discourse community, teachers and professors hold the power. They often use that power to speak for and about students and, consequently, construct an image—a critical image—of students. Critical representations of students are further supported by the type of student the discourse community of composition chooses to discuss in their essays. Struggling or poor writers remain the focus. The preoccupation with "poor" and "struggling" students establishes these writers as the norm and disregards other students, such as competent college writers. We would argue that the traditional representations of students have undervalued and even ignored "competent" writers. As we will demonstrate, much can be learned from the "competent" writer. Therefore, the traditional representations of students are problematic and need to be altered in the current discourse on composition.

THE LITERACY NARRATIVE

For the past 12 years, as part of an extensive training program, Writing Associates have been required to compose literacy narratives in which they each reflect upon their own development as individual writers throughout their educational histories. The literacy narrative assignment differs for new and experienced Writing Associates. Newly hired Writing Associates reflect on their entire writing history, told as a story in chronological order. In order to facilitate such reflection, new Writing Associates are asked to consider eight areas:

1. their first writing experiences
2. the material conditions under which they have written (such as the type of classes they have taken and the writing instruments used)
3. the types of writing they have been required to do
4. the types of writing they have done on their own
5. the reactions of others to their writing
6. how they feel about their writing and the reactions of others
7. how such feelings might have changed over the years
8. their experiences with academic writing at the college level

Experienced Writing Associates focus their reflection on the past year's writing experiences. Additionally, the assignment is designed to prepare them to help the year's new Writing Associates. Experienced Writing Associates are also given prompts to help focus their thoughts. They are asked to consider any (or all) of the following six ideas, divided into two main topics: their experiences as writers and their experiences as Writing Associates:

1. what classes have they taken and how might these have influenced their attitudes towards writing and how do they understand and perceive this work
2. in what instances could they see their writing identities or writing processes change or develop and to what do they attribute these changes
3. what experiences as a Writing Associate did they find to be challenging, formative, rewarding, etc.
4. how has being a Writing Associate changed their attitudes towards writing or their writing processes
5. how do they discuss writing with the students to whom they were assigned and how have these discussions influenced their own writing or attitudes towards writing

RESEARCH AND ANALYSIS

Our research project focused on literacy narratives written in 1999, 2000, and 2001. We read and examined the narratives from two different perspectives. In the first, we looked for attitudinal changes over time, noting the assumptions about writing, tutoring, and education that the Writing Associates brought with them to the position and then how those assumptions changed from year to year. In the second, we looked for statements about "identity," focusing on the ways in which Writing Associates view themselves as students, tutors, and tutors-as-students.

ATTITUDINAL CHANGES

In the first approach, we examined literacy narratives for attitudinal changes over time. To assess such changes, we compared and contrasted the literacy narratives written by the same Writing Associate over the period of his or her employment (typically two or three years). Since we believe that it is necessary, when talking about students, to listen to what the students themselves have to say, we have selected a few passages from two of the literacy narratives, written by two Writing Associates, Greg Stazowski and Kate McGovern.

One assumption that many of the Writing Associates brought to the position is that academic writing is confining and creative writing is unrestricted. In Greg Stazowski's first literacy narrative (written the summer before he became a Writing Associate), he makes several assumptions about writing, including the assumption mentioned above. In this, he suggests that creative writing is free from form and structure, while academic writing is confined by form and structure. In his literacy narrative he states:

> From various newspaper-like articles, to comic book selections, I had found a way to disguise the subject matter in a means that stood out from others. Using these different presentation methods made writing fun for me because it could be personal and not a form style. Difficulties arose, however, when other teachers forced me to write their specific styles.

As his literacy narrative indicates, Greg views academic writing as formulaic and impersonal. Additionally, he identifies style with form. For Greg, writing should portray one's individuality; he felt that certain required forms eliminated that individual and personal aspect.

If we now turn to Greg's third literacy narrative (written after his second year as a Writing Associate), we can see how his assumptions and ideas about writing have changed. Within this narrative, Greg acknowledges that different genres have different purposes, and thus different forms, as well. He explains that he no longer views the required forms of academic writing as negatively as he portrayed in his first literacy narrative. In fact, Greg shows appreciation for such required forms in his statement: "In many instances, a 'typical' style of writing is exactly what these students need to develop, in order to eventually become successful in the world of design engineers." As can be seen, Greg's assumptions about the confining nature of structure and form present in his first literacy narrative are almost completely reversed in his third.

It is apparent that Greg's views about writing changed somewhere between his freshman and senior years. Quite possibly, this would have occurred even if he had not become a Writing Associate. As a student,

Greg encountered various forms of writing; his work as a Writing Associate introduced him to the writing of other disciplines. By introducing him to the conventions of writing in many disciplines, working as a Writing Associate allowed him to understand and appreciate the differences in form and convention between the different disciplines. We can speculate that this increased exposure to and education about various kinds of writing is what led Greg to understand and value the required forms of academic writing and, ultimately, changed his perceptions and assumptions about writing.

As can be seen by reading Kate McGovern's literacy narratives, her perceptions about writing also change, but in a different way. While Greg's assumptions were focused on writing, Kate's were more concerned with the work of a Writing Associate and who was qualified to do that work. In her first literacy narrative she writes, "I never considered myself a good writer. I just like doing it." Kate, like many other first-year Writing Associates, felt that, as a Writing Associate, she was supposed to be a perfect writer. She did not feel as though she was a "good writer" and therefore questioned her qualifications. Similarly, other Writing Associates questioned their ability as WAs, wondering how they could be expected to advise other students about writing when they did not believe that they were good writers themselves. This was the predicament that Kate faced. However, in her second literacy narrative, Kate explains how she reconciled this difficulty:

> Coupled with my work with my assigned class through the WA program, I realized one of the most common misconceptions about the WA program, particularly the people involved in it. This is that all WA's must be excellent writers. . . . When I wrote my essay to become a WA, I placed a large amount of emphasis on the lack of self-confidence I had in my writing. . . . I still do not consider myself a good writer. What I have discovered, however, is that there is a large difference in my views about what a 'good writer' is. . . . Instead of being a good writer, I have come to the realization that I have developed a decent understanding of how a paper should come together.

As the result of her experience of working with other writers, Kate has come to recognize and denounce the "trap" that she, herself, fell into: the idea that Writing Associates must be perfect writers. Furthermore, through her realization that Writing Associates should not, and cannot, be perfect writers, Kate learned a greater lesson: good writing is not easy to define and, in most cases, lacks a clear definition. As we have seen, Kate's work as a Writing Associate has changed her views about being a Writing Associate and, correspondingly, has changed her views about writing in general.

THE THREE IDENTITIES OF A WA

While the first strategy allowed us to focus on attitudinal changes over time, the second produced, for us, the most interesting results. We learned that while most Writing Associates clearly understand their work as tutors as requiring complex negotiations of several kinds, they also had a difficult time articulating the exact nature of those negotiations. We believe that Writing Associates define themselves in three ways: student, tutor, and tutor-as-student. The student identity we understand as one who learns through classes, writing assignments, class work, and guidance from professors. The role of tutor we understand as one who teaches and helps others because they have expertise or knowledge that others need help accessing. The role of tutor-as-student we understand as one who combines both of these identities at the same time and learns through teaching or helping others. By providing help to students, the tutor is also learning something about himself or herself and his or her own writing processes.

If we examine the literacy narratives looking for these three identities, we can see how Writing Associates struggle with the tutor-student binary as traditionally understood, that is the tutor as a kind of teacher and the student as the learner. The tutor-student binary is of importance because it so heavily permeates composition discourse community. While students are not members of the discourse community who hold power— teachers and professors hold the power—they are still members of the discourse community so they too are still influenced by its ideals. Therefore, it is difficult for Writing Associates to escape traditional teacher and student roles, reflect upon them, and call them into question.

We will first consider the student identity. Andrew Platt explains, "My past year of writing has been characterized by roughly three experiences— one a class, one my personal writing, and one my poetic writing." He then continues to explain how being a student changed his perceptions of writing. The only mention of being a Writing Associate comes in the final paragraph when he mentions, "Of course, the implications of this for my work as a WA (or vice versa) are not terribly clear." Andrew appears to solely identify with the student face. He attributes any change in his writing to class work, personal writing, and poetic writing. He makes no mention of his Writing Associate work until the end of his paper, and even then, he does not clearly relate his student status with his Writing Associate status.

Other Writing Associates represent themselves primarily as students but also touch upon their experiences as peer tutors. For example, one Writing Associate explains, "Due to the nature of the writing assignments I completed over the past year, I have begun to see writing more as a tool and means for exploration rather than a task."

On the last page, this WA finally discusses how being a Writing Associate influenced her own writing:

Over the past year, my work as a Writing Associate has also contributed to the evolution of my writing identity. After, "WA-ing" for a first year seminar class and reading numerous papers with no thesis, structure, or organization, I learned to appreciate a writing tool I previously disregarded, outlining. Although I always would scribble a few ideas down on paper before I began to write, I never really made much of an outline for my papers until I saw, first-hand, how beneficial it was to the student with whom I was working. This technique proved essential to me when I set out to tackle my own structural disaster in my Renaissance Literature paper.

Within her narrative, this Writing Associate focuses on her student identity; however, she does mention how the tutor position helped her appreciate outlining. Still it is interesting to note that she ends this passage by referring to her Renaissance Literature paper. Therefore, she still seems to view herself primarily in a student position.

The second identity we will consider is the tutor identity. Art Lathers, for example, explains:

When I met with the class for the first time, I warned them about the different writing style involved. I said that the format of the papers was different than other forms of writing and told the class not to worry excessively. Professor X immediately said to me in front of the class, "Art, we're going to have to work on these introductions." I questioned him about it later, and he explained that the writing style was not much different than other classes; I never believed that. My conferences with the students only revealed the truth of my initial warning. . . . Unfortunately, the majority of my WA conferences did not focus on the body of the paper. I spent all of my effort focusing and narrowing the thesis, which I could not effectively do anyway.

Within this excerpt, Art discusses how he tried to help students in the class. Through the words "I spent all my effort," Art suggests that he is teaching the students by exerting his effort to help them. Not only does Art identify himself as a teacher, he also seems to struggle with the professor for "teacher" power and status. Art seems to keep himself firmly planted within the tutor position and gives no recognition that he learned from being a Writing Associate.

Mark Coslett's narrative slightly varies from the first example. He discusses some of the dangers of locating oneself in the tutor position. He explains:

I did mention that I must be careful when talking about structure and style. I have caught myself pressing my style onto the papers I read as a WA. Only after my first semester as a WA did I notice this dictatorship. Now I let the writers be themselves. I merely provide a crutch for their writing. While reading the paper, I note the style. In the conference I discuss the style of the paper with the writer. I make the writer aware that he or she has a style, and I point out some details found in that style.

Mark appears to be aware of his power as a tutor. He recognizes that he was pressing his style onto students, perhaps "helping" the students too much. Yet it is interesting to note that even after he recognizes his "dictatorship," he continues to talk about himself in the tutor position. He remains in the tutor position; he just seems more aware of the problems that might result in the tutor situation. Mark's excerpt shows how powerful the traditional binary is to escape.

The last identity to consider is that of tutor-as-student. Writing Associates who identify themselves as tutor-as-students often understand and attempt to transcend the traditional binary. Vilas Menon writes:

> The WA-writer interdependence grew even stronger in the spring of 2001. Prior to the semester, the last time I had written a non-engineering paper in English was the spring of 1999. Thus, when I had to write a 12-page paper for my politics class, I found, to my shock, that it was going to be a major challenge. I could not rely on a present organization sequence (as in most engineering reports), and I had to develop my own outline. Here, being a WA was a tremendous help. Although I had not written such a paper for the last 18 months, I had read plenty of them. When I had my next set of conferences, I focused on the organization and progression of each student's paper. During the actual meetings, I asked the students how they had decided to structure their paper. A week later, I got to write my own paper and tried many of the different organizational techniques I had learned during the conferences. I asked myself, "what about this method?" and "why do this?"

Vilas acknowledges that Writing Associates and writers share some sort of interdependence connection. He explains that he learned from the writers he worked with, which indicates that Vilas views himself as a learning student. Even though he was being a tutor and asking questions to help the students, he was also acting as a student and learning at the same time. Furthermore, Vilas seems confident that he can and will learn from the students he is helping.

And, finally, Scott Featherman also identifies as a tutor-as-student. He writes:

> All kidding aside, my experiences over the past year have demonstrated how valuable being a WA has been for my own writing. I remember that in one of the conferences I had this year, I was trying to explain to a student that the writing lacked a certain "flow." When

I used that word, she asked me to articulate, and after thinking for a few moments, I told her that her writing lacked flow because through asides, she was varying from the logical proof of her thesis that was the point of her paper. After saying those words, I immediately realized that I had made a personal revelation on a weakness in my own writing. It was at that moment that I realized why I am a WA, knowledge of self, rather than the rather large increase in stipend."

Within this excerpt, Scott notes that he learned from being a Writing Associate. By explaining to a student, Scott became a student himself. So, even though he at first puts himself in the tutor position, he combines roles and acknowledges he can learn and be a student. Therefore, Scott appears to have broken the traditional binary and crossed into the tutor-as-student role.

As our analysis reveals, each Writing Associate has learned something about himself or herself and his or her own writing processes through the experience of working to help other students with their writing. While the Writing Associates may not always consciously understand what they have learned and while they might have difficulty articulating what they have learned, the literacy narratives serve to highlight much of what the Writing Associates have learned and the processes through which they have learned.

In fact, what the literacy narratives ultimately show is that Writing Associates learn from being WAs; they learn about writing, in general, and their own writing processes from the work they do to help other students. First, Writing Associates learn merely because they are introduced to different disciplines and genres. Because they are relied upon to advise other students with their writing, Writing Associates must become informed themselves. Most Writing Associates are not familiar with all the intricacies and conventions of all the disciplines that they will work with. Therefore, they learn about the particulars of a given discipline so that they can better help the students with whom they are working. Second, Writing Associates learn while directly helping those students. They learn the definitions of grammatical terms and how to articulate what the writing needs in order to help other students. This sharpens their own understanding of writing. Furthermore, by constantly surveying the writing of others with a critical eye, Writing Associates begin looking at their own writing more critically. They tend to see some of the same mistakes in their own writing and they then follow the same advice that they give to the students with whom they are working. Because of this process, Writing Associates learn about what their own writing needs and how to improve them, as well as the process of writing in general.

CONCLUSIONS

Our research has brought to light the importance of studying both literacy narratives and competent college writers. In fact, we would argue that any writing program that involves undergraduate tutors (and possibly even graduate teaching assistants) would benefit from the incorporation of the literacy narrative assignment into its training program. The literacy narrative allows students an opportunity to create their own narratives and to speak in their own voices. It also allows students to explore and reflect on the often-unconscious learning process. And it invites students to step back and examine their roles, which allows students a greater level of self-reflection.

But another point we want to make is the importance of such work—the careful reading and interpretation of "proficient" writing by "proficient" writers—for the field of composition studies as a whole. As we noted earlier in our essay, the composition discourse community tends to render the "good writer" invisible, focusing instead on the ill prepared writer—the "basic" writer who "lacks" certain skills or is unfamiliar with the conventions of academic discourse. That emphasis is not surprising, and we do not mean to disparage it. After all, narratives that move from failure to success, from lack to fulfillment, are good stories, interesting to write and compelling to read. Certainly, there is much to learn about writing from challenges faced by the unprepared or confused writer.

Still, we would argue that there is a great deal that can be learned about writing from listening to what the "good writer" has to say. For example, from our research we learned that the traditional understanding of the teacher/student relationship is powerfully imprinted on students. To transform this relationship from a binary into a dialogical one, much work must be done, and this work, we would argue, is best initiated through extended self-reflections provided by such instruments as literacy narratives. Still, this is not all we learned about "good writing" from examining these narratives. We also learned that students' conceptions about writing abilities and writing components change over time due to various forces. Most importantly, we learned that student writers need to foster self-reflection by questioning and reflecting upon how their writing histories and their understandings of writing influence their work as student writers and peer tutors.

All these considerations point to the importance of educators' listening to what students themselves have to say about their development as writers. We sought to do the same in our essay and studies. The literacy narrative is one tool that allows students a forum through which they can explore their development as writers. But there are certainly others, such as portfolios and journals. These devices of writing, reflecting, talking back, talking about, and self-representing all have in common the ability to serve as what Linda Alcoff refers to as a "countersentence." Alcoff believes that instead of speaking about or for others, we should speak to others so that they can "produce a countersentence that can suggest a new historical narrative" (23). In other words, students need to be allowed the opportunity to engage in the rhetoric of the composition field so that they can create more accurate representations of themselves.

As we have explored throughout this essay, when students are allowed to create "countersentences," we see a new image of the student appear. We see students with intelligent, well thought-out ideas concerning writing, individuality, and learning. The discourse community of composition can then learn about the concerns of student writers and student writing from the writers themselves. Just as we, as students, listened to our student colleagues' voices and learned a great deal, so do we, in turn, invite you to listen to the voices of others.

Acknowledgments: We would like to thank Professor Bianca Falbo, Professor Beth Seetch, Professor William Carpenter and, especially, Professor Patricia Donahue for all of their support and assistance during our research project. We would also like to give a special thanks to all of the Writing Associates: without their words, we would have no research.

NOTES

1. We will be referring to our peer tutors throughout the essay as "Writing Associates" and "WAs," not peer tutors. Within the College Writing Program at Lafayette College, we have made a conscious decision not to use the term "tutor" because students at Lafayette College have come to associate tutors with those who work with remedial students. At Lafayette, we wished to depart from that common understanding; we chose "associate" so that both students would have the understanding that they are considered as equals, working together towards a common goal.

2. We found approximately 94 articles that were relevant to our study. We have selected a few articles that we found most helpful.

Daniel, Beth. 1997. "Narratives of Literacy: Connecting Composition to Culture." *College Composition and Communication* 50: 393–410.

Davies, Ruth. 1951. "A Defense of Freshman." *College English* 12: 441–448.

Elbow, Peter. 1973. "A Method for Teaching Writing." *College English* 30: 115–125.

Farmer, Frank. 1996 "Dialogue and Critique: Bakhtin and the Cultural Studies Writing Classroom." *College Composition and Communication* 49: 186–207.

Henderson, Lois Taylor. 1942. "Democratic Procedure in Freshman English." *College English* 4: 191–195.

Kelly, Lou. 1973. "Toward Competence and Creativity." *College English* 34: 644–660.

Lu, Min Zhan. 1994. "Professing Multiculturalism: The Politics of Style in the Contact Zone." *College Composition and Communication* 45: 442–458.

Miller, Richard. 1994. "Fault Lines in the Contact Zone." *College English* 56: 389–408.

Mills, Barriss. 1953. "Writing as a Process." *College English* 15: 19–26.

Mortensen, Peter, and Gesa E. Kirsch. 1993. "On Authority in the Study of Writing." *College Composition and Communication* 44.4: 556–569.

Rothwell, Kenneth S. 1959. "Psychiatry and the Freshman Theme." *College English* 20: 338–342.

Whitter, Gale. 1978. "Transforming the 'Same Paper' Syndrome." *College English* 40: 151–156.

WORKS CITED

Alcoff, Linda. 1991–1992. "The Problem of Speaking for Others." *Cultural Critique* 20 (Winter): 5–32.

Davies, Ruth. 1951. "A Defense of Freshmen." *College English* 12: 441–448.

Helmers, Marguerite H. 1994. *Writing Students: Composition, Testimonials, and Representations of Students.* Albany: SUNY Press.

Lu, Min Zhan. 1994. "Professing Multiculturalism: The Politics of Style in the Contact Zone." *College Composition and Communication* 45: 442–458.

Whitter, Gale. 1978. "Transforming the 'Same Paper' Syndrome." *College English* 40: 151–156.

APPENDIX 1

NEW WRITING ASSOCIATES

Your Literary Narrative Project for Workshop Due

Format: 1 diskette and 1 hard copy

Describe your history as a writer, from your first attempts to write in (or even before) elementary school to your experiences as an "academic writer" in college courses. (PLEASE do not refer to faculty members at Lafayette College by name.) Focus most intensely on the experiences— positive and negative—that are most meaningful to you.

To construct such a personal history—a narrative of your growth in literacy—you should consider the material conditions under which you have written (the kinds of classes, the kinds of implements such as pen, pencil, typewriter, and computer), the types of writing you have been required to do or have done on your own, the reactions of others to your writing, and your feelings about writing and about the reactions of others to your writing (and whether or how such feelings have changed over the years).

Rather than record every detail and capture every memory (though we do want you to be thorough), you may want to identify a handful of **formative** experiences from your earliest school years to college courses that have shaped you into the kind of writer you now believe you are.

Here are some questions to start you thinking. Please do not attempt to answer them all. Also, please construct this story as a story, arranged in chronological order ("my earliest memories are . . . " "in fourth grade Mr. Grimley . . . " "my high school physics teacher assigned . . . " "my first year seminar was like a bucket of cold water thrown in my face . . . ").

What was your very first writing act, and when did it occur? What are your earliest memories about writing? What kinds of "school writing" (genres like argument and research paper) have you been asked to produce over the years, and how clearly have these genres been explained to you? Have you ever used "creative" writing forms or more informal types of expression, like journals and freewriting (and if so, when), and did you do this kind of work on your own or was it assigned? What kinds of comments have teachers made about your writing over the years? Have you ever shown your writing to friends or family? How have their comments or teacher comments made you feel? Have you tended to agree or disagree with them, and why? When you graduated from high school, did you feel you were "adequately prepared" for college writing (and what did the idea of "adequate preparation" mean to you)? What expectations about college level writing did you have? Did your first year writing experiences at Lafayette College confirm or challenge those expectations, and how? What has been your best experience as a writer? Your worst experience?

The purpose of writing such a narrative is to reflect on your own history as a writer. It is a rare opportunity to understand how you got to where you are today, as a new Writing Associate who will soon serve as an informed reader of other peoples' writing. As a Writing Associate you will have to deal, implicitly or explicitly, with the effects of other writers' histories.

Your narrative should be approximately 7 typed pages, double-spaced.

APPENDIX 2

RETURNING WRITING ASSOCIATES

Writing Like a WA Project for Workshop Due

For this year's project, describe your history as a writer **over the last year**. Since in the past we received from you a "global" history of yourself as a writer, it makes sense to ask for a focused and detailed history of the recent past, which could serve as an addendum—but also as a development of some of the questions posed and discoveries made previously. It also makes sense to focus only on the 2000–2001 year since some of you have already written about '99–'00. Finally, we ask you consciously to include new WAs in your audience and to think of this paper as a presentation to them of what it might be like to "Write Like a WA"—at least the way you have done.

As you compose, you should apply in detail many of the same questions from the first assignment to your work as a writer from August 2000 to the present. (The old assignment is provided here for you.) You may refer to some of the same instances about which you wrote previously, and you may recall new early experiences, but if you do you should attempt to place them in a new context, as background to the featured discussion of 2000–2001.

In this paper you should review in detail the most crucial writing and WA experiences you had last year.

For example: Which, if any, writing experiences would you call formative? Typical? Difficult? Rewarding? In which experiences could you see yourself developing, changing, or establishing a writing identity? A different writing process? What obstacles did you encounter? New disciplines? New expectations from different audiences? New research methodologies or theories to apply? New expectations of your own? Give some serious thought, too, to how working as a WA played a role in last year's writing history. Did you find yourself challenging the advice you give out to other writers? Breaking rules you had thought were absolute? Turning to other WAs for advice? Mirroring any behaviors of the writers you conferred with? Asking different questions of your professors?

When you saw your first student writers in conference, what authority did you draw on to help them? Did any of last year's writing experiences bring your WA-work into clearer focus? Or prompt you to approach your conferences differently? How do you see yourself beginning the academic year now? What kinds of summer experiences might play a role in your writer's history? What is some of the most valuable advice you could share with new WAs?

Once again, the purpose of writing such a narrative is to reflect on your own history as a writer—this time your recent history as both writer and WA. Doing so will heighten your awareness of the fact that each writer you see has his or her own history, much more than what the single draft you work with in a conference will reveal. Furthermore, your reflection on your recent WA/writer experiences will prepare you to lend a hand to the new WAs coming on board this fall.

Your narrative should be approximately 7 typed pages, double-spaced.

Student Activity

READING, ANALYSIS, AND REFLECTION

Read the Bastian and Harkness essay. Reflect on their approach to the research through the following questions:

1. Why did Bastian and Harkness undertake this research? What was their research question?
2. What kinds of textual analysis did the authors use in their research process? Would you advise them to add other analyses to their approach?
3. Why do the authors include information about their institutional context? How is that important?
4. A review of literature, summarizing research foundational for the current project, is included. How would you describe these sources? What do you think of the authors' approach to how these works are cited?
5. What did the authors learn as a result of their research?
6. Are there policy or practice implications from the research?
7. What did you admire about this research project? What would you do differently if you were researching this same topic?
8. These student-researchers are working with human participants and their texts. How did they protect these participants through principles of responsible conduct of research (RCR)?

6

Conducting a Case Study

The *case study* is a qualitative approach used to look at a single case, a small group of participants, a class, or a program. It involves description and analysis and is often used to make recommendations. Although the case study has its roots in sociology and anthropology, it has also been used in the medical profession by clinicians.

Case studies have become the research of choice for teachers, as this method taps into a skill that every teacher has already: observation. Informal observation can lead to beliefs about what works and what doesn't work for individual teachers. But systematic observation can produce results that can be used not only to improve instruction in the teacher's classroom but also shared with other teachers. For instance, what is the percentage of teacher talk and student talk in a classroom? If a teacher wishes to have a student-centered classroom, it seems important that teacher talk not dominate. To test the percentage of teacher talk as opposed to student talk, one student might be deputized to keep a record of time during a class period. Or, perhaps the teacher wants to test whether they truly focus on global issues as opposed to surface issues in teacher-student conferences. An audiotape of conferences can reveal whether the teacher is practicing what is being preached. Comments are labeled according to topics discussed—paragraph development, sentence structure, coherence, punctuation—and then tabulated.

Another advantage of the case study is the relatively small number of subjects or participants involved. Collecting the data can involve observing but also interviewing, testing, or analyzing writing samples. Reading

TABLE 6.1. Types of outlines (from Emig's study)

Theme Assignment	Total Number of Expository Themes Written	Total Number of Outlines	Number of Informal Outlines	Number of Formal Outlines
1.	25	15	9	6
2.	14	6	6	0
3.	23	6	5	1
4.	22	4	3	1
5.	25	9	8	1
Total	109	40	31	9

transcripts of a peer-response group may employ the same kind of textual analysis as is found in literary criticism. Who are the characters? What is their motivation? Is there conflict? For single-subject research, multiple measures taken over a period of time are used.

Janet Emig watched eight students writing, interviewed them, and then analyzed the data. The students developed writing autobiographies and talked aloud while composing. The result was *The Composing Processes of Twelfth Graders* (Emig 1971), which influenced the teacher-researcher movement. Emig's thick description relied on multiple details, and the study helped change the way writing is taught.

Emig's study included tables that quantified the types of outlines that accompanied 109 expository themes written by twenty-five eleventh-grade students in order to get at the concept of planning (see Table 6.1).

To test the hypothesis that formal planning—an outline—influenced the quality of the writing, Emig asked three evaluators to read and grade the themes. The result? There was no correlation between the grade the student received for organization and the use of an outline (Emig 1971, 26–27).

In this instance, Emig used quantitative data to support a hypothesis and a finding. On the other hand, the profile of one of the participants, Lynn, is written as a thick description in narrative style, and it is an excellent example of how storytelling is important to case study.

> The community in which Lynn lives is one of the few truly cross-cultural districts within Chicago. The local couplet, like the area, runs "From the mill/To Pill Hill." The mills are the steel mills of South Chicago; near them lie, often on relief, blacks and newly arrived Mexicans and Puerto Ricans. "Pill Hill" is the residential area where many Jewish doctors, dentists, and professors live. Between lie several miles of small brick bungalows owned by second generation Polish- and Serbian-Americans. . . .

Lynn lives on "Pill Hill," the oldest of four children of a Jewish lawyer. Her mother is a high school history teacher at the same high school Lynn attends. (45)

The profile of Lynn also includes texts she has written, essays, and poetry. In addition, Emig includes Lynn's comments on writing: "Yeah, I can sort of wrap it up here by saying like, 'Throughout the interview which involved the math test blah, blah, blah'" (57). Emig also includes behaviors she observes. In other words, Emig assembles multiple data sources in order to draw conclusions.

The family tree of writing research that began with Emig extends to many other important researchers and studies. Donald Graves's (1975) examination of the writing processes of seven-year-olds, Sondra Perl's (1979) "The Composing Processes of Unskilled College Writers," Nancy Sommers's (1980) work on revision strategies, and Flower and Hayes's (1981) "A Cognitive Process Theory of Writing" helped move the focus from the written products to the writing process itself—all in an effort to help writers improve.

The popularity of case-study research is evident in the number of studies undertaken post-Emig. For instance, Glenda Bissex (1980) studied her own son's literacy development in *GNYS AT WRK*. Nancie Atwell (1987) began testing her assumptions about teaching junior-high-school students in her *In the Middle*. That work has made her highly respected among those who teach "tweens."

TEACHER RESEARCH: IMPROVING PRACTICE

The teacher-researcher movement grew, in part, out of a belief that teachers could best observe and analyze situations in their classrooms and, as a result, become better teachers and also add to the knowledge base. Classroom research can be a powerful professional-development experience for the teacher. *Action research*, a common approach to teacher research, is grounded in the belief that individual practitioners can see an issue or problem and, by gathering information and analyzing it, can then improve practice and perhaps even influence policy.

More often than not, teacher research relies on the case study, as the case is close to hand, and teachers can test out theories and then put them to use. Teacher research includes an important reflection element that structures this activity for a teacher and is essential to pedagogical change. It means making time for reflection.

Bissex and Bullock (1987) gather case-study research by several teachers in their *Seeing for Ourselves*. The essays include year-long studies as well as more short-term studies; the settings for the studies range from first grade to college writing classes. Their topics include the following and show the diverse possibilities of teacher research:

- "The Effect of Poetry in a First-Grade Classroom"
- "The Use of Commonplace Books in the English Class" (sixth grade)
- "A Learning-Disabled Child in a Writing-Process Classroom"
- "Who's Responsible for Finding and Correcting Mechanical Errors"
- "Roles and Strategies in College Writing Conferences"
- "Observing a Would-Be Novelist"
- "A Writer Composes Aloud: Tracing Cognitive Processes in Writing"

Daiker and Morenberg's (1990) edited volume on teacher research includes more examples of possible classroom research projects.

- "Children's Choices: The Topics of Young Writers"
- "Multigenre Research Paper"
- "Storytelling in a Technical Writing Class"
- "Observing Students' Reflective Thinking"
- "Interaction and Assessment: Some Applications of Reader-Response Criticism to the Evaluation of Student Writing in a Poetry Writing Class"
- "Negotiating Authority in Peer Response"
- "The Teacher as Eavesdropper: Listening in on the Language of Collaboration"
- "Teaching Writing Using Networked Computers"
- "Tutoring Dyslexic College Students"

While teacher research might fall under the definition of ethnography, some teacher-researchers believe they do not have the distance typical of the ethnographer even though they can be characterized as participant-observers. MacLean and Mohr (1999) believe that when teachers become teacher-researchers, the "traditional descriptions of both teachers and researchers change. Teacher-researchers raise questions about what they think and observe about their teaching and their students' learning. They collect student work in order to evaluate performance, but they also see student work as data to analyze in order to examine the teaching and learning that produced it" (x).

Teacher research carries with it the possibility of empowering teachers, but the roles of both teacher and researcher may take a toll on the person. The teacher takes on a dual role—and perhaps at times dueling roles. The teacher must stay true to the research project and be consistent according to the study's methods; however, this is more burden on what is generally a heavy workload already. The teachers who engage in research, though, talk about the experience as life changing.

Teacher research is sometimes termed *action research* although the latter is intentionally structured so the researcher can take action as a result of an investigation. The overarching goal is to improve instruction. The process of action research is similar to assessment and the feedback loop: a situation is studied and an issue or problem identified; a change to improve the situation is introduced; the situation is studied again, and the change is assessed for efficacy; and the process starts all over again. Action research has been linked to continuous-improvement assessment.

As with any research project, the topic often is derived from reflection and discussion with colleagues. A review of literature reveals whether or not solutions have already been uncovered. If not, a study is designed with a working hypothesis and put into place. The results are monitored and analyzed. If the outcome is significant, it's expected that the teacher would make changes in the classroom or other learning space based on those results and also share with colleagues. The topic may be about a question or puzzle about learning, or it may focus on teacher behavior itself. Likewise, teaching techniques may be interrogated through action research.

The National Writing Project (NWP), established in 1974 in the Bay Area, was created to improve the teaching of writing K–16. One of its primary principles is that teachers make the best teachers of other teachers in a teachers-teaching-teachers philosophy. The professional development offered through NWP sites across the nation demonstrates that teachers are effective leaders and researchers. The National Writing Project has been a leader in the revolution to move teaching writing from a product stance to a process approach. While teachers can certainly take up a variety of methodologies in teacher research—historical, text analysis—most commonly, the case study is the go-to method.

Tutor-researchers and teacher-researchers share a common goal: to tutor or teach better and to improve learning. Practitioner inquiry offers the possibility of transformative change, not just for learners but also for the practitioners themselves.

CASE-STUDY PROCESSES

Reading case-study research is helpful before beginning a research study. The NCTE journal *Research in the Teaching of English* (*RTE*) provides examples, too. The *Qualitative Studies in Education, Anthropology and Education Quarterly* and ERIC are other good sources of case-study research.

Where do research questions come from? It may be that there is something in the classroom or another writing environment that has been nagging at a practitioner. Why does one assignment work better than another? Curiosity can be a good friend to finding a worthwhile topic.

Several subject communities come to mind: students in a class, yourself as a writer, mature writers, reluctant writers. The participant(s) is then crossed with a topic, such as coherence, errors, student-teacher conferences, revision, or technology. Once the topic is established, it's time to begin prewriting about the project, jotting thoughts in a journal or log. What does the researcher know about the topic already? What is known from others?

Once the researcher's personal stake is ascertained, a review of the scholarly literature reveals the history of ideas on the topic. Developing a list of key terms (e.g., *peer editing, sentence length, writing tutors, digital writing*) makes a search easier. It's important in a review to differentiate among the types of literature written about the topic. Is it a research article? A textbook? A popular article? A prescriptive website?

Reading the literature serves many functions, primarily to find out where the holes are—areas where there are gaps in the knowledge base that a new case study may fill. A review also suggests methodology. Finally, the review of literature provides the foundation that can convince others of the findings of the final project.

To summarize the case study approach:

- Who are my subjects/participants? A single student, a group of students, a classroom, an administrator, yourself?
- What is the topic? Literature response journals in junior high; frequency of homophone spelling errors in college-aged students; publishing in-school literary magazines?
- What time frame will the study cover? A school term, a few days, four years?
- What data are collected and by what methods?
- How will results be reported?
- What theory informs the research?

Here are some examples of how specific projects were defined.

The researcher will look at the writing of *three students* to see how *a revision approach the teacher developed* influences their writing; the researcher will *collect a draft of each text* as well as *two journal entries* that include their reflections on their own writing; in addition, the researcher will keep *notes on what students say during writing conferences.*

Another researcher traced her evolution as a writer, drawing on a storage trunk of papers written from elementary school through college.

Yet another researcher studied *collaborative writing* in a writing-intensive anthropology class (Lancy, Rhees, and Kinkead 1994). Data came from instructor-designed *student-feedback forms, the university's standard student-evaluation forms, and interviews.* The results of the case study provided information for evaluating the innovative curriculum and suggested revisions.

Writing up the study means providing contextual background, a review of literature, a summary of data used (e.g., samples of student writing, tables, figures, summaries, or descriptions), and interpretation.

While the case study uses a qualitative approach, quantitative analysis may also be included as is clear from some of the "counting" examples used earlier in this chapter. The researcher may make recommendations based on the results. Any problems or limitations to the study are also included. And, typically, the researcher suggests directions for future research.

Case studies seek to explain, describe, and explore. Some researchers (e.g., Lauer and Asher 1988) believe that case-study research lays the foundation for the question or issue to be studied further through empirical designs and that case-study research may not be an end in itself. Case studies are often used to "study interventions or innovations" (Lancy 1993, 140). While a case study may be used as an evaluative tool, the definition of case study has become less precise, similar to ethnography.

Profile of a Student Researcher: Natalie Cheney Homan

Natalie worked with Global Village Gifts, a volunteer-run fair-trade store that sells handcrafted items of artisans from countries all over the world, to analyze and update its website. As a nonprofit organization, Global Village Gifts has little money to devote to the hosting and maintenance of their website but wanted to improve the site, to make it work better for their needs and to reach out to a larger audience. Before creating a new website, Natalie analyzed the original version, conducting user research to determine how users perceived the credibility of the organization based on its website. Drawing on her review of literature, Natalie chose an appropriate model as the basis for assessing credibility. Rigorous scholarship informs the design of a communication product that meets the needs of a real organization committed to a fair-trade mission.

Approved by the Institutional Review Board (IRB), the study drew on information from a focus group. The revised website, designed and developed by Natalie, was informed by user research and her own expertise developed through the professional and technical writing program. The new website features an e-commerce option so products can be sold online in the future (see http://www.globalvillagegifts.org/). Technical-communication research involves designing and conducting user research and then translating the data into design requirements that balance the needs of users and the desires of the client.

While case-study research may be difficult to generalize or aggregate, it does carry with it several advantages, which speak to its popularity. Lincoln and Guba (1985) note these attributes of case-study research:

- Builds an "emic" reconstruction of the respondents' constructions, in contrast to an "etic" one that would reinforce a positivist's

a priori inquiries; [*emic* refers to an insider's perspective while *etic* is an outsider's (read: objective) perspective; in essence, the researcher enters the study with an open mind and no preconceived conclusions (even if a hypothesis is present)]
- Builds on the interaction between the reader and the research; the narrative is presented as holistic and lifelike descriptions of events, not unlike those the reader would normally experience;
- Exposes the interactions between the inquirer and the participant;
- Allows the reader to challenge the work by searching for internal consistency, trustworthiness;
- Provides "thick description" or triangulated data, thus improving the likelihood that the reader can see implications for new settings;
- Provides a grounded picture of context. (quoted in Bridwell-Bowles 1991, 106)

A case study of one—the researcher—may be an apt way to begin to become accustomed to the method. The writer/researcher may take a long-range view, looking back on a trunk full of writing assignments and interviewing parents about literacy development, or the investigation may focus more succinctly on a few weeks, perhaps charting how the writer progressed (or did not) in a writing-focused class. Such a case study of one gathers the artifacts of writing—the texts themselves—categorizes them, and looks for themes or threads. Informants may include tutors, teachers, peers, or family members. Such self-analysis may be enlightening and exciting. And it is definitely good preparation for undertaking a formal study.

A reminder about research ethics. Whenever human participants (other than self) are involved, a proposal to the Institutional Review Board (IRB) is necessary, even if there is minimal risk to the participants. The IRB will determine status—perhaps exemption from full-board review—and assist the researcher with informed-consent forms and processes.

Sara Mulcahy's (2012) essay accompanies this chapter as an example of a case study that appeared in volume 10 of *Young Scholars in Writing*. As a case study, it includes multiple data-collecting methods: surveys, interviews, and text analysis. In the conclusion Mulcahy discusses implications and makes recommendations for policy and practice. Mulcahy wanted to see how well what a student learned in first-year writing courses transferred to other classes. The study increased in complexity when the subject chosen was an ESL student. *Transfer* of knowledge and practices of writing is increasingly a topic of scholarly research. Teaching for transfer focuses on curricular initiatives to ensure students understand that what they learn in the first-year writing course has an effect on writing they do in other contexts (Yancey et al. 2014).

REFERENCES AND FOR FURTHER READING

Atwell, Nancie. 1987. *In the Middle: Writing and Reading with Adolescents.* Portsmouth, NH: Heinemann.

Bissex, Glenda. 1980. *GNYS AT WRK: A Child Learns to Write and Read.* Cambridge, MA: Harvard University Press.

Bissex, Glenda L., and Richard H. Bullock. 1987. *Seeing for Ourselves: Case-Study Research by Teachers of Writing.* Portsmouth, NH: Heinemann.

Bridwell-Bowles, Lillian. 1991. "Research in Composition: Issues and Methods." In *An Introduction to Composition Studies*, edited by Erika Lindemann and Gary Tate, 94–117. New York: Oxford University Press.

Chewning, Bill. 2007. "The Expanding Center: Creating an Online Presence for the UMBC Writing Center." *Young Scholars in Writing* 5:50–62.

Daiker, Donald A., and Max Morenberg. 1990. *The Writing Teacher as Researcher.* Portsmouth, NH: Heinemann.

Emig, Janet. 1971. *The Composing Processes of Twelfth Graders.* Urbana, IL: NCTE.

Flower, Linda, and John R. Hayes. 1981. "A Cognitive Process Theory of Writing." *College Composition and Communication* 32 (4): 365–87. http://dx.doi.org/10.2307/356600.

Graves, Donald. 1975. "An Examination of the Writing Processes of Seven-Year-Old Children." *Research in the Teaching of English* 9 (3):227–41.

Hull, Glynda, and Mike Rose. 1990. "'This Wooden Shack Place': The Logic of an Unconventional Reading." *College Composition and Communication* 41 (3): 287–98. http://dx.doi.org/10.2307/357656.

Lancy, David F. 1993. *Qualitative Research in Education: An Introduction to the Major Traditions.* New York: Longman.

Lancy, David F., Alan Rhees, and Joyce Kinkead. 1994. "A Sense of Community: Collaboration in a Large Anthropology Class." *College Teaching* 42 (3): 102–6. http://dx.doi.org/10.1080/87567555.1994.9926834.

Lauer, Janice M., and J. William Asher. 1988. *Composition Research: Empirical Designs.* New York: Oxford University Press.

Lincoln, Yvonne S., and E.G. Guba. 1985. *Naturalistic Inquiry.* Newbury Park, CA: SAGE.

MacLean, Marion S., and Marian M. Mohr. 1999. *Teacher-Researchers at Work.* Berkeley, CA: National Writing Project.

Mulcahy, Sara. 2012. "'I Realize Writing Is a Part of My Daily Life Now': A Case Study of Writing Knowledge Transfer in One Section of ESL Writing." *Young Scholars in Writing* 10:43–57.

Perl, Sondra. 1979. "The Composing Processes of Unskilled College Writers." *Research in the Teaching of English* 13 (4): 317–36.

Sommers, Nancy. 1980. "Revision Strategies of Student Writers and Experienced Adult Writers." *College Composition and Communication* 31 (4): 378–88. http://dx.doi.org/10.2307/356588.

Yancey, Kathleen Blake, Liane Robertson, and Kara Taczak. 2014. *Writing across Contexts: Transfer, Composition, and Sites of Writing.* Logan: Utah State University Press.

"'I Realize Writing Is a Part of My Daily Life Now': A Case Study of Writing Knowledge Transfer in One Section of ESL Writing"

Sara Mulcahy, Bridgewater State University

Abstract

Most college and university students must complete first-year composition (FYC), including English as a second language (ESL) students. Many researchers in the field of composition and rhetoric question, though, whether FYC prepares beginning undergraduate students for courses they will take later in their academic careers. The question of FYC's effectiveness is heightened when considering its effect on ESL students, who must grapple with learning to write in a second language as they try to transfer their writing knowledge from FYC to their other courses. This paper examines the components of a successful FYC course for ESL students and whether students in a specific section of FYC for ESL students can transfer their writing knowledge from FYC to other courses they are taking the same semester.

First-year composition (FYC)'s role in the college curriculum is under constant scrutiny because of uncertainties as to whether the course is truly beneficial to new college students. One of the major reasons for speculation about FYC's value lies in ambiguities surrounding the transference of writing knowledge. Scholars in the field of composition and rhetoric are unsure if students are transferring what they learn in FYC courses to the writing they complete in courses across the curriculum—some researchers are concerned that the courses might not facilitate the application of learning outcomes for students writing in later courses.

Sara Mulcahy, "'I Realize Writing Is a Part of My Daily Life Now': A Case Study of Writing Knowledge Transfer in One Section of ESL Writing," *Young Scholars in Writing* 10(2012):43–57.

There are many reasons to believe there is a lack of learning transfer in FYC courses, and scholarship that emerged from what is called the "abolitionist movement" in the field of composition and rhetoric exposes these reasons. "Abolitionists" are scholars who find FYC to be flawed and seek dramatic changes to it. Sharon Crowley's article "A Personal Essay on Freshman English" served in the early 1990s as an inspiration for the abolitionist movement as many scholars embraced her critiques of FYC's role in colleges and universities. Crowley asserts that problems in FYC are curricular, finding that students are not even learning the "traditional essay" but rather are being drilled on their grammar skills via rote memorization. They cannot develop as writers because their focus on the mechanical aspects of writing impedes their ability to look at writing as a whole and develop rhetorical awareness (157).

While the current abolitionist movement can be traced to Crowley's essay, this movement has grown quite diverse in its goals. Maureen Daly Goggin and Susan K. Miller tackle some of the aspects of this abolitionist movement in their article "What Is New about the 'New Abolitionists': Continuities and Discontinuities in the Great Debate." They establish that many abolitionists, rather than seeking to abolish FYC, are calling for a dramatic reconstruction of it in colleges and universities. In this new model, instructors move beyond the typical framework of the academic essay. Some of the suggestions people have made in this new movement are

1. replacing first-year composition with writing intensive courses;
2. replacing first-year composition with freshmen writing seminars;
3. linking writing courses to other general education content courses;
4. reforming first-year composition through specifying a content for it. (96)

All of these suggestions offer a variety of writing opportunities to students. Goggin and Miller find new abolitionists split into three main groups: those who want to abolish FYC requirements, those who do not want to abolish the requirement but rather want to reinvent the course, and those who want to move the course out of the first-year (97).

The abolitionist debate covers a wide spectrum of FYC programs and certainly contributes to arguments about lack of learning transfer; however, none of these abolitionists include English as a second language (ESL) students in their research. The effectiveness of FYC for ESL students is certainly a topic worth pursuing, as ESL students are routinely entering American colleges and universities. The beliefs that shape the abolitionist movement also carry over into the discussion of the effectiveness of FYC for ESL students. Ilona Leki has argued provocatively against requiring FYC or EAP (English for Academic Purposes) programs for ESL undergraduate students. In "A Challenge to Second Language Writing Professionals: Is Writing Overrated?" Leki tackles five pro-writing claims which people in academia frequently make concerning the value of writing. Among these: "Writing can be, is, or should be personally fulfilling" and "Students will have to do a lot of writing in other courses in college in English" (318). Leki finds the first claim to be highly exaggerated because learning to write in English can be very stressful for ESL students, and they will find nothing fulfilling about it (319). Leki also believes the other claim is false. Based on her longitudinal study, Leki found that students she had worked with were not doing much writing outside of their composition courses. Further, if writing was required of them, it was often two years later, and many students no longer retained the information they had acquired in first-year composition courses (321). While Leki does not directly discuss learning transfer, her research indicates there is a lack of writing knowledge transfer from students' early undergraduate careers to their late undergraduate careers.

Keeping in mind the criticisms of FYC for both native English speakers (NES) and ESL students, below I will examine the effectiveness of an FYC course geared to instructing ESL students. I will combine a literature review and a case study of an FYC section designated for ESL writers, breaking both down into four major components to analyze writing knowledge transfer. Ultimately, I argue that writing knowledge transfer can occur if certain conditions are established and maintained.

EXPLORING FYC TRANSFER

While there is debate about whether FYC and EAP type instruction is successful in promoting transfer, there does seem to be agreement by abolitionists, supporters of FYC, and ESL composition researchers that certain strategies are more effective than others in promoting transfer. Based on my literature review, I developed a framework for the essential components of a university writing program that supports writing transfer. I argue that in order to promote the transfer of students' writing knowledge, ESL students should be enrolled in a university writing program that requires them to write often and in a variety of genres for a variety of rhetorical situations; learn writing strategies transferable to many different writing tasks; receive explicit writing instruction; and experience a positive campus atmosphere supportive of writing.

WRITING OFTEN AND VARIOUSLY

Perhaps one of the most difficult challenges ESL students encounter in their acquisition of writing knowledge is the infrequency of their chances to practice writing, as Lee Ann Carroll encounters in her research on FYC for NES students. "[T]he number of opportunities, outside of composition courses, that students have to practice in response to complex literacy tasks is very inconsistent from semester to semester" (51). While Carroll focuses on NES students in her research, the problem she presents would certainly have a negative impact on ESL students too. Such inconsistency makes it difficult for students to practice transferring their writing knowledge.

As important as frequent writing is the need to write in a variety of genres for a variety of rhetorical situations. While students might not need to write in all genres during the rest of their undergraduate careers, the experience of writing in a range of genres better equips them for encountering new writing tasks. One way of exposing students to a variety of kinds of writing is to implement a program in which the writing course is linked with a content area course. Ann M. Johns discusses the effectiveness of linked courses in her article "Teaching Classroom and Authentic Genres: Initiating Students into Academic Cultures and Discourses." Johns' university offers what she refers to as a "transition package" (281), in which English adjunct classes are attached to classes from the core curriculum. Johns finds that in FYC students are often taught "classroom genres" such as research papers and annotated bibliographies (282). She fears many students will not move past classroom genres and learn "authentic genres," texts "that serve real communicative purposes among professionals in the discipline" (283). Johns believes the linked courses at her university will promote effective writing in both classroom and authentic genres. She concludes that linked English courses prepare students to

> ask appropriate questions of content faculty . . . understand the limited purposes of CGs [classroom genres] . . . understand the nature of authentic genres and the purposes they serve within communities . . . be flexible—not cling to one referencing style, one summary style, or one text organization . . . [and] begin to understand the importance of audience in writing. (289)

Of course, an FYC course does not have to be a linked course in order to establish the variety of genres that John's linked courses promote. FYC teachers of ESL students can elect to teach a variety of "authentic genres" rather than the typical "classroom genre" alone. As authentic genres are simply those that serve real communicative purposes, an example could be something as simple as writing a brochure.

EXPLICIT INSTRUCTION

Dana Lynn Driscoll believes instructors can play an integral role in promoting students' writing transference skills. In "Connected, Disconnected, or

Uncertain: Student Attitudes about Future Writing Contexts and Perceptions of Transfer from First-year Writing to the Disciplines," Driscoll outlines six suggestions for writing instruction to promote transfer. One is "Do not assume transfer occurs—always directly address transfer through explicit teaching." Essentially, instructors should demonstrate to their students how their writing knowledge can transfer from course to course. Driscoll also suggests that instructors "ask students to think directly about, or engage with, writing situations they will encounter outside the writing classroom," "ask students to learn about how writing is done in their chosen professions by asking them to investigate writing in their fields," and "ask students to bring in and talk about the kinds of writing assignments they are doing in other courses." All of these approaches can help students make concrete connections between different writing situations, which will help them transfer their writing knowledge.

Mark A. James, a linguist who specializes in ESL writing transfer, is also an advocate for explicit teaching for transfer in ESL writing courses. In "'Far' Transfer of Learning Outcomes from an ESL Writing Course: Can the Gap Be Bridged?" James found, "Transfer can be stimulated by factors like explicit instruction in a task prompt . . . or the explicit structure of a task prompt" (78). Not only can instructors make explicit connections in course content and discussion, they can also implement explicit instruction on the actual writing prompts by giving clear specifications and providing definitions for any complex words within the prompt (79). Based on research conducted by Driscoll and James, then, it seems instructors should explicitly explain to their students how what they are learning in the class can transfer to other courses.

TEACHING STRATEGIES

Many comp/rhet scholars deem it difficult to anticipate the writing genres and assignments that undergraduate students, both ESL and NES, will complete during their undergraduate college careers. Though it may be difficult to transfer writing knowledge in the sense that one might never write in a specific genre again, it is possible to transfer writing strategies and various approaches to writing.

Carroll believes it is FYC instructors' ability to teach students writing strategies that makes it a useful course. She argues that if the tools students learn in FYC "help the novice writer take on more difficult literacy tasks in the time and space of the first-year composition course, then these strategies have value in this setting even if students do not continue to use them in quite the same ways in the future" (75). Here, Carroll emphasizes the importance of FYC, postulating that there can be transfer even if that transfer is not overt. Carroll believes FYC is "most valuable, then, not in teaching one particular genre of writing but in creating situations in which students must consider different forms of writing for different, often complex, purposes and employ the kinds of writing strategies that enable them to complete challenging literacy tasks successfully" (78). If instructors create these situations for their students by requiring students to write in different genres and discuss writing strategies (e.g., drafting) that could be applied across these genres, their students should be able to transfer this knowledge from one writing situation to another.

Ilona Leki is not an advocate for requiring ESL students to write frequently as undergraduate students ("A Challenge" 318). However, in her article "Coping Strategies of ESL Students in Writing Tasks across the Curriculum," she examines how students use writing strategies to negotiate various writing tasks in courses across the disciplines. While her article was not meant to advocate for FYC, the strategies Leki identifies serve as examples of writing strategies worth teaching in FYC classrooms. They consist of clarifying strategies, focusing strategies, relying on past experiences with writing, using current experience or feedback to adjust strategies, and using current or past ESL training in writing, among many others. Clarifying strategies involve students talking specifically to teachers in order to understand an assignment better and, in turn, understand the teachers' purposes for assigning it (247). Focusing strategies involve students reading assignments over many times, even sometimes writing an essay question for themselves to reach a better understanding of the assignment. Relying on past experiences helps students gauge how to approach a writing assignment (248). When using current experience or feedback to adjust strategies, students look at the assessments they received on shorter assignments from earlier in the semester as they construct longer pieces of writing. Only one student out of five in Leki's study said he/she used current or past ESL writing training when developing strategies for writing for other courses. Although Leki reported that three of her students did not see a link between their English courses and the writing demands across the curriculum, I argue that teaching these "coping strategies" in a FYC course for ESL students would promote transfer in writing for courses across the curriculum. It seems that the students in Leki's research did invent and "employ the kinds of writing strategies that enable them to complete challenging literacy tasks successfully," as Carroll suggests; thus they did employ knowledge transfer, whether the students were conscious of it or not.

POSITIVE CAMPUS CULTURE

ESL research indicates that the classroom atmosphere or "transfer climate" is also important to learning in the class and learning transfer. The attitudes of instructors and classmates can have a significant impact on what students learn and retain. Classroom atmosphere is not important only in FYC and EAP courses, but also in courses across the college curriculum. James argues it is important for the instructor to understand students' perceptions of writing in order to create a classroom environment that will promote transfer. James conducted studies on classroom environments at his university and, unfortunately, found many instances of a negative climate for transfer. ESL students stated that many of their peers made negative references to the course they were taking, including comments that writing was "a waste of time." Students also became discouraged because instructors did not value certain qualities (like proper grammar usage) of student writing ("Transfer Climate" 140). Students encountered limited amounts of writing across the curriculum, and they found that the writing they were doing for their major was unrelated to their current course (141–42). Overall, James determined that students may not be "receiving the message that learning outcomes from an EAP course might help. . . . Students may or may not feel support for transfer of learning outcomes from EAP courses" (143). James's troubling findings indicate how important a university's atmosphere is for writing knowledge transfer. A university needs to establish a campus-wide atmosphere that encourages writing for all students, regardless of their English-speaking backgrounds, and instructors need to create positive classroom environments and educate their colleagues across the curriculum about positive writing development.

IMPLICATIONS

The sources I consulted in my literature review did not present a consensus as to whether writing knowledge transfer is consistently occurring in FYC courses. However, they do demonstrate a potential for learning transfer to occur. I established the previously outlined framework while keeping in mind what each scholar's examination of FYC and ESL students suggested. This framework will serve as the basis for the following case study, in which I examine how one section of FYC for ESL students adheres to the beliefs and arguments surrounding writing knowledge transfer.

METHODOLOGY

Setting

This study occurred in the fall 2011 semester at a medium-sized suburban state university. Students in the study were enrolled in single section of Writing Rhetorically (ENGL 101), the first class in a two-semester FYC sequence at the university. Students who pass ENGL 101 in the fall take Writing Rhetorically with Sources (ENGL 102) in the spring. ENGL 101 focuses on the writing process and persuasive writing, while ENGL 102 focuses on research methods and incorporating source material into various genres.

The ENGL 101 class in this study is a targeted section of the course offered to ESL students. The targeted course is offered to students who score low on the Accuplacer reading test and an in-house writing assessment. These sections have the same learning outcomes as other sections, but students get an additional course credit for participating in a weekly book club and writing consultant meetings. ESL students placed in a targeted course have the option of self-selecting into the section of 101 reserved for second-language students. In this section of ENGL 101, students complete an array of writing assignments including a personal narrative, a persuasive op-ed, a profile, and a collaborative review article.

Participants

A total of nine people participated in this IRB-approved study: seven students (representing 63% of total enrollment), a peer writing consultant for the class, and the instructor of the course. All students in the study were in their first semester of their freshman year. Language backgrounds included Chinese, Haitian Creole, and Spanish. The peer writing consultant is a senior in the English department who works for the university's writing center.

Data Collection

Primary research for this study included classroom observations, surveys, and interviews. Data was collected throughout the semester. Classroom materials included assignment descriptions, syllabus, course readings, workshop materials, and the course Blackboard site. I attended the ENGL 101 course six times in order to understand the classroom environment. Midway during the semester, I handed out surveys to the students, which they had two weeks to complete. The purposes of the survey were to learn the students' perspective on what they were learning about writing from this section of ENGL 101, to determine what students were writing for their other courses, and to determine if students were transferring their writing knowledge from one course to the next. The questions were multiple choice and, in most instances, students could select more than one answer.

In addition to the survey, I conducted in-depth interviews of approximately thirty minutes with two of the students. These allowed me to elaborate on my data from the surveys and reach a greater understanding of the students' experiences with writing. In addition, I conducted individual thirty-minute interviews with the peer writing consultant and the course instructor. The interview with the peer writing consultant provided insight on the students' writing experiences not only in ENGL 101 but in their other classes as well, because the instructor encouraged the students to bring the peer consultant writing from all of their courses. I interviewed the instructor to better understand her philosophy and approach to writing instruction.

Research Objectives

I used the framework I developed through my literature review to analyze data from the above sources. I reviewed notes I had taken, course materials, information on the university's website, interview transcripts, and survey results. I then mapped this information onto the four pieces I had outlined in my literature review—frequent writing, explicit instruction, teaching strategies, and campus writing culture—and was able to draw connections between the literature I read and the observations I made.

Analysis

While conducting primary research in Dr. Maggie Jones's FYC course for ESL students, I observed many aspects of positive writing instruction. (All names used in the case study are pseudonyms.) My data from survey results and interviews contributed to the positive feedback I was receiving about the course. After connecting my observations from the case study with my notes on the secondary research, I concluded that transferable knowledge was being taught in Dr. Jones's course. In the analysis that follows, I organize my data into four sections linked to the four key components I have identified that promote transfer.

WRITING OFTEN AND VARIOUSLY

"Dr. Jones is asking you to write, write, write, all the time."

The students in this study wrote very frequently, and they wrote in a variety of genres and for a variety of rhetorical situations, both in their courses across the curriculum and in this course. The university puts a strong emphasis on writing and the writing process through its writing across the curriculum (WAC) program, which scaffolds writing throughout students' undergraduate studies. As a part of the general curriculum, students are required to take a writing-intensive (WI) first-year seminar, a WI or speaking-intensive second-year seminar, a WI general education course, and a WI upper-level course within their major. In WI courses, students are also required to complete at least fifteen pages of writing during the semester, which can be broken up into separate papers amounting to or surpassing fifteen pages. These fifteen pages of writing can include journaling, free writes, and homework activities in addition to formal writing assignments. WI courses also have to incorporate peer or instructor feedback during the writing process. WI classes are offered across numerous disciplines so students have frequent exposure to writing, and the WAC program offers a variety of faculty development opportunities throughout the academic year, contributing to a campus-wide culture of writing. The FYC writing program at the university is meant to provide a foundation of writing knowledge and skills that students can use in these WI courses. With this program in place, students write consistently during their undergraduate careers; however, none of the students in this study were taking first-year seminars or WI courses during the semester the survey was conducted. Regardless, many of the students indicated they were writing in a variety of genres and writing often in their other courses. Five of the seven students who completed the survey reported they had graded writing assignments in other courses in a variety of modes and genres:

MODES OR GENRES OF GRADED WRITING ASSIGNMENTS

Number	Types of Writing
0	Presentations (e.g., PowerPoint)
0	Analytical
0	Narrative
0	Creative
1	Case studies
1	Reviews
1	Persuasive
2	Lab reports
2	Journaling
2	Compare/contrast
2	Summaries
2	Research
3	Argumentative

Based upon these results, it appears students were writing in a range of genres across the curriculum at this university. Not only were the students writing frequently and in a range of genres in other courses, they were also writing a substantial amount for Writing Rhetorically. Dr. Jones implemented a variety of writing assignments, both informal and formal. The following are some from the syllabus that were essential assignments of the course:

Reading Reflections: For each set of readings, write a reading reflection—a 300-word reflection that makes connections among the readings and reflects on the question I pose in the syllabus. After you write this reflection, post it in Blackboard in the appropriate forum and print a hard copy for an in-class activity: ink-shedding. Ink-shedding is an activity in which we will read each other's reflections and give written feedback. Here's the process: Pass your reflection to the right. Read your neighbor's writing all the way through and then underline a sentence or two that stands out as interesting or intriguing. Then, flip the page over, and write a response. This response should not be evaluative (i.e., "good job!"), but written to continue the conversation on paper—to continue the writer's thinking, pose questions raised by the writer's thoughts, reflect on what the writer said . . .

Snapshots of Our Literacies: The first writing project of the course focuses on the writing process. During this project, you will write and revise a number of pieces, choosing from a list of writing prompts about writing, reading, language communities, discourse communities, and literacies. At the end of the project, you will select about five of these short pieces to develop a "snapshot" essay and write a cover letter about your writing process.

Op-Ed Letter: The second project makes use of persuasive writing. An op-ed letter is a type of letter to the editor that is featured in an editorial section of a newspaper or magazine. In comparison to other letters to the editor, an op-ed letter is relatively long (700–1000 words), opinionated, written to persuade a particular audience on a timely issue, and draws on evidence to support its claims. I will ask you to focus on a target audience and publication venue. If you take the extra step and send your op-ed to that magazine or newsletter, you will get extra credit.

Profile: The third project asks you to write in a genre common to newsletters: a profile. This genre is rhetorically complex to write, as you will be representing another person and another person's words in writing. You may choose to profile a Bridgewater State University writing studio consultant, tutor, graduate student, staff member, instructor, or professor. During this project, you will develop a list of interview questions, conduct a face to face interview and a follow-up interview, and compose a focused and cohesive 3–5 page essay about this person.

In the survey, most of the students cited the "Snapshots of Our Literacies" and the op-ed letter as contributing to their development as writers. All of the students cited "Reading Reflections" and brainstorming activities in class as contributing to their overall course knowledge, too.

In interviews, students voiced their pleasure with the quantity of writing and many types of writing they were exposed to. When I asked one student, Michael, if he liked the variety of writing in the class, his response was:

> Yeah. I think this is why as a writer we can say that we have the skills that we can write about anything we want. . . .You're not writing all the time the same thing, the same style, or the same voice. You change the voice all the time in every assignment, you change the voice, you change the type of writing. I think it's good. It kind of balances your writing skills.

This balance seems likely to help students transfer their writing skills across different genres and different courses. When asked about the amount of writing required for the class, Michael immediately had a positive response: "Some people may see it as annoying when Dr. Jones is asking you to write, write, write all the time . . . all the time I am writing. I think this practice with writing is very important . . . this practice really helped me, you know, and I like it. I think it's good."

The peer writing consultant also saw the value of the continual writing process and the variety of genres implemented by Dr. Jones. When I asked her if the students' improvement in writing could be attributed to Dr. Jones, she responded, "Professor Jones is the main core to their improvement . . . because of the styles of writing she has had them do. She has had them do very different styles of writing." The consultant believes the students learn more about the writing process with each piece of writing. Between the writing-intensive program implemented by the university and the writing students are completing in Dr. Jones's Writing Rhetorically section, students experience frequent writing and a variety of types of writing in their first-year as college students as well as in the remainder of their college careers.

EXPLICIT INSTRUCTION
"She has faith in them . . . she knows they can succeed."

Explicit instruction also plays an integral role in students' writing transfer. In the FYC section I studied, there was explicit instruction about the writing process in other settings. Dr. Jones would frequently begin her classes by asking her students what types of writing they were completing in their other courses, and students would vocalize different problems they encountered. Dr. Jones then led the class through a discussion of how the students could negotiate these challenges, leading them to reflect on which of the strategies they were learning in ENGL 101 were effective for them and could be transferred to other courses.

While it was important for Dr. Jones to discuss the aspects of her course that could be transferred to other courses, her students would not have been able to transfer their knowledge of writing had it not been for their concrete understanding of what was being taught to them about writing and its different modes and genres. Dr. Jones believed in the importance of clear expectations for her students. With each writing assignment for the course, there was a lengthy drafting process involved. Dr. Jones provided student and professional samples of the genres her students were working on at the time. When students were beginning to work on writing profiles of members of the university community, she introduced this assignment using "Soup," the New Yorker essay that inspired the "Soup Nazi" episode of Seinfeld. After this activity, Dr. Jones handed out the assignment description, which told students specifically what she wanted them to do and gave them student examples from previous courses. In the survey, six out of seven students indicated that student writing samples contributed to their course knowledge and writing development. Conversely, four out of the seven noted that a lack of such samples in other courses impeded their ability to write. Students were able to transfer their writing knowledge to other courses because Dr. Jones provided them with such an in-depth perspective into genres to begin with.

Whereas clear expectations and explicit instructions helped students write for ENGL 101, the lack thereof in their other courses contributed to the struggle students experienced when writing for these courses. One student I interviewed, John, characterized writing instructions in other courses as vague, which was problematic for his writing. "I have to write twenty emails to my professor to ask every single thing because . . . it's on the syllabus, the assignment, but it doesn't really say . . . what should be included. So it's just like, write about this and that and it's due this date." John's confusion from the beginning of the assignment led to confusion throughout the project as he was not able to approach his work with the confidence he brought to his ENGL 101 class assignments. If students are unable to determine what is being asked of them in a writing assignment, they may not have an idea of how to approach this writing genre. This could prohibit students from using knowledge gained in ENGL 101 to help them write for other courses. But Dr. Jones would never allow such a thing to happen. The peer writing consultant told me, "She [Dr. Jones] has faith in them . . . she knows they can succeed." Dr. Jones knew her students could succeed in other courses even if her students did not have instructors who had clear expectations for their students. In order to combat any discrepancies, Dr. Jones used explicit instruction to help students realize how their writing knowledge will translate, and thus her students were able to successfully complete writing tasks across the curriculum.

TEACHING STRATEGIES

"As a writer we can say that we have the skills that we can write about anything we want."

Perhaps some of the most important aspects of an FYC course that teaches for transfer are the writing strategies students are taught and the instructional methods the teacher uses. Those were successful aspects of Dr. Jones's ENGL 101; in my survey, students were given a checklist of strategies that were implemented in their other courses.

Do your other courses use any of the following writing strategies or instructional methods to support your writing? (Check all that apply.)

---

0   The teacher asks us to bring in early drafts for peer review sessions.

0   The teacher requires that we make an appointment with the writing studio to get feedback from a tutor on our writing.

0   None

1   Writing about course readings (such as reader response or notes in a specific format)

1   Journaling

1   The teacher provides sample student essays for use as models for writing assignments.

1   The teacher asks us to hand in an early draft so that the teacher can provide written comments.

2   The teacher creates opportunities during class to discuss an upcoming writing assignment.

2   Prewriting (such as freewriting or listing) to brainstorm in preparation for the first draft of a writing assignment.

Five students completed this part of the survey, and the most checks any given category received was two. With the small numbers for each selection, it appeared teachers were not giving students class time to develop their writing. Although the writing strategies being implemented in their other courses were limited, no student selected "none" as an option, indicating all students were having at least one strategy taught to them or implemented when they wrote in their other courses.

While the strategies and useful instructional methods were limited in other courses, students did use knowledge of strategies taught in ENGL 101 to complete writing elsewhere. The survey asked students what writing strategies they used in their other courses voluntarily, and many students reported using strategies from Dr. Jones's class in their other courses.

Strategies from ENGL 101 Used Voluntarily in Other Courses
0   None
0   Used journaling to reflect on course material
0   Formed a writing group with friends in other classes
1   Used writing (such as note-taking strategies) while reading assigned texts to better understand and remember the material
1   Asked the teacher to provide sample student essays written for the same assignment
1   Asked the teacher to meet in order to discuss an early draft
1   Asked the teacher to give written feedback on an early draft
2   Formed a writing group with other students from the same class
3   Looked for samples of the genre on your own when given an assignment for an unfamiliar type of writing
3   Used writing (such as freewriting or listing) to brainstorm before writing a draft

Based on these results, students appear to be taking the initiative to use writing strategies from ENGL 101 in order to help them write for other classes. While many of the options show only one or a few students transferring the strategy, none of the students who completed this survey elected the option of "None," indicating that all students were transferring at least one strategy from ENGL 101 to their other courses. So while a given approach to writing might show limited transfer, every student responding to this portion of the survey was transferring at least some portion of ENGL 101 learning elsewhere in the undergraduate curriculum. The strategies included voluntarily forming a writing group, which takes a lot of effort on students' parts. (These results are similar to the coping strategies Leki refers to in her article "Coping Strategies," as these students were contacting their professor for guidance and looking for writing samples on their own.)

The survey concluded by asking students, "What have you taken from ENGL 101 that has been helpful in preparing you for the writing completed in other courses?" This was another question with multiple answer options, and this survey generated a lot of positive reinforcement from the students, further establishing the importance of FYC.

What have you taken from ENGL 101 that has been helpful in preparing you for the writing completed in other courses?	
2	I am able to critically respond to course readings.
3	I am able to determine what genre I should be writing in before I approach the assignment, and I know the rhetorical approaches of the genre.
3	I am a more independent writer.
3	I plan ahead and am able to manage my time for writing assignments.
3	I learned to go to the writing studio when I need assistance with an assignment.
3	I am able to define who my audience is without the instructor telling me.
3	I am able to develop a thesis and support it through argument and evidence.
3	I am able to develop my own voice in my writing.
4	I am more confident in writing for other courses.
4	I know how to ask questions when I do not understand a writing assignment.
4	I construct multiple drafts before handing in a final copy.
4	I feel that I am better able to communicate my ideas.

Four of the five students who were concurrently writing in courses across the curriculum reported that they felt more comfortable writing for other courses after taking this course. Four out of five students also stated they now knew how to ask questions when they did not understand a writing assignment and how to construct multiple drafts before handing in a final copy. These are two essential aspects of the writing process. When students do not understand a question, they may feel insecure about the writing assignment; however, their FYC course provided them with the knowledge they need to ask questions so they can approach an assignment with confidence. This kind of learning and transfer of knowledge about writing might be missed in a transfer study that looked only at a student's writing itself or focused only on what students wrote—but it is crucial knowledge about the nature and activity of writing that would seem to be among the most important principles students could learn in ENGL 101 and transfer.

The interviews I conducted with the students also indicated that they were using writing strategies from ENGL 101. When I asked Michael if he used strategies from Dr. Jones's course in his writing, he excitedly replied, "That is what I do! 'Cause, you know, in the English 101 class, we covered a lot of things, a lot of styles of writing. I've learned a lot. . . . I got the skills so when I need to write something I say, okay, this is what I am going to write. . . . Those things I have learned from English 101." When Michael receives an assignment, he immediately analyzes the prompt or requirements. John mentioned without my prompting that he incorporated some of the techniques from FYC in his anthropology course. When I asked him for details, he replied, "Like incorporating the research . . . for like the review article, and the profile essay we kind of added quotes from people and, you know, different points of views. I never did that before and I think it is like, so cool. I actually did that on my essay and my professor thinks that's really unique." FYC has taught John how to incorporate secondary and primary research into his writing, a skill that will surely help him for the remainder of his undergraduate career.

In my interviews with John and Michael as well as with their peer writing consultant, all stated that the writing tasks they encountered across the curriculum were not similar to the writing they were completing in their FYC course. However, according to the data collected from my research, the students were nonetheless able to use the writing strategies they had learned in order to complete such assignments with success.

POSITIVE CAMPUS CULTURE

"Dr. Jones uses a strategy to make her connected to her students."

The classroom and campus cultures in this study fostered positive learning environments. Bridgewater State University, where this study took place, offers a lot of writing support to students through its writing center, a resource frequently used by Bridgewater's ESL students, as confirmed by the writing consultant. It promotes student writing through its general education requirements and WAC programming. I've noted the university's WAC program requirement of three writing-intensive courses with at least fifteen pages of writing during a semester; it also offers workshops for faculty who are implementing writing in their courses. There is also a well-funded undergraduate research program, which offers numerous avenues of publication and presentation opportunities for students. The opportunity to publish and present one's own work would certainly qualify as the kind of "authentic" writing genre that Ann Johns refers to, as writing that is published does serve "real communicative purposes." Bridgewater offers a midyear symposium and an undergraduate research symposium, both of which allow students to present their written work. The midyear symposium is specifically designed for first- and second-year students to showcase their work, offering an encouraging writing environment for students early in their undergraduate careers. Not only are students encouraged to present their work on campus, there are also opportunities for students to present their work nationally. The university also offers publication opportunities for students. Students can get their work published in the university's undergraduate research journal as well as in the first-year writing program's annual volume of student work, the student newspaper, and the student literary journal. All of these wonderful opportunities reinforce the value of writing.

In addition to the positive campus culture was a very warm and welcoming classroom atmosphere. There were only eleven students in Dr. Jones's course, and they all formed close relationships. The writing consultant reported that she frequently saw students from this class eating together in dining halls. The students were continually offering advice and constructive criticism on each other's writing. For example, when students were discussing the person at the university they wanted to interview, one student did not know whom to profile. The whole class discussed this issue and offered numerous suggestions. Finally one student, who had planned to interview the class's writing consultant, told his classmate she could have that opportunity and he would find someone else.

Adding to the positive classroom environment was students' relationship with their professor. In my interview with Michael, I gained great insight into how the students viewed Dr. Jones. Michael smiled as he recalled his first day in her class: "When she was teaching that first day, I could not stop smiling, you know, because I felt comfortable. This is exactly what I was looking for, a professor who was comfortable with the students, telling them what we are going to do for the semester and the things we are going to do and the things we are going to cover . . . and I was like, oh God, thank you, God!" He also went on to say, "Dr. Jones uses a strategy to make her connected to her students." While the students in James's study ("Transfer Climate") faced negative attitudes from instructors, the students in this class did not encounter this problem. Dr. Jones's positive attitude reinforces the importance of writing.

In our interview, Michael continued to compliment his instructor: "One thing I like about her [is] she not only cares about her class . . . she just wants you to succeed in every class you are in. . . . You know, it is kind of interesting when another professor [is] asking you about another class you are taking. . . . She show me she cares about me, not only her class, so she want us to succeed in other classes, so I think it's good." Such support from the teacher encourages students to feel that they can approach her for help with their writing development not just in her class but also in all classes. Michael expressed a fundamental indicator of the positive classroom atmosphere Dr. Jones established with her ESL students: "She's a professor [who is] easy to talk to. You don't need to be afraid. Even though I have an accent as an ESL student, she doesn't care about your accent. She wants everyone to participate in the class." Although many students may feel self-conscious of their accent, this problem is eliminated in Dr. Jones's class because of her welcoming attitude. After witnessing Dr. Jones's impact on her students and hearing these statements, I do not think transfer would have been possible without her extraordinary teaching. While my framework and a thorough curriculum makes transfer possible, it is equally important to have a competent and enthusiastic instructor.

IMPLICATIONS AND CONCLUSION

This article began with a brief outline of arguments against first-year composition then moved to the problems ESL students encounter with FYC programs. Based on the framework I created and evidence from my case study, I assert that it is indeed possible to develop an FYC course that will promote writing transfer among ESL students. Many of the grounds FYC abolitionists have offered for the ineffectiveness of mandatory comp instruction simply did not appear in the case I studied. For example, Dr. Jones did not teach the "mythical" classroom genres or "traditional" classroom essays criticized by Crowley; rather she incorporated many different genres that required students to become familiar with the characteristics of many different styles of writing. In addition, many of the abolitionists' suggestions for improving FYC were already in place at this university, such as writing-intensive courses or freshman writing seminars. Here, eliminating FYC would eliminate some of the writing preparation for these WI courses. Leki criticizes FYC when an institution's students will complete little other writing during their undergraduate careers; however, my study demonstrates how, as a part of this university's overall writing climate, even courses not designated as WI require significant writing from students. In these ways, both the university at large and Dr. Jones's course defy many of the criticisms of writing in college put forth by FYC abolitionists.

What both such criticisms and my research do suggest, however, is that in order to develop an effective FYC course for ESL students, universities must first have a successful writing across the curriculum program in place. An effective WAC program will benefit not only the writing development of ESL students but also the writing development of NES students. Still, while a positive campus culture conducive to writing is the first step to a successful writing program that will promote transfer, it cannot determine what occurs in the individual sections of a course, so individual section factors are also important. When preparing individual sections of FYC targeted for ESL students, teachers should create a curriculum that will help students transfer their writing knowledge and successfully grapple with the challenges of writing in a new language. To do this, instructors must have their students write continually throughout the semester, and they should always be encouraged to use prewriting and drafting activities. Instructors should provide an array of writing assignments so their students have the experience of approaching and analyzing new genres. Explicit instruction should be used to teach students particular writing skills and how to consciously transfer them to new writing situations. As in John's case, not all writing assignments given across the curriculum will have explicit writing instruction, which will lessen the benefit. However, the goal of him writing lengthy papers for courses outside of an English class does indicate promise for

WAC and the potential of writing knowledge transfer if explicit instruction is provided.

I close with two quotes, the first from John and the second from Michael:

> The course should still be part of the English department and they should keep it running so not only it can help us but others as well and international students too. It's very helpful for us. I like it.
>
> Thank God I had English 101 with Dr. Jones. Now I am not scared of any writing assignment. Honestly, I am telling you I was scared to write before, even in high school I was scared to write in my language . . . because, you know, it's different when you write something for the professor. She might not be satisfied . . . but now since I have this confidence in myself I have these skills. . . . I am not scared of any assignments . . . she covered everything.

Both these students volunteered to meet with me for an interview. They were not required to do so, but they wanted to share their positive experiences from the course. John and Michael did not have one negative thing to say about the course, and they both wanted me to know how much the course meant to them. Michael told me in our interview, "I realize writing is a part of my daily life now." This quotation cements just how important this course has been in the students' development as writers. These students came into class insecure about their writing abilities, and they left not only confident about their writing abilities but also proud. They considered themselves writers.

ACKNOWLEDGMENTS

There are certain teachers whose impact transcends their immediate classroom setting, and I think it fair to label such teachers as "inspirational." Dr. Michelle Cox is undoubtedly one of these inspirational teachers. She graciously agreed to be my mentor for my senior honors thesis. Without her, I would have never been able to develop this study. Dr. Cox encouraged me to submit my thesis to YSW, something I never would have had the confidence to do on my own. I owe immense gratitude and thanks to her. I would also like to thank all my research participants, especially John and Michael. These two students enthusiastically agreed to meet with me on their personal time. Their enthusiasm for writing is infectious, and I sincerely believe they will develop into fantastic writers. Lastly, I want to thank Dr. Doug Downs, my faculty advising editor from *YSW*. Dr. Downs eagerly agreed to help me develop my paper further and make it ready for publication. His suggestions during revision and editing were extremely helpful, and he was enthusiastic throughout the editing process. It was a privilege to work with him.

WORKS CITED

Carroll, Lee Ann. 2002. *Rehearsing New Roles: How College Students Develop as Writers*. Carbondale: Southern Illinois University Press.

Crowley, Sharon. 1991. "A Personal Essay on Freshman English." *Pre/Text* 12.3–4: 155–76.

Driscoll, Dana Lynn. 2011. "Connected, Disconnected, or Uncertain: Student Attitudes about Future Writing Contexts and Perceptions of Transfer from First-year Writing to the Disciplines." *Across the Disciplines* 8.2. Accessed 16 December 2012.

Goggin, Maureen Daly, and Susan K. Miller. 2000. "What is New about the 'New Abolitionists': Continuities and Discontinuities in the Great Debate." *Composition Studies* 28.2: 85–112. Print.

James, Mark A. 2009. "'Far' Transfer of Learning Outcomes from an ESL Writing Course: Can the Gap be Bridged?" *Journal of Second Language Writing* 18: 69–84.

James, Mark A. 2010. "Transfer Climate and EAP Education: Students' Perceptions of Challenges to Learning Transfer." *English for Specific Purposes* 29: 133–47.

Johns, Ann M. 1995. "Teaching Classroom and Authentic Genres: Initiating Students into Academic Cultures and Discourses." In *Academic Writing in a Second Language: Essays on Research and Pedagogy*, edited by Diane Dewhurst Belcher and George Braine, 277–92. Norwood, NJ: Ablex.

Leki, Ilona. 1995. "Coping Strategies of ESL Students in Writing Tasks across the Curriculum." *TESOL Quarterly* 29.2: 235–59.

Leki, Ilona. 2003. "A Challenge to Second Language Writing Professionals: Is Writing Overrated?" In *Exploring the Dynamics of Second Language Writing*, edited by Barbara Kroll, 315–31. Cambridge: Cambridge University Press.

Student Activity

READING, ANALYSIS, AND REFLECTION

Read the Mulcahy essay. Reflect on the author's approach to the research through the following questions.

1. What is meant by *transfer* in this essay? Why is it important to writing studies? (For an in-depth study of transfer, see *Writing across Contexts: Transfer, Composition, and Sites of Writing* by Kathleen Blake Yancey, Liane Robertson, and Kara Taczak (Yancey, Robertson, and Taczak 2014)

2. How does Mulcahy outline her research study? Why is it important to include details about the research design?

3. How does Mulcahy use quantitative information to support her arguments?
4. The researcher introduces the project by explaining the abolitionist movement to the first-year composition students. Is this a helpful way to frame the argument, or is it using a "strawman" argument?
5. How are human participants protected in this study?
6. The faculty member participating in this study, Dr. Jones, is portrayed very positively. How would this study change if the instructor were not viewed so favorably?

7

Undertaking Ethnography

Traditionally, ethnographers are anthropologists[1] who study at remote sites, immersing themselves in a society to describe and understand a *culture*, the daily routines of ordinary people. These researchers are outsiders, able to see with new eyes what is familiar to those in the society. Ethnographers live with the group they are studying, becoming participant-observers. They take field notes, building "thick descriptions," as noted by Clifford Geertz (1973), that provide the foundation from which interpretation can be made. In studying the natives of the group, the researcher often relies on one or more key informants. The researchers live for some time among the "tribe" they are studying, learning the language. Naturally, the work of Margaret Mead on Samoa springs to mind as a classic instance of an ethnography although Bronislaw Malinowski (1922) is credited with bringing ethnography to the fore, tasking researchers with describing an entire culture as opposed to only aspects of a society, such as kinship or mating. Malinowski put forward the concept that the entire context of a culture is essential for understanding any part of it.

The romance of ethnography is that the anthropologist undergoes a significant, perhaps even transformative, experience in being immersed in a foreign, probably exotic, culture, sometimes with very few actual research skills. In more recent times, the skills of ethnography have been addressed in the classroom as opposed to the field. In either case, ethnography is a representation of a culture's lived experiences. It is assumed that the ethnography is credible, based on the data collected, and that the interpretations are in line with those data.

Thus ethnography is characterized by the following:

- a review of what has been said of the society in the past through research and observation
- immersion in a society for a lengthy period of time by the researcher
- the researcher as outsider able to see afresh
- thick description of the research setting through field notes and interviews
- an inductive approach that builds a theory based on numerous examples
- complete and fulsome contextual information
- a focus on the subjects rather than the researcher

In the mid- to late twentieth century, ethnography came home to domestic sites, and the "natives" might be those in a school culture, with the researcher looking at how students create their own culture. Rebekah Nathan, an anthropologist, famously became a participant-observer when she went undercover as a first-year student at Northern Arizona University and wrote about it in *My Freshman Year: What a Professor Learned by Becoming a Student* (Nathan 2005). She was curious as to why the students in her classes seemed uninterested in their education, so she enrolled as a freshman to live among "the natives" and find out what had changed. She took a full load of classes, moved into the dorm, and discovered that being a student is hard work.

Harry Wolcott took educational practitioners to task for providing prescriptive descriptions of how to be a principal in a school setting when no one had truly described that role. He filled that gap in his descriptive study of *The Man in the Principal's Office* (Wolcott 1973), spending a year in close proximity with the principal. (Truly, at that time, using the gendered title was an accurate portrayal.)

In writing studies, ethnography became a more popular approach in the 1980s, particularly with the influential work of researchers such as Shirley Brice Heath (1983) and her *Ways with Words*, which documented literacy in Trackton, Roadville, and Maintown, demonstrating how students' socioeconomic status affects school success. One of the primary challenges of working in the field domestically is the researcher's familiarity with the culture. Not being an outsider means the researcher must be able to make the familiar unfamiliar in order to describe and then interpret the culture. In other words, the researcher has the job of seeing beyond the surface, questioning assumptions, and adopting a persona skeptical of that which is taken for granted. One of the reasons ethnography was immediately attractive to composition specialists is that ethnography requires skill in writing, particularly in narrative, in telling the story of the group being studied. The primacy of narrative in providing thick description and interpretation cannot be underestimated.

For writing studies and educational research, ethnography is defined more loosely than by anthropologists, for whom ethnography is the primary research methodology. One reason is that *culture* is defined more broadly, as in the "tribe" of snowboarders or the culture of a classroom. While Malinowski insisted that the entire context of a culture must be studied in order to understand its parts, contemporary ethnography has returned to what might be termed a *reductionist approach* in which a portion of the culture is under study. It's assumed that the larger culture is understood. For those studying writing via an ethnographic approach, the time period for an actual project may range from just a few days to a year or longer. And the number of subjects may range from a few—or even one—to several in the group. Thus, in an ethnographic approach to writing, the subject may be a single classroom, a lone learner, or even an event.

Another change in ethnographic approaches for those studying composition and writing is that the researcher may be visible within the study and the written report. The continuum of researcher visibility in an ethnography ranges from autoethnography, in which the researcher is very visible and their own story is included, to the study in which the subject remains the primary focus.

Wendy Bishop (1999) offered principles of ethnographic research that apply to studies in writing.

- Ethnographic writing research is ethnographic in *intent*.
- Ethnographic writing research is participant-observer-based inquiry.
- Ethnographic writing research studies a culture from that culture's point of view.
- Ethnographic writing research uses one or more ethnographic data-gathering techniques [e.g., field notes, interview, surveys, artifacts from the research site].
- Ethnographic writing research gains power to the degree that the researcher
    - spends time in the field
    - collects multiple sources of data
    - lets the context and participants help guide research questions
    - conducts analysis as a reiterative process. (35)

Jaqueline McLeod Rogers (2010) points out that researchers must ask themselves whether they are "committed to *documenting* or *critiquing* culture" (78). Knowing the researcher's stance in regards to the theoretical lens being used is important. For instance, a feminist or Marxist approach may focus more on critique than documentation. The choice of lens indicates not only the position of the researcher but also how what is viewed may be interpreted. Likewise, some researchers may undertake a project from an advocacy role, setting out to prove a hypothesis. This approach is very different from the researcher who begins a project with an open mind, willing to see what is out there. The stance of the researcher influences interpretation, the treatment of the participants in the study, and the possible outcomes.

Ethnography can begin with a simple question: what is happening here? Even when the researcher is an insider, a situation may pique this question: hey, what's going on? A first task for researchers may then be to interrogate their interest by writing about the topic, noting personal connections and theoretical knowledge. Assuming the question is inherently interesting, the researcher begins to assess appropriate methodology for answering the question and to see what has been done before—a review of the literature.

Developing a plan of attack for the research involves the following:

- identifying the problem and focusing it so the study itself is manageable and doable
- stating a research question
- locating the research question in a theoretical framework
- reviewing associated literature to determine the currency of the research topic
- choosing the site of the study, its participants, and a timeframe
- developing data-collection strategies and instruments, ensuring that data analysis is pragmatic
- making a research proposal, including a timeline for conducting and completing the study
- obtaining permission for any human-subject research
- conducting the study and analyzing the data
- interpreting the results and making recommendations if applicable
- sharing the results with others professionally

For an ethnographic study in writing, the focus most likely will be the discourse of a particular group. The range of discourse communities is large; the age of participants begins possibly with preschool and ends only at death.

It may be tempting to look only at the educational process in school settings—student learning, teaching practices—but there are other possibilities, such as school-board minutes, administrative memos, announcements, school newspapers, sports writing, public-relations brochures, admissions essays. Likewise, any school features writing not only in English classes but also across disciplines and fields of study. Walvoord and McCarthy (1990) completed a longitudinal study of college writers in their *Thinking and Writing in College: A Naturalistic Study of Students in*

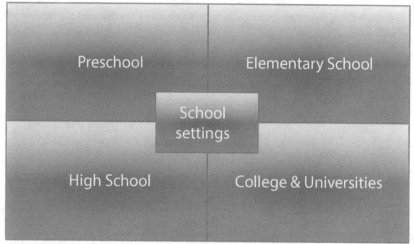

FIGURE 7.1. Settings for ethnographic research.

Four Disciplines. The participants numbered over one hundred and came from three different institutions. By using multiple campuses and a sizable number of participants, the researchers laid the groundwork for their study to be credible. Their findings included that the students were being initiated into the "club" of the particular field, being treated as professionals-in-training, and learning the discourse conventions appropriate to the field.

The workplace also offers excellent sites for inquiry into discourse. Lunsford and Ede (1990) analyzed collaborative writing in an office setting in their *Singular Texts, Plural Authors*, revealing how members of a group work together to produce a text. Their take-home message is that schools must pay more attention to how to collaborate, given that this skill is necessary for success. In effect, they challenge the assumption that writing is a solitary act.

Brenna Leath (2008) investigated student internships in the workplace but in a virtual setting, which brings onstage yet another site: the online community. Rogers refers to this as *netnography* (Rogers 2010, 83). The possibility of doing fieldwork online opens up a broad spectrum of possibilities.

As Rogers (2010) points out, the ethics of doing research in online communities is still in development, but in general, it's wise to treat anyone in an online community with the same respect and attention as those engaged in a face-to-face project. Seeking permission to study a group rather than lurking is the route that follows principles of research integrity.

Also, researchers should keep in mind that Internet users are somewhat masked. As Peter Steiner's cartoon from the July 5, 1993, issue of

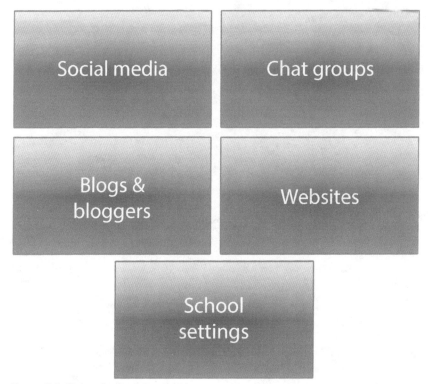

FIGURE 7.2. Types of online communities.

the *New Yorker* shows, identity is not transparent nor necessarily what it may seem in an online setting (see Fig. 7.3).

Dania Allen chose to investigate identity in the online community of PostSecret, as described by Laura Gray-Rosendale (2010). The Post-Secret site offers participants the opportunity in an anonymous forum to post secrets and to respond to others' postings. Because PostSecret was at the time a new site, it had not yet been studied; consequently, there existed a gap that Allen's research could fill. But another essay on this cultural phenomenon appeared in the 2008 issue of *Young Scholars in Writing*, "From Souvenir to Social Movement: PostSecret, Art, and Politics" (MacAulay et al. 2008), demonstrating that researchers must stake out their territory early, particularly when it focuses on popular culture.

Leath (2008), an undergraduate researcher, chose to investigate the world of virtual internships, identifying the issues, surveying participants, and eventually recommending policy and practice via a guidebook, which she authored. The survey is one tool for the ethnographer. Another one is field notes, a tool for gathering information

"On the Internet, nobody knows you're a dog."

FIGURE 7.3. Peter Steiner cartoon from the *New Yorker* (July 5, 1993)

discussed in part 1 of this book. The simple "T" or dialogic journal may be enhanced with additional coding that helps the researcher understand the notes quickly. For instance, the researcher may include codes such as PN (personal note), TN (theoretical note), or MN (method note). Notes for each event that is observed should follow guidelines for good data management, including the date and time, the scene, and participants. The discussion may be reproduced verbatim (and recorded for double-checking accuracy). Brackets [ ] can be used to note commentary by the researcher to explain a participant's statement if it needs clarification.

Another aspect of ethnography to assist with interpretation is the concept of triangulation. In sum, this means using multiple sources to arrive at an interpretation. Thus, field notes, survey, texts, observation, questionnaires, interviews, and cases provide the thick description that allows for credible and reliable analysis. Even with triangulation, the researcher should be ready to note the limitations of the study.

To summarize, the ethnography begins with the identification of a problem, most likely within a setting accessible to the researcher. Data are collected, often through multiple methods. Themes are derived from these data, which leads to interpretation. The researcher should then stand at some distance from the study and put on what Hemingway would have called a "crap detector." Has the researcher truly been open minded? Has the researcher missed any connecting points? Have the data been interpreted fairly? This is also a good point at which to bring in another reader, a second or even third pair of eyes, for a dry run of the study and its results so the researcher can be questioned. This is part of the recursive process of research: writing, reseeing, rewriting. When the researcher is satisfied with the results, it is time to share them with the professional world.

The essay that accompanies this chapter is Eric Pleasant's (2007) "Literacy Sponsors and Learning: An Ethnography of Punk Literacy in Mid-1980s Waco," published in the 2007 volume of *Young Scholars in Writing*. Pleasant engages in classic participant-observation to reveal a subculture from an insider's perspective.

NOTE

1.   It should be noted that anthropology has four subfields: archaeology, cultural anthropology, linguistics anthropology, and physical anthropology. Ethnography is centrally the province of cultural anthropologists.

REFERENCES AND FOR FURTHER READING

Bishop, Wendy. 1999. *Ethnographic Writing Research: Writing It Down, Writing It Up, and Reading It.* Portsmouth, NH: Boynton/Cook.

Geertz, Clifford. 1973. *The Interpretation of Cultures.* New York: Basic Books.

Gray-Rosendale, Laura. 2010. "Rhetorics and Undergraduate Research: A Journey into the Genre of Memoir." In *Undergraduate Research and English Studies*, edited by Laurie Grobman and Joyce Kinkead, 212–28. Urbana, IL: NCTE.

Heath, Shirley Brice. 1983. *Ways with Words: Language, Life, and Work in Communities and Classrooms.* New York: Cambridge University Press.

LaFrance, Michelle, and Melissa Nicolas. 2012. "Institutional Ethnography as a Materialist Framework for Writing Program Research." *College Composition and Communication* 64 (1): 130–50.

Leath, Brenna. 2008. "Solving the Challenges of the Virtual Workplace for Interns." *Young Scholars in Writing* 6:3–11.

Lunsford, Andrea, and Lisa Ede. 1990. *Singular Texts, Plural Authors: Perspectives on Collaborative Writing.* Carbondale: Southern Illinois University Press.

MacAulay, Maggie, Kendra Magnusson, Christopher Schiffmann, Jennifer Hamm, and Arlen Kasdorf. 2008. "From Souvenir to Social Movement: Post-Secret, Art, and Politics." *Young Scholars in Writing* 6:92–99.

Malinowski, Bronislaw. 1922. *Argonauts in the Western Pacific*. London: Routledge.

Nathan, Rebekah. 2005. *My Freshman Year: What a Professor Learned by Becoming a Student*. Ithaca, NY: Cornell University Press.

Pleasant, Eric. 2007. "Literacy Sponsors and Learning: An Ethnography of Punk Literacy in Mid-1980s Waco." *Young Scholars in Writing* 5:137–45.

Rogers, Jaqueline McLeod. 2010. "An Undergraduate Research Methods Course in Rhetoric and Composition: A Model." In *Undergraduate Research and English Studies*, edited by Laurie Grobman and Joyce Kinkead, 74–82. Urbana, IL: NCTE.

Walvoord, Barbara E., and Lucille P. McCarthy. 1990. *Thinking and Writing in College: A Naturalistic Study of Students in Four Disciplines*. Urbana, IL: NCTE.

Wolcott, Harry F. 1973. *The Man in the Principal's Office: An Ethnography*. New York: Holt, Rinehart, and Winston.

Wolcott, Harry F. 1999. *Ethnography: A Way of Seeing*. Walnut Creek, CA: AltaMira.

"Literacy Sponsors and Learning: An Ethnography of Punk Literacy in Mid-1980s Waco"

Eric Pleasant,
Texas A&M University–Commerce

Literacy is primarily something people do; it is an activity, located
in the space between thought and text. Literacy does not just
reside in people's heads as a set of skills to be learned, and it does
not just reside on paper, captured as texts to be analyzed. Like all
human activity, literacy is essentially social, and it is located in the
interaction between people.

—DAVID BARTON AND MARY HAMILTON

As you walk in, you instantly notice your surroundings. You are entering
a dark room with an almost oppressive atmosphere. Animal bones hang
from the ceiling. The walls are painted black. Flyers promoting upcoming shows have been pasted one on top of the other throughout the
room. Artwork on the flyers consists of skeletons, monsters, and an array
of unflattering caricatures of people such as Ronald Reagan, Hitler, and
the pope. Band names upon the flyers are as brash as the images: Dead
Kennedys, Millions of Dead Cops, Agent Orange, Marching Plague, and
the Offenders. Phrases such as "There is no justice, just us" and "We're
just a minor threat" are graffitied across the walls, promoting a sense of
unity outside the bounds of traditional societal values. At the opposite
end of the room is a stage. Groups of kids are standing together looking
at you with seeming tribal defiance. Most of these people have leather
jackets adorned with spikes and band names or logos similar to the ones

Eric Pleasant, "Literacy Sponsors and Learning: An Ethnography of Punk Literacy in
Mid-1980s Waco," *Young Scholars in Writing* 5 (2007):137–45.

on the walls. Some have hair that has been spiked, shaved, or colored with DayGlo hues that scream, "I am not a normal member of society!" You have just entered the netherworld of the Cave Club, Austin, Texas. The year is 1985 and you have come to see the psychedelic punk rock band the Butthole Surfers.

I am one of the people walking into the club. I look at my four best friends. We are five white adolescents aged fifteen to eighteen from Waco, Texas. How did we get here? How do we fit into this extremely closed group of people we see around us in the club? These other youths have a reputation of hating outsiders to the point of showing extreme aggression. All of a sudden, one of the people in the club sees and recognizes us. He nods and walks up. The band takes the stage and opens its set with crazy, insane sounding rants that lead into straightahead, hard-driving drums and guitar—this is stripped down, in your face music. The punk walking up grabs one of my friends. No words are spoken. He puts his arm around my friend's shoulders and pulls him into a swirling pit of kids. The music picks up. The rest of us look at each other, grin, and run to join the human maelstrom. We do fit in here!

PUNK AS LITERACY

Fitting in, in this case, means that we had acquired the requisite punk literacy necessary to survive or thrive in this environment. Acquiring the literacy of such a nontraditional, new, and relatively nonstudied or reported subculture necessitated nontraditional modes of learning. Traditional definitions of literacy are generally limited to the study of written text; such a definition limits this project to our reading of the verbal snapshot detailed above. But there is so much more going on here. As David Barton and Mary Hamilton's definition shows us, "Like all human activity, literacy is essentially social, and it is located in the interaction between people" (42). Within the context of traditional literacy, the words on the flyers, jackets, or walls are relatively meaningless. Within the bounds of the second and more relevant definition, my opening scene becomes a plethora of literacy. Every aspect of the room is a source of learning: the color of the walls, the art on the flyers, the bones on the ceiling, the interaction of the people. These things alone may not have meaning, but in this instance, the question becomes what kind of subculture would choose this setting for interaction.

In "Literacy, Discourse, and Linguistics," James Paul Gee defines what he means by "literacy studies" and pushes us beyond more traditional definitions of literacy.

> At any moment we are using language we must say or write the right thing in the right way while playing the right social role and

(appearing) to hold the right values, believes, and attitudes. Thus, what is important is not language, and surely not grammar, but saying (writing)doingbeingvaluingbelieving combinations. These combinations I call "Discourses" with a capital "D." [. . .] Discourses are ways of being in the world; they are forms of life which integrate words, acts, values, beliefs, attitudes, and social identities as well as gestures, glances, body positions, and clothes. (6–7)

In regard to my project, Gee's concept of literacy provides a frame to consider the opening scene in this paper. What are the ideas, unifying concepts, and sources of self identity among the people in the room? Every detail becomes something from which one can learn in order to blend within this unique subculture of attitudes, ideas, beliefs, and appearances. The words and art on the walls, flyers, and jackets begin to represent not just words, but the ideas and values of the culture creating them. The appearance of these groups of people in the room, from their clothing and hair to the way that they are standing, becomes a source of literacy in its own right. For those experienced in this scene, it is fairly simple to tell who is new, who is experienced, and eventually, who belongs within this group. After some time within the culture, appearance begins to assume less importance than mannerisms, slang, and ability to successfully interact.

CULTURAL SPONSORS OF LITERACY

Like Lauren B. Resnik, I am examining "literacy as a set of cultural practices that people engage in" (117). This study explores literacy practices associated with punk culture, paying particular attention to the ways in which we, in Gee's words, "acquired the Discourses" of punk culture. How did these five middle-class teenagers from suburban, Baptist Waco manage to get to this point? What drew us together and what were the different forms of sponsorship from which we assimilated different aspects of punk literacy? Therefore, this project looks at a sub-subculture of punks in mid-1980s Waco, Texas, for the ways in which my friends and I, in the words of Deborah Brandt, "pursue[d] literacy" and how punk "literacy pursue[d]" us (33).

As Brandt discusses in "Sponsors of Literacy," every aspect of our lives affects our literacy. Sponsors range from family, friends, and teachers to setting, family background, socioeconomic standing, and exposure to ideas. All forms of sponsorship direct us and influence our literacy development. Literacy itself influences the direction of further development. Sponsorship and literacy become the proverbial "snowball" within which we develop; its shape over time is dictated by the layers of learning, background, and exposure inside.

In order to study this sub-subculture, the Waco group of punks, I first detail the backgrounds of a group of five people within it: Eric (me), Matt, Harry, Judson, and Fred. Each received a survey that assessed their backgrounds, similarities, and differences—information that is invaluable in understanding the eventual development of the group. This group of friends is the direct result of the various forms of literacy sponsorship within our lives: people, setting, and backgrounds.

FAMILY BACKGROUNDS

Given the socioeconomic status of our families, we each consider ourselves to come from middle or working class backgrounds. Four of us have parents with college and postgraduate educations, and all our parents completed high school. We each view our parents as people who worked their way up to more economic stability and better social standing through their own efforts—pulled themselves up by their bootstraps, so to speak—and attained more comfortable lives by hard work and/or education. Our aspirations to attend a university were instilled in all of us by our parents. In essence, we grew up believing that hard work and education were the only ways to achieve and maintain a stable, fulfilling life. We were a fairly social group that was exposed and privy to the benefits of a decent education. Some of us attended public schools while others attended private schools, and all were active in student government, social, and academic groups in high school.

As complex and different as our family histories were, instability in our home and family life is something to which we were all exposed. Three of us came from families that were comprised of divorced and remarried parents. Matt and I were raised much of our lives by single mothers. Many of us were drawn to each other in an attempt to create our own family of friends.

COMMUNITY CULTURE

One extremely influential force in our lives did not come from our schools, religions, or families, but from our geographical area: Waco, Texas. The significance of this location cannot be stressed enough. Waco is part of the "Southern Bible Belt"; it is very much a Southern Baptist town, dominated by Baylor University. Although only one of us was specifically raised Southern Baptist, for five adolescents beginning to develop their own identities and life philosophies, this community influence played a huge role. We were all dealing with the typical adolescent crises. The constant struggle to find our own voices often meant coming face-to-face with opposing beliefs that were generally much more conservative in nature than the beliefs we were developing on our own. As Barton and Hamilton explain, "literacy practices are purposeful and embedded in broader social goals and cultural practices" (44). Our family situations may have led us to one another, but it was the conservative climate of our hometown—a climate we found alienating—that provided the glue that held our group together and led us to punk.

Our personalities all reacted to this conservative setting with a sense of defiance and sometimes outright anger. When questioned about what attracted them to punk culture, survey respondents listed angst as a main factor. Punk was both a form of music and a collective that allowed and encouraged its members to speak openly. Freedom of expression was, in 1980s punk, a defining element of the culture. We found this liberating and highly enticing. Anger and desire to change the world around us were easily expressed through the medium of punk music and were often reflected in dress and attitude, which placed importance on shock value.

CLASS CONFLICT

This leads to another prevalent answer to the question of what attracted us to the punk culture: class conflict with our peers. Many of us grew up exposed to a class structure in which we did not necessarily fit. All of our parents had achieved a certain level of success, but we still found ourselves in conflict with some of our peers. We all came from working, middle-class families that struggled to attain their class standing. While we may have reached some small level of privilege by our high school years, we were still painfully aware at times of the socioeconomic background from which we had come. The public schools some of us attended were in the more affluent parts of town. When I attended a college prep school, I was receiving financial aid for tuition from a scholarship. Essentially, we came from fairly financially comfortable families by this time, but we were still surrounded by peers from much more affluent families than ours. This basic conflict of social standing resulted in us feeling not quite part of the same society as our classmates. We chose a culture in which class was not an issue.

One reply to the question of what drew us into this culture differed from the others: "I do not know if anything necessarily 'drew' me to any scene; rather, it is simply where my life took me. I don't think that I sought the scene; instead, the scene was secondary to the friendships. [...] Simply put, it was the friendships that brought me to the scene—the scene itself was merely a collateral aspect of the friendships." I have since asked all those surveyed and each agrees with this answer. In short, our subculture was not necessarily defined by punk. Rather, it was defined by our group of friends—who happened to be punks.

POP CULTURE

Our musical tastes prior to punk were similar: each of us listened to heavy metal and classic rock, and some listed classic country music as well. Most of us had been influenced by older siblings and parents. (Most of us had siblings who had come of age in the late '70s.)

Other media that influenced our development included television and film. We were the quintessential "Pop Culture" generation. Everyone cited horror and science fiction as an influence: growing up with the electric babysitter (TV), we were inundated with campy horror and science fiction films of the '50s, '60s, and '70s. Movies such as *Planet of the Apes, Forbidden Planet,* and *Plan 9 from Outer Space* were among our favorites; we were all seeing the *Star Wars* movies and watching *Star Trek* reruns after school. Collecting toys merchandised by these movies was also a common bond. "Disposable" entertainment such as plastic toys and low budget B-movies were often the forms of media that we were drawn to and cherished.

We grew up reading the Bible and comic books, and as we grew older, we all became intrigued by authors such as Joseph Heller, Kurt Vonnegut, C. S. Lewis, Tolkien, and John Irving. It is evident that our early and middle childhood imaginations revolved around science fiction, camp, and horror. We were all relatively intelligent youths and had all made As and Bs in school to this point. Reading was a pastime that had fueled our imaginations and begun to shape our personalities.

These developments occurred independent of each other; none of us met until high school.

This taste for comic books, science fiction, horror, and ultimately our early outlook on life had developed of its own accord, free from each other's influence. Obviously, like people are drawn to like people. In our case, some of our likes and dislikes were so similar that it seems, in retrospect, inevitable that we would become close friends. Even in a town the size of Waco, it was only a matter of time until our paths crossed and we realized we were kindred spirits.

The pop culture we grew up with was as much an influence on us as the community and "place" in which we were raised, and it was also a significant influence on the subculture to which we later belonged. Our collective tastes and similar backgrounds encouraged a mutual respect for each other, which fueled a sense of belonging and family. The common thread that was stressed by each member of the group is that we were all seeking a family of our own making. We wanted to belong with people whom we had chosen and who had chosen us. We created our own stable environment that allowed us to exchange ideas, share perspectives, and nurture our individual personalities. We had grown up in a community that didn't understand us, in homes that were sometimes unstable and volatile. Within our group, we exchanged ideas and were receptive to new concepts. We frequently shared new books, new movies, and new thinking. Thus, our various early literacy sponsors were not merely people; they were the culture of our surroundings as well as the actual place we were raised. By the time we met and formed strong bonds of friendship, we were just waiting for something new and exciting or explosive to come into our lives. That something was punk.

DEVELOPING PUNK LITERACY

Sponsors are a tangible reminder that literacy learning throughout history has always required permission, sanction, assistance, coercion, or, at minimum, contact with existing trade routes. Sponsors are delivery systems for the economies of literacy, the means by which these forces present themselves to—and through—individual learners. They also represent the causes into which people's literacy usually gets recruited.

—DEBORAH BRANDT

When studying a subculture (or, as Gee would call it, a Discourse), it is interesting to look at the origins of different behaviors, beliefs, terminology, and ultimately all of the different elements that define it. Where do people learn to behave in an acceptable manner among their peers? Various subcultures have their own social practices, which eventually become forms of literacy. Written texts, even the simplest ones, are translated into action and applied within the group, and one group's texts and practices may seem completely foreign to another. As noted at the beginning of this essay, I am attempting here to understand "the social conditions under which people actually engage in literate activities" (Resnick 117). Inasmuch as punk culture and music were hard for us to come by, it is important to understand literate activities involved in the perpetual cycle of discovery and introduction that sponsored and advanced our increasing punk literacies. That's just what I will do here. While our punk literacy was culturally sponsored, as I have analyzed, I want to look in particular at how my group of friends used different forms of sponsors and literacy in order to educate ourselves about the punk subculture and, eventually, how we became accepted into that tightknit social environment.

We had each experienced limited exposure to punk music. One of my earliest sponsors was a friend from California who had introduced me to bands such as Black Flag, X, and Fear. Judson's early sponsorship came in the form of a radio show called *The Rock and Roll Alternative*. Matt was already involved with new wave music. Harry and Fred were both exposed to punk by friends or family. Thus, we did not necessarily introduce each other to punk but had some interest in the music prior to meeting. However, once we met, we became involved in a perpetual cycle of discovery and introduction. We shared every aspect of the music or culture that we learned about with each other. This perpetuated sharing of facets of the culture that we discovered produced a geometric learning curve. In a way, we became sponsors to ourselves.

One of our primary sources of information about punk culture and music came from its actual records. We would listen to *Rock and Roll Alternative* and hear a band we liked. Then we would special order the band's records from the local music store. Most included sleeves with lyrics and occasionally pictures of the band. Listening to the band, we would read the lyrics, learning the songs and what the band was talking about. The pictures showed how the band dressed. As we eagerly exchanged records among ourselves, our own group literacy began to develop. We were learning the slang, the dress, and the fashion of another culture prior to direct, personal exposure. This gave us an advantage when we began going to see bands in Austin or Dallas, where there were established punk cultures. Because we went to see only bands we liked, we were already familiar with their music and knew most of the lyrics before we saw them perform. We were "punk literate," albeit without much real life, direct exposure to the punk scene. We adapted our dress and style from the pictures on the records and learned a new language from the music. Thus, the records were extremely influential sponsors.

Television was another sponsor for us. Although there was very little true exposure to punk culture on TV, we did manage to find a few programs, movies, documentaries, and late night videos that gave us a glimpse into the world of punk rock. A late night show called *Night Flight* played some of the more controversial, less commercial music videos. These were aired after midnight on Friday and Saturday. Some of these early music videos influenced the way we dressed and exposed us to some of the more obscure bands, whose records we could then order. The same program also offered documentaries that showed us what was going on in the larger cities on the West and East coasts. Interviews on the programs taught us about other bands and different music scenes. It was almost a continuous cycle of information from media and records leading back to more information from the same sources, all leading to more learned behavior that we put into practice within our sub-subculture and, eventually, within the larger subcultures at the music venues.

One incredibly important factor in our development was exposure to other groups at shows. The records, lyric sheets, and media had provided us with the basic tools we needed to go to the show and not stick out. However, fully assimilating into the larger scenes of Austin and Dallas took a little longer. Anyone who attends live music venues knows that there are always different groups of people standing around talking. Attending the punk shows provided us with a good way to observe different mannerisms and types of dress, and to pick up some of the different slang terms. The more events we attended, the more people began to recognize us. Eventually, we began to feel that being the "Waco guys" was something we didn't need to hide. We began to make friends within the Austin and Dallas punk community. We were no longer singled out in a bad way. Simply stated, we established our credibility and earned respect. We had progressed to the point that we were comfortable and regarded as extended members of the community. The more we were exposed to the other music scenes, the more we were accepted by the punk community.

PUNK LITERACY IN PRACTICE (AND IN THE MAKING)

Now that I have outlined our individual histories and different modes of learning and assimilation, I will review some of the characteristics of our Waco punk "sub-subculture." During the mid-1980s, we were a relatively small group, initially very isolated from the active, direct persuasion of the larger punk culture in other cities. Accordingly, we developed some distinct unifying aspects.

Philosophically, we always tried to maintain an open-minded approach to other individuals and cultures. We felt that different ideas and culture should be treated with respect. The general rule in our early days was that we wanted to be introduced to and learn concepts that originally seemed foreign to us. Our reading material was often inclined to be political or subversive in nature. We traded books by authors such as Camus, Nietzsche, and Solzhenitsyn. *The Anarchist Cookbook* provided quite a bit of enjoyment and inspiration. We freely exchanged ideas and philosophies that melded with our pop culture past. The result was that our group was drawn together on a more cerebral level than some of the larger punk subcultures to which we were eventually exposed.

As punk culture developed within some of the larger cities, I at times witnessed a somewhat "testosterone" driven form of punk. During the later 1980s, many of the people drawn to this culture were not attracted to it for the same reasons we were. As punk music and fashion became more popular, some of the people we encountered at larger music venues were like the ones who had, four years earlier, relished chasing us out of fast food establishments and trying to pick fights with us. Some had the stereotypical "jock" mentality and thought that a punk show was a great place to thrash around and beat up people. The mentality in the larger punk scene was not always similar to our much smaller and more isolated scene. Unfortunately, this mentality began to appear in scenes throughout the States. George Hurchalla observed the same thing, writing in his book *Going Underground*: "The core of people making the music and putting on the shows was tight. We all were kinda dorky kids into punk rock. We weren't into all the violence and tough guy posturing [. . .] in other scenes" (279).

It pains me that this later form of punk is so often its main image. In contrast, we had been shaped by early sponsors into a group of young people drawn to this culture by intellectual and developmental desires. We wanted to feel our own voice and learn about others, in an open-minded and unrestricted manner. Nor was this motivation indigenous to Waco; these ideas were blossoming throughout the country. According to Mark Anderson of the Positive Force record label in 1985,

> Punk is not [. . .] the latest cool trend or even a particular form of style or music, really—it is an idea that guides and motivates your life. The Punk community that exists, exists to support and realize that idea through music art, fanzines and other expressions of personal creativity. And what is this idea? Think for yourself, be yourself, don't just take what society gives you, create your own rules, live your own life. (qtd. in O'Hara 36)

In the early days of our Waco subculture, we discovered the "do it yourself" attitude of punk. This part of the early punk culture encouraged us to make our own fashion, and as our punk literacies increased, the relative inaccessibility of punk fashion further "sponsored" our do-it-yourself choices. At that time it was nearly impossible to go into a store and purchase prefabricated punk look fashion, so every aspect of our fashion was do-it-yourself. We discovered ways to buy regular, plain T-shirts and transform them into more suitable and desirable attire. We quickly learned that stencils could be made out of any material, such as paper or cardboard, and with spray paint, we were able to make shirts that said anything we wanted. Leather jackets originally came in the form of motorcycle jackets, which we would decorate with ink pens and paint. We styled our hair in the backyard with pet grooming clippers. While bright colored hair dye wasn't readily accessible to us in Waco, we figured out that our hair could be bleached white and then colored with Kool-Aid drink powder in concentrated form. The spikes in our hair were made to stand up with Knox gelatin.

We also learned to go to new places. In the formative years of our subculture, we learned from some of the bigger scenes that mainstream clubs and bars were not receptive to punk rock shows. Instead, venues often came in the form of alternative "gay" bars. An early alliance was formed between much of the gay culture and the punks; because punk culture originally embraced open-mindedness, the gay culture of the time seemed a natural ally as both were often viewed as outcasts and nonconformists. Thus, we were able to persuade proprietors of gay bars to allow "our" bands to play. Eventually, we persuaded a pre-dominantly African American club to let us bring records in once a week to play our music. Our group's determination thus caused us to form somewhat unconventional associations with others with whom we might otherwise never have connected. In retrospect, these alliances and friendships seem logical; but at the time, we were merely doing what we felt we had to do to nurture our fledgling music scene. None of us knew or suspected that these actions would introduce us to cultures that would enrich our lives and lead us to a higher state of social consciousness as we became adults.

During these years, we were introduced to soul, jazz, dance, and hip hop music. Our view of punk was that we should listen to anything we found enjoyable. At least for my group of friends, the punk culture was not defined by punk music. Classical, new wave, new age, jazz, metal, hardcore, hip-hop, etc. are all forms of music that have remained in our lives.

Another characteristic of the group from this period was the reemergence of the skateboard scene. Skateboarding had begun its resurgence in the late 1970s. Its new popularity had started on the West Coast at the same time as punk emerged there, and skate culture became interconnected with punk culture. One of our favorite pastimes was to skate drainage ditches. Eventually, we were able to acquire enough wood to build our own ramp, affording us an inexpensive way to entertain ourselves. The skate culture had great impact on our clothing fashion and slang.

LASTING EFFECTS OF SPONSORED LITERACY

The "do-it-yourself," or DIY, attitude of punk permeated every aspect of our sub-subculture. Will and determination were the means by which we had our fashion, our music, and our entertainment. This drive is still visible in each of our lives today: the entire group has gone on to realize educational and/or business success. The drive that was the catalyst to form our friendships and create our sub-subculture is the same drive that has allowed us to attain some of our goals.

Every aspect of our lives, friendships, and subculture has been a direct result of our early sponsors. The forces that drew us together—background, family, education, culture—were all aspects of sponsorship that had shaped us to that point. The tools we used to assimilate and educate ourselves on punk were further sponsors in our development. Variations of these same tools are still used today in our educational or professional endeavors. Our subculture—or, more importantly, every aspect of our lives—has been the culmination of every sponsor (positive or negative) and every action that has brought us to our current state. Such analysis makes clear why Barton and Hamilton conclude: "Like all human activity, literacy is essentially social, and it is located in the interaction between people" (42). Our group's developing punk literacy was a clear case in point.

WORKS CITED

Barton, David, and Mary Hamilton. 1998. "A Social Theory of Literacy Practices and Events." In *Local Literacies: Reading and Writing in One Community*, 6–13. New York: Routledge. (Reprinted in Carter 2007, 42–53.)

Brandt, Deborah. 1998. "Sponsors of Literacy." *College Composition and Communication* 49.2: 165–85. (Reprinted in Carter 2007, 12–38.)

Carter, Shannon, ed. 2007. *Literacies in Context*. Southlake, TX: Fountainhead.

Gee, James Paul. 1989. "Literacy, Discourse, and Linguistics: An Introduction." *Journal of Education* 171.1 (November): 5–17.

Hurchalla, George. 2005. *Going Underground*. Stuart, FL: Zuo.

O'Hara, Craig. 1999. *The Philosophy of Punk: More Than Noise*. San Francisco: AK.

Resnick, Lauren B. 1991. "Literacy in School and Out." In *Literacy: An Overview by 14 Experts*, edited by Stephen R. Graubard. New York: Noonday. (Reprinted in Carter 2007, 116–33.)

Student Activity

READING, ANALYSIS, AND REFLECTION

1. Ethnography focuses on culture. What culture is the researcher analyzing? How do you know this? What are the ways a researcher can describe a culture? What details does the researcher use to draw in readers?
2. Is this ethnography based on participant-observation? If so, what methods does the researcher use to gain information?
3. How has the researcher protected the participants?
4. What point of view (first person, second person, third person) does the author use? Why?
5. How does the researcher demonstrate that he has gone beyond simply being a participant to being able to analyze from a more objective viewpoint?
6. What types of literacy exist? Make a list of various literacies. Which are of interest to you?

8

Looking at History, Working in the Archives

Historical research draws on the humanistic tradition and often relies on archives. It asks questions such as, what was done in the past? Or how did we get to where we are today in teaching writing? Researchers interrogate materials—texts, photographs, and other objects—to answer questions and to posit interpretations. This approach is in the humanistic tradition, often with the lone scholar working among stacks of artifacts. The researcher may even be required to wear gloves to ensure that the material is not damaged or affected. Archivists and librarians are usually eager to have researchers and scholars mine these special collections, but they are also the caretakers and oversee guidelines for the use of the materials.

For *A Schoolmarm All My Life: Personal Narratives from Frontier Utah* (Kinkead 1996), I spent many, many hours in the archives. The book is the end product, but it was a project not immediately clear to me. *Schoolmarm* grew out of my interest in the schoolmarm as western icon, especially in Owen Wister's classic work *The Virginian*. Not satisfied with the fictional depiction of the frontier schoolteacher, I began looking for factual accounts—diaries, journals—by real schoolteachers. I found a storehouse of primary materials for study through the Historical Department of the Church of Jesus Christ of Latter Day Saints (LDS), which came about as a result of its emphasis on recording personal histories. As a rhetorician I was also interested in these artifacts as texts, and as a feminist I was interested in recovering the schoolteachers' stories. Finally, the last prong of my interest came from teaching courses for future teachers. Thus, interests in western American literature, rhetoric, women's studies, and English education converged in a project—and eventual book—to recover the voices of these commonplace yet important figures in early Utah. My story is illustrative of how a research question develops.

For some weeks and months, I traveled from my home in Logan, Utah, eighty-three miles to Salt Lake City to visit the LDS historical department, which held a gold mine of twenty-four personal narratives. Funded by an institutional grant and also supported by the Utah Humanities Council, I sought permission from the administration of the department to use its archives. This involved a personal interview, which probed my intentions, which were academic—to fill a gap in our understanding of western women who served as schoolteachers during the nineteenth century in the Utah territory. Seeking and gaining permission also meant the materials could be used and quoted from in the final manuscript.

During the interview the guidelines for using the archives were shared. At the time I started the research in the 1980s, no computers, particularly no portable computers, existed for transcription. No ink pens were allowed in the room where materials were delivered for study, only pencils, even though much of the material was on microfilm. (As so much information is accessible on the Internet, microfilm readers may not be well known. Figure 8.1 depicts undergraduate researcher Lenaye Howard at work reading Colonial-era documents on a microfilm reader in the archives.)

Grant funds purchased a portable typewriter. The process involved reading the entire journal or diary of the teacher, deciding on its value to the project, and zeroing in on entries that focused on teaching while still keeping some entries that provided historical or cultural context.

I entered this project with the draft of a hypothesis—that the real schoolmarms of the West might not be as depicted in western novels. For instance, in most novels the schoolmarm must resign her position if she marries; on the other hand, in the Utah territory the schoolteacher might not only be married but also engaged in a plural marriage. It was fascinating reading.

In addition to reading these *primary documents*, I also studied relevant histories—secondary sources—to help frame the context. This *review of literature* of *secondary sources* included a history of the LDS church; information about the religious environment of the United States in the early 1800s; histories of LDS women; histories of the movement, led by Catherine Beecher, to encourage women to become teachers; town-building accounts of the West; published diaries of nineteenth-century LDS women and western schoolteachers; histories of other churches in Utah; local and county histories; theoretical studies and approaches to women's history. These background readings provided the contextual information necessary to understand the diaries and journals and

FIGURE 8.1. Microfilm reader and student researcher Lenaye Howard.

then to use this information as an introduction to the edited personal accounts in the book.

The personal accounts were analyzed for commonalities, and I developed matrices charting each diarist's/journalist's life: amount of education, marital status, number of children, salary, length of teaching career. These charts helped tease out common themes and also set aside anomalies in the collections. Developing taxonomies and grids can help organize the wealth of information uncovered in an archival search.

Besides gaining permission from the special collections to use these materials in a publication, I also sought permission from the families themselves, tracing the current living relative from the earlier schoolteacher. These, too, were treasure hunts in some respects—alternately frustrating and fun. The best moment came when one relative shared with me a real artifact of her grandmother's account, a worn red-velvet-covered diary. Microfilm can never reproduce the tactile sensation of holding the original source. It was a vivid window back into the nineteenth century and a teacher who lived in the brash mining town of Park City, Utah.

SPECIAL COLLECTIONS AND ARCHIVES

From this story about my own experience of working in the archives, the process can be enumerated.

1. Develop a research question that makes use of archival materials.
2. Identify and locate primary source materials.

3. Learn about the archives where materials are housed and the rules associated with using them. Most likely, a first-time user must complete a registration form. (See Fig. 8.2 for a sample of guidelines for using archives.)

4. Seek permission to have access to the materials through the appropriate channels.

5. Develop a schedule to examine the materials and collect data and information for analysis.

6. Read widely in ancillary and secondary materials to understand the historical and cultural context.

7. Study the primary documents in the archives and begin to make sense of them through analysis.

8. Be open to paths that appear from reviewing artifacts. Follow the trail.

9. In terms of data management and research ethics, gather material and discern that which is appropriate for the study; however, do not hide material that does not support the hypothesis. Good data collection and management involves taking excellent notes and keeping track of their origin for bibliographic information.

10. Construct the narrative or analysis that arises as the conclusion of the research.

11. Obtain permission to publish from the archival source. (For an example, see appendix 8.1.)

ARCHIVAL RESEARCH IN WRITING STUDIES

Kathryn Fitzgerald (2010), who won the Braddock Prize for the Best Article in Composition Studies in 2002, focused her work on the teaching of composition in late nineteenth-century normal schools, which resulted in "A Rediscovered Tradition: European Pedagogy and Composition in Nineteenth-Century Midwestern Normal Schools." As she said in a published interview,

> In the archives at the University of Wisconsin-Platteville, I discovered a couple of intriguing collections but was not sure that either had any significance outside my own quirky interest. One was a set of grammar and composition tests from a normal-school course, and the other was a class set of papers written not for a composition course but for graduation exercises. . . . I read through both, attempting to apply any theoretical lens that might help me see significance in the papers. The set of papers for the graduation exercise was definitely more interesting. (Ramsey et al. 2010, 248)

UtahStateUniversity
UNIVERSITY LIBRARIES

Special Collections and Archives

| SCA Home | About Us | Contact | Search | Forms | Donate |

Special Collection & Archives • (435) 797-2663 • scweb@usu.edu • Today's Hours : 8:00 am - 7:00 pm   Search Web Site   [Search]

Special Collection & Archives > Using

Visiting / Using:

Please Note: Special Collections & Archives (SCA) has different hours and rules than the rest of the library. SCA is located on the lower level of the Merrill-Cazier Library in Room 35. SCA is open from:

- 8 to 5 Monday, Thursday, and Friday

If you are planning to do extensive research, contact us in advance and we will prepare materials for your visit.

Please visit http://www.usu.edu/map/ for a campus map.

Using the Reading Room:

SCA operates under a closed-stack environment and as such materials may not be checked out and must be read in the Tanner Reading Room. First time users must complete Registration Agreement form (good for 5 years) with a picture ID.

- Using the card catalog or electronic cataloging system
  - Identify call numbers for desired items
  - Fill out the Blue Paging Card.
- Only three items may be used at a time
  - (e.g. three books, or three folders).
  - Only one document box may be in use at a time.
- Personal belongings such as:
  - briefcases, backpacks
  - and coats must be stored in the lockers provided.
  - A staff attendant will give you a lock.
- For note taking, only PENCIL is allowed. No pens.
- Exercise great care in handling fragile items; white gloves may be required & provided by staff.
- No food, candy, or beverages allowed in the Tanner Reading Room.
- The use of cell phones is not allowed. To make or receive a call, please exit the Tanner Reading Room.

Scanning and copies:

A scanner has been provided free of charge for patron use (requires a USB drive: if you do not have a USB drive, SCA can provide one after a small donation). Scanning items requires filling out a photocopy request form and adherence to copyright law limits. Please read posted copyright warning. Photocopies can be made by staff for a small charge, though requests may not be filled immediately.

- Scans made by staff smaller than 8 MB can be emailed one at a time (limited resolution on tiff files)
- Copy orders placed in the Reading Room for pick-up are $0.10 each
- Copy orders that require postal mail are $0.25 per image with $5 minimum charge
- Digital printing: Prints in black and white or color
- 4 x 5 = $6 / 5 x 7 = $8 / 8 x 10 = $10 / 11 x 14 = $16 / 16 x 20 = $26 / 20 x 24 = $30
  - price does not include shipping
  - same-day service not available
  - additional charge for postage outside US and bulk orders
- Commercial / Business use fee: add $0.25 per image
- Rush orders: Add 50%

Some materials may not be duplicated due to age, fragility and/or copyright. Check the Digital Library to see if requested material has already been digitized.

FIGURE 8.2. Using special collections and the archives. (Source: http://library.usu.edu /specol/using/index.php.)

Fitzgerald found that significance by thinking about the group in the context of the time, a celebration of Wisconsin's fiftieth anniversary as a state. She "began to see the papers as writing the identity of the society emerging from the frontier" (Ramsey et al. 2010, 249). She was not only a teacher of composition but also someone who became a historian of composition through this project. Jane Greer (2015) mined archives at the University of Kentucky to investigate how rural women's literacy improved through Moonlight Schools in Appalachia in the early twentieth century. This marvelous essay tells the story of one woman's (Cora Wilson Stewart) efforts to combat illiteracy.

Likewise, Robert J. Connors (1981) conducted a fascinating study to track "The Rise and Fall of the Modes of Discourse"; the modes include narration, description, argument, and exposition. "More students have been taught composition using the modes of discourse than any other classification system," as Connors puts it (444). To conduct his research, he used textbooks out of print—but housed in special collections. He charted a paradigm shift in how writing is taught to college students and demonstrated that in spite of knowing how writers write, the outdated modes of discourse held sway for decades. Similarly, David Russell (2002) produced a comprehensive study of writing across the curriculum and its historical roots, not only in institutions of higher education in the United States but traced back to origins in universities in Germany and the United Kingdom.

Historical and archival research has also been a favorite approach in the pages of *Young Scholars in Writing*. In addition to Lauren Petrillo's (2006) essay "The Visible Rhetoric and Composition of Invisible Antebellum Female Seminary Students: Clay Seminary, Liberty, Missouri, 1855–1865," provided as a sample in this chapter, the following titles suggest the rich resources found in archival sources:

- "Speaking without Words: Silence and Epistolary Rhetoric of Catholic Women Educators on the Antebellum Frontier, 1828–1834" (Jackie Hoermann, volume 9)
- "Literacy as Independence: The Writings of Hattie Reynolds, 1870–1927" (Sarah Ashlock, volume 9)
- "Reframing the Victim: Rhetoric for Segregation in the *Greenville News*" (Jennifer E.M. Hill, volume 9)
- "'My Country! 'Tis of Thee, Stronghold of Slavery': The Musical Rhetoric of the American Antislavery Movement" (Karen Anton, volume 7)
- "'With the Flash Came a Delayed Roll of Thunder': The Discursive Struggle over the Atomic Bomb" (Andrew Erickson, volume 7)
- "From Wellesley to Yale, 1969–1979: A Textual Analysis of Hillary Rodham's Early Written Rhetoric" (Jonathan Pearson, volume 7)
- "In Two Places at Once: Nellie J. Hall Williams and the Conundrum of Gender and Travel in the Early Twentieth Century" (Amanda Clark, volume 6)
- "Black Women's Voices in the Women's Movement for Equal Rights: Pauli Murray and Patricia Williams" (Anna Rae Mitchell, volume 5)

- "The Impact of Southern Heritage on the Rhetorical Style of Myra Page" (Laura Northcutt, volume 5)
- "'I Suppose I am My Own Girl Now': The Diary of Nancy Holmes Corse, Enosburg, Vermont, 1858–1859" (Lauren Petrillo, volume 3)
- "Girls in Business Meetings: Beta Phi Theta Rho Secretaries Take charge, 1946–1950" (Kate Stuart, volume 1)

Profile of a Student Researcher: Brianne Palmer

Brianne possessed her grandmother's memoir and wanted to use it as the basis for understanding not only her grandmother's life story but for contextualizing that story through historical and cultural sources. Brianne wrote in her review of literature:

> Joan Palmer was born in Dublin, Ireland in 1920, a time when women were expected to stay home and tend to the family per the societal norms and current Catholic ideology. "In the early decades of the new Irish state, Catholic ideology and statutory developments combined to create a range of formal and informal barriers to the participation of married women in the workforce. The role of motherhood was socially and legally sanctioned as the 'natural' role for Irish women and this was clearly evidenced by the 1937 constitution" (Kieley, Elizabeth, and Marie Leane. "'What Would I Be Doing at Home All Day?': Oral Narratives of Irish Married Women's Working Lives 1936–1960." *Women's History Review* 13.3 (2004): 428–46).

Brianne found in the memoir evidence of women filling jobs vacated by men who went to war. Through the lens of one woman's story, Brianne sought to understand the role of women born pre-World War II, their family dynamics, and the social structure that changed throughout the twentieth century.

RESEARCH INTEGRITY

Ethical considerations come into play when undertaking archival research. It might seem that when materials are housed in archives, consent for their use naturally comes as part of the package. Archives are most often in an official unit of a library, but in some cases archives may be in the filing cabinets of writing program offices, perhaps hundreds or thousands of student papers kept over the decades, perhaps bearing social security numbers from a time when that was not considered a security risk. Researchers have an obligation to fairly and accurately represent the people behind archival materials. They may have given permission to have their works put in a special collection; on the other hand, they may not have, particularly if the donation occurred after a death and without preplanning. Time does help. For instance, the diary of Nancy Holmes Corse noted in the titles from *YSW* is from the nineteenth century, and any person associated with it passed long ago.

McKee and Porter (2012) offer a useful heuristic for researchers using the archives, questions to use to interrogate the integrity of the research project.

- The archive itself
  - What kind of archive is it?
  - Are there archival and institutional guidelines to protect persons associated with the material?
  - How was the material obtained and what consent was given?
- The subject of the archive
  - What were the writer's intentions and directives for the material?
  - What are the family connections and their wishes?
  - Are third parties involved?
- Legal considerations
  - Are copyrights involved?
  - Are there any community claims, as in tribal contexts?
  - Does FERPA come into play in terms of student rights?
- Other researchers
  - Have these archival materials been used by others?
  - Does the researcher's professional community have ethics guidelines (such as CCCC)?

Consulting with mentors and archivists is an excellent step for ensuring archival work is undertaken with sensitivity and integrity.

Being a historian in writing studies can be an exhilarating experience, particularly when searching through a treasure trove of archival materials that may include not only texts but also photographs and cultural artifacts. Uncovering the past is not only fun and interesting, the work the scholar produces may well become part of an archival collection. Lauren Petrillo uncovers a largely forgotten past of nineteenth-century female seminaries, something more than finishing schools, for young women. Her discovery of these female voices brings to mind Abigail Adams's plea to husband John Adams in writing the Constitution to "remember the ladies."

APPENDIX 8.1

SAMPLE PERMISSION TO PUBLISH FORM
UTAH STATE UNIVERSITY

Merrill-Cazier Library Special Collections & Archives
Logan, Utah 84322–3000
(435) 797–2663

Application For Permission to Publish and/or Reproduce

Name of Applicant:
Organization or agency (if applicable):
Address:
City, State, ZIP Code:
Phone, FAX:

MATERIAL TO BE USED
Collection Name and Number * Video/Film# * Photograph #
* Manuscript * Other

1.
2.
3.
4.
5.

INTENDED USE OF MATERIAL
Title or description of use:
Author/Producer:
Publisher:

Format: _____Book _____Magazine _____Film/Video Program
_____Advertisement _____CD-ROM _____Multimedia
_____School Project/Paper _____Other (please specify):

Estimated size of edition (number of copies/size of market):
Check all that apply: _____Commercial Use _____Non-Profit
501(c)3#:_____ _____Advertising _____Book _____Periodical
_____Dissertation _____Textbook _____Exhibition Catalog

Distribution rights desired (one-time use, one language):
_____North American rights _____World rights _____Language
_____Other use (please specify):

CONDITIONS OF USE

1) All requests to reproduce the repository's holdings, which may include photographs, film, video, manuscripts, maps and other documents, must be submitted on this application. By signing this application,

the applicant agrees to abide by all terms, conditions and provisions of this document.

Permission for reproduction is granted only when this application is countersigned by an authorized representative of the repository. Permission for reproduction is limited to the applicant and is non-transferable.

Permission for reproduction is granted only for the expressed purpose described in this application. This permission is non-exclusive; the repository reserves the right to reproduce the image or document and allow others permission to reproduce the image or document.

Any subsequent use (including subsequent editions, paperback editions, foreign language editions, *et cetera*) constitutes reuse and must be applied for in writing to the repository. Any change in use from that stated on the application (e.g., increased size of edition, change in market) requires permission from the repository. In the event that the applicant engages in unauthorized reproduction of photographic images or other documents, the applicant agrees to pay the repository a sum equal to three times the normal commercial fee*, not as a penalty but as liquidated damages agreed upon due to the difficulty in assessing actual damages incurred; the repository may in the event of unauthorized reproduction require surrender of all materials containing such unauthorized reproductions, and the applicant agrees that such materials shall be immediately surrendered upon receipt of request from the repository.

The repository reserves the right to refuse reproduction of its holdings if it feels that fulfillment of that request would violate copyright or other laws. The repository reserves the right to refuse reproduction of its holdings and to impose such conditions as it may deem advisable in its sole and absolute discretion in the best interests of the repository.

2) Beyond the permission of the repository, additional permissions may be required. Those permissions may include, but are not limited to:

Copyright: In cases of living artists and/or subject to the 1976 Copyright Law or the 1991 Visual Artists Rights Act, written permission must be secured by the applicant from the artist, his/her agent, or the copyright owner and provided to the repository before a photograph of an artwork will be released.

Warning Concerning Copyright Restrictions

The Copyright Law of the United States (Title 17, United States Code) governs the creation of photocopies or other reproductions of copyrighted material. Under certain conditions specified in the law, archives and libraries are authorized to furnish a photocopy or reproduction. One of these conditions is that the photocopy or reproduction is not to be "used for any purpose other than private study, scholarship or research." If a user makes a request for, or later uses, a photocopy or reproduction for purposes in excess of "fair use," that user may be liable for copyright infringement. This institution reserves the right to refuse a copying order if in its judgment, fulfillment of that order would violate copyright law.

Privacy: An individual depicted in a reproduction has privacy rights as outlined in Title 45 Code of Federal Regulations 46 (Protection of Human Subjects). The repository reserves the right to require a release from individuals whose privacy may be violated by the reproduction of an image. The repository extends the rights of privacy to include ceremonial objects and rites of Native Americans and requires the permission of the tribe's cultural office before releasing reproductions. *Owner of original:* In instances where the repository holds only a reproduction, the written permission of the owner of the original is required.

It is the responsibility of the applicant to obtain permission to publish from the owner of copyright (the institution, the creator of the record, the author, or his/her transferees, heirs, legatees, or literary executors). The repository will aid the applicant in contacting individuals pertaining by providing addresses, when available. However, the repository does not warrant the accuracy of that information and shall not be responsible for any inaccurate information.

In instances where the individual or organization that may grant permission cannot be contacted, the repository may consider granting permission for reproduction based on the applicant's evidence of a good faith effort to contact the appropriate individual or institution. However, the repository assumes no responsibility for infraction of copyright laws, invasion of privacy, or any other improper or illegal use that may arise from reproduction of an image.

In all instances, the applicant agrees to hold the repository and its agents harmless against any and all claims arising or resulting from the use of the material and shall indemnify the repository and its agents for any and all costs and damages arising or resulting from any such unauthorized use.

3) All reproductions must include the name of the repository in a caption or credit. The repository may also require that the artist/creator, the title of the work, and the object's catalog number appear in the caption or credit.

Credits should appear in close proximity to the image or in a special section devoted to credits. However, reproductions distributed electronically must contain the credit or caption as part of the image displayed in letters, which are at least 3/8" high in a legible typeface. When permission is granted to disseminate reproductions electronically, the repository reserves the right to require an electronic watermark or other identifying code within the scanned file.

The payment of a commercial use fee does not exempt the user from the credit line requirement. Failure to include a credit line or electronic watermark, or inaccurate captions or credits shall require the applicant to pay the sum of one hundred dollars ($100) per image, as liquidated damages and not as a penalty in view of the difficulty in assessing actual damages for this breach.

4) Copy photographs or other images supplied by the repository may not be copied, scanned, exhibited, resold, or used for any other purpose than that specified in this application. Copies shall not be deposited in another library, archives, or repository.

5) Unless approved in advance by the repository, each image must be reproduced unaltered in its entirety; the image must not be cropped, overprinted, printed on color stock, or bleed off the page.

The repository reserves the right to examine proofs and captions for accuracy and sensitivity before publication with the right to revise if necessary. The repository reserves the right to refuse any request and to impose such conditions as it may deem advisable in the best interests of the repository.

If permission is granted to distribute an electronic copy of an image, the distributed copy shall not exceed a resolution of 100 d.p.i. Scanned files must be destroyed once the final product has been produced.

The applicant covenants, represents, and warrants that the product will not contain any feature which would permit users to distort or mutilate the image, nor will the product be intentionally designed or prepared so as to be compatible with any computer program which is designed to manipulate graphic images.

6) The permission granted hereunder does not include the right to include the image in any printed or electronic materials accompanying the product, or in any advertisement for the product other than is expressly permitted below:

Solely in connection with the marketing and distribution of the product, applicant may use the image on the packaging of the product and in any advertisement, product catalogs, or publicity or promotional materials (a "Promotional Use"), provided that if the image is so used, Special Collections & Archives, Merrill Library, Utah State University shall be given a credit on the same page as the image appears. Applicant agrees that any Promotional Use will be made solely in a manner which indicates that the image is part of the content of the product, and the Merrill Library's name will not be used as an aesthetic or design element in such Promotional Use. Without limiting the generality of the foregoing, applicant shall not use the image or Merrill Library's name in any manner which creates any association between the image and/ or Merrill Library and applicant to such an extent that any goodwill towards the product or applicant arises in the image and/or Merrill Library's name, and applicant agrees that it will not have right, under any circumstances whatsoever, to claim, and will not claim, that such goodwill has arisen or the applicant is entitles to the benefits, if any, thereof.

7) Prepayment of all fees, including use fees, is required before permission is granted. Default in payment shall immediately revoke permission.

If the size of edition or number of editions exceeds the terms specified in this application, the applicant shall immediately pay the difference in use fees. If payment is not received within thirty (30) days, the applicant agrees to pay a use fee equal to twice the originally quoted use fee.

8) The applicant agrees to send the repository one copy, best edition, of the work containing the reproduction at no charge. All expenses for shipping and handling are to be borne by the applicant. **9)** *Cancellation for Conflict of Interest:* The parties agree that this contract may be canceled for conflict of interest in accordance with A.R.S. 38–511.

10) *Contract Claims and Controversies:* All contract claims and controversies arising under this contract shall be resolved pursuant to Utah State Board of Regents procurement procedures.

11) CREDIT LINE MUST READ:

Special Collections & Archives Merrill-Cazier Library Utah State University

12) Reproduction is permitted only from prints or transparencies supplied by Special Collections & Archives.

13) The permission granted terminates immediately upon publication.

14) Additional conditions or exceptions to the above requirements: Endorsements

By signing this application, I accept personally and on behalf of any organization I represent the conditions set forth above:

Signed:_____ Date:_____

When signed by an authorized agent of the repository, this form constitutes permission for reproduction as outlined in this application:

Signed:_____ Date:_____

Special Collections Staff Signature

REFERENCES AND FOR FURTHER READING

Berlin, James. 1987. *Rhetoric and Reality: Writing Instruction in American Colleges, 1900–1985*. Carbondale: Southern Illinois University Press.

Bordelon, Suzanne. 2010. "Composing Women's Civic Identities during the Progressive Era: College Commencement Addresses as Overlooked Rhetorical Sites." *College Composition and Communication* 61 (3): 510–33.

Brereton, John C., ed. 1995. *The Origins of Composition Studies in the American College, 1875–1925: A Documentary History*. Pittsburgh, PA: University of Pittsburgh Press.

Connors, Robert J. 1981. "The Rise and Fall of the Modes of Discourse." *College Composition and Communication* 32 (4): 444–55. http://dx.doi.org/10.2307/356607.

Donahue, Patricia, and Gretchen Flesher Moon, eds. 2007. *Local Histories: Reading the Archives of Composition.* Pittsburgh, PA: University of Pittsburgh Press.

Enoch, Jessica. 2008. *Refiguring Rhetorical Education: Women Teaching African American, Native American, and Chicano/a Students.* Carbondale: Southern Illinois University Press.

Fitzgerald, Kathryn. 2010. "Interview: Kathryn Fitzgerald—I'm Open to Whatever I Discover." In *Working in the Archives: Practical Research Methods for Rhetoric and Composition,* edited by Alexis E. Ramsey, Wendy B. Sharer, Barbara L'Eplattenier, and Lisa S. Mastrangelo, 248–49. Carbondale: Southern Illinois University Press.

Gaillet, Lynée Lewis. 2012. "(Per)Forming Archival Research Methodologies." *College Composition and Communication* 64 (1): 35–58.

Gaillet, Lynée Lewis, and Winifred Bryan Horner, eds. 2010. *The Present State of Scholarship in the History of Rhetoric: A Twenty-First Century Guide.* Columbia: University of Missouri Press.

Gere, Anne Ruggles. 2010. "The Teaching of Writing: 1912–2000." In *Reading the Past, Writing the Future: A Century of American Literacy Education and the National Council of Teachers of English,* edited by Erika Lindemann. Urbana, IL: NCTE.

Gold, David. 2008. *Rhetoric at the Margins: Revising the History of Writing in American Colleges, 1873–1947.* Carbondale, IL: Southern Illinois University Press.

Greer, Jane. 2015. "Expanding Working-Class Rhetorical Traditions: The Moonlight Schools and Alternative Solidarities among Appalachian Women, 1911–1920." *College English* 77 (3): 216–35.

Kinkead, Joyce. 1996. *A Schoolmarm All My Life: Personal Narratives from Frontier Utah.* Salt Lake City, UT: Signature.

Kirsch, Gesa E., and Liz Rohan, eds. 2008. *Beyond the Archives: Research as a Lived Process.* Carbondale: Southern Illinois University Press.

McKee, Heidi A., and James E. Porter. 2012. "The Ethics of Archival Research." *College Composition and Communication* 64 (1): 59–81.

Miller, Thomas P. 2011. *The Evolution of College English: Literacy Studies from the Puritans to the Postmodernists.* Pittsburgh, PA: University of Pittsburgh Press.

Murphy, James J., ed. 2012. *A Short History of Writing Instruction: From Ancient Greece to Contemporary America.* New York: Routledge.

Petrillo, Lauren. 2006. "The Visible Rhetoric and Composition of Invisible Antebellum Female Seminary Students: Clay Seminary, Liberty, Missouri, 1855–1865." *University of Missouri–Kansas City Young Scholars in Writing* 4 (Fall): 15–24.

Ramsey, Alexis E., Wendy B. Sharer, Barbara L'Eplattenier, and Lisa Mastrangelo. 2010. *Working in the Archives: Practical Research Methods for Rhetoric and Composition.* Carbondale: Southern Illinois University Press.

Russell, David R. 2002. *Writing in the Academic Disciplines, 1870–1990: A Curricular History.* 2nd ed. Carbondale: Southern Illinois University Press.

Schultz, Lucille M. 1999. *The Young Composers: Composition's Beginnings in Nineteenth-Century Schools.* Carbondale: Southern Illinois University Press.

Varnum, Robin. 1996. *Fencing with Words: A History of Writing Instruction at Amherst College during the Era of Theodore Baird 1938–1966.* Urbana, IL: NCTE.

Writing Centers Research Project. http://casebuilder.rhet.ualr.edu/wcrp/.

"The Visible Rhetoric and Composition of Invisible Antebellum Female Seminary Students: Clay Seminary, Liberty, Missouri, 1855–1865"

Lauren Petrillo,
University of Missouri–Kansas City

"There is only one boon that we ask, and that is not to be forgotten."

—HENRIETTA CLAY GEORGE, 1862

Scholars tracing the history of women's rhetoric and composition in the United States focus on the decades following the Civil War into the first years of the twentieth century (Tibbetts 236), and most hold up elite eastern institutions and educators as the measure of women's education (Farnham 1). Jane Hunter characterizes postbellum high schools as gateways for girls and young women to participate in formerly prohibited public activities (194), and Carol Mattingly establishes the late 1870s and 1880s as the period in which female students were first permitted to address a mixed audience, read their own compositions in public, or even look directly at the audience (59).

Other scholars look further into the past for women's engagement with public oratory, locating this during the colonial and early national periods. "Conventional wisdom" holds that in these early years "women received no formal elocutionary training because of their exclusion from higher education and the public sphere" (Buchanan 7). In *Imagining Rhetoric: Composing Women of the Early United States*, Janet Eldred and Peter Mortensen investigate the texts read by women and conclude they offered schoolgirls rhetorical education, even if access to

Lauren Petrillo, "The Visible Rhetoric and Composition of Invisible Antebellum Female Seminary Students," *Young Scholars in Writing* 4(2006):15–24.

the public platform was restricted. Lindal Buchanan's recent work, *Regendering Delivery: The Fifth Canon and Antebellum Women Rhetors*, presents further evidence that reading classes and textbooks of the late-eighteenth and early-nineteenth centuries introduced schoolgirls to "basic principles of elocution as well as models of civic discourse" (11). Although her study focuses on northern schoolgirls, Buchanan's work is important for scholars studying female rhetoric because it establishes the antebellum period as a time when girls gained the right to read compositions in public (47). Reading on the academic platform did not extend to all students, and often male professors read essays for them, but by the mid-nineteenth century, reading in public was an accepted pedagogical practice (47). However, other forms of oratory, including debate and declamation, were coded as masculine and therefore prohibited to girls (14). Only a few northern schools, such as Mount Holyoke, modeled after Harvard, included some form of debate and oratory in their practices. In contrast, antebellum southern educators not only required female students to read their own compositions, they also encouraged debate and other forms of oration on the public platform. Buchanan characterizes the southern tendency toward public display as a marker of elite status rather than evidence of progressive pedagogical practices. She proposes that southerners "may have been more accepting of schoolgirls' elocutionary display than northerners, in part, because southern women had few opportunities for later adapting their abilities to the professional or public sphere" (51). However, to claim that southern schoolgirls were allowed to debate in public simply because they lacked options and therefore posed no threat to the social fabric fails to explain the level of visibility experienced by female students of Clay Seminary in Liberty, Missouri.

Examining the public and private records of Clay Seminary from 1855 to 1865 and the records of other Missouri female students and teachers, as well as published testimonials and critiques in local newspapers, I argue that Clay Seminary students inhabited a sphere that conflated the private and public realms. Although "invisible" as females, students were compelled to exhibit themselves in the visible settings of the academic platform and newspapers: schoolgirls faced hundreds of spectators during examinations and continued to undergo public scrutiny for days after examinations ended. Within the secluded environment of the boarding school, students were scrutinized and censored by teachers, and some students censored themselves. Others found creative means of expression in spite of the intense oversight and declared independence in essays or put down their study books and danced when the principal went out for the evening mail. Clay Seminary students also earned money through literary exhibitions, served as teachers to younger students, published speeches and rebuttals to critics in local newspapers, and

participated in various local aid societies. Within the sheltered boarding school, in the midst of sectional conflict, they declaimed, debated,
and danced their way from girlhood to womanhood—and much of their
activity took place in the public realm.

FEMALE EDUCATION IN CLAY
COUNTY, MISSOURI

The term *boarding school* calls to mind images of nineteenth-century
schoolgirls sequestered within protective walls, far from the corrupting
influences of society. Southern female colleges and boarding schools
have been characterized as mere "finishing schools" for the wealthy
(McCandless 14), where girls acquired virtue, self-control, modesty, and
the ability to play the piano or embroider. In an age when women were
increasingly identified with the private sphere, teachers and principals
created environments analogous to the home circle, and as surrogate
parents they enforced strict guidelines. Students followed a dress code,
adhered to rigid schedules, and communicated only with individuals
approved by parents and faculty. Some schools restricted boarders from
exchanging packages or letters with day pupils, and virtually every letter
was intercepted, monitored, or censored.

The town of Liberty in Clay County, Missouri was founded in 1822,
and by the 1830s had established female schools the community considered to be on an equal footing with eastern institutions. Although Clay
County existed on the frontier, the citizens of Liberty considered themselves progressive with regard to female education, especially the education of elite daughters. As early as 1846, local newspapers commended
women whose minds are "quite as susceptible of higher intellectual cultivation as that of the male, and are quite as capable of accomplishing
great things in literature and science" (Liberty *Weekly Tribune*, May 9).
During the 1840s and 1850s, schools in Clay and surrounding counties
underscored the value of female education and uplifted woman's role
in the new Republic. She was encouraged to develop virtue and intelli-
gence, to embrace her sacred duty and raise patriot children. Previously
considered "merely an appendage to man," woman now inhabited a
higher sphere, making education a necessity (Yantis 6). As an intelligent wife and friend to man, woman must be educated. According to
Amy McCandless, "elite Southern fathers were much more willing than
their counterparts in the North to expose women to the classical curriculum" (14).

Clay Seminary was established in 1855, and continued throughout
the Civil War until 1865. Founders James and Lucy Love enforced seminary rules aimed at preserving decorum and preparing women for their

societal roles, but also included typically "male" subjects, such as mathematics, science, and public oration. Clay Seminary students were prohibited from attending "balls, parties or other places of mere amusement" (Christian College 1860). School guidelines aimed at preserving decorum were strictly enforced, and yet students also participated in highly public events that complicate traditional notions of private and public. The tendency of southern fathers to expose daughters to a classical curriculum played a major role. One might also consider the seminary and its public exhibitions as an enlarged home circle that included seminary students, teachers, and the community. In addition, the long-standing tradition of debate among the county's male citizens and the educational backgrounds of Clay Seminary's founders may have provided a further foundation.

James Love attended schools in Kentucky, graduated from the University of Missouri, Columbia, in 1853, and served as chair of mathematics and natural science at Liberty's William Jewell College from 1853 to 1855. By the time Love and his wife founded Clay Seminary in 1855, he was well established in the classical curriculum taught to men. James Love was by no means a progressive educator or herald of women's education—he spoke many years later of the crowning jewels of his career, the happy wives in many of Missouri's households (Clark 1893, 33). His primary purpose in establishing the seminary was financial; however, his journals and school records indicate a dedication to debate that undoubtedly influenced his decision to include debate in the curriculum at Clay Seminary. Lucy Ward Love attended Mount Holyoke Female Seminary in 1839–40, where young women engaged in a "demanding curriculum conspicuously free of instruction of domestic pursuits," and which included debate and current events (Mount Holyoke). She administered the two literary societies at Clay Seminary, where students accessed debate and other forms of public oration.

Another factor in the inclusion of public speaking in the curriculum, besides the influence, direct or indirect, of James and Lucy Love, was that debating already constituted a tradition in Liberty and surrounding counties. Clay County was considered frontier territory in the 1840s when citizens of nearby townships, some of them fathers of future students at Clay Seminary, formed the Franklin Debate Society. According to historian Louis Potts, "the oration, whether delivered orally or in printed form, became the American art form," and even on the frontier, Missourians engaged in "speechifying and disputation" (3). The minute book of the society indicates that "women were invited to attend the society as early as December 20, 1842, and members renewed the invitation a year later. However, records do not indicate female participation in the sessions"; instead, "females became passive members of the audience" (Potts 7). Although women did not participate directly, the invitation suggests a degree of community approval regarding women's access to public oratory. Decades later some of these men attended Clay Seminary exhibitions along with hundreds of others, where they watched, listened to, and occasionally stamped their feet in approval of young women debating and declaiming on the academic platform. Many of the topics were the same or similar to those debated by the Franklin Debate Society.

Waltus Watkins, a prominent man of the community and active member of the debate society, sent four daughters to Clay Seminary. Kate Watkins was a small child when her father attended weekly society meetings at the log schoolhouse on the Watkins property. The society's library remained in the schoolhouse after the society ceased to exist in early 1846; the library included Richard Whatley's texts on rhetoric and oration, which were also used by students at Clay Seminary as they prepared for public exhibitions.

ORATIONS AT CLAY SEMINARY

Tracing rhetorical training of women in the nineteenth century, Carol Mattingly found that educational institutions "allowed women to attend classes in rhetoric and elocution, but denied participation in public speaking" (59). With women denied public space, their compositions were read by male professors, or not at all. The experience of girls and young women at Clay Seminary challenges the notion that females were denied speaking experiences during the antebellum and Civil War years. Extant copies of school exhibitions and examination announcements provide evidence not only that schoolgirls received training in rhetoric and elocution, but that they also ascended the academic platform to read original compositions and participate in debate.

Lucy Love's earlier experience at Mount Holyoke, where she learned to compose and deliver essays and may have participated in debate, shaped her teaching methods. Enunciation, voice projection, and delivery were crucial elocutionary components at Mount Holyoke and remained important elements of public speaking throughout Love's career. In 1882, nearly two decades after retiring from teaching, she wrote to her husband as he sojourned in the Holy Land. From her cousin's Massachusetts boardinghouse Love anticipated listening to a woman speaking in public: "Tonight we are to have a temperance lecture from a lady—Mrs Knox—her subject—'A week in Washington.' I can tell you more about what I think of women as a speaker after I have heard her." A few lines later she continued that she had heard "the little woman" and that it was an interesting account of the Christian Women's Temperance Convention. Love wrote that the woman, a Methodist minister's wife, "put on no airs,—any school girl would have read her composition in about the same way. She had a soft low voice, "so low I could not quite catch the import. She did not move her hands except to wipe her face" (Love).

Based upon volume and gesture Love differentiates between a "school girl reading a composition" and a "woman as a speaker." Although some considered speaking softly "an excellent thing in woman" (Love), Love disagreed. Clearly, she does not approve of appropriating typically feminine gestures when ascending the public platform. Simply reading a composition in public does not make a woman a public speaker, but Love's reference to schoolgirls, even those of Clay Seminary, suggests that reading in public was an accepted practice. Mount Holyoke's founder, Mary Lyon, insisted on speaking voices that reached to every corner of the room. Love was educated under Lyon's direction; her earliest training imparted public speaking skills considered progressive, even if that training emphasized delivery more than content. Her letters remain silent as to whether she taught her own students to stand straight, speak loudly, and look the audience in the eye; however, evidence exists suggesting Clay Seminary students acquired public speaking skills under her guidance.

Students taught under the direction of James and Lucy Love utilized principles of elocution and engaged in public rhetoric models similar to those embraced in the 1840s by the Franklin Debate Society. Members of the society discussed contemporary issues, and later debates shifted toward the affirmative/negative model as issues tended to be charged with ideology. One of the latter topics debated was the question: Which is the greater stimulus to the actions of men—the hope of reward or the fear of punishment? (Potts 17). A decade later, in 1856, members of the Mary Lyon Literary Society at Clay Seminary took sides and debated the same question (Liberty *Weekly Tribune*). The youngest students at Clay Seminary participated in dialogue and debate typically reserved for adult males, but these schoolgirls debated during public exhibitions before hundreds of spectators. Students in Clay Seminary's Eunomian Society, comprised of advanced "collegiate"-level students, debated topics of common interest that avoided incendiary issues: Should there be a different mode of educating the sexes? (June 15, 1858); Are public examinations beneficial to the pupil? (June 21, 1860); Which enjoys life most, the man of business or the man of leisure? (June 21, 1860);

Is one out of the world when out of the fashion? (June 10, 1862); Which has achieved the greater, genius or industry? (June 18, 1863); Is truth most effective with mankind? (June 23, 1864) (Clay Seminary Papers). Eunomian announcements indicate that, as in debates conducted by men, at least two girls argued for each side, affirmative or negative. The winning side was announced according to the society president's decision, and a "Critic's Report" was presented by another member. Students also participated in soliloquies and presented original compositions and speeches.

INVISIBLE YOUNG LADIES IN VISIBLE
SCHOOL EXHIBITIONS

The *Liberty Weekly Tribune* routinely published articles of examinations and literary exhibitions held by local female schools, including students' names and the titles of their compositions and debate topics. Reviews underscore the value of Liberty's female institutions, and most reviews were positive. Commencement and examination exercises at Clay Seminary drew overflowing crowds eager to hear students answer questions, read essays, perform music, and give speeches. The Mary Lyon Literary Society conducted a debate and presented a "Port Folio" consisting of a "manuscript paper, issued monthly, filled with original contributions" (Liberty *Weekly Tribune,* June 27, 1856). The writer praised Clay Seminary students as "young ladies who could write as well as study and speak." The Board of Visitors printed testimonials of "the searching and thorough character" of examination to which the young ladies were subjected "before crowded audience, and praised their success" (Liberty *Weekly Tribune,* August 1, 1856). Another article recognized that examination exercises induced "thought, reflection, reason, discrimination, methodical preparation, logical disquisition and analysis, and mental activity and acquisitiveness" (Liberty *Weekly Tribune,* June 29, 1860). One writer also spoke of the "absence of all those clap-trap deceptions and parrot-like performances, which are too often attendant on occasions of this kind. The shadow was absent—the substance was present" (Liberty *Weekly Tribune,* June 26, 1860).

On July 25, 1862, the *Liberty Weekly Tribune* printed the only existing valedictory speech of a student at Clay Seminary. The speech was submitted and published at the request of six community members, and both the original request and the student's written response appeared before the text of the speech. Henrietta Clay George received a brief note stating that the venue at which she had spoken had been too full for all to hear her speak, and the members of the community, "having heard it highly spoken of, and being very desirous to see it in print, would respectfully solicit a copy for publication" (Liberty *Weekly Tribune,* July 25, 1862). She disclaimed "just title to the distinction" conferred upon her, but exhibited no surprise at being asked and submitted the manuscript to be disposed of at their discretion. George, often referred to as Henri or Clay, had presented a speech infused with war rhetoric, an oration that exhibits knowledge of the sectional struggle as well as its effects beyond national borders.

George's valedictory speech, written within the school walls and presented on the academic platform before teachers, parents, family, and neighbors, is hardly representative of a secluded schoolgirl unaccustomed to public speaking and refers to subjects supposedly not mentioned in school or within the home circle at Clay Seminary. She speaks of herself and other students as those who have "peacefully and without interruption gathered around the shrine of wisdom," yet acknowledges a connection with the masses "who are now enacting their part in the fearful drama, which the world's grand stage is now exhibiting to wondering and tearful eyes." School walls could not exclude "the dread tocsin of war [that] pealed aloud its thunder tones, to arouse from the lethargy of peace and security, and call to arms our once united and happy country. Its wild and thrilling notes were heard from ocean to ocean, and were reverberated from the snow clad forests of Maine, to the gulf-bound shores of the sunny South" (Liberty *Weekly Tribune,* July 25, 1862).

George speaks not as an invisible, sheltered schoolgirl or southern belle, but as female orator well aware of the present political and social struggle reaching beyond national borders:

> like a vivid flash through the gathering storm, it darted its forked tongues on the sky of astounded Europe, and excited an interest among foreign powers, most absorbing and intense, and these now gaze with eagle eye, upon the rising storm, which heaves to the very centre, the grand "Old Ship of State," which has safely braved the storms and tempests of external opposition, but to be buffeted by the waves of internal dissensions.

Turning to the graduation at hand, she speaks of drawing back the "curtain of oblivion over so soul-sickening a picture, and with tearful eye, turn to scan for a moment, that more pleasing subject, the human mind, in its relations to our future destinies, to the cultivation and improvement of which, all our powers have been directed for some years past." She directs her attention to the students remaining in school: "you will soon take your stand by our sides, recognized as sisters leagued together for the accomplishment of the same great purpose." She urges them not to shrink back from the call of duty, but to "go boldly forth clad in the armor of truth, thoroughly prepared for the struggles of life; and to give battle to the opposers of right." In conclusion she states, "There is only one boon that we ask, and that is not to be forgotten" (Liberty *Weekly Tribune,* July 25, 1862). George's speech must have made a deep impression upon those present, deep enough to ensure publication for posterity. It represents the only remaining speech written by a student at Clay Seminary, a faithful witness of their ability to write and speak, and a public testimony that girls occupied a place in the public sphere. George and the other graduates continued to find a place in Liberty's history, as the members of the graduating class of 1862 were referred to in local newspapers after the turn of the century. And for some girls, the experience at Clay prepared them for a life in public speaking.

In her autobiography, Carrie Nation suggests that debating at Clay Seminary was instrumental in laying a foundation for her future, and letters written from Kansas jail cells indicate she never forgot James and Lucy Love for the part they played. Nation is well known for her participation in the temperance movement. Scholars believe public speaking training served as the basis from which she drew authority for her public stance (Nation). In between throwing billiard balls and stones through saloon windows or wielding her infamous ax, she addressed the mothers of America on the evils of liquor (Nation). The only remaining account of a student's participation in a public discussion or debate is found in Nation's autobiography. Although written decades after the experience and crafted in hindsight, the account merits attention as evidence that southern schoolgirls participated in debate and public speaking.

As a girl of eighteen, Carrie Nation, then Carrie Moore, attended Clay Seminary for one year. Here she encountered public speaking for the first time. An argument in the classroom turned into a topic for debate to be used at the upcoming exhibition for the Eunomian Society. When Nation was called up to argue her side of the question, she was unprepared and later wrote that she "was taken by surprise and was in confusion, when I saw the room crowded." She wrote that when called to enter the debate, she looked ridiculously blank. "The president tried to keep her face straight," and Nation "got no further than 'Miss President.' All burst out in uncontrollable laughter. I went to my seat put my face in my arms and turned my back to the audience." She was humiliated and disgraced and thought of the shame she was bringing to her parents, and "how ever after this I must be considered a 'Silly' by my schoolmates. These things nerved me. I dried my tears, turned around in my seat, looked up, and the moral force it required to do this was almost equal to that which smashed a saloon" (Nation).

Nation continued with simple reasoning, discussing and debating why "animals have reason" in "homely style and spoke with a vehemence which said: 'I will make my point.' Which I did amidst the cheers of the school" (Nation). Her candid account not only represents the only written record of a student's experience at Clay Seminary, it also describes one of the last debates during its final session in 1865. Under the direction of other professors, the school continued to follow a similar curriculum, but by the late 1870s public examinations involved performances in elocution, essay reading, and spelling bees, and apparently did not require the same level of skill witnessed under James and Lucy Love. Although relatively uneducated compared with her peers and somewhat rough around the edges, as a girl Carrie Moore took part in the shared experiences of female seminary students. Their rhetoric was not as sophisticated as that of adult male members of the Franklin Debate Society or of adult women in the temperance movement, yet they debated with their peers in front of large audiences and then endured the continued public scrutiny carried out in local newspaper articles.

CONCLUSION

Southern girls and young ladies participated in rhetoric and composition in ways that differed from their northern "sisters." Their experiences as female students did not always follow the march of footsteps traveling from invisibility to the rhetorical visibility of reform and temperance movements. Instead, they trod a little softer and more often traced a path toward hearth and home. Some grew up to join the ranks of the suffrage and temperance movements, but more did not. Missouri's female seminaries prepared women for marriage, but during the 1830s and into the 1860s this meant they learned solid subjects alongside the ornamental. Clay Seminary students participated in oration, debate, and composition at a crucial juncture at the nineteenth century when the term *rhetoric* continued to be defined as persuasive public discourse (Mastrangelo 3), and teachers were trained in classical curriculum, including rhetorical principles.

Participating in debates probably prepared sixteen-year-old Minnie Withers, a Clay Seminary graduate, to deliver a public speech to the Confederate "Mounted Rangers" the day troops rode out in the spring of 1861 to report for duty at Jefferson City (Liberty *Weekly Tribune*, May 24). Cordelia Green gained skills that prepared her to teach in Liberty public schools and administer Kansas City's Drumm Institute for orphaned boys with her husband. Administering literary societies and participating in school-sponsored fund-raisers gave Kate Watkins and Mattie Denny skills needed to raise funds for the Southern Aid Society after the Civil War. And Carrie Nation built upon the rhetorical foundation laid at Clay Seminary, while other, less famous students also joined the Women's Christian Temperance Union or fought for women's suffrage.

Clay Seminary students came from Missouri, Pennsylvania, the Nebraska and New Mexico territories, Kentucky, and one student was English by birth. Their fathers were lawyers, merchants, doctors, county clerks, and judges, but many lived in farming households where they helped widowed fathers raise large families, or, like Kate Watkins, participated in household chores and family businesses. Most households owned or hired slaves, but Clay Seminary students did not live on stereotypical plantations. Their lives as "southern belles" and farmers' daughters were decidedly and permanently interrupted by a war that changed their roles as daughters and women. As residents of a border state during a time of intense sectional conflict, Clay Seminary students navigated their way through lessons and public exhibitions under the intense scrutiny of teachers and parents, while Confederate troops marched through the town of Liberty one day and Federal troops the next. And as southern females they participated in public oratory and debate more often attributed to progressive northern seminaries. Clay Seminary was an oasis in the sectional storm bearing down around them, where girls and young women negotiated a space that traversed the private and the public. Yet, Clay Seminary represents only one of Missouri's female schools, and seminary students comprise only a fraction of girls living in Missouri during the antebellum and Civil War years. Their voices, Missouri voices, have yet to be heard, and they, too, might ask with Henri Clay George, "There is only one boon that we ask, and that is not to be forgotten."

WORKS CITED

Buchanan, Lindal. 2005. *Regendering Delivery: The Fifth Canon and Antebellum Women Rhetors*. Carbondale: Southern Illinois University Press.

Christian College, Columbia. 1858–1859. "Annual Announcement and Catalogue." Missouri, Records, 1836–1986 (C0038). Columbia, MO: Western Historical Manuscripts Collection.

Clark, James G. 1893. "James Love." In *History of William Jewell College, Liberty, Clay County, Missouri*, 230–34. Liberty, MO: William Jewell College. http://digital.library.umsystem.edu/cgi/t/text/text-idxsid=440d2e824902d74e7c0f3bfb950b47f3;g=;c=wmjhist;idno=wmj000002.

Clay Seminary Papers. n.d. Liberty, MO: Clay County Archives & Historical Society.

Eldred, Janet Carey, and Peter Mortensen. 2002. *Imagining Rhetoric: Composing Women of the Early United States*. Pittsburgh: Pittsburgh University Press.

Farnham, Christie Ann. 1994. *The Education of the Southern Belle: Higher Education and Student Socialization in the Antebellum South*. New York: New York University Press.

Hunter, Jane H. 2002. *How Young Ladies Became Girls: The Victorian Origins of American Girlhood*. New Haven: Yale University Press.

Liberty Weekly Tribune Newspaper. n.d. Historic Missouri Newspaper Project. www.newspapers.umsystem.edu.

Love, Lucy. n.d. Papers. Liberty, MO: Clay County Archives & Historical Society.

Mastrangelo, Lisa S. 1999. "Learning from the Past: Rhetoric, Composition, and Debate at Mount Holyoke College." *Rhetoric Review* 18.1: 46–64.

Mattingly, Carol. 1998. *Well-Tempered Women: Nineteenth-Century Temperance Rhetoric*. Carbondale: Southern Illinois University Press.

McCandless, Amy Thompson. 1999. *The Past in the Present: Women's Higher Education in the Twentieth-Century American South*. Tuscaloosa: Alabama University Press.

Mount Holyoke College. 2006. "A Detailed History." 26 January. https://www.mtholyoke.edu/cic/about/detailed.shtml.

Nation, Carrie A. 1905. "The Use and Need of the Life of Carrie A. Nation."

Potts, Louis W. 1991. "The Franklin Debate Society: Culture on the Missouri Frontier." *Missouri Historical Review* 83.1: 1–21.

Tibbetts, A. M. 1967. "Argument in Nineteenth-Century American Rhetoric Textbooks." *College Composition and Communication* 18.5: 236–41.

Yantis, Rev. J. L. 1841. #572. Columbia, (Mo.) Female Academy, Address. Western Historical Manuscripts Collection, Columbia, MO.

Student Activity

READING, ANALYSIS, AND REFLECTION

1. How do the references in a research report based in history differ from other references in other approaches?
2. What is the research question for this project?
3. What are the challenges the researcher faced in undertaking this project?
4. What surprised you about this history, uncovered and recovered, by the student researcher?
5. Why is it important to undertake archival research such as this project? What do we learn from it? Why is it significant?
6. Historical research requires interpretation. Do you agree with the findings as determined by this student researcher?

9

Using Mixed-Methods Research

Writing studies is grounded in *practice*. As a result, practitioners—tutors, teachers, program administrators, technical writers, social advocates—often look to research as a way to answer questions and find solutions to problems. This chapter explores how mixed methods may be used to improve practices and products.

In previous chapters specific methods for undertaking research in writing have been examined. In this last chapter a mixed-methods approach is introduced, drawing on the chapters that have come before.

IMPROVING PRACTICE: TUTOR RESEARCH

In the seminal text *The Making of Knowledge in Composition*, Stephen North (1987) lays out three key communities of inquirers: practitioners, scholars, and researchers. Practice as inquiry can create useful knowledge for the field of composition studies. He cautions, though, against the random approach he describes in a metaphorical way as the "House of Lore." It's a charming house, but it's not necessarily useful in producing research based on empirical principles. His description of this house deserves reading:

> A rambling, to my mind, delightful old manse, wing branching off
> from wing, addition tacked to addition, in all sorts of materials—
> brick, wood, canvas, sheet metal, cardboard—with turrets and gables,
> minarets and spires, spiral staircases, rope ladders, pitons, dungeons,
> secrete passageways—all seemingly random, yet all connected. (27)

While practitioner lore is to be valued, it is not the same as rigorous, evidence-based research. Questions about practice come up frequently in tutorial practice. Take the example of four tutors who came to question the value of the plagiarism-checking software, Turnitin. Several students had approached their writing center in a panic, as Turnitin had identified their essays as plagiarized, which they swore was not true. By using textual analysis and case-study method, they demonstrated flaws in the Turnitin system. Renee Brown, Brian Fallon, Jessica Lott, Elizabeth Matthews, and Elizabeth Mentie—undergraduates with the exception of Fallon, who was a graduate student at the time—won the 2007 International Writing Centers Association (IWCA) Best Article Award for their article, "Taking on Turnitin: Tutors Advocating Change" (Brown et al. 2007).

To test their assumptions, they submitted a paper through the Turnitin software and analyzed its results. The foursome argued that Turnitin has both pedagogical limitations and ethical problems in the way it handles student writing because the software oversimplifies what it means to write with sources. In addition, students can learn how to outsmart Turnitin. Tutors and writing centers work with writers from all over the university, they argue, and need to take the lead in plagiarism and citation issues. They recommend teaching citation first and giving workshops so instructors can use Turnitin results as part of a pedagogical approach.

The Turnitin essay was a bellwether for writing center research, demonstrating emphatically that student researchers can add to the knowledge base in writing studies. The editors of *The Writing Center Journal* built upon this fact by designating a 2012 issue of the journal to focus on the disciplinary knowledge created by undergraduate research. A review of the titles of the essays published reveals a range of topics and approaches:

- "Got Guilt? Consultant Guilt in the Writing Center Community"
- "The Power of Common Interest for Motivating Writers: A Case Study"
- "How Are We Doing? A Review of Assessments within Writing Centers"
- "Bridging the Gap: Essential Issues to Address in Recurring Writing Center Appointments with Chinese ELL Students"
- "What a Writer Wants: Assessing Fulfillment of Student Goals in Writing Center Tutoring Sessions"
- "Tutoring Between Languages with Comparative Multilingual Tutoring"
- "Bringing Balance to the Table: Comprehensive Writing Instruction in the Tutoring Session"

Tutors are in unique positions to make inquiries about practice, as they are on the ground (or in a digital sphere), working individually with student writers, on a daily basis. They are often called on for spur-of-the-moment solutions to problems. Muriel Harris's (1991b) article focuses on daily issues in writing center administration, noting solutions but also trade-offs; this article inspired a group of tutors to think critically about their own work in a writing-fellows program as tutors (Kinkead et al. 1995). Writing fellows and writing center tutors usually meet to talk about their work in meetings and practica, where these kinds of conversations occur naturally. There is also the advantage that dissemination opportunities for students to share their research broadly have existed since 1984 with the *Writing Lab Newsletter*'s Tutor's Column as well as professional meetings such as the National Conference on Peer Tutoring in Writing that started shortly thereafter.

A useful taxonomy of methodologies for writing center research has been mapped by Sarah Liggett, Kerri Jordan, and Steve Price (Liggett, Jordan, and Price 2011b). Note in Figure 9.1 that they include methods that have already been addressed in this text: historical inquiry, textual analysis, case study, ethnography. Practitioner inquiry privileges the experience of tutoring and the reflection that accompanies it. Two tutors, Heather Bastian and Lindsey Harkness, wrote about the importance of self-reflection in their essay, "When Peer Tutors Write about Writing: Literacy Narratives and Self Reflection" (Bastian and Harkness 2003). This case study and textual analysis, published in the inaugural issue of *Young Scholars in Writing*, is an excellent example of practitioner inquiry—using narrative—that also draws on other methods. Bastian and Harkness make their study more than just stories about tutors by seeing implications for practice. Other examples of narrative inquiry in the context of tutoring and writing centers include *The Everyday Writing Center* (Geller et al. 2007), *Noise from the Writing Center* (Boquet 2002), *Stories from the Center: Connecting Narrative and Theory in the Writing Center* (Briggs and Woolbright 2000), and *Researching the Writing Center: Toward an Evidence-Based Practice* (Babcock and Thonus 2012).

Liggett, Jordan, and Price (2011b) believe researchers engaging in conceptual inquiry "study texts to create interpretations of what happens within writing centers and beyond in the broader contexts of writing programs and institutional hierarchies" (64). The study of texts may include "student writing, transcripts of tutorials, writing center documents such as manuals or mission statements or even the visual, oral, and technological contexts of center activities" (64).

Studying the architecture of a writing center falls into that latter category, which is just what tutor Leslie Hadfield did with two other students in interior design, a research project that resulted in a detailed analysis of what an "ideal" writing center might look like. Based on the question, can space have an impact on writing? the team interviewed tutors,

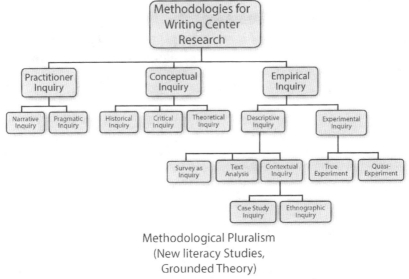

FIGURE 9.1. A taxonomy of methodologies for writing center research.

writing center administrators, and student writers using the writing center to determine the best design for a comfortable learning space (Hadfield et al. 2003). They also reviewed the literature on academic architecture to place their design within the context of architectural theory. They learned that task performance and job satisfaction are negatively affected by ambient conditions such as uncomfortable room temperature, stuffy air quality, lack of natural light, loud colors, and noise. Good rooms don't necessarily make teachers good, but bad rooms certainly don't help. Patrons of the writing center wanted a calming, nonthreatening, and easily understood space. The first-time visitor is wondering, "Will I be welcome here? Is this a situation where I might be embarrassed?" Their findings resulted in a model (see Fig. 9.2) delineating the sections of the writing center; in addition to this mock-up of the tutorial space, they also created lighting plans, plumbing specifications, and recommendations for furniture, even advocating particular fabrics.

The classification of empirical inquiry offers two tracks, one descriptive and one experimental. The former is more widely used in writing center research and relies on surveys, textual analysis, case study, and ethnography. (Note that *text* occurs here yet again as it did in practitioner inquiry, a signal of how important texts are in writing studies research.) Liggett, Jordan, and Price (2011b), in the end, argue for methodological pluralism in writing center research, using the metaphor of the global positioning system (GPS) as opposed to the linear taxonomy depicted

FIGURE 9.2A. Writing center models.

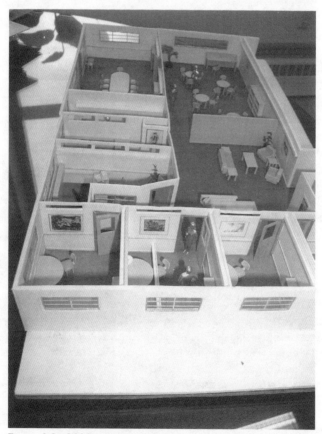

FIGURE 9.2B. Writing center models.

earlier. In this GPS version of methods, the researcher is a "traveler" who knows the destination and is "in search of a way to proceed" (81).

Here are samples of topics tutors might explore in research:

- the tutorial conversation
- English-language learners and tutoring
- tutoring spaces
- gender and tutoring
- novice and experienced tutors
- administration of writing-tutoring programs
- tutors' knowledge of writing/composition studies
- working with nontraditional students
- the institutional context of tutoring: two-year college; private, liberal-arts college; research university
- tutoring writing in international settings—beyond the United States
- histories of tutoring
- tutor-training manuals
- tutor-training seminars
- mentors and tutors
- technology and tutoring
- online writing labs (OWLs)
- synchronous versus asynchronous tutorial sessions
- group tutorials
- writing centers versus writing-fellows programs
- record keeping and tutoring
- tutorials and the relationship to classroom writing (and to the teachers of those classes)
- tutor writing and publication
- tutors and professional conferences and publications
- tutors as alumni (Where are they now?)
- students (undergraduate, graduate), paraprofessionals, staff who work as tutors
- approaches to tutoring: direct instruction, reader response
- the problem of assignments
- tutors and flexibility
- writers' needs
- proofreading and editing
- plagiarism and academic honesty
- the listening tutor
- tutorials and revision strategies
- basic writers and tutoring
- writing across the curriculum/writing in the disciplines and tutors
- titles for tutors

- errors and tutoring
- genres and tutoring
- handbooks and reference guides for tutoring
- professional journals: *Writing Lab Newsletter; The Writing Center Journal*
- the meaning of *peer* in peer tutoring
- the professional and personal development of the writing tutor
- budgets and writing centers
- schedules: drop-in, appointments
- counting beans: record keeping and tutoring
- difficult students and tutors: emergency preparedness
- writing center administration and tutor relationships
- tutoring and special-topic workshops
- tutors and graduate-school admissions

The topics for research by tutors are almost limitless. As with any research project, the tutor undertaking the project must be invested in the topic, and to truly contribute to knowledge, it must be a topic that has not yet been addressed. Expanding knowledge about tutoring and writing studies is a worthy goal, and there are multiple methodological pathways to achieve that goal.

Tutors work not only in centralized writing centers. *Writing-fellows* programs feature tutors who are attached to specific classes and work in a decentralized way. The sample student research essay that illustrates the mixed methods approach of this chapter (McMunn and Reifer 2006) grew out of their work as writing fellows at La Salle University.

Profile of a Student Researcher: Samantha Latham

A tutor in the university writing center, Samantha was intrigued when a request from the biology department asked if it were possible to have writing tutors help students with writing in their science classes. Although these students could visit the central writing center, the department felt that a specific program for its students might be efficacious. Samantha set out to find possible models for a biology writing center. Conducting a review of literature, including a review of writing center sites from around the country, she identified common tutorial models for students in disciplines other than English. The options she presented in her resulting report included keeping the status quo model but integrating discipline-specific training for tutors; a satellite writing center housed in the biology department; online tutoring with integrated discipline-specific training; and discipline-specific writing labs/workshops. Samantha created a poster to communicate these recommendations, which was also presented at the 2014 International Writing Centers Association Conference.

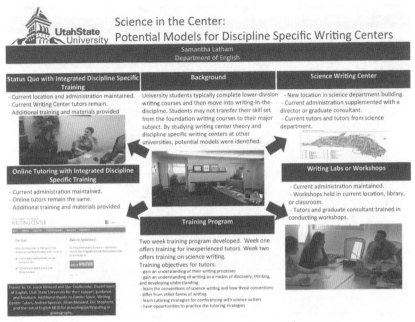

Figure 9.3. Research poster depicting models for a science writing center.

ABOUT THE RESEARCH ESSAY THAT FOLLOWS

Renee Brown, Brian Fallon, Jessica Lott, Elizabeth Matthews, and Elizabeth Mintie (2007) won the outstanding scholarship award from the International Writing Centers Association (IWCA) for their investigation, "Taking on Turnitin: Tutors Advocating Change." They sought to better understand the relationship between the plagiarism-detection service Turnitin.com and their writing center (Brown et al. 2007). To test claims made by the company, they submitted a few sample papers. From their research, they argue that there are serious pedagogical limitations and unethical dimensions to the program. This exemplary study is one of the readings for this chapter.

REFERENCES AND FOR FURTHER READING

Babcock, Rebecca Day, and Teresa Thonus. 2012. *Researching the Writing Center: Toward an Evidence-Based Practice.* Bern: Peter Lang. http://dx.doi.org /10.3726/978-1-4539-0869-3.

Babcock, Rebecca Day, Kellye Manning, Travis Rogers, and Courtney Goff. 2012. *A Synthesis of Qualitative Studies of Writing Center Tutoring, 1983–2006.* Bern: Peter Lang.

Bartholomae, David, and Anthony Petrosky. 2005. *Ways of Reading: An Anthology for Writers.* 7th ed. Boston: Bedford/St. Martins.

Bastian, Heather, and Lindsey Harkness. 2003. "When Peer Tutors Write about Writing: Literacy Narratives and Self Reflection." *Young Scholars in Writing* 1:77–94.

Bissex, Glenda L., and Richard H. Bullock. 1987. *Seeing for Ourselves: Case-Study Research by Teachers of Writing.* Portsmouth, NH: Heinemann.

Boquet, Elizabeth H. 2002. *Noise from the Writing Center.* Logan: Utah State University Press.

Briggs, Lynn Craigue, and Meg Woolbright, eds. 2000. *Stories from the Center: Connecting Narrative and Theory in the Writing Center.* Urbana, IL: NCTE.

Brown, Renee, Brian Fallon, Jessica Lott, Elizabeth Matthews, and Elizabeth Mentie. 2007. "Taking on Turnitin: Tutors Advocating Change." *Writing Center Journal* 27 (1): 7–28.

Chewning, Bill. 2007. "Recent Activity in the Expanding Center: Creating an Online Presence for the UMBC Writing Center." *Young Scholars in Writing* 5:50–62.

Cochran-Smith, Marilyn, and Susan Lytle. 2010. *Inquiry as Stance: Practitioner Research for the Next Generation.* New York: Teachers College Press.

Cooke, Deanna, and Trisha Thorme. 2011. *A Practical Handbook for Supporting Community-Based Research with Undergraduate Students.* Washington, DC: Council on Undergraduate Research.

Daiker, Donald A., and Max Morenberg. 1990. *The Writing Teacher as Researcher.* Portsmouth, NH: Heinemann.

Doucette, Jonathon. 2011. "Composing Queers: The Subversive Potential of the Writing Center." *Young Scholars in Writing* 8:5–15.

Dryer, Dylan B. 2012. "At a Mirror, Darkly: The Imagined Undergraduate Writers of Ten Novice Composition Instructors." *College Composition and Communication* 63 (3): 420–52.

Fels, Dawn, and Jennifer Wells. 2011. *The Successful High School Writing Center.* New York: Teachers College Press.

Geller, Anne Ellen, Michele Eodice, Frankie Condon, Meg Carroll, and Elizabeth H. Boquet. 2007. *The Everyday Writing Center: A Community of Practice.* Logan: Utah State University Press.

Gillespie, Paula, Alice Gillam, Lady Falls Brown, and Byron Stay, eds. 2002. *Writing Center Research: Extending the Conversation.* Mahwah, NJ: Erlbaum.

Goswami, Dixie, and Peter R. Stillman, eds. 1987. *Reclaiming the Classroom: Teacher Research as an Agency for Change.* Portsmouth, NH: Heinemann.

Grobman, Laurie. 2015. "(Re)Writing Local Racial, Ethnic, and Cultural Histories: Negotiating Shared Meaning in Public Rhetoric Partnerships." *College English* 77 (3): 236–58.

Hadfield, Leslie, Stephanie Ray, Joyce Kinkead, Tom Peterson, and Stephanie Morgan. 2003. "An Idea Writing Center: Re-Imagining Space and Design." In *The Center Will Hold: Critical Perspectives on Writing Center Scholarship*, edited by Michael Pemberton and Joyce Kinkead, 166–76. Logan: Utah State University Press.

Harris, Muriel. 1991a. "Assignments from Hell." Conference on College Composition and Communication *Word Works* 45 (September). Accessed May 30, 2008. http://www.boisestate.edu/wcenter/Word%20Works%2045.pdf.

Harris, Muriel. 1991b. "Solutions and Trade-Offs in Writing Center Administration." *Writing Center Journal* 12 (1): 63–80.

Hudson, Sue. 1991. "Rites of Passage: Assignments that Work." *Word Works,* 46 (October). http://www.boisestate.edu/wcenter/wordworks19861994.html.

International Writing Centers Association. n.d. http://writingcenters.org/.

Kinkead, Joyce. 1993. "Taking Tutoring on the Road." In *Writing Centers in Context: Twelve Case Studies,* edited by Joyce Kinkead and Jeanette Harris, 210–15. Urbana, IL: National Council of Teachers of English.

Kinkead, Joyce, Nanette Alderman, Brett Baker, Alan Freer, Jon Hertzke, Sonya Mildon Hill, Jennifer Obray, Tiffany Parker, and Maryann Peterson. 1995. "Situations and Solutions for Tutoring across the Curriculum." *Writing Lab Newsletter* 19 (8): 1–5.

Kinkead, Joyce, and Jeanette Harris, eds. 1993. *Writing Centers in Context: Twelve Case Studies.* Urbana, IL: National Council of Teachers of English.

Liggett, Sarah, Kerri Jordan, and Steve Price. 2011a. "Makers of Knowledge in Writing Centers: Practitioners, Scholars, and Researchers at Work." In *The Changing of Knowledge in Composition: Contemporary Perspectives,* edited by Lance Massey and Richard Gebhardt, 102–20. Logan: Utah State University Press.

Liggett, Sarah, Kerri Jordan, and Steve Price. 2011b. "Mapping Knowledge-Making in Writing Center Research: A Taxonomy of Methodologies." *Writing Center Journal* 31 (2): 50–88.

McLeod, Susan H., and Margot Soven, eds. 1992. *Writing Across the Curriculum: A Guide to Developing Programs.* Newbury Park, CA: SAGE.

McMunn, Andrea, and Jessica Reifer. 2006. "Determining the Effectiveness of La Salle University's Writing-Across-the-Curriculum Requirement in the Biology Major." *Young Scholars in Writing* 4:73–93.

MacLean, Marion S., and Marian M. Mohr. 1999. *Teacher-Researchers at Work.* Berkeley, CA: National Writing Project.

Mauriello, Nicholas, William Macauley Jr., and Robert Koch. 2012. *Before and After the Tutorial: Writing Centers and Institutional Relationships.* Cresskill, NJ: Hampton.

Mohr, Marian M., and Marion S. MacLean. 1987. *Working Together: A Guide for Teacher-Researchers.* Urbana, IL: NCTE.

North, Stephen. 1987. *The Making of Knowledge in Composition: Portrait of an Emerging Field.* Montclair, NJ: Boynton/Cook.

Schendel, Ellen, and William J. Macauley Jr. 2012. *Building Writing Center Assessments That Matter.* Logan: Utah State University Press.

Smith, Frank. 1982. *Writing and the Writer.* New York: Holt, Rinehart.

Soven, Margot K. 1996. *Write to Learn: A Guide to Writing Across the Curriculum.* Cincinnati, OH: South-Western.

"Taking on Turnitin: Tutors Advocating Change"

Renee Brown, Brian Fallon, Jessica Lott, Elizabeth Matthews, and Elizabeth Mintie

Like many writing centers, ours trained us to respond to writers whose papers might involve plagiarism; we learned to show students how to use various paraphrasing techniques and how to cite sources. In staff meetings, we talked about why it was more important to understand the causes of students' plagiarism than to judge them for it. Then one day, a student walked into our writing center and said that she had submitted a paper to her professor online, as required, only to learn a little later that her paper had been reported to her professor as plagiarized. Visibly upset, this student asked that we help her with this paper so that she could resubmit it and avoid failing the course. She also showed us this statement in the course syllabus: "Students agree that by taking this course all required papers/reports/tests may be subject to submission for textual similarity review to Turnitin.com for the detection of plagiarism." This was the boilerplate language recommended to professors at our institution who chose to use Turnitin.com, a web-based plagiarism detection service, in their courses (Sherwood). Before our tutors had time to decide how best to respond to this experience, other panicked students came in with similar stories. We felt helpless to do anything for these students because we understood so little about Turnitin or their professors' literacy expectations and values. Were the students really plagiarizing? Could Turnitin point the finger at them and cause them to fail

Renee Brown, Brian Fallon, Jessica Lott, Elizabeth Matthews, and Elizabeth Mintie, "Taking on Turnitin: Tutors Advocating Change," *Writing Center Journal* 27, no. 1 (2007): 7–28.

the course? How does Turnitin work? The answers to these questions, we discovered, were not to be found easily. Our director, Ben Rafoth, suggested that we investigate and then share what we learned with others at the university and in the writing center community.

As both students and tutors, we had concerns about the Turnitin software being used at our university. It was easy for us to identify with students who felt helpless when dealing with a software program that could seal their fates. We found it harder to identify with the values of their professors and of the Turnitin officials who made students use the program without providing important background information and without helping them to interpret the results. As we began to learn more about the program—more, actually, than we suspected even the faculty knew—we had to confront another question: How much should tutors tell students about Turnitin? If we decided to say nothing, we were tacitly supporting the way Turnitin was being used. If we told what we had learned, we were entering a realm of discourse that we might not be able to sustain and could even get in trouble for. With some encouragement, we decided to keep investigating and to go wherever our search led us.

We began our mission with two goals: What did our writing center staff need to know about Turnitin? And, how could tutors help students who must deal with Turnitin and the professors who require it? As we delved into these questions, we felt a growing sense that we were looking at very different values and expectations when it comes to student writing than we had learned during our training and our combined years of experience. We combed through websites and talked to students and faculty, collecting evidence that was sometimes technical, frequently changing, and often confusing. Our aim was to learn as much as we could about Turnitin and how it affects our peers so that we could tell students, faculty, and others in the writing center community what we had learned and how it might affect them. Although the students who visited the writing center concerned about Turnitin prompted our inquiry, we felt that our findings were best used when we considered the pitfalls and possibilities for tutoring involved. As a foundation for the work we embarked on, we held to some notions about plagiarism, writing centers, and tutors that we feel are important for grounding this discussion.

PLAGIARISM, TUTORS, WRITING CENTERS: A COMPLICATED TRIO

Our research began with the practical challenge of what to say to students who brought papers to us that had been identified by Turnitin as containing plagiarized material. In some cases students had received papers back from their professors because Turnitin had flagged them as plagiarized, and they were now being asked to correct plagiarized passages and submit revised versions. These students came to our writing center and said, "Here's what Turnitin said I plagiarized, so how do I fix it?" In other cases students were about to submit their finished papers to Turnitin, as they were required to do, and were worried that the program would accuse them of plagiarism. This challenge, though, soon led us in a number of directions that would help us to offer the best advice possible to students and to discover what kinds of roles we as tutors and the writing center play in campus conversations on plagiarism. In order to find the right words to say to students who visit with Turnitin concerns, we had to understand plagiarism better, the stance writing center literature takes on plagiarism, and what kinds of institutional roles tutors can play.

As students, we began to feel that our own perceptions on plagiarism, mainly that it is academic dishonesty, were problematic because what Turnitin had flagged as plagiarism didn't seem to suggest that students were intentionally being dishonest. With the help of our assistant director, we looked to composition studies for some answers and considered some of Rebecca Moore Howard's thoughts on plagiarism. Through an exploration of her work, we began to expand our understanding of plagiarism by taking into account Howard's attention to patchwriting in her *Standing in the Shadow of Giants: Plagiarists, Authors, Collaborators.* Students are often criminalized for being patchwriters, Howard argues, when, in actuality, even the most professional writers are merely sophisticated patchwriters. She establishes a pedagogical space for patchwriting, which she refers to as, "a process of evaluating a source text, selecting passages pertinent to the patchwriter's purposes, and transporting those passages to the patchwriter's new context" (xviii). Furthermore, Howard, elsewhere, calls for the replacement of plagiarism with the categories of *fraud, citation,* and *repetition* ("Sexuality, Textuality" 488). In addition to Howard, Kurt Bouman has strongly suggested that differences in cultural and academic expectations can lead some students, particularly international students, to make choices that would be deemed wrong by an American academic audience. Given what we learned from our initial exploration into discussions of plagiarism in composition studies and what we've witnessed from students with Turnitin concerns, we have decided to reserve the term *fraudulent plagiarism* for instances in which there is, beyond a doubt, true intent by writers to submit work that is not their own. We have made this decision primarily because any discussion on plagiarism should not automatically assume that any text that imitates another text or lacks originality is a result of a criminal act.

With a better sense of how experts in the field define plagiarism, we began to think carefully about what the writing center's stance is when it comes to plagiarism. As we noted at the beginning of this article, an issue for us as tutors centered on what we would say to a student whom we knew was plagiarizing. Luckily for us, this scenario has not happened very often, but we still had to consider what kinds of positions we could possibly take on this issue. Would we establish a set of procedures like tutors Jennifer Herrick and Mark Niquette did in their "Ethics in the Writing Lab: Tutoring under the Honor Code"? Would we casually take a walk with the writer and describe to them what's at stake by choosing to plagiarize? As our research developed, we realized that we had to take a step beyond our training, that our response to such a situation had to be informed by what scholars were saying about the writing center's tempestuous past and present relationship to plagiarism. In their "Plagiarism, Rhetorical Theory, and the Writing Center: New Approaches, New Locations," Linda Shamoon and Deborah H. Burns provided not only a history of this relationship but some answers to the questions we had about how the writing center might approach the issue of plagiarism in general.

According to Shamoon and Burns, the writing center literature mainly focuses on defending our institutional spaces against accusations that writers receive too much help when they visit. They present three responses to charges of plagiarism that the writing center literature has provided: "[W]e recount the nature of the writing process, we explain the importance of feedback for all writers, and we offer pointers about how peer tutors can negotiate the border between the 'legitimate' practice of giving advice and the 'illegitimate' practice of writing too much on the paper" (184). However, Shamoon and Burns are quick to point out the philosophical discrepancies inherent in these three responses when they are measured against our beliefs about writing and the realities we face while tutoring. The perspective they ultimately endorse is a *social-rhetorical* one that "would make interpellation more conscious because it articulates the constructed nature of subject matter, of disciplinary thinking and questioning, of the related features of the discourse (including paper features), and of the values and expectations of a specific reader or audience" (191). In line with their recommendation to approach tutoring from this perspective, we believe that our job as tutors is to help students come to new meanings, understandings, and ideas through their writing and to do so while situating themselves in the kinds of disciplinary conversations their teachers expect of them.

This is not an easy task, but what we've learned about plagiarism, particularly in Howard's explanation of patchwriting, tells us that complicated plagiarism issues most likely happen in the writing center more frequently than we may have thought. That is, if all writers are essentially patchwriters and if students are particularly prone to having their patchwriting critiqued as cheating, then we, as tutors, have a dilemma on our hands every time we work with students who are already under suspicion for plagiarizing. Since our job entails walking the line between what type of writing is expected in the student's discipline and how the student is prepared to meet those expectations, we may find ourselves wandering into disciplinary conversations about plagiarism that aren't so pretty. In taking this approach, how we respond to plagiarism cannot be framed in terms of ethics or a misconception of writing center practice, as Shamoon and Burns suggest, because a *social-rhetorical* approach to writing center pedagogy "views the issue of plagiarism as a social and rhetorical construct, and rather than sidestep the issue of plagiarism by claiming to build a fence around collaboration and tutoring, such a writing center inserts itself into a conversation about the rhetorical and social nature of the disciplines" (192). We are left to ponder how tutors, as the main practitioners in our writing centers, might insert themselves into such a conversation, especially now that Turnitin has presented us with new challenges to our tutoring and to our institutional positions.

Of course, the time we spent researching Turnitin was extensive, and we had the opportunity to present our findings both locally and nationally, but the persistent issue of who is really listening to us, the tutors, kept nagging us throughout this project. During our first presentation to the English faculty here at Indiana University of Pennsylvania (IUP), we became aware that showing professors what Turnitin is all about and how it is influencing their teaching could potentially put us in the political hot seat. How would they respond to us, their students, but also their other students' tutors? At the end of the day, the information we had to share was well received, and the faculty in our audience were there because they wanted to hear what we had to say, hut this was the first time we had to ask ourselves about the potential risks involved in becoming advocates for students who have had bad Turnitin experiences. In considering a political and pedagogical space for our research, we found it necessary to step outside the traditional roles of writing center tutors in order to make claims about how Turnitin was influencing teaching on our campus. Thinking about Shamoon and Burn's social-rhetorical approach to writing center work led us to the conclusion that there was, or at least should be, an arena for tutors to discuss campus-wide issues that affect tutoring. In Harvey Kail and John Trimbur's "The Politics of Peer Tutoring," they argue that, "[locating the sources of knowledge in the social fabric rather than in the power lines of generation and transmission offers a way to talk about peer tutoring that goes beyond the operational model of plugging tutors into the grid" (207). We began to consider the kind of knowledge we could bring to the social fabric of our institution and other ways that Kail and Trimbur's statement informs our situation almost twenty years after they originally made it.

We are not interested in being plugged into the Turnitin grid just because some faculty and administrators on our campus have chosen to use the program. Instead, we would like to offer up our voice along with the voices of students who have been informed about this decision as a way to cautiously approach what Turnitin means for learning and teaching on our campus. Although the debates about peer tutoring may have focused on collaborative learning in the university, we have reinterpreted our goals in line with Kail and Trimbur in that "[t]he experience of co-learning changes students and helps them to see that the power ascribed to the faculty depends on the students' own sense of powerlessness and [the faculty's] need for omnipotent authority" (209). What we came to recognize at our writing center is that we had an opportunity to inform students about what Turnitin does and how their teachers are using it so they could make informed decisions on how to approach their professors and engage their own texts. If we took the time, together, with students to pose problems with what Turnitin said they plagiarized and explained why it had said so, then we'd be doing productive work in our writing center rather than working to just fix the supposed problem areas of flagged texts. We would, in a sense, have to forgo how the institution intended to use Turnitin and help students in these situations to see the choices they have, to feel more confident in how they use sources, and to identify themselves as writers who intricately manipulate and synthesize texts for their own purposes.

With this complex nexus of plagiarism, writing centers, and tutor roles as a base, we will now turn our attention to how Turnitin works from technological, legal, and ethical perspectives; how students seem to be responding to the increasing use of plagiarism detection services; and how Turnitin limits pedagogical options and opportunities. Finally, we will offer some perspectives on what tutors can do both in their sessions and on their campuses to have their voices heard in a discussion on plagiarism detection services.

HOW TURNITIN WORKS

Understanding how Turnitin functions and the purposes for which it is used by an institution proved vital to any discussion we had about the program. We should note, however, that Turnitin updates the information it provides online regularly and has done so since we first began our research. The information provided from Turnitin's web site in this article was collected in March 2006. Likewise, the information we present throughout this section is also influenced by the kinds of programming parameters set for our institution, which means that different institutions can customize aspects of the program for their own purposes. What we present in this piece demonstrates the issues that we have dealt with here at Indiana University of Pennsylvania (IUP) with our new subscription to Turnitin.

For starters, we found that the corporation behind Turnitin claims to have an educational purpose. In fact, banners on their website tout that they are "focused on education" ("Products and Services"). Turnitin's website hosts an online interface where students can submit work to professors, comment on their peers' work, and review their grades. Although these services are similar to those provided by other educational resources such as WebCT and Blackboard, Turnitin is unique because as "the standard in online plagiarism prevention," Turnitin also claims to "help educators and students take full advantage of the internet's educational potential" by scanning every paper submitted for "measurable rates of plagiarism" ("Plagiarism Prevention").

Bill Marsh's "Turnitin.com and the Scriptural Enterprise of Plagiarism Detection" offers a thorough description of how Turnitin operates, specifically dealing with the way Turnitin "maps identity, codes writing, and manages transgression in the service of broader, historically entrenched values of authorial propriety and educational achievement" (427–428). Our analysis echoes much of the work done by Marsh, and we recommend his article for those who are investigating Turnitin, but we have included our observations since they were not only the results of researching the Turnitin website but also our own experimentation with the program.

Turnitin's capacity to detect plagiarism is actually based on the matches it makes between similar sequences of text ("Product Tour"). When students or professors submit work on Turnitin's interface, proprietary algorithms convert the text into what Turnitin calls a "digital fingerprint," a unique sequence of code that has meaning only within Turnitin's technological interface. Turnitin's web crawlers compare these "fingerprints" to the 4.5 million student papers and archived websites Turnitin claims to have in its proprietary database. The database then retains a copy of the "fingerprint" to compare against future student submissions. When the code sequence of a submitted paper matches a file within Turnitin's database, Turnitin highlights the matching text and creates a link to the source in its database. The instructor receives an originality report with a color-coded Similarity Index that shows the total percentage of text in the submitted document that matched text from sources in the database. (Again, see Marsh's article for a thorough explanation of Turnitin's scriptural similarity and originality reports).

Once a paper is submitted to Turnitin, its "fingerprint" remains in the proprietary database indefinitely ("Product Tour"). This feature distinguishes Turnitin from other plagiarism prevention programs, such as Essay Verification Engine and IntegriGuard, because other programs do not maintain a database of student work. Turnitin claims that retaining these fingerprints does not infringe upon students' copyrights because the proprietary algorithms it applies convert the text into a new product, the fingerprint, even though they convert it back to its original format to produce originality reports ("Legal Document"). Turnitin's lawyers explain this sleight of hand as follows: "The fingerprint is merely a digital code, which relays the unprotectable factual information that certain predefined content is present in the work . . . the fingerprint does not include any of the work's actual contents, and is therefore neither a copy nor a true derivative of the original text" ("Legal Document"). In other words, according to Turnitin's legal team, the code products of Turnitin's algorithms contain information about the text rather than the actual text, just as a physical fingerprint contains information about a finger rather than the actual finger. This analogy is questionable, however. A student's text can, and is, reconstructed from Turnitin's "digital fingerprint," whereas a physical finger cannot be reconstructed from a fingerprint.

This reconstruction of text poses an ethical dilemma pertaining to students' ownership of their work, as well as a privacy issue. Tutors in our writing center found that students who are enrolled in classes using Turnitin are not always aware that the database retains a fingerprint of their work. When we experimented with the program in December 2005, we created a fictional student and then later submitted a small portion of an actual paper that was written for a graduate-level criminology course in April. When we obtained consent to use the paper, we asked the writer whether her professor used Turnitin. She replied that to the best of her knowledge, none of her work had ever been submitted to Turnitin; she had never even heard of the program. However, this was not the case because her professor had submitted her work to Turnitin without her knowledge, and, in submitting her paper for our experiment, we had unwittingly alerted her professor to the possibility that she might he attempting to submit the same paper for another course. To prevent this misconception, we contacted the professor to explain that we had used the student's paper with permission as part of our research on Turnitin.

In this situation the original report flagged 24% of the student's text as matching a document within the database. After selecting Turnitin's option to obtain more information, we received an e-mail message stating that the professor from the course in which the matching paper had been submitted granted permission for Turnitin to send us the original paper from which our submission had ostensibly been "plagiarized." Turnitin forwarded us a copy of the entire paper, including the personal information the writer had included in her heading, specifically her full name and course number. In many courses students are required to put their identification numbers, e-mail addresses, and even contact numbers on their papers; *we* had now discovered that this student information can be forwarded by Turnitin to third parties as long as the original professor—not the student author—grants permission. We had not only obtained the student's entire original paper without her knowledge or permission, but also her full name and course number.

In addition, Turnitin claims to save professors time ("Plagiarism Prevention"). Instructors who use the program still must look at Turnitin's report of the student's paper because this report does not distinguish between properly and improperly cited information. While the option exists to omit marking material within quotation marks and in the bibliography, Turnitin cannot verify that citations are formatted correctly or that students have quoted correctly. As we have noted, Turnitin is able to detect only copy-and-paste plagiarism from within its database; the instructor must still check for copy-and-paste plagiarism from outside of the Turnitin database. Turnitin, however, is not clear about these limitations in the scope of its database, simply stating that it uses "exhaustive searches of billions of pages from both current and archived instances of the internet, millions of student papers previously submitted to Turnitin, and commercial databases of journal articles and periodicals" ("Plagiarism Prevention"). Furthermore, since Turnitin detects only this type of plagiarism, professors must scrutinize papers for other types of plagiarism on their own. Therefore, the timesaving claim made by Turnitin is dubious.

The more we delved into the institutional aspects of Turnitin, the greater our concerns became. The money that institutions use to pay for the license to use Turnitin can come from various sources, depending on the institution. At our university the funds come from the technology fee that all students are required to pay. This fee is meant to enhance student learning, provide equitable access, and make graduates competitive in the workplace ("Pennsylvania"). Turnitin charges between $4,000 and $10,000 a year for the use of their program, depending on the institution's enrollment. Bigger schools pay more for the service because it is expected that they will submit more papers to the program. In 2004–05, with approximately 13,500 students, our university paid $8,100. Meanwhile, Turnitin is a for-profit company that charges licensing fees to institutions that want access to their program, Turnitin's parent company, iParadigms, had 3,500 member institutions in 2004 and earned $10 million in annual revenue (Dodnga).

iParadigms reports that it receives over 20,000 papers on a peak day from users in 51 countries ("About"). iParadigm's other services include iThenticate, a commercial version of Turnitin; plagiarism.org, a website that provides information about online plagiarism and Turnitin; and Research Resources, a website about plagiarism and the Internet ("Products"). Turnitin, backed by its ever-expanding proprietary database, is the star of iParadigm's corporate agenda. Every new subscription not only generates revenue for the company through licensing fees, it also increases the size of its proprietary database and thus the market value of its product. Student papers remain in the database even after students graduate or schools cancel their subscriptions, so that every paper that enters the database puts iParadigms a step ahead of aspiring competitors. iParadigms' CEO Tom Barrie boasts, "In very short order, we'll have it all wrapped up. We'll become the next generation's spell checker. . . . There will be no room for anybody else, not even a Microsoft, to provide a similar type of service because we will have the database" (Masur).

"Having the database" is crucial to Turnitin's business model, which depends upon adding value to its product by continuously expanding the amount of original work it collects from students and other sources and then holds forever. Each sales transaction to a college or university then creates a dependent economic relationship between Turnitin and the university, leaving institutions that might want to choose a different software company to decide between losing access to all of their students' papers and renewing their licenses with Turnitin.

Furthermore, the legal issues surrounding Turnitin concern the Copyright Law and the Fair Use Law. The Copyright Law covers items such as literary works, musical compositions, musical records, screenplays, and works of art. Items not eligible for protection under the Copyright Law are ideas, facts, dates, names, short phrases, and blank forms. The Fair Use Law determines whether the use made of a work is fair, and several factors are considered in this decision. One is the purpose and character of the use, such as whether the item in question is being used for commercial or nonprofit purposes. Another is the nature of the copyrighted work and includes the amount and substantiality of the portion of the work in question relative to the copyrighted work as a whole. Finally, there is the effect of the use upon the potential market for or value of the copyrighted work. Turnitin argues that the purpose of the digital fingerprint is to enable the evaluation of works for plagiarism; the purpose of the work itself is to express an idea or information for an academic purpose. Therefore, the purposes of use are not prohibited under the Fair Use Law. This also means that the use of the students' work will not affect its potential market value.

As of December 2005, there was no clear legal precedent for the situation created by Turnitin. Turnitin, however, markets itself largely as an educational tool. It is conceivable that Turnitin attempts to use its affiliations with educational institutions to gain leniency in copyright and fair use laws. Programs affiliated with educational pursuits often argue that special circumstances are required to fulfill their educational mission. Actions that are used to advance that goal are often able to infringe on possible copyrights and are justified because the purpose is the greater goal of education. Turnitin proclaims to be working for education, and the company claims that it should be able to make use of these legal leniencies; others contest the view that Turnitin has the educational system in its best interests.

On its website, Turnitin publishes a statement by its law firm, Foly & Lardner, to reassure readers that Turnitin infringes on no copyrights ("Legal Document"). The statement claims that using Turnitin "does not pose a significant risk of infringement of any copyright in written works submitted to Turnitin for evaluation." Perhaps in anticipation of questions about the violation of copyright laws, Turnitin defends their program on their website in a section called "Legal Document," where they pose a series of questions. The first one asks: "Does Turnitin infringe on student's [*sic*] copyrights to their work?" Their response to this question is as follows:

> Determining whether a copyright exists in a particular work or is infringed by a particular use of the work is difficult [. . .] [C]asual analysis of these issues will not suffice, especially when the use in question is novel, as is the Turnitin system for plagiarism detection. For that reason, iParadigms [. . .] sought expert legal advice before launching the Turnitin system, and have continued to do so during its operation.
>
> Based on extensive analysis of all aspects of the Turnitin system, we have concluded that its use does not pose a significant risk of infringement of any copyright in written works submitted to Turnitin for evaluation. ("Legal Document")

Readers of this response may agree with us that it is vague and evasive, relying mainly on reassurances that the company has received expert legal advice and conducted an extensive analysis, but offering no supporting evidence. The evasiveness continues on page three of their legal document, when Turnitin poses the question, "Is Turnitin's use of student work ethical?" They respond first by noting:

> Each faculty user of the Turnitin system must decide whether the advantages of detecting plagiarism quickly and efficiently, coupled with the ability for peers to efficiently and anonymously review each others' work, is outweighed by any reservations the faculty user may have about bow Turnitin accomplishes those goals. ("Legal Document")

This statement seems to ignore the question of using students' original work and focuses instead on the convenience afforded to faculty, suggesting that students will simply have to defer to their instructors' wishes about handling their work. Students' rights are often subordinated to the decisions of teachers and administrators, and Turnitin may believe it has the backing of most legal opinions. The question of whether or not it is ethical for Turnitin (and the faculty and institutions who subscribe to it) to use students' work in the way that Turnitin seems to encourage is left unanswered. The "Legal Document" goes on to state:

In that respect, we believe it helpful to bear in mind that academic institutions and their teachers are not only encouraged, but obliged, to award grades to student work based on student input, rather than the intellectual contribution of others. Students should know that not only the content, but also the integrity of their work is subject to evaluation.

Once again, we see Turnitin shifting the focus of the question to what they believe students must do, namely, maintain the integrity of their work. The integrity of students' work is precisely what is at stake, however, when Turnitin encourages faculty to require that all students submit their work to Turnitin's proprietary database and holds these works there indefinitely, even sending out copies of the students' work with personal, identifying information to those who wish to examine it, as we found in our research.

STUDENT PERCEPTIONS ON TURNITIN

What do students think about Turnitin? In addition to the panicked writers we met with and the students whose frustration we've discussed thus far, we visited an online conversation forum called "Students Hate Turnitin.com." Some of the posts were supportive. One student wrote, "I think the concept of Turnitin is good—as somebody who doesn't plagiarize then I've got nothing to worry about. What I don't like though is the thought of my work being kept on file for future comparison." Another student believed that if people were against Turnitin, it must be because they themselves plagiarize. "Why else would anyone complain about such a service?" she asked. Also surprising was the seemingly low regard students had for their own work. At least three posts indicated feelings of surrender, suggesting that the moment they submit their papers, the work is no longer theirs. After all, they said, the papers were never copyrighted or protected in any way, and whatever the professors decide to do with the papers is fine with them; this, they felt, was the "cost" of the grade they received in return. On the other hand, there were two responses expressing dislike for Turnitin. One student wondered what happened if "[a] student isn't comfortable with their assignment being put through this system?" Another student observed the long-term effects of submitting work and "how the information can/will be used."

Students who deliberately choose to plagiarize are often well aware of Turnitin's shortcomings. Some of our tutors who are English education majors doing their student teaching had the opportunity to speak with a number of the high school students in their classes about their thoughts on Turnitin. One fifteen-year-old student told us that due to "the paper mill plagiarism problem," his high school required students to submit all papers through Turnitin. We asked if the requirement had stopped students from downloading papers, and he laughed. He explained:

> Really, it's so worthless. Everyone knows how it catches you, so it's easy to figure out how not to get caught. All you have to do is move things around in a sentence to change the order, or put in some extra words, or put in words that mean the same thing. They say a lot of times it fixes the paper up, actually, because those papers you get online aren't so good when it comes to grammar or using vocabulary. (Anonymous)

So perhaps, after all, Turnitin leads some students to edit their plagiarism more carefully, even as it poses little obstacle for determined plagiarists.

We wonder whether students realize the full extent of the obstacles Turnitin creates. Consider students who feel attached to their work, whether it is creative or research based. Do they understand how Turnitin benefits financially from having their work in the database? Or, do they realize that their work is easily reproduced whenever a paper is submitted that matches what they've written? We found few who expressed serious reservations about Turnitin and what it might mean for them in the future. Those who favored Turnitin seemed to do so because they respected those who do not plagiarize and wanted people who *do* to get caught. There were occasional complaints on student blogs about the unauthorized retention of student work, but they were relatively mild.

If these scant complaints have failed to get much attention, a 2004 court case involving a student at McGill University in Montreal seems to be having an impact. College sophomore Jesse Rosenfeld failed his assignments when be refused his professor's instructions to submit his work to Turnitin, citing "ethical and political problem[s]" with the system (Grinberg). "I was having to prove I didn't plagiarize even before my paper was looked at by my professor," Rosenfeld stated. A Canadian court sided with the student, and many authorities agreed with his position. Ian Boyko, national chairman of the Canadian Federation of Students, stated, "Of the 20 Canadian universities currently using the site, not one consulted with students in the decision-making process when signing on with Turnitin.com . . . that in itself shows a lack of respect for students' rights" (qtd. in Grinberg). Boyko further states that students, as authors, should be able to decide where their work goes, period, especially considering that the company makes money from the submissions. This last piece of evidence may be the most damaging to the credibility of Turnitin, which bases the legality of its operation on its purported educational mission.

Tom Barrie, founder and president of Turnitin.com, had strong reactions to the accusations: "This is the first time since our inception in 1998, since millions of papers have gone though our site, that this issue has come up . . . , we are following the letter of the law, and not one of the 3,000 universities who use our service would have signed contracts with us if we weren't" (qtd. in Grinberg). He also disputes that Turnitin withholds student work. Because the papers are imprinted digitally into the system, rather than in written form, he says there is no need for concern. "We don't harm the free-market value of the work—a student can take their Macbeth essay to the market and make millions," argues Barrie. But the claim is at least debatable because once a work is in the database, its content is available to others, even unscrupulous users who could claim the work as their own and take it to the market. Whether the input of the saved work is manifested digitally or otherwise seems beside the point if it is being stored against the will of the writers who crafted it.

Given the responses we've provided from students and the scenarios offered that led to poor solutions to plagiarism issues in student writing, we do not believe the program actually helps to solve the problem of plagiarism. Boyko argues that it does not: "We see the use of sites like Turnitin.com as means of cutting corners . . . we think they are a poor substitute for trained individuals" (qtd. in Grinberg). Most teachers feel an obligation that goes beyond producing graduates who have simply met the requirements; writing teachers and tutors, in particular, believe that each student's experience with writing is at least as important as the ability to follow the rules of writing. And yet the sheer power of electronic solutions is hard to match. Turnitin's president says there is little choice but to rely on a digital solution because "[h]uman beings cannot detect plagiarism . . . unless you apply a digital solution, it's impossible. We have 13 seven-foot computer racks to determine if a student has lifted one line in an essay from the internet" (qtd. in Grinberg).

Turnitin does make a compelling argument when it observes that human brains do not have the capacity to scan billions of pages to detect every instance of plagiarism; on the other hand, detection is not a simple matter of matching. Whether or not a student has plagiarized requires knowledge of the student, the assignment, and other factors for which human judgment trumps computer power. The controversy over Turnitin will likely continue, and it is bound to find its way back to the courtroom, and much more research is needed on how students perceive and are being informed on Turnitin at their schools. For now, we'd like to take the controversy to spaces where writing is taught, learned, and done.

SOME PEDAGOGICAL LIMITATIONS OF TURNITIN

In a typical session dealing with the topic of plagiarism, tutors at most writing centers try first to understand what students do and don't know about the topic. They explain what plagiarism is and how to avoid improperly using the words, ideas, and research of others. The session might last thirty minutes to an hour. The tutor and writer review when information should be cited, how to handle direct quotes, and how to acknowledge someone else's words or ideas. Tutors show students how to do relatively easy things like using signal phrases and harder ones like creating summaries and paraphrases. While we may not always he experts on the pedagogy of teaching citation, tutors have developed effective skills for teaching skills related to the use of sources. Sometimes we ask writers to read the original source aloud, and then we use this as a basis for teachable moments, as when a writer struggles to read passages he or she did not write. Sometimes tutors remove the original text by minimizing the computer screen or turning over the paper and asking the writer to recap what he or she has just read. Tutors write or have the student write notes based on what the student is able to remember. These strategies, which Howard advocates in her work on helping students to learn paraphrasing skills, provide students the opportunity to expand how they think about incorporating sources into their own writing ("Plagiarisms" 801).

At the same time, tutors are trained to steer students away from certain practices. Tutors generally do not teach students to use the computer's thesaurus as a paraphrasing tool. We do not encourage them simply to substitute words like "splendid" for words like "great" to create an acceptable paraphrase. Avoiding the thesaurus becomes problematic once students understand bow Turnitin defines and detects "plagiarism," however. While most people would agree that a thesaurus can be helpful, it becomes downright essential to using Turnitin when writing something that involves a set of standard or agreed upon terms that professional writers repeat without quoting or citing. We discovered this as we spoke to students who were required to submit papers to Turnitin and had figured out that a thesaurus was almost essential. We wrote and submitted a passage to Turnitin (in December 2005) that used standard terms to define a concept: "Freud discussed hidden emotions and drives as a person's libido, a type of psychic energy." When we made minimal changes to the sentence—"Freud talks about concealed emotions and drives as a person's libido, a kind of psychic energy"—and resubmitted it, Turnitin did not recognize the text as plagiarized. Similarly, we found that changing the syntax of the sentence could also outwit the software. "As defined by Freud, the id is the psychic energy that . . . " was not flagged as being plagiarized from the original, "The id, as defined by Freud, is the psychic energy that . . . "

Turnitin is marketed as a campus-wide "technological solution," so various departments in schools, colleges, and universities across the nation ask students to submit their papers to their instructors through the program. Many instructors use Turnitin to compare "textual similarity," meaning identical or nearly identical strings of words and phrases, which they believe is a key step in the detection of plagiarism (Sherwood). Considering only textual similarity as a way to identify plagiarism is a limited way of looking at the problem, however, and causes distress for students who seek to learn the appropriate discourse practices of their field of study and the writing center tutors trying to support them. In our writing center we have met several students who were writing field-specific papers in the sciences and social sciences. These papers relied heavily on precise definitions and standard vocabulary. In a paper on Attention Deficit Disorder that one of our tutors wrote in December 2005, the three types of ADD, as defined by the DSM-IV (American Psychiatric Association), a widely accepted psychological manual for diagnosing disorders, were listed. The section of text that Turnitin flagged as plagiarized was, "the DSM-IV: predominantly inattentive, predominantly hyperactive-impulsive, and combined." This string of words matches other strings of words that exist with high frequency in cyberspace because these are the precise names of the subcategories of the disorder ADD, in the order in which they appear in the DSM-IV. The paper was not plagiarized, but the terminology being used was too specific for the software to interpret intelligently. Tutors and students will continue to struggle through sessions with papers like this one because concerned students have determined that they must change the order in which the subcategories are described in order to circumvent the identical binary coding that Turnitin matches and marks for "textual similarity." Should students have to change what they know is right because their institution's computer software does not?

Even when students deliberately copy text from another source, Turnitin does not consistently identify this type of fraudulent plagiarism. Kurt Bouman points out that there are many levels of plagiarism. There is a clear difference, for example, between a student who inadvertently paraphrases a source incorrectly and a student who fraudulently downloads a paper from a paper mill and submits it as his or her own writing. Since Turnitin cannot distinguish a student's intent as it scans the paper, the program often marks appropriate paraphrasing as inappropriate and lets inappropriate paraphrasing slide. As part of our investigation, we conducted a test to determine whether we could submit a plagiarized text without being detected by Turnitin. We began with a text from DigitalTermPapers.com, an online paper mill. We were able to view, on the mill's website, the first 150 words of a sample essay written on *The House on Mango Street,* and so we copied and pasted this publicly available text into a word processor and submitted the document to Turnitin in February 2005. Surprisingly, the originality report came hack with only the first sentence flagged and a similarity index of 10%. When we clicked on the highlighted text to see what Turnitin had matched to our text, it displayed a page of nonsensical strings of words and sentences from an obscure website. An instructor evaluating the originality report would not have been able to determine that we had directly copied the text from a publicly available Internet paper mill, even though that is the type of website Turnitin claims to target with its web crawlers.

Most paper mills require accounts and passwords, thereby placing them beyond the reach of Turnitin's web crawlers. Turnitin claims that this is not a significant weakness of their program since it retains a copy of every paper submitted within its database. As soon as a student submits a paper purchased from a paper mill, that paper can be compared to future submissions ("Turnitin Virtual Tour"). In response to this, paper mills have begun to offer custom-written papers that are guaranteed not to be detected by services such as Turnitin. The website EssayMall.com advertises "original, well-balanced, and thoughtfully-written custom essays" which are checked by a "licensed plagiarism detection program to ensure one hundred percent originality and authenticity of work" ("Custom Essay Value"). Prices range from $11.79 per 330-word page with five days' notice to a steep $29.79 per page for twelve hours' notice; however, the company assures prospective buyers that the quality of its products, coupled with its originality and confidentiality guarantees, is worth the price. As long as the company is true to its guarantees, students who fraudulently plagiarize through custom paper mills such as EssayMall.com are safe from Turnitin detection.

Thus, we question Turnitin's ability to be a campus-wide "technological solution" to plagiarism, which brings us to even more serious questions about the program's pedagogical limitations. From the information we've presented here, the program itself is in no way a panacea for plagiarism issues. From our discussion throughout this section, we would like to point out two major differences between students who accidentally plagiarize and those who, as in the cases of students who buy papers off the Internet, fraudulently plagiarize. Believing that Turnitin will function as a "cure-all" detracts our attention from asking why or how students plagiarize and places an emphasis on what they plagiarize. The danger in such a focus is that the teaching of proper paraphrasing may be overlooked for the simplest solutions to preventing plagiarism that we've demonstrated, such as using the thesaurus function in Word. This approach may not happen in composition classrooms, but we wonder about those students with whom we met who were simply required to fix the problems rather than being told how to paraphrase and cite properly. Turnitin offered no advice to these students on how they might begin to cite and paraphrase properly. Furthermore, in our more extreme example of fraudulent plagiarism, Turnitin failed to catch the work that was purchased from paper mills. The question for us, then, is whether or not Turnitin actually has any pedagogical purposes on its own? A teacher can surely use the program to some pedagogical ends, but what does it say about the pedagogical claims being offered by Turnitin when the program is more than likely going to flag issues of accidental plagiarism and totally miss cases of severe fraud? The point is that we cannot and should not forget about the kinds of responsibilities we have to young writers as tutors and teachers just because we now have the ability to compare cases of textual similarity.

WHAT'S A TUTOR TO DO? SOME THOUGHTS ON PRACTICE AND ADVOCACY

Back in the comfort of our own writing center, we pondered one more question: To what extent can the writing center change the momentum when an institution has decided to adopt a program like Turnitin? At the very least, tutors and directors can try to make their faculty aware of the limitations of Turnitin and the need to interpret its reports carefully.

Tutors who begin to learn about Turnitin software soon confront the question of what to tell others. To what extent, for example, should tutors become a political voice for or against the program? Arguably, knowing more precisely what Turnitin can and cannot do could strengthen its support among faculty, students, and perhaps even tutors. Some might say that it is helpful to know that Turnitin cannot determine fraudulent from inadvertent plagiarism, and that it cannot even be counted on to help detect fraudulent plagiarism. And then there is the cost. Is it appropriate for tutors who learn the price their institutions pay for a Turnitin license to share this information with their peers? Are the stakes in this debate higher if Turnitin is funded entirely through student fees?

At times, we felt it was our duty to take what we had learned, and the discourse we had developed to articulate it, and become politically active on our campus. The more students who go to their professors and complain about Turnitin, we reasoned, the more likely the professors would be to unite and to ask the university to curtail its use or at least to request better training measures that critique the use and implications of Turnitin. On the other hand, many of the students using Turnitin are first- or second-year undergraduates. Is it appropriate for their tutors to increase the anxiety level of these students by telling of *potential* horror stories about the "plagiarism detector"? At our university, as in many others, tutors are employees of the school. As university employees—and without tenure—do we have license to speak against an institutional practice? If we were to publicly oppose Turnitin, how might this impact the writing center and the broad support our center enjoys from faculty and administrators? Would we reduce ourselves to "bitching buddies," willing to trash professors who use Turnitin and possibly creating the misconception that we believe plagiarism should be tolerated?

What we found in our own tutoring was a space for honest discussions about the program and approaches to dealing with a professor who may not be entirely aware of how the program works. Initially, during sessions that dealt with Turnitin issues, we told students everything we had learned about the program; we told them, as we have addressed earlier, how it works and what this means for the work that they are doing. There was something empowering about these conversations because students were given the kind of information they needed to address seriously how they were being implicated in the mix between their writing, their teachers' beliefs about plagiarism, and the use of the program. We shared the stories and the writing we had collected, not to strike fear in the hearts of anxious students but to give them a sense of what they're really dealing with and the kinds of options they had. As we saw more students with similar issues, our Turnitin information blitzes turned into focused pieces of advice that worked well for students at our university.

In efforts to be both honest and supportive to students, we first told them that it was important to speak with their professors about the situation. Beyond teaching students bow to properly paraphrase and cite, the students here needed to know that it was ok to ask professors questions to point out that Turnitin was flagging parts of their papers that they had merely cited or in which discipline specific discourse was being used that would represent common knowledge in their field. In addition to trying to open up lines of communication between students and teachers, we also encouraged students to share their stories about Turnitin with other students, to let others know that there's much more than meets the eye with this program and that students have a stake in how this program is being used because it affects them both scholastically and financially at our institution. Our approach, in a nutshell, was to create avenues for discussions on Turnitin that tutors and other students could take in discussing problems of plagiarism and plagiarism detection services with faculty and other members of the University community.

As for us, we dealt with the questions we articulated earlier about the political implications of our exposé of Turnitin, our outreach to faculty, and our relationship to other students with the utmost seriousness. With our initial questions about the program and how it was used answered, we decided to become intellectually engaged with what we had learned. We presented our findings to faculty and students at our institution, and in doing so, we posed ethical, legal, and financial problems with the program that prompted faculty to think carefully about how to use Turnitin in their classes. In addition to the outreach we did locally, we brought what we had learned to the IWCA/NCPTW conference in Minneapolis, where we heard even more stories about Turnitin, both positive and negative, that have helped shape our current approaches to the Turnitin dilemma on our own campus. We would recommend that other tutors do the same—to find out more about how things on their campuses work and to become engaged in conversations about various campus issues at both local and national levels. As tutors, we see a lot that other people at our institutions either take for granted or barely recognize, but we do have the ability and opportunity to speak up on those often glanced over issues and to reach out to fellow students and our faculty.

Coming back to our own research, we think that writing centers have a greater obligation to the Turnitin debate, however, which begins by acknowledging that many students are never taught what plagiarism is or how to avoid it. Many high school teachers decide that citation skills can be taught in college, while many college teachers outside of English departments decide it is not their responsibility to teach writing. For students who have had little or no instruction on how to cite sources, Turnitin is not the answer. Writing center staff should press their faculty and administration to offer all students the opportunity to learn how to document their sources before they require them to use Turnitin. Second, writing center staff should promote in-service education for all instructors who use Turnitin so that they are familiar with the program and learn to use it in limited, pedagogically sound ways. And, finally, we believe that all members of the writing center community need to keep up with technological innovations related to plagiarism detection so that faculty can he warned against and tutors can be prepared to deal with programs that are potentially detrimental to the educational process in composition.

NOTE

We would like to thank our writing center director Ben Rafoth for his support and guidance while we researched, wrote, and presented this piece. We would also like to thank our fellow tutors Anna Bloom, Gretchen Burger, and Jon Derr, who embarked on this research project with us and have since graduated. Their efforts set the foundation for our presentations and this publication.

WORKS CITED

Anonymous. 2005. Personal Interview, 3 October.
"About Us." 2005. iParadigms. 9 December. http://www.turnitin.com /about_us/.

America Psychiatric Association. 1994. *Diagnostic and Statistical Manual of Mental Disorders DSM-IV.* 4th ed. Washington, DC: American Psychiatric Association.

Bouman, Kurt. "Raising Questions about Plagiarism." In *ESL Writers: A Guide for Writing Center Tutors,* edited by Shanti Bruce and Ben Rafoth, 105–116. Portsmouth: Boynton/Cook.

"Custom Essay Value." 2005. *Essay Mall.com.* 3 December. http://www.essaymall .com.

Dotinga, Randy. 2004. "Electronic Snoops Tackle Copiers." *Wired.com,* 2 April. Accessed 14 February 2005. http://archive.wired.com/techbiz/media/news /2004/04/62906?currentPage=all.

Grinberg, Emanuella. 2004. "Student Wins Battle against Plagiarism-Detection Requirement." *CNN.com,* 21 January. Accessed 3 October 2005. http://www .cnn.com/2004/LAW/01/21/ctv.plagiarism/.

Herek, Jennifer, and Mark Niquette. 1990. "Ethics in the Writing Lab: Tutoring under the Honor Code." *The Writing Lab Newsletter* 14.5: 12–15.

Howard, Rebecca Moore. 1995. "Plagiarisms, Authorships, and the Academic Death Penalty." *College English* 57.7: 788–806.

Howard, Rebecca Moore. 1999. *Standing in the Shadow of Giants: Plagiarists, Authors, Collaborators.* Stamford, CT: Ablex.

Howard, Rebecca Moore. 2000. "Sexuality, Textuality: The Cultural Work on Plagiarism." *College English* 62.4: 47391.

Kail, Harvey, and John Trimbur. 1995. "The Politics of Peer Tutoring." In *Landmark Essays on Writing Centers,* edited by Christina Murphy and Joe Law, 203–210. Davis, CA: Hermagoras.

"Legal Document." 2005. *Turnitin Legal Information.* Accessed 10 October 2005. http://www.turnitin.com/en_us/ static/legal/legaLdocument.html.

Marsh, Bill. 2004. "Turnitin.com and the Scriptural Enterprise of Plagiarism Detection." *Computers and Composition* 21: 427–438.

Masur, Kate. 2001. "Papers, Profits, and Pedagogy: Plagiarism in the Age of the Internet." *Perspectives Online,* November. Accessed 8 November 2005. http://www.historians.org/perspectives/issues/2001/0105/0105new3.cfm.

"The Pennsylvania State System of Higher Education Technology Policy." 2002. Indiana University of Pennsylvania, 3 September. Accessed 9 December 2005. http://www.iup.edu/aog/DOCUMENTS/Technology-Fee.doc.

"Plagiarism Prevention." 2006. *Turnitin.com.* Accessed 6 March 2006. http://www.turnitin.com/en_us/ static/plagiarism.html.

"Privacy Pledge." 2006. *Turnitin.com.* Accessed 6 March 2006. http://www.turni tin.com/static/privacyhtml.

"Products and Services." 2005. iParadigms. Accessed 9 December 2005. http://www.turnitin.com/products_services/.

"Product Tour." 2006. *Turnitin.com.* Accessed 6 March 2006. http://www.turni tin.com/en_us/static/flash/tii.html.

Shamoon, Linda, and Deborah H. Burns. 1999. "Plagiarism, Rhetorical Theory, and the Writing Center: New Approaches, New Locations." In *Perspectives on Plagiarism and Intellectual Property in a Postmodern World,* edited by Lise Buranen and Alice M. Roy, 183–192. Albany: SUNY Press.

Sherwood, Kenneth. 2005. "Syllabus-ENGL 202—Research Writing-Fall 2005." Indiana University of Pennsylvania, August. Accessed 5 April 2005. http://www.chss.iup.edu/sherwood/courses/ENGL202F05/index.htm/.

"Students Hate Turnitin.com." 2005. *Webhosting Talk*, 3 October. http://www
.webhostingtalk.com.

Turnitin.com. 2006. iParadigms. Accessed 15 March 2005. http://www.turnitin.com/.

Student Activity

READING, ANALYSIS, AND REFLECTION

1. What methods do the authors employ in their research study?
2. How does this fit or not action research?
3. The authors write: "Believing that Turnitin will function as a 'cure-all' detracts our attention from asking why or how students plagiarize and places an emphasis on what they plagiarize. The danger in such a focus is that the teaching of proper paraphrasing may be overlooked for the simplest solutions to preventing plagiarism that we've demonstrated, such as using the thesaurus" (24). Do the authors have an agenda in undertaking this research project? How do they remain objective and thus credible?
4. What practices can be improved or strengthened through these research findings?
5. In terms of research integrity, what are the issues in undertaking a project such as this?

"Determining the Effectiveness of La Salle University's Writing-Across-the-Curriculum Requirement in the Biology Major"

Andrea McMunn and Jessica Reifer, La Salle University

Andrea McMunn and Jessica Reifer, writing fellows at La Salle University, undertook a study to determine if the writing-across-the-curriculum requirement in their university's biology department was truly efficacious. To do so, they surveyed both students and faculty members. They also conducted a review of literature about writing in science. Their results influenced policy and practice on their campus. In granting permission to reprint this essay, McMunn and Reifer particularly wished to acknowledge Margot Soven for her support through the research, writing, and publication process. In doing so, they acknowledge the impact a good mentor may have on student researchers.

In 1988, La Salle University incorporated a writing emphasis requirement within each major to provide more effective writing instruction in every discipline. By 1991, La Salle's biology curriculum required all biology majors to complete a writing component consisting of two assignments. The first required students to write a scientific review article on a topic of personal interest. The biology faculty expected students to use about thirty primary sources from contemporary journals to compose this twenty- to twenty-five-page paper. The second assignment entailed condensing the information discussed in the review paper into a shorter, popular science format that would convey the same scientific information

Andrea McMunn and Jessica Reifer, "Determining the Effectiveness of La Salle University's Writing-Across-the-Curriculum Requirement in the Biology Major," *Young Scholars in Writing,* 4(2006):73–93.

to the general public. In 1996, Margot Soven and Craig Franz evaluated the biology writing component in a descriptive study to determine if the goals of the requirement had been met and whether the assignment was effective. The evaluators at the time concluded that the writing component was, indeed, an effective means of teaching biology students how to write well within their discipline.

Since the 1996 evaluation, the biology writing component has changed slightly, because the department has altered the course curriculum. The assignment had originally been incorporated into a two-semester biochemistry class, providing students with an entire academic year to work on these two essays. This modification in the curriculum resulted in a one-semester condensed biochemistry course and an independent one-semester molecular biology course into which the professors decided to transfer the writing assignment requirements. The faculty then removed the second assignment designed for the general public from the curriculum because of the shortened timeline for completion. The longer review paper, however, remained generally the same.

The authors of this article designed and conducted a new study to assess the effectiveness of the current biology writing component based on the perspectives of both students and professors of the La Salle biology department, as well as scholars in the field of writing-across-the-curriculum (WAC) assignment design and implementation. The investigators in this study determined that the current biology writing assignment meets the criteria of a quality assignment according to WAC scholars. It can also be classified as an effective assignment that meets the needs of biology students and professors at La Salle University. While the assignment is effective in its current form, it deviates from the original goals instituted in 1988. The new assignment excludes other biological writing styles, such as the popular science essay, from the former assignment. This study explores possible shortcomings of the new assignment's lack of representation of the variety of biological writing styles, and the investigators have provided some suggestions for the biology department to consider when reviewing the assignment for aspects that can be improved.

THE IMPORTANCE OF WRITING IN SCIENCE

In order to be successful as professionals, students must learn the basic inquiry strategies common to most disciplines and incorporate these into their writing. Such strategies include examining assumptions and prior knowledge, posing questions, making and interpreting inferences, establishing working hypotheses, testing interpretations, and imagining. In fact, imagining is perhaps the most powerful gateway of all, the foundation for original discovery and insight (Nagin 55). These strategies lie at the core of the critical thinking that students must practice in academia, in a profession, and as adult citizens beyond school.

In addition to acquiring communication skills required of successful professionals, students can also utilize writing to learn the subject matter of the discipline. A complex educational tool, writing is a means of inquiry and expression for learning in all disciplines (Nagin 3). For example, clear, precise statements, closely reasoned arguments, and unambiguous language are valued among scientists. Practitioners argue that problem solving through writing leads students to come to grips with their incomplete understanding in an active and self-stimulating fashion (Tobias 48). Moreover, instructors intend for students to construct a personalized understanding of the subject by means of the written or spoken phrase. Writing as a means of self-exploration in mathematics and science learning achieves two important goals: it provides classroom-based specific feedback, and it gives students the opportunity to identify and to unravel their own misconceptions (54). If students write about the material, especially from some personal vantage point, they come to own the material. Open-ended writing assignments in the sciences allow for individuality and creativity, while more specific assignments ensure that certain concepts are understood. Research demonstrates that students who associate the material with images or ideas of their own creation increase their recall. Furthermore, a case study by Kathryn Martin indicated that writing on a daily basis encourages students to review biological concepts (114).

Scientists' composition processes typically involve the discovery of new ideas and information about their research and its meaning. When instructors assign research papers, they intend for the students to experience the satisfaction that comes from discovering new ideas and the exhilaration that comes from exploring the sources. These educators also hope that students will discover that sifting through the information and organizing it into coherent statements, though difficult and often frustrating, in the end can be a rewarding experience (Lutzker 1).

DESCRIPTION OF WRITING IN THE SCIENCES

Writing in the sciences may not differ radically from the writing processes of other kinds of professionals. The conventional notion of non-scientists is that the writing task is one in which scientists simply record laboratory procedures and results. Those outside of the field assume that scientists' perspectives are developed from a preconceived frame of reference, which determines the observations they make about the world. Contrarily, scientists regard the experimental paper as the vehicle both for giving meaning to their observations and for persuading the scientific community that those observations are truths (Rymer 212).

Scholars have observed routine laboratory practices and shown how a scientist's writing imposes a logical structure on the mass of confusion in the lab. Thus, the written works of scientists establish their credibility and persuade the community that the claims asserted in their works should be accepted as facts (Rymer 212). Additionally, as Harrington and Rivers identify, the scientist is ever seeking to systematize knowledge by stating general laws; some may be amended by new discoveries, but the substance of science is a body of general propositions (11). The professional scientist selects all the relevant information, tests deductions, and evaluates the results in the light of many facts or general propositions that bear upon the issue (12). Geller adds that scientists also write to show nonscientists what is important about their work, no matter how specialized the subject material (84).

Scientists choose to represent their actions and beliefs in discourse using a wide array of genres and styles. However, the depersonalized, objective, scientific style of experimental papers plays a significant role in the discussion of material expected to be accepted as scientific knowledge (Rymer 212). Rymer illuminates how the conventions of scientific texts operate, explaining that the genre dictates certain choices of form and content while serving to justify the writer's belief that the scientific enterprise leads to reliable and valuable knowledge about the natural world (213). However, Rymer also presents evidence that scientists use multiple approaches in writing experimental papers. In addition to linear models focused on detailed planning, scientists use a full range of strategies, including recursive models focused on revision. Rymer's study also suggests that scientists frequently discover new ideas about their experimental results and what the underlying science means while composing their journal submissions (244). An undergraduate writing assignment in the sciences must be representative of these aspects of scientific writing without overwhelming students.

USING WAC IDEOLOGY TO DEVELOP
EFFECTIVE WRITING ASSIGNMENTS

In the 1970s, WAC programs appeared in reaction to the dominant view that language has only one function—to inform. The precedent at the time suggested that the only language activity useful to education is the finished report or essay. WAC programs challenged this idea and sought to use writing to improve the teaching techniques of faculty members and expand the realm of learning activities for students. Learning to write in new ways allows students to intensify their involvement with the different areas of study in their educational program. Similarly, faculty members believe WAC is ultimately about finding textual pathways to help students enter and eventually transform powerful organizations of people (Russell 331). Other premises of WAC programs include writing to promote learning, writing as a complex developmental process, and the idea that the universe of discourse includes a broad range of writing functions and audiences (Freisinger 3).

The writing assignment quickly became a major tool for transforming teaching practices at the undergraduate level. However, promoters of WAC programs now faced the challenging project of creating quality writing assignments for a diverse range of disciplines. After years of planning and trial and error, WAC advocates established some requirements for designing an effective writing assignment. According to these standards, developed over time, an effective writing assignment does more than ask students to write about what they have read. Rather, such an assignment engages students in a series of cognitive processes, such as reflection, analysis, and synthesis, so that they are required to transform the information from the reading material (Nagin 47). Furthermore, an effective assignment gives students a framework for developing ideas and organizational guidelines that help them analyze and synthesize the information with which they are working. The most successful assignments offer the student a genuine opportunity to communicate with a real audience (48).

Marilyn Lutzker has also contributed helpful guidelines for designing effective writing assignments. Lutzker suggests that most educators now realize that learning takes place during the process of researching and writing a paper, and the final product is, at best, a report of that learning. Professors also increasingly recognize that more will be learned during the writing process if they actively monitor and review each stage of students' writing. As a result, Lutzker concludes that structured assignments are vital to WAC programs. The best format seems to involve a number of small, interrelated projects completed sequentially to culminate in a larger product. Such an assignment is valuable because it permits multiple deadlines as well as early and frequent feedback so that teachers can identify flaws in the writing and research early. In addition, such a process takes advantage of the recognized efficacy of incremental learning (9). Finally, Lutzker believes instructors should also build opportunities for students to practice several different types of writing, such as analysis, classification, comparison, criticism, evaluation, justification, and summarization (10). In 1988, La Salle instructors took on the challenge of developing a biology writing assignment that meets these criteria.

INITIAL GOALS AND EXPECTATIONS OF THE BIOLOGY WAC ASSIGNMENT AT LA SALLE UNIVERSITY

Previous research shows that WAC programs seek to enhance students' higher-order thinking or habits of mind, to make students more active learners, and to evaluate student work more effectively (Dowling et al.

50; Russell 264–69). Prior to the institution of writing emphasis requirements at various colleges, most science students across the nation had
very little experience in thinking about how to communicate scientific
information to nonspecialists. Although some of these students had previously completed creative science projects meant to encourage writing
to learn, and most of them had composed some form of research paper
in the humanities, science students had virtually no experience writing
scientific research articles (Geller 84). At La Salle specifically, laboratory
reports were the primary writing activity of biology majors. Some biology
students also had experience in answering essay questions, but they had
almost no experience in writing lengthy research papers. Furthermore,
professors rarely required students to translate highly technical material
into popular science terms to prove their understanding of the material
and show that they could convey this knowledge to others. Clearly, the students needed more specific instruction in writing scientific papers as well
as experience writing for a nontechnical audience (Franz and Soven).

Each scientific discipline has rhetorical conventions specific to its subject, so the importance of discipline-specific writing instruction in biology was evident. The university recognized this need because students
were not learning specific discipline-related writing in undergraduate
first-year composition classes (Franz and Soven). Also, in the past, science professors were often more concerned with the interpretation and
presentation of scientific data than the style in which it was written. This
deficit led to the 1988 implementation of a writing emphasis requirement at La Salle University. The establishment of a WAC program at
the University was undoubtedly beneficial, but a discussion of its specific
goals is necessary to gauge its success.

Realizing that successful scientific writing develops from experience and guidance, La Salle faculty sought to incorporate writing projects into the biology curriculum to encourage students to develop and
improve the skills needed to write within their discipline. Faculty members worked together to create a common writing experience for students based on typical writing in the biological field. By 1991, La Salle
faculty had developed a writing component, which all biology majors
were required to complete regardless of concentration within the major.
The writing component consisted of two assignments: a scientific review
article twenty to twenty-five pages in length with approximately thirty
primary source references from contemporary journals and a shorter
summary of the review written for the general public. The first essay was
to be an in-depth exploration of a topic that interested the student. The
second paper involved adapting the content of the first essay to a shorter,
popular science format. Biology professors served as faculty mentors to
assist students with organization and scheduling of the project. The
department chairperson assigned students to their mentors according

to their topic choices, so that each student would have access to a specialist in the subdiscipline he or she chose with whom to discuss the research process as well as subject matter. Writing fellows reviewed the rough drafts, and the biology department archived the final copies for future student reference (Franz and Soven).[1]

The 1996 Franz and Soven study evaluated the goals of the senior writing component in biology and concluded that the program was effective. The former writing requirement gave La Salle biology students the valuable opportunity to communicate with experts in their field of interest and to discuss the technicalities of scientific topics. Students also learned ancillary skills such as techniques for searching electronic databases, organizational schemas for preparation of major papers, and editorial skills for the improvement of written presentation. In addition, students learned how to translate technical terms and explain complicated processes in simpler terminology in the second assignment. The senior writing project in biology enabled students to see the connection between biology and rhetoric, to learn how to synthesize complex material into a coherent research essay, and to develop capacities for translating technical knowledge into information understandable to the general public.

The changes made to the initial writing assignment instituted in 1988 motivated the student authors of this work to conduct a small-scale research study examining the revised biology writing requirement. Expanding on the 1996 descriptive study of Franz and Soven, which confirmed that the original assignment implemented was effective, the investigators studied student surveys and professor interviews to explore the perspectives of La Salle biology majors and professors to determine if these groups find the revised assignment effective.

ASSESSING WAC PROGRAMS

Assessment is a valuable tool for the development and implementation of instructional programs. Focusing on the big picture, effective assessment relies on a set of guidelines that motivates inquiry, employs diverse methods, focuses on learning and teaching and how the two interact, and needs to be regular, systematic, and coherent (Beason and Darrow 7–8). Helpful questions to consider when assessing WAC programs are: Did the strategy help build engagement and community in the classroom? Did the strategy lead to enhanced student learning? Was the strategy consistent with teachers' time pressures and other constraints? Did the strategy fit teachers' philosophies, priorities, and styles of teaching (Dowling et al. 93)? Do students and teachers perceive an improvement in students' writing abilities because of the writing activities done in a WAC classroom? Do students and teachers perceive that these writing activities improved students' ability to understand course content? How do various writing activities compare in terms of improving either students' writing or their understanding of course content (Beason and Darrow 99)? These questions will be useful in examining the new biology writing requirement at La Salle.

When assessing WAC programs, there are several types of analysis to consider. One focuses on the writing program itself, such as the interaction among social context, institutional context, and program structure. This analysis takes into account the attitude of the general society toward the students in the program, the learning institution's commitment to the education of those students, and the organization of a writing program that distinguishes between developmental and nondevelopmental students. Another type of analysis focuses on evaluation—for example, the evaluation of the effects of writing on the society. Does the writing program affect the value its students place on written language once they leave college? Does it make the public aware of the different uses of language for different purposes? Does it send students into the world better able to adapt the processes and products of writing to novel situations? Do the theoretical underpinnings of a curriculum affect what students learn? Do students' attitudes toward writing change as a result of the program? (Faigley and White 64–65). In evaluating the current WAC biology requirement, finding answers to many of these questions is crucial to assess accurately whether or not this writing assignment is a productive and useful tool from the perspective of both students and teachers.

METHODOLOGY

To assess the effectiveness of the writing-across-the-curriculum assignment for biology majors, the investigators constructed a student survey. The survey consists of nine statements referencing writing in biology, writing in English, preparation for writing in a variety of disciplines, and the biology writing component itself. The authors asked students to rate their opinion of each statement on a scale of 1 to 5 (1—strongly disagree, 2—somewhat disagree, 3—neither agree nor disagree, 4—somewhat agree, 5—strongly agree). The researchers also asked students to complete three open-ended questions to determine the level of importance writing holds for each particular student, whether or not the purpose of the biology writing component was effectively conveyed to students, and what students learned from the biology review paper. (See appendix A for the full survey.)

The study developers distributed this student survey to thirteen of the twenty-seven students who completed the writing component in the Spring 2005 semester. (The other fourteen students were not surveyed because they had already graduated or could not be contacted to participate.) The researchers also distributed the survey to the eleven students currently involved in writing the assignment for the Fall 2005 semester. These students had already submitted a rough draft whose return they were awaiting at the time of the survey. These students had yet to review their mentors' comments and complete the revision process. The investigators separated these surveys from the surveys of students who had already completed the course and assignment to see if there were any major differences between students commenting retrospectively on the assignment and students commenting while undergoing the writing process. Out of these eleven students, seven chose to participate in the survey, making a total of twenty student surveys from which the authors tabulated results.

To evaluate the biology writing component through the perspective of biology professors who are actively involved in the scientific field, the study creators constructed a questionnaire consisting of ten questions. Out of the seven biology professors who serve as mentors in this writing program, four chose to participate. Two of these professors chose to complete the survey in interview format and the other two provided written responses to the questions listed in the questionnaire. (See appendix B for a complete copy of the mentor questionnaire.) After compiling the information from the surveys and the questionnaires, the researchers then reviewed and analyzed the data to determine whether or not the current biology writing component is an effective requirement.

RESULTS STUDENT SURVEY SUMMARY

Of the twenty biology students surveyed, 95% somewhat or strongly agreed that the necessity of writing well is not limited to English and literature courses. To further ascertain the writing experience of biology majors in English courses, one statement in the survey required students to rank whether or not they agreed that they learned everything they need to know about writing from their first-year composition course at La Salle University. In response to this statement, 85% of the students strongly or somewhat disagreed, suggesting that they understand that there is more to learn about writing than the material covered in one introductory-level writing course. However, 15% of the students surveyed somewhat or strongly agreed that they learned everything they need to know about writing from their first-year composition course. Similarly, 55% of the biology majors surveyed believe that they learned skills to prepare them for writing in other disciplines from their first-year composition course. Interestingly, however, 20% of these biology students believe they did not learn skills for writing in other disciplines from their first-year composition course, and 25% of those surveyed neither agreed nor disagreed in regard to this statement.

Furthermore, 95% of the biology majors surveyed believe that writing is a necessary skill in the biological sciences. When asked to rank how often biology majors at La Salle write within their major, the results varied significantly depending upon whether or not students considered lab reports a form of writing. Several students commented on this in their open-ended questions, noting that the lab reports for biochemistry were useful writing experiences—possibly even more effective than the current writing-across-the-curriculum requirement. Here it is important to note that biochemistry is the only required biology course at La Salle University for which the lab report must be written in a scientific format as if it were to be submitted to a scientific journal. To meet these constraints, biochemistry lab reports cannot exceed five pages, but require students to very thoroughly address the subtopics Introduction, Methods, Results, and Discussion and to include diagrams, graphs, and charts that are relevant to convey the results of the experiment. In order to condense all of this pertinent information into only five pages, the writer must be very concise and make use of formatting tools that will make the final work as brief, yet thorough, as possible. Some of the other biology electives require lab reports of the same structure (e.g., cell biology), but these lab reports have no page limit, and not all biology majors take these elective courses.

Of all the biology majors surveyed, 55% somewhat or strongly agreed that the WAC requirement is the first academic paper they have written in their field, while 40% somewhat or strongly disagreed with this statement, indicating that they have had other academic writing experiences within La Salle's biology department. This discrepancy can be attributed to the decision of some students to include lab reports as writing assignments when responding to the statement. The survey also required students to rank whether or not they found the biology WAC requirement helpful. The majority of students somewhat or strongly agreed, indicating that most students extracted a valuable learning experience from this writing process. Out of the twenty surveys completed, 60% of the students felt that the WAC requirement taught them a lot about writing in the discipline of biology, while 20% felt the writing assignment did not. Also, 20% of the students neither agreed nor disagreed with the statement. This variation can be attributed to several factors, including whether or not students had learned the same skills in their first-year composition course, and whether or not the biology students surveyed learned how to write in the biological field from other writing assignments at La Salle or even from outside experiences, such as research.

Of the students surveyed, 70% did not find it difficult to write in courses outside of their major, 15% did find it difficult to write in nonbiology courses, and the remaining 15% neither agreed nor disagreed that they struggle to write in courses outside of their major. The investigators designed this statement to determine if the styles of writing for biology are too drastically different from the writing styles of other disciplines for students to excel in writing outside of their major. It appears, from the survey results, that most students do not come across a problem when asked to write for their courses in other disciplines.

STUDENT OPEN-ENDED RESPONSES

The authors designed the open-ended questions of the student survey to determine if students accurately understand the purpose and objective of the biology writing assignment, what value each student attributes to the importance of writing, and what specifically this writing assignment has taught the students about writing in the discipline of biology. The majority of students questioned understood that this writing assignment is geared toward helping students become familiar with writing in the discipline of biology by giving them experience in researching and reviewing scientific papers, learning the format for scientific review papers, learning scientific citation conventions, and becoming familiar with a complex scientific topic that students may not have studied otherwise. However, one response—"pass molecular and graduate"—revealed that some students can go through the entire writing process and never understand the preparatory implications of the WAC biology requirement.

When questioned on the importance of writing, most students concurred that writing is a necessary communication tool used to express thoughts, opinions, experiences, and knowledge. Several students also agreed that writing is a powerful skill for all disciplines that gives authority to the writer's ideas and is crucial in many careers. The question of what the WAC biology requirement at La Salle taught students about writing in their discipline brought a variety of answers. One student learned the necessity of the revision process, while several other students learned that academic writing in the biological field must be short and concise, yet still complete. Many students learned the scientific citation convention, and one student noted the difference between a review and a research paper. Students also learned the importance of finding credible sources and being able to comprehend the material in the resources in order to write about this information effectively. Biology majors also noted that the format and style of this paper was somewhat different from their English research papers, but they were still able to make use of English skills such as word choice and sentence structure to make their arguments clearer and stronger. Some students noted that lab reports are more helpful in preparing students for their future careers than this particular assignment, because biological research papers and review papers are generally much shorter than the WAC assignment. One student found the short and concise nature of scientific writing to be a flaw, stating, "The problem is that general understanding is often sacrificed for this brevity. Contrary to other fields, scientific writers assume their audience can interpret data on their own. Failing to thoroughly explain their research, however, scientists widen the gap between the scientific and nonscientific communities." Another student less eloquently criticized the assignment, complaining, "Academic writing in Biology is very boring and has no leeway for emotion or style—and—I'll never use it again."

PROFESSOR QUESTIONNAIRE RESPONSES

The questionnaires distributed to the professors in the biology department consisted of ten open-ended questions. The professors responded to these questions in written form or verbally via an interview. When the professors were asked if writing is an important skill for biologists, the response was a unanimous "Absolutely!" or "Yes!" Stefan Samulewicz affirmed that writing is "the best way to reach the widest audience with their [biologists'] ideas, research, results, and arguments." Also, as Norbert Belzer noted, "if one cannot convey his or her work in writing, regardless of the field, the work becomes useless because no one else can benefit from it."

Next, the questionnaire asked the professors what types of writing are typical in biological fields of study. To this question, the professors provided a variety of responses, including primary research articles (typically three to five pages in length); textbooks; review books; articles for nonscience journals, magazines, or newspapers; review articles; grant applications; and laboratory notebooks.

The final question in the first segment of the questionnaire asked professors to describe which of these types of writing the current WAC requirement most resembles. To this each professor had similar yet slightly different responses. O'Connor believed: "It most resembles a chapter in a text or a review article for a science journal." Belzer found it to be most like a research article except that the paper requires students to review primary research articles and synthesize them into a longer review instead of conducting and writing about their own research. Similarly, Samulewicz found the WAC biology requirement to fall between the extremes of a primary research article and an article designed for a lay audience, because while "it should be written in the language of experts," the paper is composed of a review of primary research, not the research itself—similar to a newspaper or magazine article.

All four professors agreed that the goals of the biology WAC requirement are to learn to read scientific material, put this information into one's own words while still maintaining a scientific voice, learn proper documentation for scientific papers, and allow students to explore a topic that may not be covered in the typical classroom setting. As mentors for this program, all four professors believe that the students they advise, for the most part, typically meet these goals. O'Connor stated, "students take their assignment seriously and put forth the effort to do a good job. The procedure that is in place gives students the opportunity to be successful." Belzer agreed, because the first drafts, though complete, often have many errors in grammar, spelling, syntax, style, and other writing skills. Once students correct these errors, Belzer believes the scientific content of the papers is generally very successful at meeting the goals of the requirement. Gerald Ballough concurred, stating, "the only deficit is the students are not required to describe the empirical methodologies at the same level that is necessary.

The next question asked professors to describe their expectations of biology students' writing skills. O'Connor, Belzer, and Ballough expect biology students to be "competent writers," have "the same skills as [students in] any other major," and show "a willingness to improve," respectively. Samulewicz emphasized, "I expect the papers to be an effective synthesis of multiple aspects of a topic, taking into account different points of view and different lines of research. I expect the sentence structure to be complex, similar to the articles the students are referencing." When the professors were asked if students usually meet these expectations, they agreed that most often they do. If not in the first draft, then certainly by the final draft the students are able to meet these expectations and often exceed them.

Next, the professors were asked if the WAC biology requirement is useful to the future careers of students. All four professors agreed that this is a very useful assignment. O'Connor stated, "There is almost no way they [biology majors] will go through life without using writing skills developed here [La Salle University]." Samulewicz also noted "the value of the reading that goes into this paper." On this topic he wrote, "It's the most concentrated scientific reading assignment they [biology students] have in college, so they learn to read as well as write." Most of the professors did not find anything about the WAC biology requirement ineffective when questioned about this. However, Samulewicz mentioned, "Sometimes the topics chosen are not supported by a great deal of literature. This makes it frustrating for the students, but it's still a good learning experience of how science works."

Finally, the professors were asked if they had any suggestions for improving the WAC requirement in the biology major. O'Connor suggested shortening the length of the paper to allow the faculty mentors to dedicate more time to reviewing the first drafts of their students. Similarly, Belzer wished the semester were longer, so there would be more time for the writing process. Samulewicz thought the deadlines should be earlier, "so there's more time for revision. A real scientific report goes through numerous revisions—this should as well." Ballough added, While the molecular paper is a very good exercise, I think it is more similar to a review paper or a scientific term paper and does not require the absolute highest level of a student's critical thinking. Perhaps if a laboratory report were to be presented as a scientific research paper, students would have a better opportunity to precisely describe methodologies and, more importantly, write a research discussion that requires their highest ability for conjecture.

CONSENSUS OF RESULTS

Overall, this study determined that, for the majority of biology students, the WAC requirement effectively reaches the goals of the WAC program. Students learn how to write a paper that reflects a range of typical biological writings, they learn the proper documentation style of scientific papers, and they learn to write in the style of a scientist, in a short, concise manner such as will be expected of these students in their professional careers. It is interesting that all professors interviewed and the majority of students surveyed agreed on this point. Another interesting point that several students and professors made is that this assignment is not in the format of a primary research article, a type of writing that, the consensus seems to be, students will be involved with in their future careers. This suggests that even though the writing assignment is effective, there are certainly aspects that can be improved.

SUGGESTIONS FOR IMPROVEMENT

Although the investigators expected that professors would have a clear understanding of the importance of writing in the biological fields, it was surprising to find that a significant majority of the students surveyed effectively understood the implications and relevance this writing assignment holds for their future careers. Despite the overwhelming consensus among the biology mentors and students concerning the effectiveness of the research assignment, several faculty members and students hinted at some minor problems and various ways to improve the guidelines of this process. O'Connor suggested shortening the length of the paper so faculty members can revise and return drafts in a timely manner. Belzer recognized the stressful time constraints as well, wishing for a longer semester. Similarly, Samulewicz recommended setting earlier and more frequent deadlines so students experience the arduous process of writing, submitting, revising, and resubmitting more comprehensively—and in a process more similar to what they will encounter in their future careers.

All of these suggestions deal, essentially, with the time constraints of such a large project. In addition to all their other coursework, students must find time to sift through a significant number of primary resources to choose thirty that are most relevant to their topic of choice. Biology majors must then perform a close reading of all thirty primary resources to develop an understanding of the complex material. Students then take notes translating the complicated language of the scientific articles into their own words, and finally, they must formulate their notes into a coherent twenty- to twenty-five-page synthesis. Once mentors return the rough drafts, students are back to work with revisions to complete the final draft before the deadline.

In addition to time constraints, a number of students observed that this paper is only a review of scientific material and, therefore, does not teach students how to write a true scientific research paper. One student also noticed the contradictory nature of the paper's style, explaining that scientific research papers are typically "much shorter and require concise explanations" of laboratory research, whereas review articles tend to be "targeted more for the lay audience" in magazines and newspapers. However, this paper is a "long review of scientific studies" requiring scientific, rather than common, language. Another student explained the paper "did not teach me too much about writing in my field." This student thought, "writing for labs . . . is more helpful." Ballough recognized this flaw in the writing assignment as well, acknowledging, "laboratory reports might be more effective" for teaching students "to describe empirical methodologies." Along these lines, Ballough discussed the possibility of having students treat a traditional lab experiment as their own research, reporting the information in a short article as if it were to be submitted to a scientific journal. This would emphasize the significance of empirical data and require "the absolute highest level of a student's critical thinking" and "ability for conjecture."

While all four professors mentioned writing about science for the general public as one of the many genres of scientific writing, students and professors alike failed to recognize the lack of this experience in the current biology WAC requirement at La Salle University. Since the change in curriculum in the 1994–95 academic year, biochemistry was converted to a one-semester course, and molecular biology was added to the curriculum. The shorter popular science article was removed from the assignment and the remaining review essay was incorporated into the new course. Belzer explained that the biology department chose to eliminate the "common assignment" because the goal of the WAC program is to help students write in their own field. The faculty felt the longer review paper was more representative of a biologist's writing than the shorter popular science essay. While this may be true for students going into research or industry, a student interested in writing for a science column in a newspaper or for a popular science magazine would benefit more from the shorter essay. Even though the current review essay appears to be effective from the results of this study, it fails to represent other genres of biological writing.

Since the current WAC assignment is incorporated into a one-semester course, it would be difficult to add anything else to the assignment to address other areas of science writing, especially since students and professors both feel the pressure of the current timeline in its present form. To help relieve some of this pressure for professors and students, the investigators have three suggested options to offer La Salle's biology department. The first requires very little change in the course curriculum, but alters the assignment somewhat. The second spans the assignment over two semesters, similar to the previous requirement, but alters the assignment slightly. And the third involves the addition of a writing laboratory course to draw more attention and focus to the various aspects of writing in science.

To address the time constraints of the current assignment, one option for the biology department is to shorten the assignment from a twenty- to twenty-five-page essay referencing thirty sources to a ten- to twelve-page essay referencing fifteen sources. With a shorter essay, faculty members can develop a new timeline with earlier and more frequent deadlines, as Samulewicz suggested. Another, much shorter assignment could then be incorporated to address other areas of scientific writing. The best way to institute a second assignment is to provide several genre options, allowing students to choose the essay format that seems most representative of their personal career interests. For example, a student going into industry, research, or graduate school might be interested in treating a laboratory report as his or her own experimental investigation and writing a three-to five-page research paper modeled after those submitted to scientific journals. However, a student with goals to "interest and inform non-experts about important biological phenomena" may be more interested in writing a two- to four-page article for the general public (Samulewicz). A student struggling to understand primary research articles may be interested in using his or her second assignment to focus on closely examining such an article and writing a second, but much shorter review essay. La Salle biology faculty members can incorporate this second assignment in one of two ways: they can allow students to design their own assignment to meet their own needs (with approval and direction from their mentor), or the faculty members can work together to develop several shorter writing assignment options from which students can choose the most appealing.

If faculty members feel shortening the review essay is somehow detrimental to the effectiveness of the assignment, then another option entails spreading the assignment out over two semesters in the higher-level required courses of biochemistry and molecular biology. This will allow students an entire academic year to complete the longer paper, and a second essay can be reincorporated into the assignment. This format was shown to be effective in the previous descriptive study conducted by Soven and Franz, so the efficacy of the requirement will not be compromised. The timeline and deadlines can then be reorganized appropriately to give students time for multiple stages of revision for each writing piece. The second assignment, as described in the previous instance, can either be something students choose from a list designed by the faculty, or an assignment students design individually based on their career goals with guidance and approval from their mentors.

The final suggestion places a much larger emphasis on writing in the biological sciences than the others. The current curriculum for molecular biology includes an optional laboratory through the chemistry department. Since the laboratory can be taken at another time for those students interested, a writing laboratory can be instituted to place more emphasis on the importance of writing in the sciences. In this laboratory, either one consistent professor or rotated faculty members can teach students about different writing styles and genres each week. Professors can also assign readings such as primary research articles, newspaper articles, magazine articles, journal essays, reviews, excerpts from textbooks, and other forms of scientific writing for class discussion. In these discussions the professor and students can address various writing techniques and styles, discussing the similarities and differences present in these styles. Teachers can also create brief writing assignments to summarize, evaluate, analyze, criticize, replicate, or compare and contrast the styles studied. This course design would not only help students to improve their writing but also help them to develop their reading comprehension skills. Like the molecular biology science laboratory, this writing laboratory can also be optional—students can opt to take the science lab instead or neither lab. In this circumstance the existing curriculum, or one of the other two options suggested, would have to remain in place for students who do not choose to take this writing lab. Or the writing laboratory can be instituted as a requirement and some laboratory time can be dedicated to a peer revision process for the longer review paper, with either writing fellows or classmates. In this instance, students interested in taking the science lab would be instructed to take it at a later time. Another option would be to require an independent writing laboratory encompassing everything described above as well as the longer review paper, which could then be removed from the molecular biology curriculum altogether. Each of the three suggestions requires a different level of preparation to implement and may work best if changed gradually from one to another, studied for efficacy, and then altered accordingly to meet the needs of biology majors. However, the ultimate decision lies within the biology department. Faculty members must consult with one another and WAC specialist Soven to determine what changes, if any, are most feasible and beneficial for both the faculty and students.

LIMITATIONS OF THE STUDY

After analyzing the data, several limitations of this study became obvious. The most prominent limitation is the small sample of students and professors surveyed in order to conduct the study. La Salle is a teaching university, so class sizes are generally small to guarantee each student a personalized educational environment and to ensure that professors can dedicate enough of their time to helping and guiding students through their coursework. The biology department itself is also relatively small, consisting of only seven full-time faculty members who serve as mentors for this writing project. Although this feature is an asset for La Salle's students and faculty, it limits this study extensively. In order to create a large enough sample size to provide accurate results, this study would need to be conducted over a period of several years. Unfortunately, the researchers were limited to one semester of research, touching base with as many students who had previously experienced the biology writing requirement as possible in order to expand the study. While twenty students and four professors are not enough to provide a thorough and accurate analysis of the efficacy of this writing assignment, it certainly provides a glimpse into the perspectives of La Salle students and faculty and offers an introductory review of the value of the La Salle biology department's WAC requirement.

Additional insight could also have been offered to this study had demographics been surveyed. For example, it would be interesting to know the influence of future career expectations—medical school, graduate research, education, industry—on students' perspectives of the importance of writing in biology, as well as which types of writing are most applicable to their fields of interest. It would also be interesting to examine students' GPAs in biology and English courses to determine if students who struggle or those who excel academically in either or both subjects benefit equally from the biology writing assignment.

Furthermore, results from several survey questions indicate that additional research may be necessary to learn what constitutes writing for biology students. The responses to the survey statements "I write often for my biology classes" and "The senior biology paper was the first time I wrote an academic paper in my major" illustrate the various interpretations of writing among biology students. Moreover, faculty responses indicate that future research to expand this study might include inquiries into what types of writing biology professors find most important to teach at the undergraduate level, as well as how the role of writing varies in different types of biology courses: for instance, the role of writing in introductory-level courses in comparison with upper-level courses, or the role of writing in different specialties in biology, such as ecology versus physiology.

Ultimately, this study contributes to the discussion of writing-across-the-curriculum programs. It provides an introductory inquiry into a department's major writing requirement and opens the door to continued research in La Salle's biology department. It may also lead to the examination of WAC assignments in other departments at La Salle University and in other schools as well.

NOTE

1.   Writing fellows at La Salle University use the skills they learn in the course Writing and the University to review and edit student drafts for the class(es) to which they are assigned. Typically, writing fellows make written comments on the drafts and then meet with students to discuss ways to improve organization, grammar, spelling, and style for the final draft, which, after revision, is submitted to the professor by each student writer.

   We would like to thank Dr. Margot Soven for all of her direction and encouragement throughout the writing process, as well as all of the biology professors and students who contributed to our study.

WORKS CITED

Beason, Larry, and Laurel Darrow. 1997. "Listening as Assessment: How Students and Teachers Evaluate WAC." In *Assessing Writing across the Curriculum: Diverse Approaches and Practices*, edited by Brian Huot and Kathleen Blake Yancey, 97–121. Greenwich, CT: Ablex.

Dowling, H. Fil, Jr., Linda Lawrence Hunt, Joan D. McMahon, and Barbara E. Walvoord. 1997. *In the Long Run: A Study of Faculty in Three Writing-across-the-Curriculum Programs*. Urbana, IL: National Council of Teachers of English.

Faigley, Lester, and Stephen P. Witte. 1983. *Evaluating College Writing Programs*. Carbondale: Southern Illinois University Press.

Franz, Craig, and Margot Soven. 1996. "Writing in Biology: The Senior Project." *JCST* (November): 111–14.

Freisinger, Randall. 1982. "Cross-Disciplinary Writing Programs: Beginnings." In *Language Connections: Writing and Reading across the Curriculum*, edited by Toby Fulwiler and Art Young, 3–13. Urbana, IL: National Council of Teachers of English.

Geller, Anne Ellen. 2005. "'What's Cool Here?' Collaboratively Learning Genre in Biology." In *Genre across the Curriculum*, edited by Anne Herrington and Charles Moran, 83–108. Logan: Utah State University Press.

Harrington, Susan L., and William L. Rivers. 1988. *Finding Facts: Research Writing across the Curriculum*. Englewood Cliffs, NJ: Prentice Hall.

Lutzker, Marilyn. 1988. *Research Projects for College Students: What to Write across the Curriculum*. New York: Greenwood.

Martin, Kathryn. 1989. "Writing 'Microthemes' to Learn Human Biology." In *Writing to Learn Mathematics and Science*, edited by Paul Connolly and Teresa Villardi, 113–21. New York: Teachers College Press.

Nagin, Carl. 2003. *Because Writing Matters: Improving Student Writing in Our Schools*. San Francisco: Jossey-Bass.

Russell, David R. 2002. *Writing in the Academic Disciplines: A Curricular History*. Carbondale: Southern Illinois University Press.

Rymer, Joan. 1998. "Scientific Composing Process: How Eminent Scientists Write Journal Articles." In *Writing in Academic Disciplines*, edited by David A. Jolliffe, 211–50. Vol. 2 of *Advances in Writing Research*. Norwood, CT: Ablex.

Tobias, Sheila. 1989. "Writing to Learn in Science and Mathematics." In *Writing to Learn Mathematics and Science*, edited by Paul Connolly and Teresa Villardi. New York: Teachers College Press.

APPENDIX A—STUDENT SURVEY

S = Spring semester, 2005; F = Fall semester, 2005

- Describe the purpose of your senior biology paper.
- How is writing important to you?
- What did the senior biology paper teach you about academic writing in your field?

TALLY RESULTS OF STUDENT SURVEY

Responses tallied are in the format of: Total (Spring 2005, Fall 2005)

Writing is an important skill only in English/literature courses.

16 (11, 5)	strongly disagree
3 (2, 1)	somewhat disagree
0	neither agree nor disagree
1 (0, 1)	somewhat agree
0	strongly agree

Writing is a necessary skill for my discipline/major course of study.

0	strongly disagree
1 (0, 1)	somewhat disagree
0	neither agree nor disagree
7 (3, 4)	somewhat agree
12 (10, 2)	strongly agree

I write often for my biology classes.

3 (1, 2)	strongly disagree
1 (1, 0)	somewhat disagree
5 (3, 2)	neither agree nor disagree
6 (5, 1)	somewhat agree
5 (3, 2)	strongly agree

The senior biology paper was a helpful experience.

0	strongly disagree
3 (2, 1)	somewhat disagree
4 (1, 3)	neither agree nor disagree
8 (6, 2)	somewhat agree
5 (4, 1)	strongly agree

All I need to know about writing I learned from my freshman English class.

12 (8, 4)	strongly disagree
5 (4, 1)	somewhat disagree
0	neither agree nor disagree
2 (1, 1)	somewhat agree
1 (0, 1)	strongly agree

In my freshman composition course, I learned skills that helped me write in other courses.

1 (1, 0)	strongly disagree
3 (2, 1)	somewhat disagree
5 (4, 1)	neither agree nor disagree
7 (4, 3)	somewhat agree
4 (2, 2)	strongly agree

I find it difficult to write in classes other than my major.

9 (5, 4)	strongly disagree
5 (3, 2)	somewhat disagree
3 (2, 1)	neither agree nor disagree
1 (1, 0)	somewhat agree
2 (2, 0)	strongly agree

The senior biology paper was the first time I wrote an academic paper in my major.

4 (3, 1)	strongly disagree
4 (3, 1)	somewhat disagree
1 (0, 1)	neither agree nor disagree
5 (3, 2)	somewhat agree
6 (4, 2)	strongly agree

The senior biology paper taught me a lot about writing in my discipline.

1 (0, 1)	strongly disagree
3 (2, 1)	somewhat disagree
4 (3, 1)	neither agree nor disagree
8 (6, 2)	somewhat agree
4 (2, 2)	strongly agree

APPENDIX B—MENTOR INTERVIEW/
QUESTIONNAIRE

1. Is writing an important skill for biologists?
2. What types of writing are typical in the biological fields?
3. Is the biology WAC requirement reflective of any of these types of writing?
4. What are the goals of the biology WAC requirement?
5. As a mentor for the program, do you feel these goals are reached, for the most part? Why or why not?
6. What are your expectations concerning the writing skills of biology students?
7. Do students meet your expectations in writing these papers?
8. Do you think this particular requirement is useful to students for their future careers?
9. Is there anything about the WAC requirement in biology that you do not like, or find ineffective?
10. Do you have any suggestions for improving the WAC requirement for biology majors?

Student Activity

READING, ANALYSIS, AND REFLECTION

1. What methods did the authors use to determine the efficacy of the WAC requirement in biology?
2. Are there additional methods you would recommend to the researchers?
3. The researchers felt it necessary to review literature in several different areas. What were they, and why was each important?
4. What surprises did the researchers find in conducting their study? What assumptions did they hold that led to these unexpected results?
5. An improving-practice approach usually results in advice for improvement. What did these researchers recommend?
6. The researchers end with a limitations-of-the-study section. Why is this important? What does it communicate about the researchers and the project?
7. This study was conducted at one institution of higher education. Are its findings applicable to a wider audience? If yes, how so?

IMPROVING PRODUCTS: USABILITY STUDIES

We have been focusing primarily on writing as it relates to school and academe. Writing studies is a large field and includes subareas such as technical and professional writing. For students entering the workforce as experts in this field, it's important to understand usability studies and their methods. Usability refers to a focus on the *user.* How will users approach and evaluate products? Will users find a website or an app easy to use or frustrating? All of us have experienced such technological aids that are not user friendly. Will the user like it? Find it attractive? Enjoy it? Get pleasure from using it? In the case-study chapter, Natalie's work on reconceiving a design for a fair-trade gift shop was profiled. Her goal was to ensure that the end users found information on the website of value. Placing users in positions of priority can also help with the overall goals of a business.

Research may be applied to all stages of the design process, including what the product is to look like from the start. Surveys solicit information that may be used in the design. Brainstorming sessions also provide useful advice. For some products, end users may even participate in the design process, drawing images and imagining layouts. Charrettes are designs generated by stakeholders—from as many groups as affected as possible—over an intensive planning period. Another approach is to put information—such as that to be used on a website—on a variety of cards and then ask users to sort the cards. The researcher notes the layout and can use this information in design.

To begin a usability study, there must be a design to be tested. It may be revised as feedback is received. Usability studies employ mixed-method strategies to the maximum and to good effect. Users not only test-drive the product—technological tools, equipment—but also provide evaluation in a number of other ways. Interviews may focus on a single individual, or focus groups can provide information as the participants build on each other's comments. The classic concept of heuristics, asking probing questions to understand all aspects of the product, provides a global analysis of usability.

Evaluation of the usability of a product may take place in a lab setting or on-site. Ethnography comes into play in usability studies in which the researcher watches users in their natural environment interacting with the product. It's important to date and time such observations. A less intrusive method uses cameras to record user interaction. And the researcher may also photograph settings.

Accessibility involves social and ethical issues. People with disabilities are important users of products, and their needs should be incorporated into any research on usability. Are there roadblocks on websites that makes access more difficult for someone who is blind? Can the technology be used by someone who is unable to physically move? What assistive technology must be taken into account?

As with any research involving human participants, responsible conduct of research through approved channels is required. Consent forms indicating any risks—even if minimal—are required, and these forms should clearly state the purpose of the research and how the results will be used.

To undertake a usability study, the researcher must first submit a proposal explaining the design and goals of the study. An outline of the proposal might look like this:

- product description
- audience (users) description
- areas of concern to evaluate (e.g., functionality)
- context of use defined
- methods of research to be used (e.g., how information will be gathered)
- scripts to be used by the researcher
- goals, motivations, and fears of the user
- background sources relevant in a review of literature

The users evaluating the product fill out a user profile, including demographic information (e.g., age, gender, education, socioeconomic status, first language, and geographical location). They also note their familiarity or experience with the product or technology. To avoid conflict of interest, they also disclose any relationship with the product's organization or company.

The final report begins with an executive summary—a type of abstract—that efficiently reveals the purpose of the study, its key findings, and recommendations. A table of contents lays out the parts of the report for easy reference:

- Introduction
  - Research problem defined
  - Participant profile and how participants were recruited
- The study
  - Tasks, procedures, and results
- Summary of recommendations
- Evaluation and reflection on the efficacy of the study
- Appendices
  - A copy of the proposal (revised as needed)
  - Documents used in the study
    - Prestudy questionnaires, surveys, interviews
    - Script for administering the study
    - Data collection forms
    - Consent forms

Illustrate the final report with pictures and graphs to illustrate the project. These may include photographs of the setting or even of the participants' doodles and notes. Do use quantitative data, but never forget the power of narrative to communicate messages. Imagine the user who says "I was afraid to try that maneuver with the equipment" or "I didn't realize there was more information at the bottom of the screen and that I needed to scroll down." After all, stories are what we remember.

Student Activity

RESEARCH: INTERROGATING PRODUCTS

Find a product (e.g., some kind of equipment, technology) with which you are unfamiliar. Set up a usability protocol you will use to test the user experience, drawing on a profile of yourself as a user, setting up a series of tasks to undertake, and recording your reactions. How difficult or easy is the product to understand and use? While this is a brief entry into usability study, it will give you an idea of how a product is interrogated.

IMPROVING COMMUNITIES: COMMUNITY-BASED RESEARCH

Community-based research (CBR) is the union of research and service learning. Such research is beneficial to the community and also includes participation by members of the community, making the project collaborative. In keeping with principles of service learning, a nonhierarchal approach is used in which all participants are equal. A reflective piece by the researcher at the conclusion of the project is also required.

CBR may also draw on a philosophy of *social justice*, the view that everyone deserves equal economic, political, and social rights and opportunities. The following are characteristics of community-based research:

- The relevance of the research topic is identified or verified by community members.
- The resources of research are shared with community members, particularly those most affected by the research topic.
- The research process recognizes and utilizes the expertise community members have.
- The research process recognizes and addresses power imbalances between researchers and community members.

- The research process is driven by values, including empowerment, supportive relationships, social change, learning as an ongoing process, and respect for diversity.
- The research process and results are accessible and understandable to community members.
- The research process and results consider and adapt to the context in which the research is conducted.
- The research leaves a legacy, in terms of both the utilization of research results and future collaboration among partners. (Source: Centre for Community-Based Research in Waterloo, Ontario, http://www.communitybasedresearch.ca/Page/View /CBR_definition)

Cooke and Thorme's (2011) *A Practical Handbook for Supporting Community-Based Research with Undergraduate Students* addresses the benefits and challenges in undertaking change-oriented community-based projects. Issues include developing and maintaining partnerships, developing research questions, collecting and analyzing data, and reporting findings. Laurie Grobman (2015), a leader in CBR, addresses ethical challenges in working with community participants, particularly in ensuring that their voices are heard and acted upon. Her students have developed book-length projects that fulfill a hallmark of CBR, leaving a legacy for the community: *History of the Jewish Community in Reading and Berks County; Woven with Words: A Collection of African American History in Berks County, Pennsylvania;* and *The Future's Past: Life Histories of 17 African American Residents of Berks County, PA.*

REFERENCES

Cooke, Deanna, and Trisha Thorme. 2011. *A Practical Handbook for Supporting Community-Based Research with Undergraduate Students.* Washington, DC: Council on Undergraduate Research.

Grobman, Laurie. 2015. "(Re)Writing Local Racial, Ethnic, and Cultural Histories: Negotiating Shared Meaning in Public Rhetoric Partnerships." *College English* 77 (3): 236–58.

Appendix

CWPA GUIDELINES FOR SELF-STUDY
Guidelines for Self-Study to Precede CWPA Visit

This document is published by the Council of Writing Program Administrators and is available open-access at the following website: http://wpacouncil.org/consultant.

The purposes of this self-study are, through the process of writing it, to help you understand more clearly the reasons for the visit and to acquaint the consultants with your institution.

Ideally, this self-study will be prepared by a team, including the writing program administrator at your institution and others who are directly involved in your writing program—and not by one individual.

The self-study should be largely a narrative report that focuses on the main concerns you have about your writing program. The questions below are intended to help you think of all the possible facets of your program you might want to describe in your self-study. You need not answer all these questions, and they are not intended as an outline for your report. You might also find that related issues (current uses of technology, for instance) are implied if not directly asked; please discuss your program and its related institutional contexts as directly and specifically as possible.

The final self-study should be about 10 pages in length, not including any supporting documents.

I. GENERAL BACKGROUND

A. Focus of the Visit

1. What are the program's current concerns?
2. What changes in the program are being contemplated?
3. What issues would you like the consultant-evaluators to address?

B. Current Institutional Conditions

1. What specific institutional changes are affecting your writing program?
2. What specific characteristics of your student body affect your program?

C. Missions

1. What is the mission of your institution?
2. What is the mission of your writing program?
3. How does the mission of your program support the mission of your institution?

D. Philosophy and Goals

1. What are the principles or philosophy of the writing program(s) at your institution?
2. What are the goals of your program?
3. How do these goals reflect the program's philosophy?
4. How do your program's practices enact the philosophy and goals?

II. CURRICULUM

A. Philosophy and Goals

1. What are the philosophy and goals of the writing program(s) at your institution?
2. Do the goals of the writing program(s) accord with the goals of the institution as a whole?
3. How are the philosophy and goals communicated to the teachers, the students, and the appropriate administrators?

B. Courses and Syllabi

1. What writing courses are currently taught in your institution? By what departments are they taught?
2. How are these courses sequenced or otherwise related? Which courses are required, and of whom are they required?
3. If your institution identifies some students as "basic writers," how are their needs addressed?

4. Are the syllabi for the courses uniform or different for each teacher? (Or do some teachers follow a uniform syllabus, while other teachers follow their individual syllabi?) If the syllabus is uniform within each course or for several sections within each course, who is responsible for developing it?

5. If the syllabus is uniform within each course, what opportunities do individual teachers have for experimentation with the syllabus? If the syllabi are individual, what ties or links make the course cohere across the sections?

6. What is the logical basis for the sequence of assignments within each course? How does that sequence relate to the goals and philosophy of the program?

7. How much writing, and what kinds of writing, must students do for each course?

8. What kinds of reading are assigned in the writing courses? What instruction is given to students in the reading of these texts? In the reading of their own drafts?

C. Instructional Methods and Materials

1. What events or activities typically take place in the classrooms of the program's writing courses?

2. What textbooks are used in each writing course? Why is the program using these textbooks? What instructional materials other than textbooks does the program use? How do these textbooks and other materials fit the goals and structure of the course(s)? Who chooses the textbooks and other instructional materials used in the courses?

3. How much time do teachers devote to individual conferences?

D. Responses to and Evaluation of Student Writing

1. At what point(s) in their composing do students receive responses to their writing? What kinds of responses do they receive? At what points during the course(s) do students receive evaluation of their progress?

2. What procedures do faculty use in evaluating students' writing (e.g., letter grades on each paper, letter grades on some papers only, no grades until the end of the course)? On what bases (standards) do faculty evaluate papers?

3. What processes are used to assure consistency across sections in evaluation of students' writing? How does the program assure that the bases for evaluation cohere with the goals of the program?

4. How does the evaluation of students' work reflect their achievement of the stated goals of the course?

E. Assessment

1. What tests and testing procedures are used in the writing program for such purposes as placement, exemption, determination of readiness to exit from a course or from the program, determination of eligibility to enter a more advanced program? What procedures are used to correct errors in placement? How do these procedures relate to the goals of the program?

2. Under what conditions are the assessment procedures conducted? Who conducts them? Who interprets and uses the results? What training do those who conduct the assessment have? If tests are scored by humans (i.e., not machines), what training do the scorers have?

3. What methods are used for continued monitoring of the assessment instruments to assure their current reliability and validity for the students and the purposes they are to serve? How frequently is the monitoring conducted?

III. FACULTY

A. Status and Working Conditions

1. What percentage of full-time faculty at each rank, adjunct faculty, and graduate students teach writing? How many writing courses do faculty at each rank or status teach? What percentage of the writing courses are taught by faculty at each rank or status?

2. What are the qualifications for writing faculty, and how are they established? What training and experience in teaching writing do the writing faculty have? What professional organizations do they belong to? What is their record of research, publication, conference participation, and professional activity in composition and rhetoric?

3. What are the salary ranges by rank and category? How do these salary ranges compare to comparable departments? To neighboring, comparable institutions?

4. How are teaching, administration, and research in composition rewarded in terms of salary, promotion, and tenure?

5. How are adjunct faculty appointed? By whom? When in relation to the opening of a term? How are they evaluated? What is the length of their appointment? How are they reappointed? What percentage have multiple-year contracts? How are the adjunct faculty compensated in terms of salary and benefits? Are there step raises or cost of living increases for adjunct faculty? Are adjunct faculty compensated for preparation if a course does not fill or is covered by a full-time faculty mem-

ber? Is there a departmental policy on percentage of part-time faculty? Do adjunct faculty attend department meetings and writing program meetings? Serve on departmental or writing program committees? What opportunities exist for adjunct faculty to develop curriculum, choose textbooks, formulate policy and procedures? What arrangements are made for office space, telephones, mailboxes, and clerical support for adjunct faculty?

B. Faculty Development

1. How is faculty development defined as a goal of the institution, the department or administrative unit, and the writing program? What are ongoing plans for faculty development in teaching writing?

2. What courses, speaker programs, workshops, teaching awards, etc., does the writing program offer or support to encourage excellence in teaching writing?

3. What opportunities for faculty development in teaching writing already exist? Who uses them? How do faculty find out about them? In what ways are faculty encouraged to avail themselves of these opportunities?

4. Are these opportunities available to adjunct faculty and teaching assistants?

5. Are issues of race and gender addressed in faculty development?

6. What financial resources are available for travel to workshops, conferences, and institutes related to teaching writing?

7. What avenues exist for writing faculty at each rank and status to design, implement, and evaluate faculty development programs best suited to their needs and interests? How are faculty encouraged to develop their skills in composition research and teaching writing? What opportunities exist for learning about faculty development programs in writing at other institutions?

8. Does the department or institution support faculty development by offering paid leaves or sabbaticals for further education in composition studies and rhetoric, by publishing journals, by developing software or other media for use in teaching writing?

9. What support does the department or institution give for development of institutional and individual grants to improve writing instruction and curricula and for released time, overhead, and other support to carry out the grant?

IV. PROGRAM ADMINISTRATION

A. Institutional and Program Structure

1. What writing programs are there on campus (e.g., first-year composition, writing across the curriculum, technical writing)?

2. What is the size and make-up of each of the departments or administrative units in which these programs are housed? What is the governing structure of each? How are these related administratively?

3. What are the internal governing structures of the writing programs? Are there writing program administrators (e.g., director of first-year composition, composition committee chair, director of the writing center)? If so, what are the WPAs' administrative relations to other levels of administration? To whom are the WPAs responsible?

4. If there are night school, continuing education, or non-degree programs, who determines how writing is taught in those programs? How is control exercised? Who is responsible for the teaching of writing in other departments or colleges within the institution?

5. How are the teaching and tutoring of writing funded? Who controls these funds? On what are these funds spent? How does the funding of the writing programs compare to the funding of other programs on campus?

6. Are institutional grant funds available for program development (e.g., curriculum development and assessment)? If so, have WPAs applied for and been awarded any of these grants?

7. Who hires, promotes, and tenures the writing faculty throughout the institution? Who determines their salaries and assigns courses to them?

8. How are new teaching positions determined and by whom?

9. Who determines such things as class size, curriculum, and teaching load in the various programs?

10. How are internal problems solved? Who decides on syllabi, testing procedures, textbooks, etc.? What procedures are in place for full-time faculty, adjunct faculty, teaching assistants, and students to shape policies?

11. What permanent or ad hoc committees related to writing programs exist? How are these committees appointed? Who serves on them (e.g., full-time faculty, adjuncts, students)? What do these committees do?

12. What are the procedures for negotiating student and faculty complaints about grading, teaching, harassment, learning atmosphere, and administrative processes and policies?

13. What administrative, clerical, and technical support is there?

14. How are the writing programs' histories documented (e.g., annual reports, status reports on progress toward multi-year development plans)? Who writes these histories and who reads them? How are they used?

B. Writing Program Administrators

1. How are the WPAs chosen and what are the lengths of their appointments?

2. What are the terms and conditions of appointments of the WPAs? Are these terms in writing?

3. What are the academic and professional qualifications of the WPAs? What are the WPAs' ranks and tenure statuses? Who decides the WPAs' tenures, promotions, and salaries?

4. What are the WPAs' teaching loads and how do they compare with other faculties' loads?

5. How much and what type of research are WPAs expected to do? To what extent are the WPAs' efforts in program development and institutional research considered scholarship?

6. How and by whom are WPAs evaluated? How are WPAs rewarded?

V. RELATED WRITING PROGRAMS AND INSTRUCTIONAL UNITS

In many institutions the English Department's composition program is not the only place where writing instruction takes place. Other sites charged with teaching writing may include many of the following: technology/IT centers, writing centers, reading centers, learning centers, testing centers, disabled student centers, Writing-Across-the-Curriculum Programs, ESL and bilingual programs, tutoring services, correspondence and extension courses, telecommunications and long-distance learning courses and programs, high school bridge programs, writing proficiency programs and exams, and discipline-based writing programs in colleges of education, business, nursing, law, the arts, and engineering.

Please address the relationships with the programs that are most pertinent to this visit. (Also include relationships that may become significant in the immediate or long-term.) Briefly tell how you perceive the relationships between your program and the other academic units charged with writing instruction.

A. Administration

1. To what extent do services offered by the writing program and other units overlap? Do their common goals and procedures reinforce each other or conflict? In what formal and informal ways (through scheduling, a coordinating committee, etc.) is each unit related to the writing program?
2. How is each unit funded?
3. How does each unit follow up on students who have used its services?
4. How is credit determined for work in these units?
5. What arrangements exist for the evaluation of each unit?

B. Curriculum

1. How many students and faculty are associated with each unit?
2. What is the profile of the students?
3. How are students placed in or referred to each unit?
4. What kinds of materials (books, computers, television) and techniques (tutoring, workshops) does the unit use?
5. How do students learn about the unit?

C. Personnel

1. What are the job descriptions for the director and teaching staff of each unit? How are the director and staff selected?
2. What is the institutional status (faculty, full-time, part-time, graduate student, etc.) of unit personnel? How are they compensated for their work? How is their work evaluated?
3. What provisions exist for training and professional development of unit staff?

   Include the following in an appendix to the narrative report:
   - Statistical information for the previous and current academic year: enrollments, class sizes, makeup of the teaching staff, final grade distribution.
   - A description of each course within the program(s) to be evaluated (objectives, syllabuses, texts, placement and exemption procedures, grading criteria).
   - Copies of evaluative instruments.
   - Materials pertaining to teacher training (both faculty and graduate students or adjuncts), including orientation meeting agendas, workshop descriptions, and syllabuses for training courses.
   - School catalogues, department handbooks, and departmental student materials.

Glossary of Terms in Writing Studies

Abolitionist Movement. A term applied to a group of scholars who advocated removing composition classes from departments of English and integrating writing requirements across the curriculum and in the disciplines.

abstract. A summary of the research that provides the reader a sense of its methods, processes, and outcomes.

action research. Research undertaken by the practitioner in order to improve a situation. In the case of education, teachers engage in action research to improve teaching and learning.

annotated bibliography. A list of sources collected by the researcher that offers not only the bibliographic information but also summary of the sources.

APA. The American Psychological Association citation style, which is commonly used in writing research.

applied writing. Generally refers to real-world writing applications outside of academe.

archive. An assemblage of historical documents, records, and data, including personal narratives, letters, journals, and photographs, that has been gathered into an organized collection. Artifacts, including books from various historical periods, are housed in an archive to be preserved and stored. Archives may be housed with a unit called Special Collections. Most libraries include an archive section.

audience. A concept used by mature writers to help in the invention process through the choice of format. An audience may be real or imagined, or it may be an audience of one: the self.

authorship. The person or people who get credit for the research. Generally, the person who conceives the project and does most of the work is deemed *first author*. Determination of authorship is one of the standards in responsible conduct of research.

autoethnography. The researcher's exploration of personal experience through self-reflection and writing. In order to be significant, this autobiographical story is examined for its relationship to wider cultural, political, and social meanings.

blind review. Evaluation through a peer-review process in which identifying information about the authors is removed from a submission for publication before it is evaluated.

budget. The financial costs of a research project. These should be defined before undertaking a project. Grant programs for student research exist on many campuses.

case study. A social scientific research tradition that looks at a small group; its findings often lead to recommendations in practice or policy.

CCC and CCCC. College Composition and Communication, a professional organization within the National Council of Teachers of English (NCTE) whose members include those engaged in composition, rhetoric, and writing teaching and study at the college level. An annual conference—CCCC—convenes each spring. The organization issues policy and practice statements, such as the Ethical Conduct of Research in Composition Studies.

citation chaining. A pre-Internet search strategy in which a list of references in a source is mined for further reading.

CITI. The Collaborative Institutional Training Initiative, which provides training modules for certification in human-subjects research.

common rule. A federal policy regarding human subjects protection. The main elements of the Common Rule include (1) requirements for assuring compliance by research institutions; (2) requirements for researchers' obtaining and documenting informed consent; and (3) requirements for Institutional Review Board (IRB) membership, function, operations, review of research, and record keeping.

community-based research (CBR). The intersection of research and service learning in which participants from the research side as well as members of the community collaborate to improve a situation or process. CBR requires problem definition and negotiation by those involved.

composition studies. The professional field of writing research and instruction with a specific focus on writing at the college level. Composition scholars study the theory and practice of postsecondary writing instruction, how different writing conventions and genres influence writers' composing processes, and how these conventions change over time. More recently, the term *writing studies* has supplanted composition studies.

CompPile. A database of scholarly work published in composition studies since World War II. A group of volunteers oversee additions to this database. URL: http://comppile.org/.

content analysis. Explanation of the meaning of texts.

critical discourse analysis. The study of writing and speaking that emphasizes their social implications, particularly issues of power. This approach is used by multiple disciplines to analyze political, social, and economic subjects.

data. Information collected, sorted, interpreted, and given meaning after a hypothesis is formed. This information is called *data*. *Datum* is the singular form of the word.

database. An organized collection of information. A database of interest may focus on education, poetry, or communication and media.

demographical information. Essential information about informants, such as age, gender, ethnicity, educational level, income, geographical location.

digital humanities. The intersection of computing and humanities in relationship to both teaching and research.

discourse community. A community that adheres to certain conventions for the presentation of its theories and research.

ELL. English-language learners, students for whom English is a second language (ESL).

elocution. The study or art of formal public speaking or oral delivery including pronunciation, grammar, style, and tone. In classical times, *elocutio* (style) focused on using rhetorical techniques such as figures of speech and was one of the five components of delivering speeches, an art called *pronunciation*. The four other canons of rhetoric include *inventio* (invention—developing the argument), *dispositio* (arrangement—organizing the argument), *memoria* (memory—delivering the argument without the use of notes), and *actio* (delivery—using hand gestures and voice control).

emic/etic. Two differing methods used in the reconstruction of cultural, anthropological, or group occurrences. The emic method builds a view based on an insider point of view while the etic method relies more heavily on observation by an outsider, most likely a researcher, to come to hypotheses about the occurrences.

empirical research. Research that uses studies and data from observation or experimentation. Scholarly research papers are often written from this type of research and include a hypothesis, tests, and results.

ERIC. A database started in 1954 that catalogs educational research and information in an Education Resources Information Center.

error. A mistake, quite simply. Error was a major concern in teaching writing prior to a shift from writing product to writing process. Error can even be a positive sign as writers take on more complex and challenging tasks.

ethnography. A qualitative approach to research that draws upon anthropological ties to the subject. Research is performed by observation, and observations are recorded and analyzed. Researchers may view the subject internally as an observing participant or externally as an observant onlooker. As it pertains to writing, ethnography may deal with writing as it influences and is influenced by societal surroundings.

exempt review. Research deemed exempt by virtue of not involving vulnerable populations (e.g., minors, the mentally disabled, pregnant women, prisoners), and not including audio- or videotaping, may be reviewed by the IRB chairperson and approved. Research that takes place in educational settings may be exempt. Researchers must check with their IRB for specific criteria.

expedited review. A review conducted when research is deemed to have minimal risk not warranting full review by the IRB. To qualify, the project must meet certain criteria, including minimal risk and not involving vulnerable populations such as children, pregnant women, or prisoners. Other criteria must be met as well.

generalizable knowledge. Information derived from research that can apply to other settings or situations.

genres. Generally types or kinds of texts with specific conventions: comedy, tragedy, film noir, ballad.

heuristics. A research inquiry with origins in ancient Greece that asks a set of questions that investigate and generate content. The questions asked help to fill a gap in the knowledge and create a clear path in doing research and gaining information.

human-subjects research. Research involving human beings. Participants in research projects are protected by federal law. Research involving people must be approved through an Institutional Review Board (IRB). The term *subjects* is not favored by many researchers, who prefer *participants* and may even invite participation in the project, particularly through response or reflection.

ideology. A set of ideas that makes up a person's goals and influences actions and behaviors.

IMRAD. An organizational structure for research reports, particularly popular in the sciences, that uses this format: introduction, methods, results, and discussion.

inadvertent disclosure. The accidental exposure of information—such as field notes, interview transcripts, medical records, or other classified documents corresponding to a research project—to a person who has not been given subject authorization to access these materials. Any such risk should be explained to a subject in the form of a consent document to be signed before research begins on a subject.

incubation. The process of thinking about a topic for writing before writing, a term put forward by Flower and Hayes in their cognitive research on writing processes.

informed consent. Permission from people to involve them in a research study. They must be informed of the amount of risk—even if it is minimal, the measures the researcher will take to maintain confidentiality, and how the results of the research will be used and disseminated.

intellectual history. A biography of influential scholars, researchers, or thought leaders and their ideas.

interrater reliability. The degree of agreement among the raters. A score is given that shows how much consensus there is in the ratings given by the judges. It is useful to determine whether a certain scale is appropriate for measuring a particular variable. This scale is usually used in statistics for different types of measurement. Interrater reliability is often used in holistic or primary-trait scoring of essays.

interviews. A tool to gather information from sources.

invention. A classical rhetorical term that describes the process of deciding what to write about. In contemporary parlance, this is referred to as *prewriting.*

IRB. A board that provides oversight to ensure that research is conducted ethically. The Institutional Review Board is comprised of institutional and community members, including medical and veterinary experts.

IWCA. The International Writing Centers Association, which started in 1983 as the National Writing Centers Association and is the professional organization for staff in writing centers. *The Writing Center Journal* and *WLN: A Journal of Writing Center Scholarship* are linked with IWCA.

Likert scale. Named after Rensis Likert and most commonly used with questionnaires. A scale that specifies a level of agreement or disagreement in order to capture the intensity of feelings for a given item. The distances between each item are assumed to be equal.

literacy. Historically, the ability to read and write but more recently embracing more areas such as digital literacy.

literature review or review of literature. The process of reading, analyzing, evaluating, and summarizing scholarly materials on a specific subject. It may be compiled in a report or be included in a research paper or article, thesis, or grant proposal. There should be clear links between the research and the literature review. *Literature review* refers to any collection of materials on various subjects. It discusses published information in a particular subject area.It does not refer to *literature* in the sense of fiction.

longitudinal study. A correlational research study that involves repeated observations of the same variables over long periods of time—often many decades. For a writing study, the time period might extend over an undergraduate's career of four years. Walvoord and McCarthy did a longitudinal study of writing across the curriculum in their *Talking and Writing in College.*

marginalization. A term used in many parts of the world to characterize contemporary forms of social disadvantage. Also called *social exclusion*, it refers to processes in which individuals or entire communities are blocked from rights, opportunities, and resources that are normally available and are key to social integration. It is associated with social class, educational status, disabilities, minorities, all sexual orientations and gender identities, the elderly, and the young.

mentor. A person who guides a novice in research practices, policies, and ethics.

methodology. A systematic philosophical or theoretical approach to research. A methodology employs methods for gathering information to be used in the research.

methods. Tools for gathering information such as interviews, surveys, and observations.

mixed-methods research. A procedure for collecting, analyzing, and mixing quantitative and qualitative research methods in a single study to understand a research problem.

MLA. A professional organization comprised of teachers and scholars in English and foreign languages that focuses primarily on a scholarly agenda and convenes annually for a convention. The Modern Language Association provides a documentation style for citation of sources used in literary research.

multimodal. The various modes that come together to produce meaning and that can include traditional text, digital words, images, sound, and design.

narrative inquiry. A qualitative research approach based on a researcher's narrative account of the investigation.

National Writing Project (NWP). An organization that grew out of a group of teachers and professors who met for what was called the *Bay Area Writing Project* in the 1970s. The NWP is a nationwide set of teachers who come together, generally by state or by region, and who share the philosophy that teachers are the best resources for each other.

NCTE. National Council of Teachers of English. The NCTE is a professional organization of teachers, kindergarten through college, who share a common interest in issues of teaching English.

NCUR. An annual meeting dedicated to student research attended by about three thousand participants. A small strand of the conference is devoted to FAN sessions, a faculty-administrative network. The National Conference on Undergraduate Research is part of the Council on Undergraduate Research (CUR), which has national offices in Washington, DC.

netnography. An Internet ethnography that focuses on computer-mediated environments (e.g., blogs, chat rooms, social media). Ethically, the researcher must disclose identity and purpose upon entering the group, gain consent from participants, ensure anonymity, elicit feedback on the project, and gain permission prior to publication.

observations. Accurate notes taken by the researcher on a situation or venue noting carefully time, date, behaviors, and other information that will inform the research.

oral history. Information about the history of a topic, place, person, and so forth that is gathered by researchers using interviews.

participant-observation. A research methodology whereby the researcher functions as a member of the group and records what is viewed.

pedagogical. A term that describes practice and theory having to do with education.

peer review. A process of self-regulation and evaluation by a profession involving qualified individuals within the relevant field. Peer-review methods are employed to maintain standards, improve performance, and provide credibility. In academia, peer review is often used to determine an academic manuscript's suitability for publication. Peer review is a standard in responsible conduct of research.

portfolio. In terms of writing, a compilation of writing tasks and products, generally coupled with reflections by the writer. The portfolio may be accumulated over a single term or a much longer period to measure growth in writing. It may be electronic or in print.

primary documents. Original documents that provide the most reliable and close source of historical information. Secondary documents are those written about primary documents.

private collection. A collection of works of writing owned by an individual rather than a university or library. Private collections may have a specific focus or contain works that are rare. Scholars can often appeal to the owner to gain access to the collection for research.

process. The primary writing pedagogy since the 1970s. It focuses on process—how one develops a product. Stages in the writing process include coming up with an idea (prewriting), drafting, getting feedback, revising, and editing. Although these appear to be linear stages, they may loop back on one another in a recursive way.

proposal. A document that delineates a plan for research. It is reviewed and refined before the project is started.

protocol analysis. A cognitive research strategy that asks participants to verbalize their thoughts while engaged in a process.

quadrivium. Arithmetic, geometry, astronomy, and music in classical studies.

qualitative research. A research tradition that focuses on the observation of *qualities* or aspects.

quantitative research. Research bolstered through the use of numbers, data, and quantities.

RAD criteria. Replicable, aggregable, and data supported. RAD refers to a standard to which research should be held. Replicable means the research should be capable of being repeated by another researcher using the original research. Aggregable means the research should be the sum total of all information gleaned from the research. Data supported means the data gathered from the research should support the research findings (or the researcher's conclusions). For more information, see "NCTE/CCCC's Recent War on Scholarship" by Richard H. Haswell (*Written Communication* 22.2 [April 2005]: 198–223).

recursive process. An indefinite loop that characterizes the writing process. Writers can choose to go back to previous stages at any point during their writing to revise their work. This same process applies to research, in which the researcher may return to a previous stage to get more information or revise an existing section of their work.

reflection. Often journals, field or lab notes, or writing that occurs over time. Reflection can be used to evaluate the research process, particularly in defining limitations of a study and planning for improved research processes.

response rate. The percentage of responses received weighed against the number sent. If sixty-five people respond to a survey sent to one hundred, then the response rate is 65 percent.

responsible conduct of research (RCR). Ethical guidelines for doing research. Integrity in research is important and is often defined in nine standards, ranging from treatment of human and animal subjects to relationships between mentors and mentees.

review essay. A professional, scholarly article that provides an overview of several sources on the same or similar topic.

REx. The Research Exchange Index (http://researchexchange.colostate.edu) is a searchable database of researcher-authored, peer-reviewed reports on contemporary research.

rhetoric. The art or science of all specialized literary uses of language in prose or even verse, including figures of speech, for the purposes of writing research, although contemporary definitions of rhetoric may lean toward "empty" rhetoric as bombast that is overly exaggerated. Rhetoric also refers to the study of writing or speaking effectively. A *rhetor* is a speaker.

rhetorical analysis. A qualitative research method used to understand how well words and phrases instruct, inform, entertain, move, arouse, perform, convince, or persuade.

rubric. A document used to communicate expectations for an assignment but also used to evaluate. Criteria on which a text or project will be evaluated are identified, and descriptions of poor to excellent demonstration of those criteria may be included.

secondary documents. Those writings that focus on primary documents, discussing previously touched-upon topics.

service learning. The combining of classroom instruction with meaningful community service to emphasize civic engagement. A project is addressed in a collaborative manner among the academics and members of the community. At the end of the project, students engage in self-reflection. Campus Compact is a national organization dedicated to service learning.

surveys. A quantitative approach to gathering information. The survey (written, oral, electronic) offers a standardized questionnaire to a certain segment of a population targeted by the research project.

tagmeme. The basic functional unit in the structure of a language in a form of grammatical analysis called *tagmemics*. A tagmeme is the speech element that will fulfill the same grammatical role in a sentence. This is also the correlation of syntagmatic function (subject or object of the sentence) and paradigmatic fillers (nouns, pronouns, etc.). Multiple tagmemes are grouped together into syntagmemes.

thick description. A research tool popularized by anthropologist Clifford Geertz in which human behaviors as well as contextual information such as setting are described in rich detail. The goal is to make the research topic more meaningful.

transcript. A document that accurately captures interviews or conversations and can be coded for themes.

transfer. The skills and knowledge a writer takes from a composition classroom to other writing settings.

translation rules. A set of rules by which less general concepts will be translated into more general ones when a researcher chooses to generalize concepts during coding. These rules must be developed so the research method is transparent.

triangulated data. The use of multiple sources of information to validate a study. Researchers can overcome biases and weaknesses by using multiple sources.

trivium. Grammar, rhetoric, and logic in classical study.

tutors. Students who are trained to assist student writers with their writing projects, often in a centralized campus location.

usability studies. A method used particularly in work settings that emphasizes reactions by users and that influences design decisions.

validity. A characteristic of strong research. *Valid* is derived from the Latin *validus*, meaning strong. Can a study scientifically answer the questions it is intended to answer? Is the method used one that can truly measure the question and result in strong assertions? A checklist to determine validity might include the following: (1) the proposal has a valid research hypothesis and appropriate objectives; (2) the design uses appropriate participant selection; (3) the duration of the study and enrollment of participants is feasible; (4) the review of literature provides justification for the study; (5) the sample size is appropriate; (6) the safety of participants is assured; (7) the objectives are defined; (8) sufficient resources exist to conduct the research; (9) the researcher has no conflict of interest.

verisimilitude. The semblance of truth. In research, it refers to the probability that the research findings are consistent with occurrences in the real world.

WebGURU. The Web Guide to Research for Undergraduates funded by the National Science Foundation: http://www.webguru.neu.edu/. Although the interactive website is specifically for students in the sciences, it contains valuable information for others as well.

WPA. A writing program administrator. The Council of Writing Program Administration is also referred to as the CWPA; this professional group hosts an annual conference and publishes a quarterly journal as well as providing consultant-evaluators to writing programs on a contractual basis.

writer's block. The inability of a writer to create a new work or continue a work due to internal or externally perceived distractions.

writing across the curriculum. Strategies used to improve learning and writing in all content areas.

writing centers. Centers for individualized tutoring in writing. They have been in existence for many, many years, but they became more widespread in the 1970s due to increasing enrollments in colleges and universities. They may be housed within departments of English/writing, in more generic learning centers, or at satellite locations.

writing fellows. Special writing tutors assigned to specific classes to support writing and learning in discipline-specific classes.

writing in the disciplines. A field that focuses on conventions of the specific discourse communities in learning the language, formats, and styles of the field.

writing programs. Typically used as a term to describe the collection of required writing classes at an institution of higher education. It may have a more expansive meaning, such as all writing classes offered in a departmental unit, including upper-division courses. It may or may not include courses in creative writing. Often, a single person is charged with directing the writing program and is termed a WPA, a writing program administrator.

writing studies. The term that supplanted *composition studies* as the primary term to refer to research on writing in the twenty-first century, due in part to the growing number of degree programs in writing and increased attention by researchers such as Charles Bazerman, Douglas Downs, and Elizabeth Wardle.

About the Author

My own passion for asking questions about writing and how writing is taught has been a hallmark of a career extending over thirty years, during which time I've used many of the methods and approaches included in these chapters. My intention is to share that enthusiasm for inquiry and also to impart what I've discovered as a researcher and scholar of writing. As a result, I've written in first person—perhaps an unusual choice for a textbook but one that exemplifies the kind of relationship I hope to establish with readers. Please consider me a mentor.

As a researcher of writing, I've drawn on two research traditions, one based in humanistic scholarship and the other in social sciences research. Historical research—sometimes called *archival research*—draws on the former. Being a detective in the archives can be exciting, as manuscripts from previous times reveal information and fascinating stories. Such research was key to one of my projects, *A Schoolmarm All My Life: Personal Narratives from Frontier Utah* (Kinkead 1997b). That book arose from my curiosity about the reality of the schoolmarm icon as exemplified by Owen Wister's *The Virginian*. Etta Place, the schoolmarm in the classic western *Butch Cassidy and the Sundance Kid*, seems to suggest that perhaps the attributes of Wister's schoolmarm are not universal. To find the answer to my question about how realistic schoolmarms are in fiction, I located and analyzed the personal narratives of three dozen real schoolteachers from the nineteenth century. In the process of analyzing these diaries rhetorically, I learned a lot about the history of the West and the history of the teaching profession.

Textual analysis can draw on both humanistic and social sciences methods. An article I coauthored, "The Administrative Audience: A Rhetorical Problem," for the *WPA Journal*, a publication of the Council of Writing Program Administrators, drew on the classic concept of audience, a key component of *rhetoric*, which was introduced by Aristotle (Kinkead and Simpson 2000). My coauthor, Jeanne Simpson, and I used our vantage point of administrative roles at a university to demystify and unpack terminology important to the institutional mission but perhaps not as well known to directors of writing programs. That project may not sound as exciting as research on schoolmarms, but we were intrigued by how technical vocabulary can make a person an insider or an outsider. We felt that engaging in critical discourse analysis helped those who were in less powerful positions.

A researcher who studies writing draws from multiple traditions. *Ethnography* has its roots in anthropology. This *qualitative* approach focuses on *culture*, looking at the daily routines of ordinary people. For researchers of writing, most often the technique of *participant-observation* is employed. This approach is particularly appropriate for *teacher* or *action research* as I describe in the article "Looking for Yourself: The Classroom Teacher as Researcher" (Kinkead and Lancy 1990). In this project I wanted to empower teachers who are sometimes timid about engaging in research. By demonstrating that English teachers, who are skilled in literary analysis, can use those same kinds of skills to analyze classroom behaviors, I aimed to help them become more reflective and intentional practitioners.

Sometimes, researchers look at a *case* rather than at the overall culture. The *case study* is yet another qualitative approach that involves description and analysis. It may also use quantitative tools such as surveys. While the case study has its origins in anthropology and sociology, clinicians have also used it. I used the case-study approach to investigate "The Role of Gender in Writing Center Tutoring" by coding and analyzing videotapes of tutoring sessions. For this study, I had two simple questions: Does gender matter? Are there attributes of different communication styles that can be used to improve all tutoring? In undertaking this research, I was influenced by Deborah Tannen's fascinating research on male/female communication styles in her *You Just Don't Understand* (1990).

Because I have administered writing programs, improving practice has been a key concern throughout my career. How can we as professionals ensure that our students have the best writing experiences and instruction possible? At times I found that using multiple approaches, called *mixed methods*, was the right way to proceed. Can the architectural layout of a writing center have an impact on tutoring (Hadfield et al. 2003)? I was fortunate to work on an interdisciplinary project with a writing tutor and interior-design major to investigate that question. In directing a writing-fellows program, I worked with them to analyze all syllabi on campus to investigate writing in the disciplines (Kinkead 1997a). How can we use research to do better work?

My view of undergraduate research expanded significantly when I was appointed to oversee our university's undergraduate research program, the second oldest in the nation. Seeing firsthand the power of undergraduate research to transform lives in every discipline in the university was a breathtaking experience. I learned so much from my students and the projects they undertook—from bioremediation of toxic soils to the creation of a sculpture.

Key to this textbook is the notion that students researching writing can produce results that add to the knowledge base. Thus, an exemplary research essay accompanies each chapter, several derived from the excellent peer-reviewed journal *Young Scholars in Writing: Undergraduate Research in Writing and Rhetoric* (*YSW*). Venues for students doing research in writing studies are increasing, including *Kairos,* an online journal that explores the intersection of technology and rhetoric, and *Jump,* another multimedia outlet. Research is not finished until it is shared or disseminated. It is the intent of this volume that students will engage in authentic, hands-on research and share that research—not just reading and critiquing research but conducting research.

I have been thinking about this book for a long, long time. In writing-process theory, that might be called *incubation.* This is an exciting moment with the burgeoning number of writing studies majors and an increased interest in writing about writing. It's a fascinating field that has been my life's work, and I'm eager to share it with you in this volume.

Index